Cultural Atlas of
ANCIENT
EGYPT

Editor Graham Speake
Art Editor Andrew Lawson
Map Editor John-David Yule
Design Bernard Higton
Production Clive Sparling

For revised edition
Project Manager Richard Watts
Editor Lauren Bourque
Map Editor Tim Williams
Picture Research Claire Turner
Design Chris Munday
Typesetting Brian Blackmore
Index Ann Barrett

AN ANDROMEDA BOOK

Planned and produced by Andromeda
Oxford Limited, 11–13 The Vineyard,
Abingdon, Oxfordshire, England OX14 3PX
www.andromeda.co.uk

Published by Checkmark Books,
an imprint of Facts On File

**Library of Congress Cataloging-in-
Publication Data**

Baines, John, 1946–
    Cultural atlas of Ancient Egypt / by John
    Baines and Jaromír Málek. Rev. ed.
        p. cm. — (Cultural atlas series)
    Includes bibliographical references and
    index.
    ISBN 0-8160-4036-2
    1. Egypt—Antiquities. 2. Egypt—
Civilization—To 332 B.C. 3. Egypt—
Civilization—332 B.C.–638 A.D. I. Málek,
Jaromír. II. Title. III. Series.

DT60 .B34 2000
932—dc21   99–057588

Printed in Hong Kong by Hong Kong
Graphics and Printing Ltd.

Distributed in China and Hong Kong by
Hong Kong Graphics and Distribution

10 9 8 7 6 5 4 3 2 1

This book is printed on acid-free paper.

ISBN 0–8160–4036–2

Frontispiece Ornamental titulary of Ramesses
VI (c. 1145–1137), on the pillars of a hall in
his tomb (KV 9) in the Valley of the Kings.
Adapted from the illustration in Ippolito
Rosellini, *I monumenti dell'Egitto e della
Nubia,* Vol. I: *Monumenti storici* (Pisa, 1832).

Cultural Atlas of
ANCIENT
EGYPT

by John Baines
and Jaromir Malek

Revised Edition

Checkmark Books™
An imprint of Facts On File, Inc.

CONTENTS

Part One – The Cultural Setting

Part Two – A Journey down the Nile

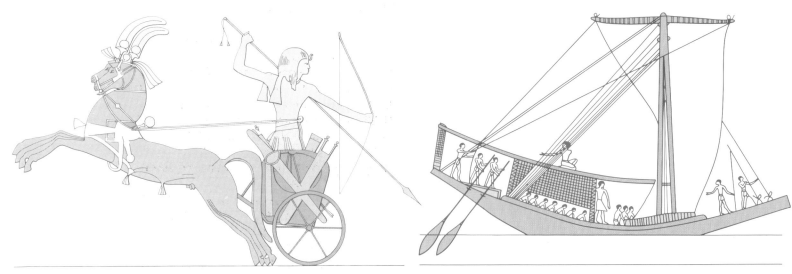

Part Three – Aspects of Egyptian Society

List of Maps

CHRONOLOGICAL TABLE

Dates marked * are absolute. All others are subject to margins of error. A king list appears on pp. 36–37.

	6500 BCE	4500	4000	3500	3000	2500
EGYPT	Late Paleolithic	Badarian (Nile valley) Merimda (delta) Faiyum A & B	Naqada I (Nile valley) Ma‘adi/Buto el-‘Omari (Memphite area)	Naqada II (Nile valley)	**Foundation of the Egyptian state** (Naqada III) **c. 3100** and invention of writing **Early Dynastic Period c. 2950–2575** 1st Dynasty c. 2950–2775 2nd Dynasty c. 2775–2650 3rd Dynasty c. 2650–2575	**Old Kingdom c. 2575–2150** 4th Dynasty c. 2575–2450 5th Dynasty c. 2450–2325 6th Dynasty c. 2325–2175 **1st Intermediate Period c. 2125–1975** 9th–10th Dynasties (Herakleopolis) c. 2125– 11th Dynasty (Thebes) c. 2080

Painted terracotta figure of a dancing woman. Naqada I Period.

The Step Pyramid of Djoser at Saqqara. c. 2650.

Painting of geese from the tomb of Itet at Maidum. c. 2550.

	6500 BCE	4500	4000	3500	3000	2500
LOWER NUBIA/ UPPER NUBIA	Late Paleolithic	Neolithic Abkan Post-Shamarkian Khartoum Variant *Khartoum Neolithic*		Early A Group	Classic A Group Terminal A Group Little settled population	C Group *Kerma culture*
SYRIA/ PALESTINE	*Neolithic Jericho 8500*			Urban society: Habuba el-Kebira	Early Bronze Age *Egyptian contact with Palestine* Ebla	Egyptian contact with Byblos Destruction of Ebla Middle Bronze Age
MESOPOTAMIA/ IRAN	*Neolithic 6500* Neolithic 6000	Late Neolithic ‘Ubaid 5000 Irrigation farming 5500		Urban society: Uruk IV Invention of writing *Proto-Elamite expansion (writing)*	Jamdat Nasr Early Dynastic Period	Sargonid Dynasty 3rd Dynasty of Ur Isin Larsa Babylon
ANATOLIA	Neolithic Catal Hüyük 6500					
AEGEAN	Neolithic 6500				Early Bronze Age	Middle Bronze Age

ddle Kingdom c. 1975–1640
1th Dynasty (all Egypt)
  c. 1975–1940
  12th Dynasty 1938–1756
  13th Dynasty c. 1755–1630
**2nd Intermediate period
  c. 1630–1520**
  15th Dynasty (Hyksos)
    c. 1630–1520
    17th Dynasty (Thebes)
    c. 1630–1540

New Kingdom c. 1539–1075
  18th Dynasty c. 1539–1252
   Amarna Period c. 1353–1332
  19th Dynasty c. 1292–1190
  20th Dynasty c. 1190–1075
**3rd Intermediate Period
  c. 1075–715**
  21st Dynasty c. 1075–945

22nd Dynasty c. 945–715
  23rd Dynasty c. 830–715
  24th Dynasty c. 730–715
  25th Dynasty (Nubia
    and Theban area)
    c. 770–715
Late Period c. 715–332
  25th Dynasty (Nubia and
    all Egypt) c. 715–657
    26th Dynasty *664–*525

27th Dynasty (Persian)
  *525–*404
  28th Dynasty *404–*399
  29th Dynasty *399–*380
  30th Dynasty *380–*343
  2nd Persian Period
  *343–*332
**Greco-Roman Period
  *332–*395 CE**
  Macedonian Dynasty
    *332–*304
    Ptolemaic Dynasty *304–*30 BCE

Roman
emperors
  *30 BCE–395 CE
**Byzantine
Period
  *395–*640**

of Ma'rya, relief in
Theban tomb of Ra'mose
55, c. 1360).

Detail of facade of the Great
Temple of Abu Simbel. c. 1260

Inlaid gold funerary
mask of Tut'ankh-
amun. c. 1325.

Inlaid bronze figure
of the Divine
Adoratrice
Karomama. c. 850.

The "Berlin Green
Head," from a
nonroyal statue of
schist. c. 75 BCE (?).

Facade of the temple of
Hathor at Dendara.
Construction dedicated
17 November 34 CE (the
decoration is later).

Egyptian occupation *Kerma state* Kerma conquest Pan-grave culture	Egyptian conquest (Lower and Upper)	Depopulation *Egyptian withdrawal* *Rise of Napata–Meroe (the later 25th Dynasty)* 25th Dynasty Napata–Meroe state –4th century CE	Meroitic- Egyptian condominium in Dodekaschoinos *Meroitic writing*	Meroitic settlement *Fall of Meroë* X Group (Ballana culture) *Tanqasi culture*
Egyptian contact Hittite with Byblos incursions	Late Bronze Age: city states Egyptian occupation c. 1520–1200 Mitanni c. 1500–1330 Hittite domination	*United Israelite monarchy* *Kingdoms of Israel and Judah* Assyrian expansion Neo-Hittite states *Joshua and Judges* Babylonian captivity Jews in Egypt	Persian rule Revolt of Satraps Alexander the Great Seleucid Empire *Ptolemies*	*Roman Empire* *Byzantine Empire*
1st Dynasty of Babylon *Old Elamite Kingdom* Fall of Babylon (1595 or 1531) Kassite Dynasty	Independence of Assur c. 1380 *Elamite expansion* 2nd Dynasty of Isin	Assyrian Empire *Persian conquest* Fall of Nineveh Neo-Babylonian Empire *Medes*	Alexander the Great Seleucid Empire *Parthian Dynasty*	Parthian Dynasty *Sasanid Dynasty*
Hittite Old Kingdom	Hittite Empire Fall of Hittite Empire	Urartu SW Anatolian states Gyges of Lydia	Persian rule Alexander the Great Seleucid Empire Ptolemies	Roman Empire Byzantine Empire
Late Bronze Age	Linear B Cretan destruction Mycenaean destruction Sub-Mycenaean	Protogeometric Geometric Orientalizing Period Greeks in Egypt Archaic Period	Classical Period Wars with Persia; aid to and from Egypt Alexander the Great *336–*323 Macedon Seleucid Empire Ptolemies	Roman Empire Byzantine Empire

INTRODUCTION

The monuments – pyramids, temples and tombs, statues and stelae – represent some of the most valuable sources for our knowledge of ancient Egypt. A study of monuments, either still at various sites all over Egypt, or in their new locations in museums and collections, is also a happy meeting-ground of specialists and non-specialists. No great scholarship is required in order to be impressed by the grandeur and technical accomplishment of the Great Pyramid at Giza, to be enchanted by paintings in the Ramessid tombs at Deir el-Medina, or be left dumbfounded by the extravagantly opulent taste shown in the objects from the tomb of Tutʿankhamun in the Valley of the Kings, and now in the Cairo Museum. Nonetheless, knowledge adds significantly to our appreciation and enjoyment.

So the aim of this book is easily defined: to provide a systematic survey of the most important sites with ancient Egyptian monuments, an assessment of their historical and cultural importance and a brief description of their salient features, based on the most up-to-date Egyptological knowledge and thoroughly revised for this new edition. Further chapters and special features deal with general aspects of Egyptian civilization. These enable readers to find their bearings quickly in the initially bewildering mass of names of places, kings, and gods, and at the same time help them to understand broader issues in the development of Egyptian society and the fluctuating fortunes of Egyptian towns and temples.

Geographically, the limits of the book are set by the frontiers of Egypt along the Nile, as far south as the first cataract and as far north as the Mediterranean; the main exceptions are Egypt's traditional imperial extension into Lower Nubia, Sinai, and the oases in the western desert. The maps present much of the book's content topographically, and supplement the information in the text at many points. Those in Parts One and Three are organized by theme and period. In Part Two the maps for each section present a detailed, large-scale view of the successive stages of our journey, including both ancient and modern features.

The period covered by the native Egyptian dynasties of kings (with the brief interruptions of foreign rule), about 2950 to 332 BCE, provides the temporal setting. But some knowledge of Predynastic Egypt is essential for understanding the earliest stages of dynastic history, while for centuries the culture of the Greco-Roman Period remained largely Egyptian; these two phases, sometimes treated as separate units, are referred to and discussed where appropriate.

In writing this book we have envisaged our "typical reader" as anyone interested in ancient Egypt. The book is arranged in such a way that there is no need to read it straight through for its individual sections to remain comprehensible. There is a firm geographical framework, and the sites are discussed proceeding from south to north. The ancient Egyptians themselves used this scheme, and began their systematic lists at Elephantine (Aswan). Many modern books are arranged from north to south, which was the approach experienced by travelers of the last century who arrived by boat at Alexandria, went from there to Cairo and, provided they were adventurous and prepared to accept some discomfort, further south. We have decided instead to follow the Egyptians, so that we can see the country as far as possible from their own viewpoint. Readers are, of course, free to begin their personal journeys wherever they wish. One of our aims has been to help those intending to visit Egypt by "briefing" them in advance. Those who have already seen that fascinating country might like to refresh their memory, and perhaps broaden their understanding of it, while those who simply like reading about civilizations of long ago may enjoy a new approach to one of the greatest. We hope that students in related disciplines will find this book useful when seeking reliable information about ancient Egypt.

Last, and most important, we hope that we have communicated to our readers some of the enjoyment that brought us to the subject in the first place.

Part One is largely the work of John Baines and Part Two of Jaromir Malek; Part Three is shared between us. This division has been retained during the work on this revised edition, for which we wish to thank Susanne Bickel, Colin Hope, Andrea McDowell, and Mary Ann Pouls for their help. We are particularly grateful to Helen Whitehouse for updating her "Egypt in Western Art," in which she is a leading expert.

PART ONE
THE CULTURAL SETTING

THE GEOGRAPHY OF ANCIENT EGYPT

Ancient Egypt was exceptional in its setting and unique in its continuity. The setting is the extreme case among several cultural and physical oases which were the great states of antiquity. It is almost impossible for us to recapture a feeling for this situation, with its mixture of geographical and human elements, just as we find it difficult to comprehend the time-span involved, half as long again as the Common Era. The position of the designer of the first pyramid, who created the earliest stone building on its scale in the world and lived in the only large, united state of the time, can never be recovered. Any understanding of ancient Egypt must include an awareness of these and other enormous differences between antiquity and our own times. Yet human beings are in many ways the same everywhere, and much of our detailed knowledge of different civilizations will include material as ordinary as anything in our own lives. When approaching an alien civilization we need to know about both the ordinary and the exotic. Both are affected by the environment. One exploits it in a routine fashion, the other more creatively; neither is independent of it.

In its geographical context Egypt is part of the larger area of northeastern Africa, and within this wider region its proximity to the heartlands of agricultural development in western Asia was initially of great significance. Dynastic Egypt was largely self-contained in most periods, but this was only because its economy was very heavily agricultural; for many important raw materials and for the requirements of high civilization foreign trade or travel into the desert were necessary, so that the perspective of the wider region is essential for understanding Egyptian culture. The same is true for the population, which probably came from all the surrounding areas, and was always ethnically heterogeneous.

The boundaries of ancient Egypt
A definition of the boundaries of Egypt in antiquity – a theme of which the ancient texts are very fond and which reflects an Egyptian concern with demarcations in general – is not simple. The basic areas of the country, the Nile valley, the delta, and the Faiyum, were supplemented by parts of the surrounding regions over which the Egyptians exerted particular rights, such as those of mining. The southern frontier, traditionally at the first cataract of the Nile at Aswan, moved further south in some periods; New Kingdom texts sometimes use words for Egypt to refer also to parts of Nubia, which were then incorporated into the state. Apart from these extensions of Egyptian territory, the line of oases that runs from Siwa in the north to el-Kharga in the south, approximately parallel to the Nile and about 200 kilometers west of it, was settled and governed by Egyptians during most of the Dynastic Period, reaching the peak of its prosperity in Roman times.

The main areas of Egypt form a river oasis in the desert. As such, the country was isolated from its neighbors to a greater extent than the other major states of antiquity, and its exceptional stability was no doubt fostered by this isolation, a striking indication of which is the complete absence of mention of Egypt in texts of the third millennium BCE from Mesopotamia and Syria. Egypt was a magnet for settlers, but not for a concerted invasion, until perhaps the 13th century BCE, and immigrants were absorbed quickly into the population. But while much of Egyptian history is internal history, this is less true of the more sweeping, imperfectly known changes of prehistory. Although the oasis of Egypt was fully formed by the end of the third millennium, it is necessary to relate this stage of climatic evolution to the more extensive alterations in earlier periods.

In the millennia after the end of the last Ice Age (about 10,000 BCE) the Nile valley was one of the areas that attracted population from the Sahara and much of North-east Africa. During the Pleistocene era the valley was frequently swampy and river levels were generally higher than now. As the Sahara dried out at the end of this phase, it became progressively less hospitable to the nomadic bands which had originally spread over much of its area. From as early as 15,000 BCE there is a concentration of Paleolithic sites on the low desert on the edge of the valley, and one detail of these cultures may indicate that they were already experiencing shortages and population pressure. Some flint blades from sites in both Egypt and Nubia show traces of use for gathering grasses, probably wild grasses that could yield cereal grains. This is perhaps the earliest indication of cereal consumption known in the world, earlier than incipient sedentary sites in Syria-Palestine. It is not evidence for a settled, agricultural life, but rather for an intensified use of resources by a still nomadic population.

This isolated apparent innovation seems not to have had any long-term influence. From about 10,000 to 5000 BCE late and epi-Paleolithic modes of life continued without any clear transition to the succeeding cultures. The earliest Neolithic remains found in Egypt are in the Western Desert at Nabta, where traces of incipient agriculture may date to 6000 BCE or still earlier. It is likely, however, that cultivated crops were introduced to Egypt from Western Asia and that early Neolithic sites remain to be discovered within the Nile valley and delta. Egyptologists term the settled, partly agricultural cultures of the floodplain and of the oases "Predynastic". They date from perhaps 5000 BCE to the beginning of the Dynastic Period around 3000 BCE. The Egyptian setting of later Predynastic times offered opportunities for exploitation not fundamentally different from those found at the beginning of the 19th century BCE. That analogy is important, because most settlement has always been within the Nile valley and the delta, not on the desert edges (unless irrigated, all areas not reached by the inundation are desert, or at best desert savanna). The precise location of settlements has probably not changed very much, since there is the advantage in building on an earlier site that any accumulation of

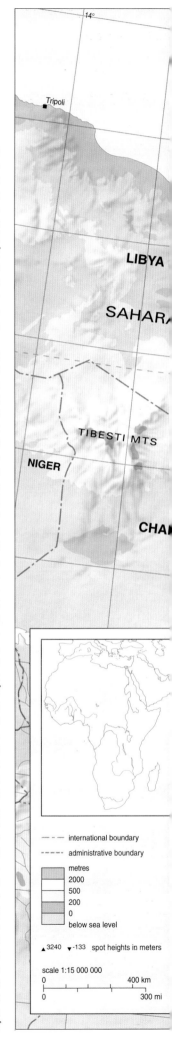

LIBYA

SAHARA

TIBESTI MTS

NIGER

CHAD

Tripoli

---- international boundary

---- administrative boundary

metres
2000
500
200
0
below sea level

▲3240 ▼-133 spot heights in meters

scale 1:15 000 000
0   400 km
0   300 mi

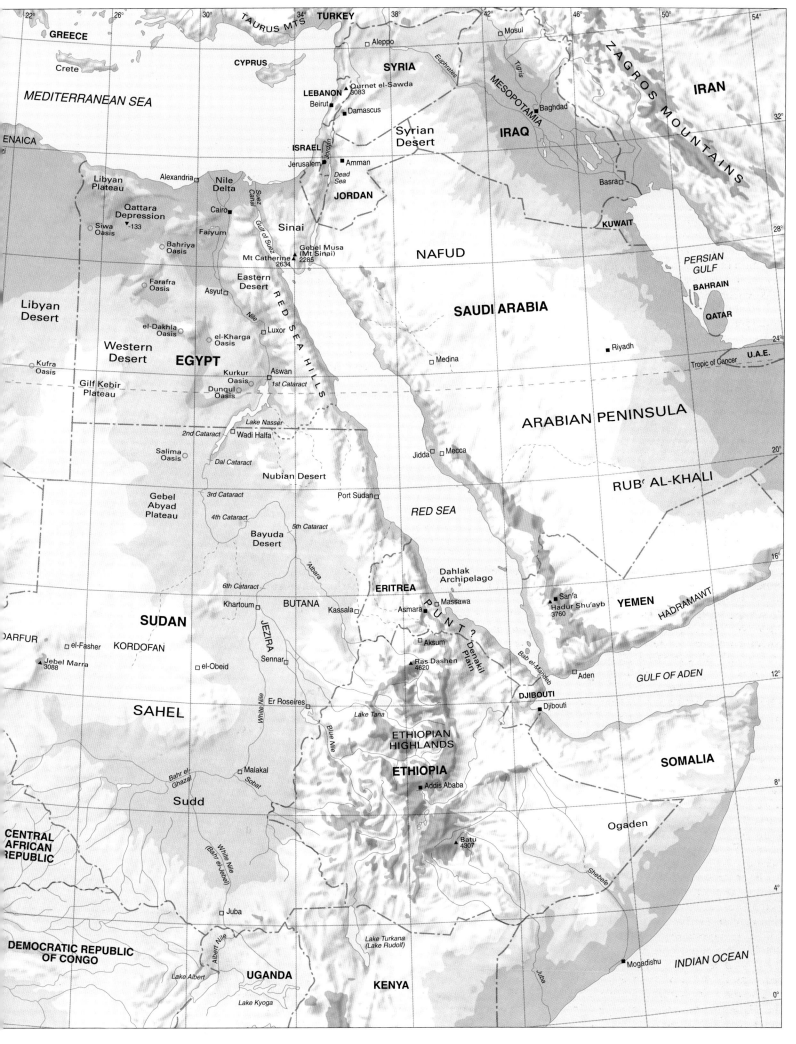

GREECE

Crete

MEDITERRANEAN SEA

CYRENAICA

zi

TAURUS MTS

TURKEY

CYPRUS

SYRIA

Aleppo

LEBANON
Beirut

Qurnet el-Sawda
3083

Damascus

Euphrates

MESOPOTAMIA

Mosul

Tigris

Baghdad

ZAGROS MOUNTAINS

IRAN

IRAQ

Syrian
Desert

ISRAEL

Jerusalem

Amman

Jordan

Dead
Sea

JORDAN

Basra

KUWAIT

PERSIAN
GULF

Libyan
Plateau

Alexandria

Nile
Delta

Cairo

Suez
Canal

Sinai

Gulf of Suez

Qattara
Depression
▼ -133

Siwa
Oasis

Faiyum

Bahriya
Oasis

Gebel Musa
(Mt Sinai)
2285

Mt Catherine ▲
2634

NAFUD

SAUDI ARABIA

BAHRAIN

QATAR

Libyan
Desert

Farafra
Oasis

Asyut

Eastern
Desert

Nile

RED SEA HILLS

Western
Desert

EGYPT

el-Dakhla
Oasis

el-Kharga
Oasis

Luxor

Medina

Riyadh

Tropic of Cancer

U.A.E.

Kufra
Oasis

Gilf Kebir
Plateau

Kurkur
Oasis

Dunqul
Oasis

Aswan

1st Cataract

ARABIAN PENINSULA

2nd Cataract

Lake Nasser

Wadi Halfa

Jidda

Mecca

Salima
Oasis

Dal Cataract

Nubian Desert

RUB' AL-KHALI

Gebel
Abyad
Plateau

3rd Cataract

Port Sudan

RED SEA

4th Cataract

5th Cataract

Bayuda
Desert

Atbara

6th Cataract

Dahlak
Archipelago

San'a
Hadur Shu'ayb
3760

YEMEN

HADRAMAWT

DARFUR

el-Fasher

KORDOFAN

Jebel Marra
3088

Khartoum

BUTANA

JEZIRA

Kassala

ERITREA

PUNT?

Massawa

Asmara

Denakil Plain

Bab el-Mandeb

Aden

GULF OF ADEN

SUDAN

el-Obeid

Sennar

Aksum

Ras Dashen
4620

DJIBOUTI

Djibouti

SAHEL

White Nile

Er Roseires

Blue Nile

Lake Tana

ETHIOPIAN
HIGHLANDS

SOMALIA

Bahr el-
Ghazal

Malakal

Sobat

ETHIOPIA

Addis Ababa

Sudd

Ogaden

CENTRAL
AFRICAN
REPUBLIC

White Nile
(Bahr el-Jebel)

Batu
4307

Shebele

Juba

DEMOCRATIC REPUBLIC
OF CONGO

Albert Nile

Lake Albert

UGANDA

Lake Turkana
(Lake Rudolf)

KENYA

Juba

Mogadishu

INDIAN OCEAN

Lake Kyoga

13

debris will raise a village above the valley floor and the danger of high floods. Both because earlier sites will be buried under modern ones and because three or more meters of silt have been deposited over the whole valley since 3000 BCE, the archaeological record of settlement within the inundated and cultivated area is rather slight. Much of Egyptian archaeology is therefore somewhat hypothetical.

The Nile valley of the Predynastic and later periods was a focal point in north-east Africa for the development of agriculture and later of urban society. The whole region from the confluence of the Blue and White Niles to the delta may at first have been culturally similar (there were separate developments farther south), but differences became marked by 3000 BCE. The concentration of population from various sources brought innovation from different directions, notably the Near East. The majority of elements of the civilization, however, developed in Egypt itself. In most periods Egypt was not very innovative in technology. The prodigality of the land and its water may not have encouraged invention.

In these formative periods contact between Egypt and neighboring areas was easier than in later times, because the desiccation of the Sahara was not yet complete and the desert on either side of the Nile valley supported a wider variety of flora and fauna and perhaps a larger nomadic population than now. Even for the inhabitants of the valley itself these regions had some significance. During the later fourth and third millennia the desert became progressively more arid, a development that may be significant for the formation of the Egyptian state. The political collapse at the end of this climatic phase (c. 2150 BCE) could have been triggered off – but not entirely caused – by low inundations, which might be a symptom of a dry phase over the whole of northern Africa, rather like the drought in the Sahel in the early 1970s, another time of low floods.

Climate and geography played an important part in these developments. They did not determine their direction, for different results can be imagined, but they ruled out a continuation of older subsistence patterns. The Nile and its flooding were vital factors in the organization of the newly formed Egyptian state.

The Nile valley and agriculture

Rainfall in the Nile valley is insignificant in volume, and it is no more than 100–200 millimeters per year in the delta; without the Nile, agriculture would be impossible in Egypt, except perhaps on the Mediterranean coast. The river is a more regular and predictable source of water than other great rivers whose valleys are used for floodplain farming. In antiquity its annual inundation between July and October covered most of the land in the Nile valley and the delta; with careful management the water deposited could produce an abundant crop. The pattern of the inundation can no longer be seen in operation, because the river has been checked by a whole series of dams and sluices built since 1830. These provide regulation of water levels from the Ethiopian border on the Blue Nile to the apex of the delta north of Cairo. The construction of the Aswan High Dam in the 1960s eliminated the inundation entirely, and water management and the area of land under cultivation continue to be expanded. Instead

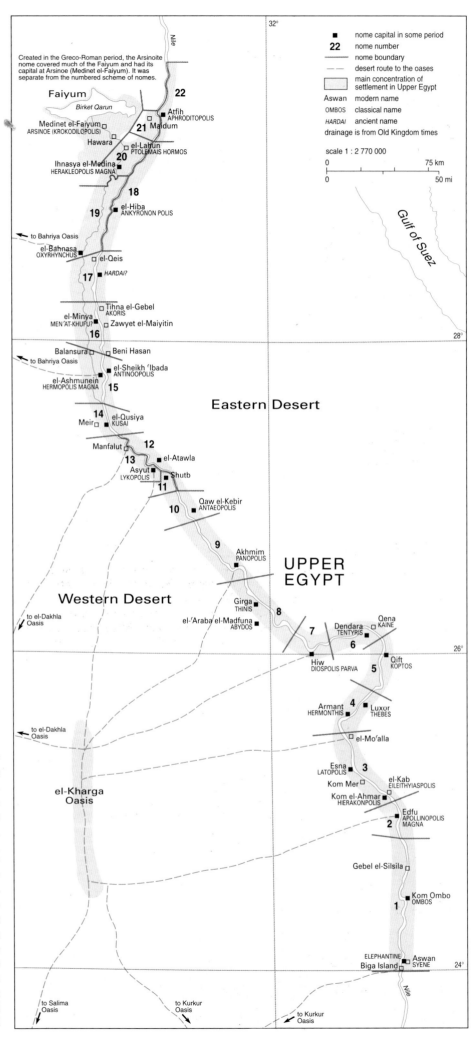

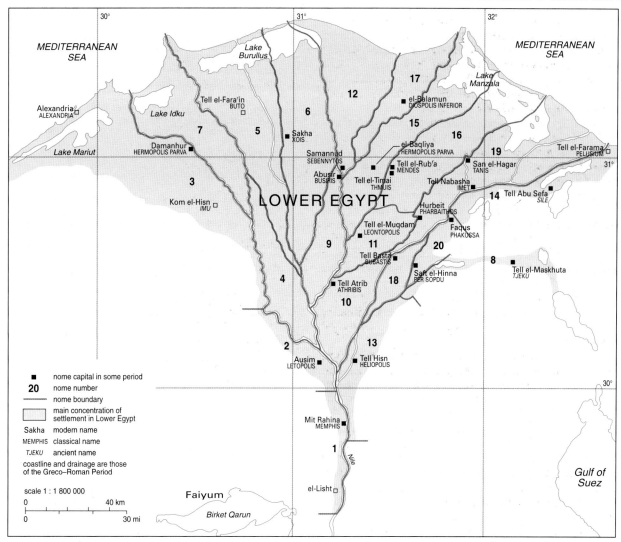

Left: The nomes of Upper Egypt
The nomes were the administrative divisions of Egypt, whose origins go back to the Early Dynastic Period. The 22 nomes of Upper Egypt were fixed by the 5th Dynasty, and their lengths along the river are recorded in the White Chapel of Senwosret I at Karnak. The divisions on this map are based on an interpretation of these measurements and are valid only for some periods. For Lower Egypt, the definitive number of 20 nomes was not established until the Greco-Roman Period. The Faiyum and the oases were not part of the original scheme.

The total number of 42 had a symbolic value: there were 42 judges of the dead, and the early Christian writer, Clement of Alexandria (2nd century CE), stated that the Egyptians had 42 sacred books.

Locations of nome capitals are indicated by a solid black square. Where more than one square is present, the capital shifted or the nome division changed in some period; where none is given, the capital is uncertain.

Right: The nomes of Lower Egypt
This arrangement of the 20 nomes of the Greco-Roman Period is based on processions of figures and their accompanying texts in the temples of Edfu and Dendara. Many nome boundaries run along waterways whose ancient course is tentative.

Nomes had ensigns, which are worn on the heads of processions of nome personifications that decorate the base areas of temple walls. The ensigns of Upper and Lower Egypt are:

Upper Egypt

Lower Egypt

of observing modern conditions we must rely on earlier sources, from pharaonic documents to the *Description de l'Egypte* produced by Napoleon's expedition and the writings of 19th-century irrigation engineers. In order to establish the precise area cultivated at any time in the past it would be necessary to make detailed local studies. An estimate for early periods is shown in the map on p. 31.

The waters of the Nile come from the Blue Nile, which rises in the Ethiopian highlands, and the White Nile, which rises south of Lake Victoria in central Africa and receives water from many smaller rivers in southern Sudan. The White Nile is fed by the rains of the tropical belt and provides a relatively constant supply throughout the year, mediated by the great marshes of the Sudd in southern Sudan, which absorb much water in the rainy season. The Blue Nile and the ꜥAtbara, which flows into the Nile

some way north of Khartoum, bring vast quantities of water from the Ethiopian summer monsoon (which forms part of the Indian Ocean monsoon system), and provide almost all the water in the river from July to October (earlier in Sudan itself). This period corresponds to the time of the rains on the savanna in central Sudan. In Egypt the water in the river was at its lowest from April to June. The level rose in July and the flood normally began in August, covering most of the valley floor approximately from mid-August to late September, washing salts out of the soil and depositing a layer of silt, which built up at the rate of several centimeters per century. After the water level fell, the main crops were sown in October and November, ripening from January to May according to variety. In antiquity agriculture was possible over much of the Nile valley and in large parts of the delta, the chief exceptions being tracts of swamp.

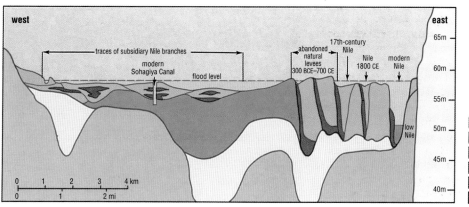

Generalized cross-section through the Nile valley between Sohag and Asyut (after Butzer). In historical times the main river has migrated eastward, leaving traces of its earlier raised banks. The vertical scale is greatly exaggerated.

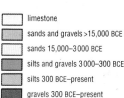

The valley and delta together form an area of about 34,000 square kilometers (1949–50 figures). Over long periods this area has varied considerably, but it has remained within the same range for the last 5,000 years. The accumulation of silt and human management of water have, however, led to a gradual increase in arable land as the swamps at the desert edge have been reclaimed for cultivation and flatter stretches of the low desert have been incorporated in the floodplain. The profile of the valley and the detailed pattern of the flooding are relevant to this process. The water in the channel itself tended to erode the bed, while the deposition of silt during the flood raised the level of the land nearest the river, where the flow was strongest. So the profile of the valley is convex and land near the river was drier and more readily settled than that further away. The flood was not a general overflowing, but ran through overflow channels onto the lower-lying land behind the banks. The flood crest ran more or less in parallel in the river and on the main area of the plain.

Agriculture involved controlling this flow pattern as well as possible. The areas of the plain were leveled as far as practicable and formed into a series of basins of considerable size that "terraced" the land for irrigation in stages both down river and away from the banks. Each terrace was only imperceptibly lower than the last: the drop in river level from Aswan to the sea is no more than 85 meters. Because of the large size of irrigated units, some large-scale organization must have been needed for optimal exploitation of the land. Effective groups of basins would have been about the size of the ancient provinces or nomes, of which there were just over 20 from the first cataract to south of Memphis. In the Dynastic Period the irrigated area in the valley increased gradually – with occasional setbacks, especially around 2100 BCE – through the reclamation of low-lying and swampy land, and to some extent through improved water-lifting technology that seems mostly to have been introduced from the Near East. Swamps provided a habitat for wildlife that was hunted by the elite, and were the source of reeds and papyrus, which was made into a writing material and into mats, boats, and utensils. These resources were gradually replaced by those of intensive agriculture. Papyrus died out in the Middle Ages (it has recently been reintroduced) and most swamp areas have been reclaimed, except in the northern delta.

The main crops were cereals, emmer (*Triticum dicoccum*) for bread, and barley for beer (wheat, *Triticum durum*, was introduced in the Greco-Roman Period). In addition to these there were pulses such as lentils and chickpeas; vegetables – lettuces, onions, and garlic; fruit, especially dates; an uncertain amount of fodder crops for animals, which were important for hides as well as meat and other products; and plants grown for oil, such as sesame. Rather little is known about herbs and spices. Honey was the chief sweetener, and bee keeping was evidently important. Meat was a luxury. Herds were probably grazed on swampy, marginal land, especially in the delta. The most prestigious meat was beef, but mutton, pork, and goat were also eaten, as was the flesh of various species of antelope. Fowl, too, was the food of the wealthy, who ate pigeon (probably raised in dovecotes), ducks, geese, and

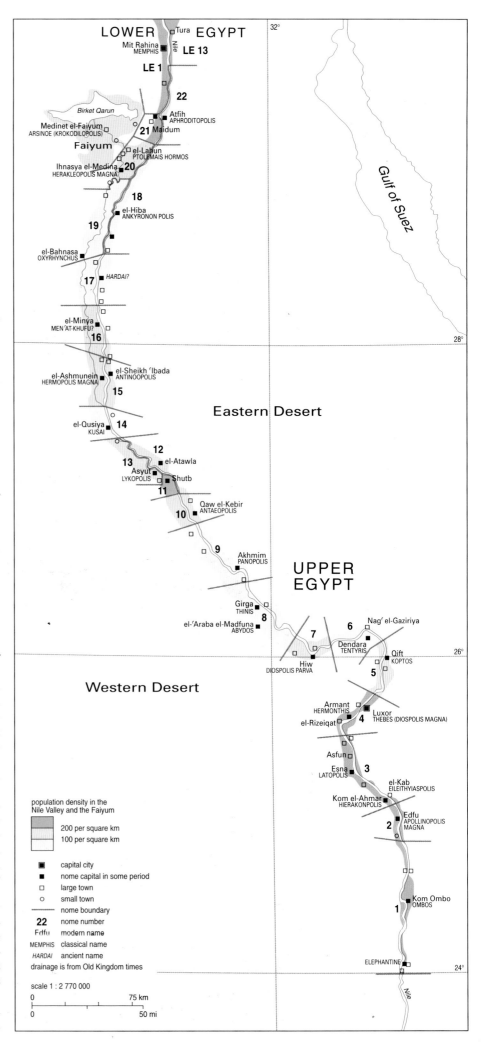

Population density in the Nile valley
Estimated population densities in the nomes of the Nile valley in dynastic times (after Butzer). The densities are higher near the capital and in narrow parts of the valley, probably because these areas were fully settled at an earlier date; the narrow parts may also have been easier to exploit. The evidence does, however, favor them, because sites are preserved more easily where the desert is closer to the river; the result may therefore be a little exaggerated. The population of the delta, where there is no basis for a detailed estimate, probably overtook that of the valley no later than the New Kingdom.
  Large settlements are indicated according to approximate size, giving a rough supplementary guide to population; all are attested from Dynastic sources. Villages are not shown.

various game birds. Chickens were unknown before the New Kingdom and probably became common only in the Greco-Roman Period. Grapes, which were grown chiefly in the western delta and in the oases, were made into wine, which was a luxury product; red wines are well attested, and white ones are found in Greek sources. The normal alcoholic drink was a coarse barley beer, which was made in the home; pomegranate and date wines are also known. Finally, two very important plant crops were papyrus, swamp areas of which were actively managed, and flax, which was used for almost all clothing and for sails and ropes (and possibly linseed oil), and also exported. The date palm was an additional important source of fiber.

The delta
The delta presents a generally similar picture to the Nile valley, but must have been a more difficult challenge for reclamation for agriculture. Even now large areas remain unsuitable for cultivation, but some swamps and lagoons may have been created by later incursion of the sea. Land reclamation was probably significant for development in all periods. This was true already by the 4th Dynasty, when the delta is prominent in the lists of estates inscribed by members of the elite in their Memphite tombs. Through its agricultural strength the delta increasingly dominated Egyptian economic and political life from about 1400 BCE on. The potential amount of usable land in the delta was double that in the Nile valley, and the delta was closer to the Near East, contacts with which played an ever-greater part in later Egyptian history.
  The delta was created by interplay between the sea, in periods of high sea levels in earlier geological ages, and the mud deposited by the Nile. The areas most suitable for permanent settlement were

Early photograph of a Nile boat with a cargo of water pots. Because of the ease of river transport, which is many times more efficient than movement of goods by land, cheap and bulky objects such as these are sent great distances and probably always have been. These pots are made near Qena, where there are suitable clays for slightly porous jars that keep water cool by evaporation. The horse in the water on the right was probably sheltering from the heat.

Old photograph of a pair of *shadufs* – weight arms with buckets – being used to lift water for irrigation (the women in the foreground are collecting it for domestic use). The *shaduf*, which was introduced in the New Kingdom, could lift water as much as 3 meters, or more when used in tandem as here, but it is so labor-intensive that it is valuable only for garden crops or for topping up the water level of inundated areas.

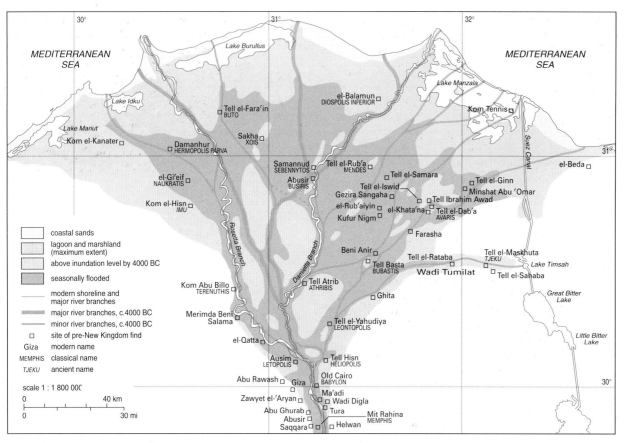

Delta topography
The topography of the delta reconstructed for c. 4000 BCE (after Butzer), and compared with the modern situation.
The northern delta was formerly lagoon and swamp, and was gradually coated with layers of Nile silt, slowly increasing the area of land that was seasonally above water. The northernmost margin may, however, have been more attractive for early settlement than this might imply; there are early sites in the northeast and a nome around Lake Burullus. As is suggested by submerged sites on the coastline, this area may later have warped downwards in relation to the southern delta, roughly on the axis of the Wadi Tumilat.
The overall development of the river branches – probably much influenced by human action – has been to reduce their number and to shift the main discharge westward (in the Nile valley, by contrast, the river has moved toward the east).
Areas above inundation level by 4000 BCE are composed of sand and silt, and are often known by the Arabic word *gezira* "island." Their edges are particularly favorable for settlement. The sites marked have produced significant pre-New Kingdom finds. Further place names that are known only from texts are omitted.

sandy ridges, known as turtlebacks, between the Nile branches and other water channels. Some of these were probably occupied from far back in prehistory. The land around the ridges could be used for crops or, if wetter, for grazing, while the swamps contained far more wild life, fish, and papyrus than those in the Nile valley. The agricultural exploitation of the two main regions evidently differed, and there is evidence for trade between them. No large cities of earlier periods have been found in the delta. This relative paucity of centers of population may be due in part to the relative proximity of Memphis, south of the delta apex, but it is also likely to be illusory, because so many delta sites are lost beneath the floodplain or destroyed by later development. It is not surprising that the archaeological material from the delta is only a small fraction of that from Upper Egypt and does not reflect the area's true importance.

The Faiyum
The third sizable area of ancient settlement was the Faiyum. This is a lakeside oasis west of the Nile valley and south of Memphis, which is fed by the Bahr Yusuf, a branch of the Nile that diverges westward north of Asyut and terminates in the Birket Qarun, Lake Moeris of Classical antiquity. The lake has dwindled gradually from its Neolithic extent, which may have been little less than that of the entire Faiyum. The lake was a focus for settlement in the late Paleolithic (about 7000 BCE) and Neolithic periods, and is also attested for the Old Kingdom. Intensive exploitation of the area depended on lowering the lake level to reclaim land, using the water that would otherwise have filled it to irrigate both above and below the natural level. Major works were undertaken by 12th-Dynasty kings, who must, to judge by the siting of some of their monuments, have reduced the lake considerably and won back about

450 square kilometers for cultivation. Later the Ptolemies made it into one of the most prosperous and heavily populated parts of the country, with about 1,200 square kilometers of agricultural land, much of it settled by the ethnic Greek population; some sectors irrigated then are now desert. A different form of irrigation is required in the Faiyum from the rest of Egypt, relying on large amounts of labor rather than any very advanced techniques. In the lower-lying areas it will have been possible to produce two major crops per year and there is some evidence for this being done in the Greco-Roman Period.

An area analogous to the Faiyum but much less significant is the Wadi el-Natrun, a natural oasis close to the delta, northwest of Cairo and south of Alexandria. The word "Natrun" in its name refers to the salt lakes there. These were the chief ancient source of natron (sodium carbonate/bicarbonate), which was used for cleaning, ritual purposes including mummification, and the manufacture of Egyptian faience and of glass. The oasis is poor in agricultural resources; in the Byzantine Period it became a refuge for Christian ascetics and it still contains the most important Coptic monasteries.

The western desert
The remaining areas to be discussed were more peripheral and could be held only when Egypt was powerful.

The oases of the western desert produced valuable crops such as grapes and the best dates, and were also important as links in trade with more remote areas. From south to north four main oases were governed by Egypt: el-Kharga, el-Dakhla (west of el-Kharga), Farafra, and Bahariya, of which the first two were by far the most significant. El-Dakhla and el-Kharga were settled no later than Neolithic times. The more remote westerly oasis of Siwa, which was incorporated into Egypt in the Late

Period, acquired world renown through the abortive mission of the Persian conqueror Cambyses to it in 525 BCE and Alexander the Great's subsequent consultation of the oracle there. There are various smaller oases west of the Nile; the more southerly, Kurkur, Dunqul, and Salima, are staging posts on long-distance caravan routes, but have not produced significant ancient remains.

In the Middle and New Kingdoms some people fled from justice or from persecution to el-Kharga and el-Dakhla oases, while in the 21st Dynasty political opponents were banished there. The area was one of those exploited for the harsher purposes of Egyptian governance, another being the mines of the eastern desert, where there was forced labor in appalling conditions, with great loss of life.

In antiquity "Libya" was a designation for the entire region west of the Nile valley. The coastal area west of Alexandria, particularly Cyrenaica, probably contained the majority of the Libyan population, and was less inhospitable than it may now seem. Most of the Egyptian evidence from here dates to the time of Ramesses II, who built forts along the coast as far as Zawyet Umm el-Rakham, 340 kilometers west of Alexandria, and to the Greco-Roman Period, when the Ptolemies ruled Cyrenaica, building in both Greek and Egyptian style at Tolmeita, about 1,000 kilometers from Alexandria.

For most of Egyptian history the oases were an Egyptian outpost against the Libyans, who tried to infiltrate in many periods. In the reigns of Merenreʿ and Pepy II the expedition leader Harkhuf made several journeys to Yam, a country perhaps around the fifth Nile cataract. On one occasion he took the "desert road," leaving the Nile valley near Abydos and no doubt passing through el-Dakhla, where there was a major late Old Kingdom settlement with governors' residences and large mastaba tombs. When he arrived in Yam he found that its ruler had gone to "smite the ruler of the Libyan land to the western corner of the sky". This detail suggests that for Egyptians "Libya" signified regions extending for as much as 1,500 kilometers south from the sea. Remains from the Fezzan, probably dating to Roman times, show the possibilities of settlement in southern Libya in antiquity, while the Uweinat area was settled in the third millennium BCE. In early periods some Libyans were culturally similar to the Egyptians and may have spoken a closely related language, but contacts during the Dynastic Period were mostly wary or hostile.

From the western oases a trail now called the Darb el-Arbaʿin ("40-day track") leads to el-Fasher, the capital of Darfur province in western Sudan. Harkhuf used the first part of this, but it is possible that its entire length was opened up to trade in antiquity. Harkhuf traveled with donkeys, but effective exploitation of such routes may have depended on the camel, which seems not to have become common in Egypt until Roman times.

The eastern desert

To the east of Egypt were a number of important sources of minerals. The northernmost is the Sinai peninsula, which supplied turquoise, mined by the Egyptians from the 3rd Dynasty to the end of the New Kingdom, but not later (finds of the beginning of the Dynastic Period have been reported, but it is not clear whether they relate to mining). The main

sites with Egyptian remains are in western Sinai at Maghara and Serabit el-Khadim, where at times there was semipermanent Egyptian settlement. Sinai is also a source of copper, and copper mines contemporary with the Egyptian 18th–20th Dynasties have been excavated at Timna near Eilat; these were probably worked by locals under Egyptian direction. There is no evidence that the Egyptians themselves mined copper anywhere in Sinai but, as with trade in grain with the Near East, the Egyptians may have worked the mines but not have considered the

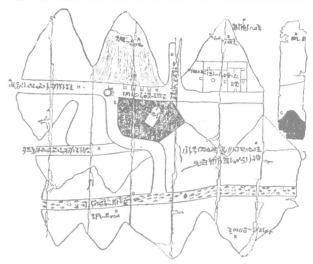

activity prestigious enough to record. They may also have employed local labor, as at Timna, traded with local people for copper, or acquired their principal supplies elsewhere.

The eastern desert of Egypt yielded many stones for building and statuary, as well as semiprecious stones, and was the route to the Red Sea. Some quarries were near the Nile valley, like Gebel Ahmar for quartzite and Hatnub for calcite (also known as Egyptian alabaster or travertine), but others, especially the sources of graywacke (or siltstone, a hard, blackish stone) in the Wadi Hammamat and the gold mines, most of which are south of the latitude of Koptos, required significant expeditions. They could not have been exploited without Egyptian domination of, or collaboration with, the sparse local nomadic population. The Egyptians also needed control in order to use the three main routes to the Red Sea. These run by way of the Wadi Gasus to Safaga, the Wadi Hammamat to Quseir, and the Wadi Abbad to Berenike; there is also a minor route from about 80 kilometers south of Cairo to the Gulf of Suez. The earliest evidence for their use is from the end of the Predynastic Period (Wadi el-Qash, leading from Koptos to Berenike); this may relate to Red Sea trade or to mining or quarrying. The northerly routes are attested from all the main historical periods, and the southernmost from the New Kingdom on.

At the termination of the Wadi Gasus was a temple of the 12th Dynasty, as well as a nearby Egyptian port. Renewed evidence comes from the 25th and 26th Dynasties (700–525 BCE), and the pattern probably continued in the Persian Period (6th–5th century BCE), when a route to Iran around the Arabian coast was opened up. The Roman Period is represented at the sites of Quseir and Berenike, which were ports for trade with East Africa and India. Although there is no evidence that the earlier Egyptians had contacts so far afield, such ports were probably used for trade with the fabled and idealized land

Right The only surviving Egyptian map. A fragment of a sketch map that probably shows the central area of the Wadi Hammamat, where there are graywacke quarries and gold mines. Additional fragments (not shown) give a long track with few topographical details. The hieratic captions describe manmade and natural features and the whole is related to the extraction of a partly worked statue that was taken to the Theban West Bank in year 6, perhaps of Ramesses IV. Turin, Museo Egizio.

of Punt, which is mentioned in texts from the Old Kingdom on. If the term "Punt" designated any single location, it is most likely to have been in the region of modern Eritrea, where finds of the Hellenistic and Roman Periods have been reported. The articles obtained from there were all exotic or luxury goods, the most important being incense; Punt may also have been an entrepôt for materials traded from much further away. Whether the Punt trade was the only reason for navigation on the Red Sea, apart from access to some areas of Sinai, is uncertain. Egyptian 18th-Dynasty beads have been reported on the East African coast south of the river Juba near the Equator; but this does not mean that the Egyptians themselves penetrated this far.

Nubia

The political boundary of Egypt at the first cataract was established in late Predynastic times, replacing an earlier natural frontier at Gebel el-Silsila, where the limestone hills to either side of the Nile give way to sandstone, which is the basic element in the rock as far south as the Butana in central Sudan. At Gebel el-Silsila the sandstone comes down to the river on either side, and the site was the main quarry for building stone for Upper Egypt from the New Kingdom on. Limestone allowed the Nile to carve a relatively broad floodplain, whereas the area of arable land beside sandstone reaches is very narrow.

South of Gebel el-Silsila was the first Egyptian nome or province, the main towns in which were Aswan and Kom Ombo. Its early separate status was recorded in its name "Nubia"; this area has always been culturally mixed. Between the first and second cataracts lay Lower Nubia, which was Egypt's prime target for conquest. For much of the third millennium BCE evidence for a settled population in Lower Nubia is lacking. An Egyptian settlement at Buhen north of the second cataract implies hegemony, if not rule. In the 6th Dynasty the Egyptians yielded to local inhabitants, but control was regained in the 11th Dynasty and again at the end of the 17th. The 18th-Dynasty kings extended Egyptian rule as far as Kurgus, south of the caravan route across the Eastern Desert from Korosko to Abu Hamed. This acquisition of territory was significant for later times, when an Egyptian-influenced civilization arose and established its center at Napata, the capital of Upper Nubia, producing the 25th Egyptian Dynasty and the state of Napata–Meroe, which survived into the 4th century CE.

Lower Nubia seems to have been regarded almost as being Egyptian by right, and was significant for access to raw materials, principally hard stones and gold, in the desert to either side of the Nile. It can never have been agriculturally important, because the cultivable area is no more than a narrow strip on either side of the river. It was also, however, the route through which came many of the southern products the Egyptians prized. These included spices, ivory, ebony, ostrich feathers, and certain species of baboon; pygmies figured in the stereotyped landscape of the Nile in Classical antiquity, and must have been traded as human exotica in some periods. It is not known what the Egyptians offered in return for all this, and hardly any archaeological evidence for ancient trade with Egypt has so far been found in sub-Saharan Africa. The ultimate provenance of many of the goods is unknown – pygmies probably never spread north of the Nile–Congo watershed, while commodities such as ebony must have come from the rain forest – and they may have passed through numerous intermediaries before reaching Egypt. It is difficult for us to evaluate the importance of these products for the Egyptians, which was often religious, but they were made into a focus for prestige comparable to precious stones and rare exotica in the modern world.

Palestine and Syria

The last major area to be considered here is the coastal region of Palestine and Syria. Contacts between Egypt and the Near East are attested from Predynastic times, and the name of Naʿrmer, the latest king of Dynasty 0, has been found at several sites in Palestine. Trade in lapis lazuli, whose main ancient source was Badakshan in Afghanistan, flourished from still earlier, and Egypt may already have been importing metal from Asia. Connections between Egypt and Byblos in Lebanon are attested in the Old Kingdom, and the funerary boat of Khufu, the builder of the Great Pyramid, was made of Lebanese cedar. Egyptian wood is sparse and of poor quality, so that good timber always had to be imported from the Near East. The Middle Kingdom saw an intensification of these links, while in the New Kingdom the Egyptians conquered large parts of the area and held them for more than two centuries, exploiting vassal city-states and trading with neighbors. During resurgences of Egyptian power in the 22nd and 26th Dynasties parts of Palestine were again conquered, as they were also in the Ptolemaic Period. The possession of part of Syria-Palestine was a natural goal for a strong regime in Egypt, but its achievement was far more difficult than in Nubia.

Many advances in Egyptian material culture came from the Near East. In return for these "invisible" imports and for wood, copper, possibly tin, silver, precious stones, wine, and oil, the Egyptians could offer four main resources: gold, linen, food surpluses, and, particularly in later periods, papyrus. Trade in gold and the bartering of African goods imported into Egypt are well known, but exports of food and other non-prestige products can be proved only in exceptional cases. They leave little or no mark in the archaeological record and are almost never mentioned in texts, the best-known textual allusion being a gift of grain by Merneptah to the Hittites during a famine, which is not trade. But Egyptian agriculture was far more secure and productive than any in Syria-Palestine, and just as Rome's granary in imperial times was Egypt, so may the Near East's have been in some earlier periods. Grain was very important in Late Period foreign relations, especially with the Aegean.

In various periods Egypt also had relations with a number of more distant areas, including Mesopotamia, Anatolia, Iran, Arabia, the Aegean, Cyprus, Rome, and India. Whereas earlier Egypt was rather self-contained in culture, politics, and economy, from the mid second millennium BCE onward it was increasingly integrated into the Near East and the Mediterranean world. Both its naturally well defined boundaries and its position at the bridge between Africa and Asia, the tropics and the temperate zone, are vital to understanding its civilization.

Below Granite outcrop near Aswan with quarry marks. The rows of tooth-like indentations are where slots were cut in the quarrying process. The exact method of extraction of the granite is not fully understood. The scorings on some surfaces were probably made with iron tools. These workings therefore date no earlier than c. 700 BCE.

Bottom Landscape in the southern part of the eastern desert. Although this area is somewhat less arid than the western desert, the organization of expeditions to mine or collect minerals in it must have posed formidable problems. Even so, exploration was very thorough; few significant mineral deposits have been found that were not exploited in antiquity.

Natural resources of ancient Egypt
The sites indicated are places where there are ancient workings of the minerals named. It is often impossible to date workings precisely, but several are exclusively Greco-Roman, such as the sources of emerald or beryl, porphyry, and the granite of Mons Claudianus.

Further semiprecious stones and minerals occur in small deposits scattered over the eastern desert: agate; breccia; calcite (for 140 km north of Asyut); carnelian; chalcedony; felspar; garnet; iron; jasper; rock crystal (quartz); serpentine.

Gypsum is found west of the Nile for 100 km south from Cairo, and flint is widespread on either side of the valley, especially from Luxor to el-Kab. The hills near the Nile are composed of limestone as far south as Gebel el-Silsila; only quarries of good-quality building stone are marked.

Commodities imported from further afield included incense and myrrh from Punt (perhaps in the region of Eritrea and conceivably Yemen on the opposite shore of the Red Sea), obsidian from southern Ethiopia or possibly from the Aegean, silver from Syria, and lapis lazuli from Badakshan in northeastern Afghanistan. Tin may have come from Anatolia. Most of these were luxury products; the chief requirement of peasants for non-local materials was for flint or metal tools.

The area under cultivation fluctuated in extent, while the land available for grazing varied with long-term climatic changes.

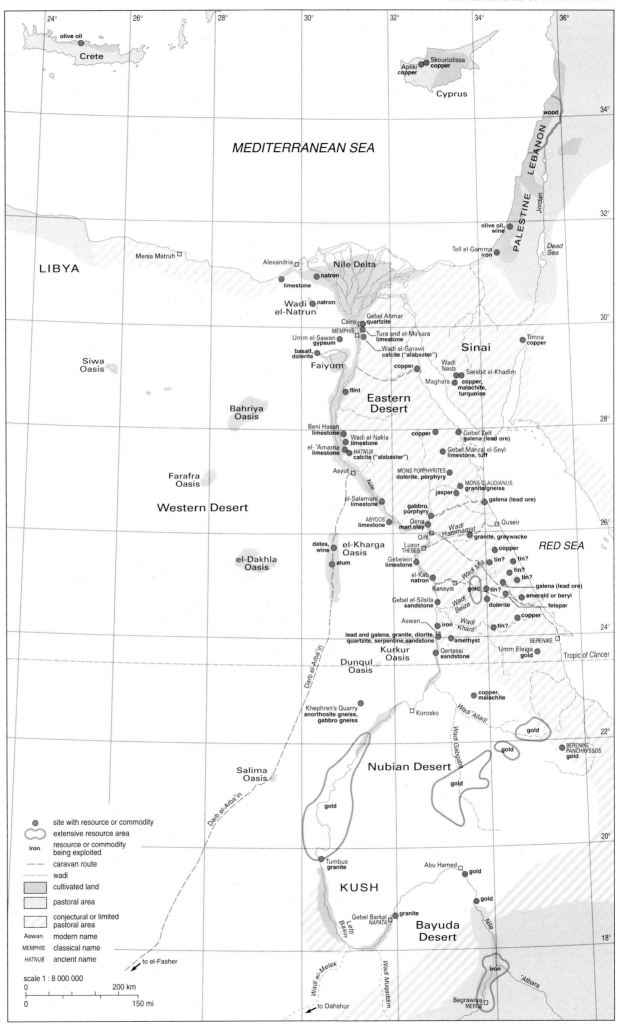

THE STUDY OF ANCIENT EGYPT

Egypt has been of almost continual interest to people of other cultures, and has been written about by authors from the Greek Hekataios of Miletos in the 6th century BCE (whose book is lost) to today. When ancient Egyptian civilization disappeared in the Byzantine Period it could no longer be an object of contemporary study, but it was remembered throughout the Middle Ages for its monuments, notably the pyramids. A number of medieval pilgrims to Palestine and Jerusalem visited Egypt, mostly to see sites associated with Christ's stay there; even the pyramids were believed to relate to the Bible, being the "granaries of Joseph."

The first stages

Interest in Mediterranean antiquity and knowledge of it revived in the Renaissance, and among the first Classical texts to be rediscovered and circulated in the 15th century were two products of the early centuries CE that were probably composed in Egypt in the Greek language. The first was the *Hieroglyphica* of Horapollo, which gives symbolic elucidations of a number of hieroglyphs. The second was the *Hermetic Corpus*, a set of philosophical tracts that contain Neoplatonist and other material as well as genuine Egyptian ideas. Texts of the latter type tended to support the assumption, which goes back to early Greek philosophers, that Egypt was the fount of ancient wisdom. The same is true of the *Hieroglyphica*, which was held to describe a method of encapsulating profound truths in pictorial signs.

In the 16th century antiquarians studied the physical remains of antiquity rather more. In Rome, the chief center of their researches, they were immediately confronted with Egyptian objects, most of which had been imported for the prestigious Isis cult in the early Empire, and included them in their publications. This material formed, with the obelisks that are still a striking element in the Roman scene, a nucleus that was generally recognized as being Egyptian, and was interpreted with the aid of writings about Egypt by authors of Classical antiquity. Illustrators of the time had no conception of the differences in character between their own methods of pictorial representation and those of ancient Egypt, so that many of their reproductions resemble the originals only very remotely.

The late 16th and early 17th centuries brought the first visits to Egypt in search of antiquities. Pietro della Valle (1586–1652) traveled all over the eastern Mediterranean from 1614 to 1626, bringing Egyptian mummies and important Coptic manuscripts back with him to Italy. The manuscripts were in the latest form of the Egyptian language, written in Greek letters, which was regularly learned by priests in the Coptic Church in Egypt, where it is used to this day in the liturgy. They could therefore be studied by those who knew Arabic, the language in which primers of Coptic were written. Two centuries later Coptic was fundamental to the decipherment of the hieroglyphic script. It was also the initial study of the

Block statue of the Chief Lector-Priest Petamenope: engraving in G. Herwart van Hohenburg, *Thesaurus Hieroglyphicorum* (1620), the earliest published collection of hieroglyphic inscriptions. Herwart showed the same object as two different ones, using two 16th-century manuscript sources as his models. From Rome (?), originally from Thebes; c. 650 BCE. Paris, Musée du Louvre. Another statue of the same man is illustrated on p. 198.

Obelisk and elephant: illustration of an imaginary mausoleum from Francesco Colonna, *Hypnerotomachia Polifili* (Venice, 1499). The "hieroglyphic" inscription is mostly after a Roman temple frieze that was believed to contain Egyptian hieroglyphs.

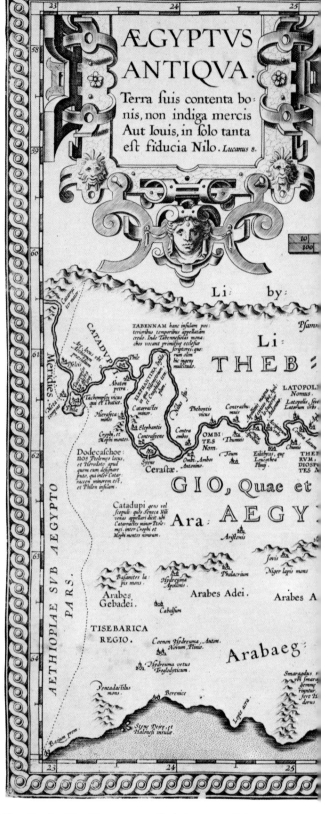

Map of ancient Egypt by Abraham Ortelius, Amsterdam, 1595. The motto reads "Rich in natural resources, Egypt places all her trust in the Nile, and so has no need of either foreign trade or the rain of heaven" (Lucan, *Civil War* 8.446–47). As on many other pre–1800 maps, north is placed on the right in order to give a "landscape" of the Nile. The map is a remarkable achievement, showing most towns and nomes in their correct relative positions, including Thebes 125 years before its site was identified on the ground. The information is almost all from Classical sources, the only ones then available for ancient Egypt, so that, for example, the Classical river mouths are shown. Note the list of unidentified places. The topography is not based on a survey and is inaccurate. London, British Library.

great Jesuit polymath Athanasius Kircher (1602–80), who wrote numerous works about ancient Egypt and was one of the first to attempt a decipherment.

A byway in the development of European knowledge of Egypt is revealed by a manuscript recording the travels of an unidentified Venetian in 1589 through Upper Egypt and Lower Nubia as far south as el-Derr. His is one of dozens of accounts by visitors to, and residents of, Egypt, but the only one to proclaim a disinterested fascination for the ancient monuments. The author stated that he "did not travel for

any useful purpose, but only to see so many superb edifices, churches, statues, colossi, obelisks, and columns." But "even though I went a great distance, none of the buildings I saw was worthy of admiration, except for one, which is called Ochsur [Luxor, within which he included Karnak] by the Moors [the Italian word for North Africans]." His evaluation foreshadowed the 19th century, when Luxor became a center of tourism. Of Karnak he said: "Judge whether this tremendous building is superior to the seven wonders of the world. One of them still exists, one of the pyramids of the pharaohs; in comparison with this construction it is a small thing. I am not sending anyone who wishes to see this monument to the end of the world; it is only ten days' journey from Cairo, and one can go there quite cheaply." This astonishing work was not published until the 20th century and seems to have had no influence on other writers.

In the next century the most nearly comparable text, known from secondary publications, is a narrative of the visit of two Capuchin friars to Luxor and Esna in 1668 where, they stated, "in human memory no Frenchman had ever been." Like their predecessor, they were pressed for time, but they succeeded in crossing to the west bank at Thebes and seeing the Valley of the Kings, the prime later tourist attraction that had eluded the Venetian.

Travelers and antiquaries
Explorations like those just mentioned cannot be termed archaeological. The word can, however, be used for the work of John Greaves (1602–52), an English astronomer who published his *Pyramidographia, or a Discourse of the Pyramids in Aegypt* in 1646. Greaves visited Giza on two occasions in 1638–39, measured and examined the pyramids thoroughly, and made a critical analysis of ancient writings about them; he also went to Saqqara. The resulting work was more penetrating than any other of its time on ancient Egypt; a notable feature is its use of medieval Arabic sources. Essentially Greaves followed the example of humanist scholarship of the Renaissance, but his application of the methods to Egypt was scarcely imitated by others.

From the later 17th century onward the number of travelers to Egypt increased gradually, and their writings started to incorporate usable drawings of the monuments. The most significant advance in knowledge was made by the Jesuit Claude Sicard (1677–1726), who was commissioned by the French regent to investigate ancient monuments in Egypt. His studies were never finally completed and survive mainly in the form of letters and a map. He visited Upper Egypt four times, and was the first modern traveler to identify the site of Thebes, and to attribute correctly the colossi of Memnon and the Valley of the Kings – on the basis of Classical descriptions. His most important successor was the Dane Frederik Ludwig Norden (1708–42), who visited Egypt in 1737–38, and whose posthumously published volume of travels, magnificently illustrated with his own drawings, appeared in various editions from 1751 to the end of the 18th century.

The increase in the numbers of visitors to Egypt went together with an improvement in the treatment of Egyptian artifacts – and of antiquity and exotic cultures as a whole – in major 18th century works, of which the most important are the multi-volume compilations of Bernard de Montfaucon (published in 1719–24) and the Comte de Caylus (1752–64). Both devoted a notable amount of space to Egyptian objects, while also assigning to Egypt much that came from elsewhere. Considerable collections of Egyptian antiquities already existed; some, like a small group that was in the Bodleian Library in Oxford in the seventeenth century, even included forgeries.

Decipherment of the hieroglyphic script
Throughout the 18th century the hieroglyphic script continued to be studied, although little progress was

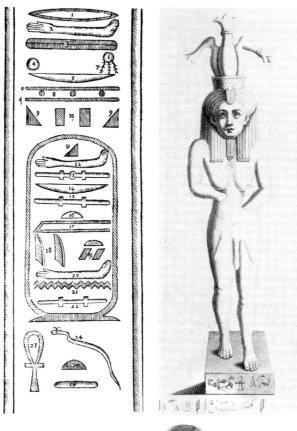

Far left Part of the titulary of the Roman emperor Domitian (81–96 CE) on the obelisk in Piazza Navona in Rome; engraving from Athanasius Kircher, *Obeliscus Pamphilius* (Rome, 1650). The small numbers refer to allegorical explanations of the signs in the text of the book.

Left Bronze statuette of Haʿpy, the inundation, dedicated by Tjahapimu, son of Ptahirdis; engraving from B. de Montfaucon, *L'Antiquité expliquée et représentée en figures. Supplément* (Paris, 1724). The object, then in Montpellier, was acquired by the Musée des Beaux-Arts in Lyon in 1835.

Below Group of small objects that were in the Bodleian Library in Oxford, including some received from the collection of Archbishop William Laud (1573–1645) in 1635. The two figures on the left are genuine, but those on the lower right are forgeries. No. 32 may imitate an "Isis-knot" amulet; D is a seventeenth-century pseudo-shawabty. Oxford, Ashmolean Museum.

Bottom View of rock-cut shrines and inscriptions at Gebel el-Silsila, from F. L. Norden, *Voyage d'Egypte et de Nubie* (Copenhagen, 1755).

Vue des Chapelles taillées dans le roc près de la Pierre de la Chaine à Tshibel Esselsele. a La dite Pierre le Bloc de Granit, avec une inscription en Hieroglyphes. Chapelles pleines de Hieroglyphes. Rochers de Granit.

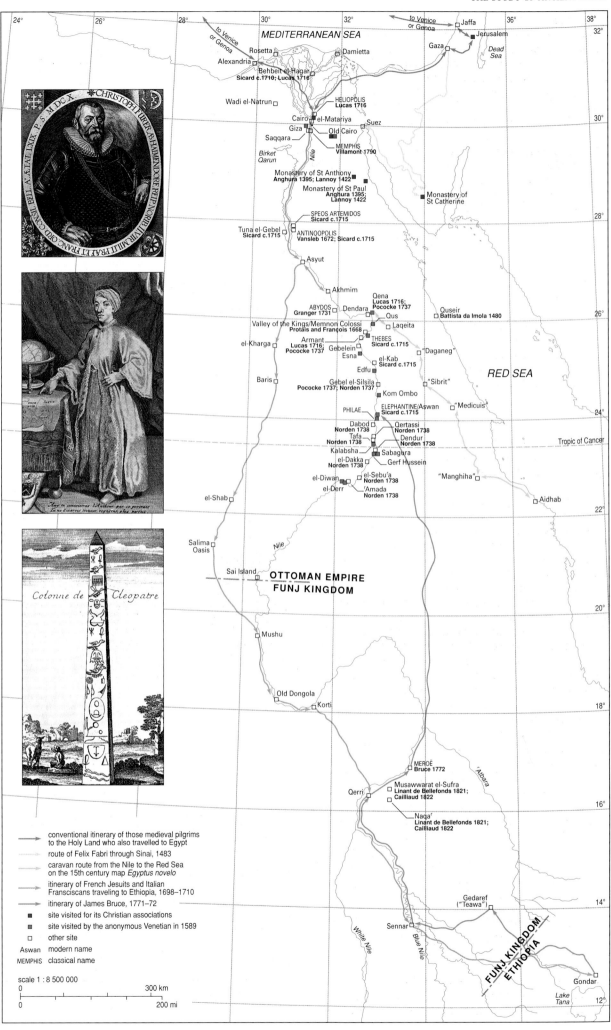

Travelers to Egypt and Sudan before 1800
The towns and sites marked are prominent in the records of travelers before Napoleon's expedition of 1798. Some of their names and the dates of their visits are given in bold type.

Inset Illustrations from the books of less well known travelers, published on their return to Europe. More than 200 accounts of travelers whose journeys included Egypt survive from 1400–1700.

Top Christoph Fürer von Haimendorf, aged 69, dated 1610; from *Itinerarium Aegypti Arabiae, Syriae, aliumque regionum orientalium* (Nürnberg, 1610).

Center Jean de Thevenot (1633–67), frontispiece of *Voyages de M. de Thevenot en Europe, Asie & Afrique* (Amsterdam, 1727; originally Paris, 1665). The inscription says "Friend, you may know the author from this portrait; /you could not find a traveler more perfect."

Bottom Obelisk of Senwosret I at Heliopolis; the hieroglyphs are legible but quite un-Egyptian in style, and the landscape is European. From Gemelli Careri, *Voyage du tour du monde* (Paris, 1729), whose text implies that the obelisk was in Alexandria.

made toward a decipherment. Antiquarian and linguistic interest in Egypt culminated with the Dane Georg Zoëga (1755–1809), whose two major works, a treatise on obelisks, which includes a section on the hieroglyphic script, and a catalog of Coptic manuscripts in the Vatican collections, are of lasting value. The 1797 work on obelisks marks a peak in Egyptian studies before Napoleon's expedition in 1798. Although the script could, and no doubt would, have been deciphered without the discovery of bilingual inscriptions, Egyptology as we know it is a product of that expedition, during which the Rosetta Stone was unearthed, of the associated surge of enthusiasm for Egypt, and of gradual changes in the intellectual climate of western Europe.

Napoleon's expedition was accompanied by a vast team of scholars who were sent to study and record all aspects of Egypt, ancient and modern. The Rosetta Stone soon passed into British hands, but the team produced a fundamental multi-volume work, the *Description de l'Egypte*, first published in 1809–30. This was the last, and much the most important, such work produced before the decipherment of the script by Jean-François Champollion le Jeune (1790–1832) in 1822–24, which signals the beginning of Egyptology as a distinct subject. Champollion and the Pisan Ippolito Rosellini (1800–43) mounted a joint expedition to record monuments in Egypt in the late 1820s, but by that time they were latecomers on the scene. In the previous twenty years numerous travelers had visited Egyptian and Lower Nubian sites and had rifled them for antiquities, written books about them, or both. Prominent among them were several consuls of European nations, the Italian strongman Giovanni Belzoni (1778–1823), the French sculptor Jean Jacques Rifaud (1786–1852), the Swiss traveler Johann Ludwig Burckhardt (1784–1817), and the Franco-German Franz Christian Gau (1790–1853). The collections some of these men gathered formed the nuclei of the Egyptian sections of the British Museum in London, the Louvre in Paris, the Rijksmuseum van Oudheden in Leiden, and the Museo Egizio

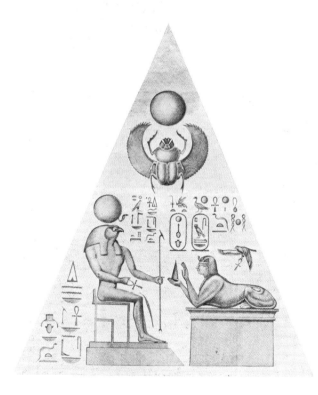

in Turin (there was no Egyptian Museum in Cairo until the late 1850s). In the first half of the 19th century digging in Egypt was primarily for objects. The recovery of information, as against objects, came a poor second.

Before his death in 1832 Champollion had made great progress in understanding the Egyptian language and in reconstructing Egyptian history and civilization, but this work had little impact, both because of delays in publication and because of its strictly academic nature. By 1840 the first generation of Egyptologists was already dead, and the subject retained a precarious existence in France, with Vicomte Emmanuel de Rougé (1811–72), in Holland with Conrad Leemans (1809–93), and especially in Prussia with Carl Richard Lepsius (1810–84). Lepsius's

Above Frontispiece of F. L. Norden, *Voyage d'Egypte et de Nubie* (Copenhagen, 1755). The central allegory shows: Fame; Ancient Egypt displaying her treasures; a lion with the arms of ancient kings of Denmark; and the Nile. There is also a Classical figure of Isis, as well as Egyptian monuments and other motifs.

Left Pyramidion of the obelisk of Psammetichus II by the Palazzo di Montecitorio in Rome; from G. Zoëga, *De origine et usu obeliscorum* (Rome, 1797). The copy is accurate and legible, but its style is rather un-Egyptian.

12-volume *Denkmaeler aus Aegypten und Aethiopien* (1849–59), the result of an expedition up the Nile as far as Meroe in 1842–45, is the earliest reliable publication of a large selection of monuments, and remains of fundamental importance. The English pioneer Wilkinson is treated in detail on pages 106–07.

The growth of Egyptology

In the mid-19th century Lepsius, his younger contemporary Heinrich Brugsch (1827–94), and a handful of other scholars continued to advance the subject, while Auguste Mariette (1821–81), a Frenchman who was originally sent to acquire Coptic manuscripts for the Louvre in 1850, placed work in Egypt on a permanent footing. Mariette entered the service of the Khedive Said in 1858, excavated at many sites before and after that date, and founded the Egyptian Museum and Antiquities Service (now Supreme Council of Antiquities). The aims of the latter were to preserve and record the monuments, to excavate, and to administer the museum. Until the Egyptian Revolution of 1952 its directors were European, the best known of them being Gaston Maspero (1846–1916).

The aims of scientific excavation in Egypt were first stated in 1862 by the Scot Alexander Rhind (1833–63), but they were not realized on any scale until the work of Sir William Matthew Flinders Petrie (1853–1942). Petrie first went to Egypt in 1880 to make measurements of the Great Pyramid for the supposed arcane secrets it embodied – a pursuit generally termed "pyramidology". He was soon convinced of the spuriousness of pyramidology and went on to excavate at sites all over Egypt, publishing a volume almost every year on the results of the preceding winter. Among his excavations were major discoveries, but his work was far more important in providing a framework of method, information, and typology about the different areas and periods, often resulting from reworking sites that had already been excavated

summarily by others. During his own lifetime Petrie's standards were overtaken, notably by the American George Andrew Reisner (1867–1942), but Reisner published relatively little of his results.

From about 1880 to 1914 there was much archaeological work in Egypt, and sites in Nubia came into prominence with the completion and subsequent raising of the first Aswan Dam (1902 and 1907). The end of the 19th century saw major advances in the understanding of Egyptian language and chronology, made in Berlin by Adolf Erman (1854–1937) and Eduard Meyer (1855–1930) respectively, and the discovery of sites from all historical periods, as well as Predynastic phases from Naqada I on. Work since then has developed knowledge greatly in all areas, but only in a few has it changed the outlines fundamentally. In comparison, the 19th century was a time of continuous change. Until about 1870 most Egyptological knowledge related to late stages of the civilization, while there was no proper division of the physical remains or of the language into periods. As knowledge advanced, interest tended to focus on the earlier, more "classical" phases of both.

Excavation in the 20th century

The public image of 20th century excavation was dominated by a few spectacular discoveries and by the salvage campaigns in Nubia occasioned by the second raising of the first Aswan dam in the 1930s and the construction of the High Dam in the 1960s. There was no systematic survey of the whole country, but increasing numbers of sites were nonetheless explored. Complementary to excavation, and as important, is the recording and publication of standing monuments, which first reached adequate standards around 1900. This does not have the glamor of excavation and has seldom attracted the same public interest or support.

Foremost in popular attention has been exploration in the Valley of the Kings at Thebes. The first

Excavations in the First Intermediate period town at Abydos, south of the Osiris temple, 1979 season. The site is dug in squares that are extended into trenches, with the sections left as a check on stratification. This is one of relatively few townsites that have been excavated in Upper Egypt. Pennsylvania–Yale–Institute of Fine Arts expedition to Abydos.

find of royalty was the discovery in the 1870s by the ʿAbd el-Rasul family of Qurna of the pit containing the mummies of a majority of the New Kingdom kings. They had been removed from their original tombs in the 21st Dynasty and reburied near Deir el-Bahri for greater security. Like many important discoveries, this was the result of the search by local inhabitants for marketable antiquities, not of systematic excavation. While Egyptologists rightly deplore the loss of information that goes with these discoveries, many of them would never have been made by orthodox expeditions.

In 1898 the tomb of Amenhotep II was discovered by Victor Loret (1859–1946) in the Valley of the Kings, and proved to contain the mummies of most of the kings missing from the earlier find. Work in the valley continued almost without interruption until 1932. The most methodical examination was by Howard Carter (1874–1939), under the patronage of Lord Carnarvon. Carter's main discovery was the tomb of Tutʿankhamun, which he found in 1922 and worked on for ten years. Although other intact royal burials have been excavated in the Near East, this is the richest single find and contained many unique objects. The rediscovery of the damaged but enormous tomb of the sons of Ramesses II by Kent Weeks in 1989 showed, contrary to some expectations, that the Valley still has surprises to offer.

Several other royal burials or cemeteries were excavated in Egypt in the 20th century. Reisner's discovery of the funerary deposit of Hetepheres at Giza in 1925 is the only major find of Old Kingdom jewelry and furniture; the recovery of the forms of decayed wooden objects was a triumph of recording. In the 1940s Pierre Montet (1885–1966) excavated several intact tombs of the 21st- and 22nd-Dynasty kings and royal family at Tanis, producing rare examples of art in precious materials from a period that has left rather few significant remains.

The most important excavated settlement sites, el-ʿAmarna and Deir el-Medina, have been extensively studied. After the clandestine discovery of the el-ʿAmarna cuneiform tablets in the 1880s Urbain Bouriant (1849–1903) worked there, producing a volume with the striking title *Two Days' Excavation at Tell el Amarna* (c. 1884). He was followed by Petrie (1891–92), whose brief stay produced much of value, but was overshadowed by a German expedition in 1913–14 under Ludwig Borchardt (1863–1938), during which the house compound of the sculptor Thutmose was found. This contained the world-famous bust of Nefertiti and other masterpieces. In the 1920s and 1930s there were several seasons of British excavation, which contributed both to the history of the later 18th Dynasty and to the understanding of the short-lived capital, which has been further illuminated by re-excavation and analysis under Barry Kemp since 1977. Deir el-Medina was a source of finds throughout the 19th century, and was excavated by an Italian expedition at the turn of the century and a German one under Georg Möller (1876–1921) in 1911–13. In 1917 the Institut Français d'Archéologie Orientale in Cairo began excavations there that continued with interruptions until the 1970s, uncovering the workmen's village and adjacent necropolis almost completely.

The Egyptian Antiquities Service and Egyptian Egyptologists have been crucial to the development of Egyptology. After the foundation of the Service

Group of foreign captives – a Libyan, a Nubian (?), an Asiatic, and another Libyan – on a relief from the causeway of the mortuary complex of Sahureʿ at Abusir. The superbly accurate drawing is from L. Borchardt *et al.*, *Das Grabdenkmal des Königs Śa3ḥu-Reʿ*, ii (Leipzig, 1913), plate 7.

under Mariette, its first Egyptian high official was Ahmed Kamal (1849–1932), who worked in the Cairo Museum and excavated at a number of sites. In the 20th century an increasing proportion of the staff of the Service was Egyptian, and Egyptians taught Egyptology at Cairo University. Since 1952 both sectors have been completely Egyptian. The Service has excavated more than any other body, and much of the material in the Cairo Museum and in other museums around the country comes from its excavations. The most striking Egyptian discoveries are perhaps those at Tuna el-Gebel, where an animal necropolis and a Greco-Egyptian city of the dead have been excavated, and the pioneer work of Ahmed Fakhry (1905–73) in the oases of the western desert.

Since the 1960s archaeology has become more prominent in Egyptology, both in the data it supplies to all aspects of the subject and, more significantly, in its contribution of a distinctive approach, especially to comprehending the society as a whole and not just its tiny elite. Standards of excavation and survey have risen greatly and the range of sites studied has increased. Because of high population levels and alterations to the environment, much fieldwork is now rescue archaeology, especially in the delta.

Surveys and publications

There have been exhaustive surveys of Nubia as far upstream as the Dal cataract. Archaeologically, Lower Nubia is one of the world's most studied areas. Only the fortress site of Qasr Ibrim remains above water, and this is still being excavated. The expansion in Nubian studies, and the wide spread of finds from the Paleolithic to the 19th century CE, have led to the creation of a virtually separate field of study.

The recording of complete monuments in Egypt was initiated by Maxence de Rochemonteix (1849–91) and Johannes Dümichen (1833–94), but neither lived to complete his work. In the 1890s the Egypt Exploration Fund (later Society) began an "Archaeological Survey of Egypt," which was to record standing monuments, while Jacques de Morgan (1857–

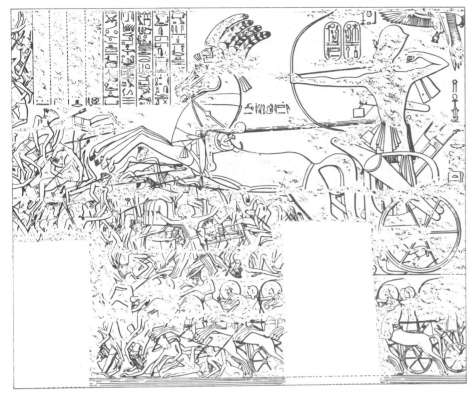

Relief of Ramesses III in battle against the "Sea Peoples" in the definitive publication by the Oriental Institute of the University of Chicago: *Medinet Habu*, i (Chicago, 1930), plate 32. This synoptic drawing is followed by two details of sections of the scene.

1924) started a *Catalogue des Monuments*, which published the temple of Kom Ombo. These projects were unrealistically ambitious, but the Archaeological Survey initiated the work of Norman de Garis Davies (1865–1941), the most prolific copyist of Egyptian monuments. He published more than 25 volumes on tombs alone, almost always presenting a complete record of their decoration; his wife Nina and others made colored reproductions of selected scenes. There are few full publications of monuments in color photographs; really effective presentation of the unique and vanishing legacy of color on Egyptian monuments has yet to be achieved.

The most important epigraphic venture to follow Davies was the foundation of Chicago House, a field station of the Oriental Institute of the University of Chicago at Luxor, in 1924. The Oriental Institute itself was the creation of James Henry Breasted (1865–1935), a major scholar and the virtual founder of American Egyptology, who gained the support of John D. Rockefeller. The Chicago expedition produced the only exhaustive record of a large Egyptian temple in facsimile (*Medinet Habu*, 1930–70) and a number of other volumes. Another work that set comparable standards, also funded by Rockefeller, was the publication of the inner parts of the temple of Sety I at Abydos by Amice M. Calverley (1896–1959) and Myrtle F. Broome (1888–1978). Methods of digital recording of the monuments have begun to be used but have not yet superseded more traditional ones.

Egyptology outside Egypt
Indispensable though it is, fieldwork is a small part of the total activity of Egyptologists, and there is often rather little contact between the field and the study. It is more difficult to select names among mainly armchair Egyptologists than it is for fieldworkers, but it is necessary for the sake of balance.

A fundamental objective is to understand the Egyptian language. Early in the 20th century F. Ll. Griffith (1862–1934) and Wilhelm Spiegelberg

(1870–1930) advanced enormously the knowledge of demotic, the cursive script and language of the Late and Greco-Roman Periods. In 1927 Sir Alan Gardiner (1879–1963) produced a renowned grammar of Middle Egyptian, incorporating discoveries of his own and of Battiscombe Gunn (1883–1950). Research on the language continues, the major figure of the later 20th century being H. J. Polotsky (1905–91); the day when the language will be completely understood is not in sight. Similarly, the 11-volume dictionary published in 1926–53 and edited by Erman with Hermann Grapow (1885–1967) was a huge advance on the pioneer work of Brugsch, but marks the beginning rather than the end of the study of Egyptian words.

Egyptologists need publications of the monuments, more detailed studies on texts – hieroglyphic, hieratic, and demotic – and numerous reference works. In these areas Kurt Sethe (1869–1934) was perhaps the leading scholar. Starting as a grammarian, he later made contributions in almost all areas, and was the most prolific editor of texts, whose work remains indispensable. Gardiner was the leading editor of papyrus texts, who with the papyrus conservator Hugo Ibscher (1874–1943) set new standards in the treatment of the papyri themselves and in their presentation. His collaborator Jaroslav Černý (1898–1970) was the outstanding worker on the ostraca and cursive documents from Deir el-Medina in particular.

As examples of more general Egyptological work it is worth singling out, more or less arbitrarily, two writers who changed whole areas of the subject; further names may be found in the bibliography. Heinrich Schäfer (1868–1957) published the fundamental work on Egyptian representational art, which analyzes how the Egyptians depicted objects and figures in the natural world (see pp. 60–61). Gerhard Fecht transformed our view of the organization of Egyptian texts, showing that the majority of them are written in a kind of meter. It seems that writing was more normally in "verse" than in "prose." Both these scholars illuminated areas that are alien to modern eyes, demonstrating features that are prerequisites to a proper comprehension of ancient sources. Everywhere in Egyptology what has been done is a prelude to what might be done. Sadly, original work in the subject has become almost exclusively confined to universities, research institutes, and museums.

Today Egyptology is pursued in academic institutions in more than 25 countries. The several hundred Egyptologists cover fields, such as archaeology, language, literature, history, religion, art, that would be separate in the study of more recent civilizations. This interdisciplinary character has the advantage of requiring the practitioner to maintain a general perspective, but can pose difficulties for detailed work or for major projects.

Ancient Egypt has participated in a general upsurge in interest in early civilizations and is now seen as an essential contributor to discussions of their nature and character; a major scholar who has been active here is Jan Assmann. The advances in archaeology outlined above have also played their part in this more thorough integration of Egyptology among the humanities and social sciences. These developments are beneficial, because no subject can be autonomous. Moreover, the legacy which ancient Egypt can offer toward the broader understanding of human societies is uniquely rich in many domains.

THE HISTORICAL BACKGROUND

Predynastic Egypt

The material culture of northern Africa was very uniform as late as the end of the last Ice Age (c. 10,000 BCE). The gradual formation of Egyptian civilization was a separation from this background, much affected by changes in climate. The most striking features of this process are the acceleration of change in the centuries before the beginning of the Dynastic Period, and the enormous gulf between the Egyptian state of the Old Kingdom and its Predynastic antecedents, perhaps half a millennium earlier. Egyptian culture did not then become static, but there was never again such a surge of growth; a continuity can be discerned from the Old Kingdom to the Roman Period that cannot be found between Predynastic and Dynastic Egypt.

The earlier Predynastic cultures were not uniform over the country, and the two main regions developed along different lines. On the delta margins the large site of Merimda Beni Salama provides evidence of two phases of a Neolithic culture dating to perhaps 5000 BCE that is likely to have spread over much of the north. On present evidence it appears slightly later than some Neolithic sites in the depressions of the Western Desert south of el-Kharga Oasis, but this seeming priority is likely to be due to the better preservation of desert sites. In the Faiyum, slightly later cultures of similar character are known from the then lake-shore. In the Nile valley the earliest Neolithic, settled, food-producing cultures are the Tarifian in the Theban area, the Tasian, and the Badarian (named for the sites at which they were first identified, as are those mentioned below); the last two may not in fact be separate (c. 4500 BCE). These are confined to an area south of Asyut and consist mainly of modest cemetery sites, perhaps near lost settlements that are likely to have been less substantial and permanent than later habitation sites. Several further Neolithic cultures are known from the second cataract area.

Naqada I (or Amratian) is, like its predecessors, a local, small-scale village culture, but toward its end signs of incipient social stratification appear. It is also known from a wider area, and is a prelude to the more expansive phase of Naqada II.

Naqada II (or Gerzean) forms the turning point in the development of Predynastic Egypt, and gradually spread over the entire Nile valley and into the delta. Social stratification is evident and significant population centers developed, notably Hierakonpolis (Kom el-Ahmar), Koptos (Qift), Naqada, and Abydos. This is the last period during which cultures north and south of the first cataract were at all comparable. The Nubian cultures of Predynastic times, which are distributed as far south as Khartoum, are not sharply distinct from those of Egypt. There was probably exchange over the whole region but no central political authority. The cultural demarcation with the Nubian A Group, which becomes noticeable in the first cataract region in Naqada II, accompanied the emergence of complex society in Egypt and the definition of a political frontier. This process led into Naqada III, the latest predynastic phase, and the Early Dynastic Period, when Egypt was united under a single ruler, within boundaries comparable to those of later periods. No sharp break in material culture can be seen between Naqada III and the Early Dynastic Period, even though the transformation over the centuries was almost total.

Some Naqada II/III motifs in art and items of technology demonstrate cultural contact with Mesopotamia, whose example could have stimulated the invention of Egyptian writing, although the two systems are not closely similar and it is

Predynastic and Early Dynastic Egypt

A number of Egyptian-type Predynastic cultures are attested. These include: Tasian/Badarian; Naqada I; Naqada II; lower Egyptian and delta cultures (contemporary with Badarian to mid-Naqada II, but not uniform); Faiyum Neolithic culture; Naqada III, leading into Early Dynastic.

Many Predynastic sites ceased to be used in the Early Dynastic Period, in part because the desert became less significant as a resource and in part through urbanization and reorganization of the population.

Rock drawings of varying dates are common in all desert areas, many of them probably carved by nomads. Mostly they are close to tracks; in Lower Nubia they are also frequent near the Nile. Their style continued to be un-Egyptian in the Dynastic Period. The hard stones of the eastern desert were used by the valley dwellers throughout the Predynastic and Early Dynastic Periods.

The political status of the capitals marked, with the exceptions of Abydos and Memphis, is uncertain.

Nubian-type sites include those of the A Group and are distinguished as either early A Group (contemporary with late Naqada I and early Naqada II), or Classic and Terminal A group (contemporary with late Naqada II–Naqada III). In the area of the second cataract, Nubian-type sites also include Khartoum Variant, c. 4500–3500 BCE; Post-Shamarkian, c. 3500 BCE; and Abkan, c. 4000–3200 BCE, overlapping with Classic A Group.

Favorable conditions and extensive surveys have led to the identification of numerous sites of all these types, which are much better attested than their Egyptian counterparts.

Far right: The second cataract area in Predynastic times

Left Objects from tombs of the Naqada I period. Left: unfired silt statuette of a woman with her right hand under her left breast, with exaggerated thighs and legs. Center: fine black topped red-ware pot with a design of uncertain meaning incised post-firing. Right: elaborately worked flint knife, probably a ceremonial object. Oxford, Ashmolean Museum.

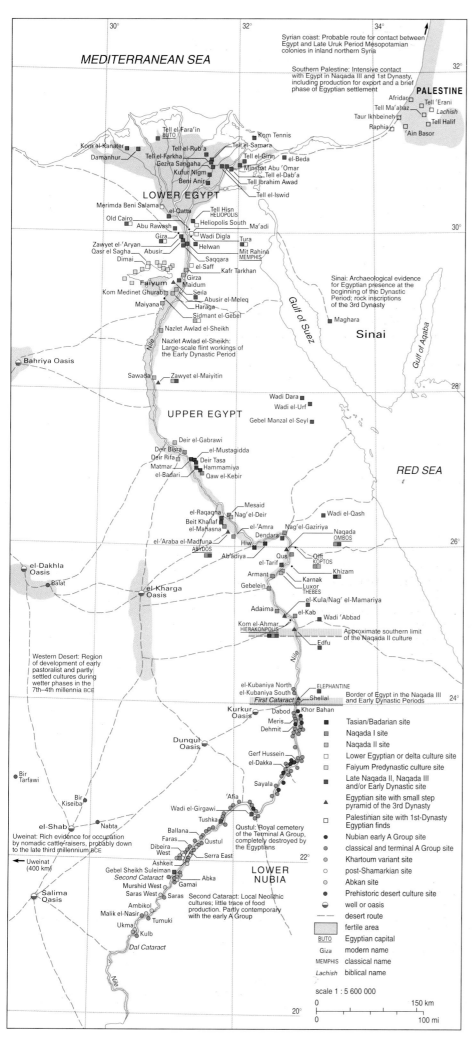

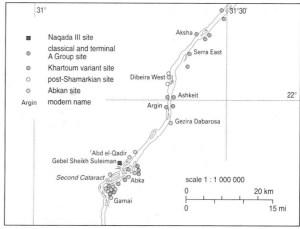

uncertain which is the older. The most likely method of transmission between the regions is trade, which had already brought lapis lazuli to Egypt from eastern Afghanistan. Mesopotamian colonies founded in northern Syria in the late Uruk period (late fourth millennium) would have provided a staging point on the way to Egypt. In Naqada III, the latter phase of which is often termed Dynasty 0, Egypt also traded with southern Palestine and seems to have set up colonies there that disappeared during the 1st Dynasty.

Later written sources suggest that there were rulers of all Egypt before the beginning of the 1st Dynasty, and that they succeeded earlier dynasties of rulers of the "Two Lands" of Upper and Lower Egypt. But the idea of two Predynastic kingdoms may be a projection of the pervasive dualities of Egyptian ideology, not a record of a true historical situation. More probably there was a gradual unification of a previously uncentralized society, reflected in the cultural uniformity of the country at the end of Naqada II, and in objects bearing early versions of the later royal emblem of the *serekh*, a brick facade whose developed form is the king's Horus name, in which a hawk surmounts a facade with a space for a name. Motifs of this sort have been found in Upper Egypt, in the area around Memphis, and in the delta. The appearance of the motif is roughly contemporary with cemeteries U and B at Abydos, which contain royal tombs of Dynasty 0 and are near the tombs of the 1st-Dynasty kings. Thus, rulers in Naqada III, centered on Abydos, seem to have controlled most of the country. Another major site of this period is Kom el-Ahmar (Hierakonpolis), but no tradition of a capital there is known. Probably during Naqada III the A Group culture of Lower Nubia, which had become stratified rather like those of Egypt, was destroyed; an Egyptian triumphal relief of the period at Gebel Sheikh Suleiman (now moved to Khartoum) suggests that Egypt eliminated this potential southern rival, suppressing settled population in the area for many centuries thereafter.

The monumental schist palettes and maceheads of the latest Predynastic kings, especially Naʿrmer, are similar in type to later royal reliefs, and appear to record victories over places in the delta and in Libya, as well as agricultural and ritual events. In later periods, however, most scenes of this sort conveyed no precise historical information; these reliefs are significant rather in showing that the king's role was defined and given a visual formulation by this date. The historical events in question probably occurred earlier.

Early Dynastic Period

Two main changes appear to mark the beginning of the 1st Dynasty: an increase in the use of writing, and the founding of Memphis, which was the country's political capital and economic center from that time on. There may also have been a change of ruling family, as is suggested by differences in the naming of the kings. Writing was used notably for year names, which recorded a salient event for each year for dating purposes; the oldest known of these is of the reign of Naʿrmer. Lists of these year names formed the first annals.

The 1st Dynasty begins with the legendary Menes, whose name occurs in later Egyptian king lists and in Classical sources. In their own time these kings were mostly known by their Horus names, the official royal element in the titulary, and not by their birth names, which are those used in the lists. As a result, both the identification and the existence of Menes are disputed, but he was perhaps the same as King ʿAha, to whose reign dates the earliest tomb at Saqqara, the elite necropolis of Memphis. The two main centers of power at this time were Abydos and Memphis, while Hierakonpolis also has substantial remains. The two guardian deities of the Egyptian king, Nekhbet and Wadjit, belonged to Hierakonpolis and to Buto (Tell el-Faraʿin) in the delta, which had been important since Predynastic times.

The duration of the 1st Dynasty is estimated at about 150 years. Large cemeteries of the period, with rich burials, have been found in many parts of the country, including the delta; the finest tombs date to the long reign of Den. Their spread implies that there was less centralization of wealth than in the central Old Kingdom, when provincial cemeteries of importance disappear.

The kings were buried at Abydos in Umm el-Qaʿab, a cemetery set well back in the desert, while near the cultivation were brick enclosures for the royal mortuary cult. The royal tombs themselves were relatively modest in size, and were thoroughly ransacked in later periods, but what remains from them is of superb workmanship.

While the kings and their court were buried at Abydos, some high officials had imposing mud-brick tombs of a different design on the edge of the desert escarpment at north Saqqara (comparable tombs have also been found at other sites). There were probably no more than one or two of these officials at one time, since the number of tombs is not much greater than that of the kings, with more tombs dating to the reigns of the longer-lived kings. The contents of some of the storage chambers in the superstructures of these tombs included a remarkable array of objects in copper and huge quantities of stone vessels in a wide variety of materials and shapes. The genre of stone vessels originated in Predynastic times, and they were the most widespread luxury product of the country until the 3rd Dynasty.

The Horus name of the first king of the 2nd Dynasty, Hotepsekhemwy, means "The Peaceful one of the Two Powers", alluding to struggle for the throne; the "Two Powers" are the archetypal antagonists among deities, Horus and Seth. Hotep-

sekhemwy also moved the royal necropolis to Saqqara. The funerary stela of his successor Reʿneb (whose name may not relate to the cult of the sun god Reʿ), was discovered near Saqqara. After the third king, Ninetjer, the record is very uncertain; there were probably rival claimants to the throne, and later traditions seem to include names from both sides. The first king of the dynasty whose name has been found at Abydos is Peribsen, the only king in Egyptian history to bear the title Seth instead of Horus. Peribsen may have altered his name from a Horus name, Sekhemib, exploiting the same religious idiom as Hotepsekhemwy had done. The change in title might refer to a belief in the triumph of Seth, or to a difference in local loyalties, among other possibilities. Peribsen's actions seem to have provoked opposition from a king Khaʿsekhem, of whom objects are known only from Hierakonpolis in the south, and who was probably the same person as Khaʿsekhemwy, whose name has been found over the whole country, on objects that presumably date from after Peribsen's death. The name Khaʿsekhem alludes to the single "power" Horus, while Khaʿsekhemwy refers to "two powers" – Horus and Seth – and is set beneath figures of both gods and accompanied by the statement "the Two Lords are at peace in him." The whole announces that the struggle is over. Architecture of this time shows great advances. Khaʿsekhem constructed a large mud-brick funerary enclosure at Hierakonpolis and as Khaʿsekhemwy a larger one at Abydos, both of which stand to this day; a still larger stone enclosure a long way into the desert at Saqqara that has been ascribed to him remained unfinished.

The first king of the 3rd Dynasty (c. 2650–2575), Djoser, is known above all as the builder of the Step Pyramid at Saqqara, the oldest stone building of its size in the world. In addition to this, fragments of a shrine of his reign from Heliopolis show a fully developed Egyptian artistic style and iconography. The Step Pyramid complex, which is not quite as large as the one nearby ascribed to Khaʿsekhemwy, shows numerous changes of plan and is in many ways a tentative composition, but it displays astonishing technical mastery and economic power.

The time of Djoser was later looked back upon as a golden age of achievement and wisdom. The name of Imhotep, the probable architect of the Step Pyramid – he held the titles of a master sculptor among others – came to be especially venerated, and in the Greco-Roman Period he was a popular deity, associated particularly with healing. His name is also found as a graffito on a stretch of the enclosure wall of the pyramid of Djoser's successor, which was buried almost at once in a modification of the original plan. Perhaps he was a hero among the craftsmen of his own time.

Djoser's buildings stood out from the group of massive mud-brick mastabas of his reign at North Saqqara; not until the next dynasty did other men have large stone tombs. But the perfection of relief work extended beyond the royal monument, and the wooden reliefs from the contemporaneous tomb of Hezyreʿ are among the finest ancient sculpture in the material; they may have been made in a royal workshop.

The still larger monument of the next king, Sekhemkhet, scarcely progressed beyond ground level, and his reign is followed by an obscure

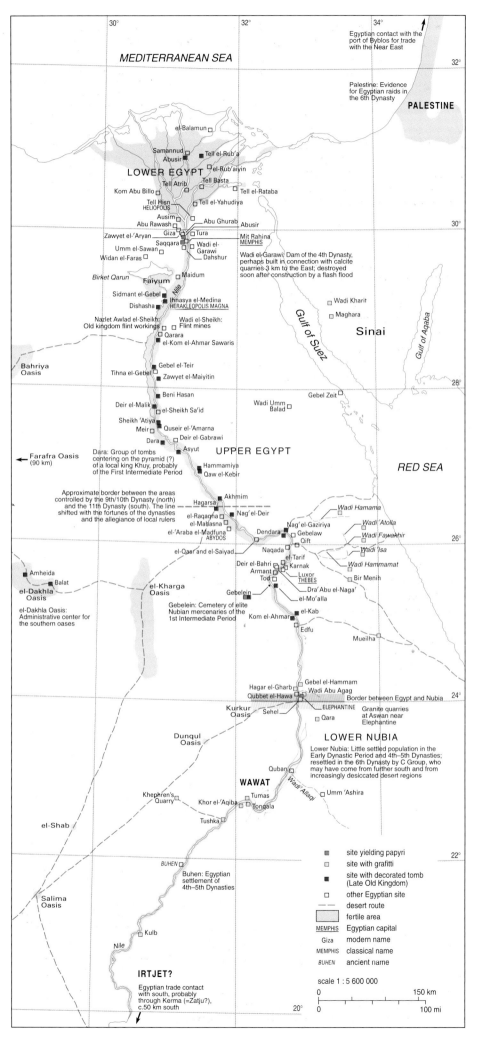

period. This interlude before the 4th Dynasty illustrates how the rulers predominate in the record and hence in our view of the history. Where the king and his organization were strong, the country's resources could be harnessed to vastly impressive effect, probably through conscripted labor. When he was weak, the normal subsistence pattern continued without either harming the country's economic fabric or reducing accumulated technical expertise, but also without dedicating its potential to the same enduring end.

By the end of the Early Dynastic Period Egyptian cultural, administrative, and technical resources had developed virtually into their classic forms. There had been a progressive centralization of power that can be seen only indirectly in the record, in a decline of provincial cemeteries. This was a precondition for the exploits of the 4th-Dynasty rulers.

Old Kingdom (c. 2575–2150)

The 4th Dynasty (c. 2575–2450) was the time of the great pyramids, but it would be wrong to allow our view of it to be dominated by their massive durability. No less than any other, it was a period of change and of political conflict.

Snofru, the first ruler of the dynasty, built the two pyramids at Dahshur and either built or completed the Maidum pyramid. This building program was on a greater scale than those of his successors, and implies at least the same level of economic productivity and organizational skill. In addition to the pyramids, there are nonroyal mastabas of his reign at Maidum, Dahshur, and Saqqara. The reliefs and paintings in these contain the earliest examples of the repertory of subjects found in later Old Kingdom nonroyal tombs.

Some details of administration are known, especially from the inscriptions in the tomb of Metjen from Saqqara. Widely separated estates were given to high officials, possibly in order to discourage the creation of baronial areas. Metjen's estates were mostly in the delta, perhaps on previously uncultivated land. Unlike the very highest officials of the time, Metjen was not a member of the royal family, which dominates other records.

During the reign of Snofru there was a major campaign or campaigns to Nubia, which is recorded in the fragmentary royal annals (the Palermo Stone) and may be linked with rock inscriptions in Nubia itself. An Egyptian settlement was founded at Buhen and lasted for perhaps 250 years, probably being used as a base for mining expeditions and for trade with regions farther south.

A major factor in 4th- and 5th-Dynasty history was solar religion. The true pyramid is most probably a solar symbol, so that Snofru himself was a solar innovator. The compounding of royal names with the sun god Reʿ and the use of the royal epithet "Son of Reʿ" are found from the reign of Reʿdjedef onward. It seems that the sun god's influence and importance grew continuously until the mid-5th Dynasty, and that different political factions were united in their adherence to Reʿ.

Of the remaining rulers of the 4th Dynasty Khufu and Khephren stand out through their pyramids; Menkaureʿ comes a considerable way behind. The placing of their monuments in a close group at Giza may show factional solidarity, while the pyramid of Reʿdjedef at Abu Rawash, the excavation for a pyramid at Zawyet el-ʿAryan (whose builder's name is uncertain) and the tomb of Shepseskaf at south Saqqara perhaps belonged to other, more ephemeral factions. The centralization of rule and the authority of the main kings can be read off the rigidly ordered groups of tombs around the pyramids at Giza. This concentration of power is not, however, the cause of power, since Snofru was as strong as his successors, but did not plan his cemeteries in the same way. It may be no coincidence that he later had a good reputation and was deified, whereas Khufu and Khephren were said in folklore to have been tyrants.

In addition to buildings, the 4th Dynasty produced much of the finest statuary of the Old Kingdom, and the scanty surviving reliefs, inscriptions, and tomb furniture are of similar quality. In terms of material culture it is the high point of the period, but of its intellectual culture and daily life we know almost nothing.

Shepseskaf built himself a massive mastaba instead of a pyramid, and this almost unique departure may be reflected in the practice of kings of the 5th Dynasty (c. 2450–2325). The first of these, Userkaf, built a small pyramid at Saqqara, east of the Step Pyramid, as well as a solar temple near Abusir; this latter practice was followed by five successors. These temples were separate institutions from the pyramids, but were closely associated with the kings who built them, and probably had a mortuary significance for them.

The architectural continuity which may be posited between the two dynasties has a parallel in the ruling families. In both respects Shepseskaf forms the turning point as much as Userkaf. Khentkaus, the mother of Userkaf and Sahureʿ, was a member of the 4th-Dynasty royal family. Their paternity is unknown, but the father(s) may have been from another branch of the same large group. Despite this continuity, the internal policies of the 5th Dynasty were different from those of the 4th. The reduction in the size of pyramids was not accompanied by a compensating increase in other construction, and the change must reflect either economic decline or an increase in the consumption of things that leave no trace. While a general decline is evident in the late 6th Dynasty, the level of activity in the two preceding centuries was roughly constant. There is no simple explanation for this pattern; one should perhaps rather ask what provoked the the extraordinary phase of building in the 4th Dynasty.

Nonroyal tombs of the 5th Dynasty were no longer regimented into rows or confined on a single site, and the amount of decoration in them increased continually. This is evidence for greater freedom of expression for the elite – within close limits – but not necessarily for an increase in their wealth. A further significant change is the location of some tombs in the provinces toward the end of the dynasty. Provincial administrators, who were in origin central appointees, turned slowly into local elites. By the end of the Old Kingdom there were large provincial cemeteries, a development that marks a loosening of royal power and a rather less unequal distribution of wealth. This slight leveling is seen rather earlier in the holders of high office, who were no longer members of the royal family, although they might marry into it. An administration based on autocracy and kinship gave way

to something like an evolving bureaucracy.

The latest royal name found at the Egyptian settlement of Buhen is that of Neuserreʿ; Egypt probably lost control of Lower Nubia soon after. From some generations later come records of Egyptian trading expeditions to the south that presumably replaced the permanent depot.

The last kings of the 5th Dynasty did not build separate solar temples, which may imply a lessening in the importance of solar religion or of its role in the king's personal destiny in the next world. Wenis appears to be a transitional figure, heralding the 6th Dynasty (c. 2325–2175). His pyramid complex, with its small pyramid, is of great interest both for the reliefs on its long causeway and for the texts on the walls of the internal chambers. The texts themselves had probably been used for earlier kings, so that they do not necessarily point to a change in belief. They continued to be inscribed until the 8th Dynasty, but the selection of spells in the different pyramids varied greatly.

More is known of the political history of the 6th Dynasty than of earlier periods, but still only a random spread of information; much of what is regarded as typical of it could have happened at other times too. This applies particularly to military campaigns, like those to the north-east recorded by the high official Weni. The location of the area attacked is uncertain – perhaps in southern Palestine – and the nature of the enemy is not clear. But even if the import of these campaigns is unknown, their occurrence is attested. Campaigns recorded in royal mortuary reliefs have no simple relationship

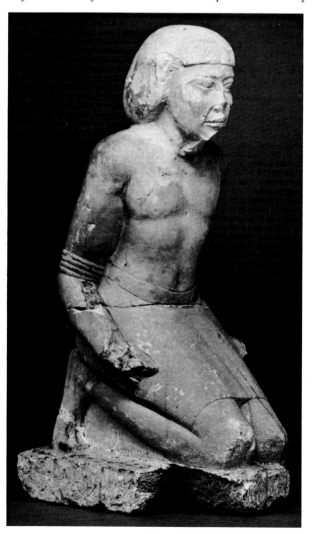

Statue of an Asiatic (?) captive, perhaps from the pyramid complex of Pepy II at South Saqqara. Large numbers of these statues depicting people from various regions have been found in 6th-Dynasty complexes, but the sites have been so ransacked that it is not known how they were arranged. They are counterparts of relief scenes of the defeat of enemies. New York, Metropolitan Museum of Art.

Roughly worked funerary stela of the Nubian Senu, from el-Rizeiqat near Gebelein. The captions state that the owner and his son, who is shown directly under him, are Nubian; both wear a distinctive, sporran-like garment. They were probably mercenaries. Height 37 cm. First Intermediate Period. Boston, Museum of Fine Arts.

with fact. A campaign to Libya depicted in the complex of Sahureʿ was repeated on monuments of Neuserreʿ, Pepy I, Pepy II, and finally Taharqa (690–664); this was a ritual event, which probably corresponded with a real campaign before the time of Sahureʿ, but with no other specific happening.

Occasional archaeological evidence highlights our ignorance of Egyptian relations with the Near East. Pieces of 5th-Dynasty goldwork have appeared in Anatolia, while stone vases of Khephren and Pepy I have been excavated at Ebla in Syria, the capital of a state that fell around 2250 BCE. Such objects might have been either diplomatic gifts or exotica traded after they had ceased to be used in Egypt. As in the Middle Kingdom, the main channel of communication was no doubt Byblos on the Lebanese coast, where Old Kingdom objects have been found.

The biographical inscriptions of expedition leaders in their tombs opposite Aswan give much information about trade to the south in the 6th Dynasty, some of it through el-Dakhla Oasis, where local governors constructed massive mud-brick tombs that are among the most impressive monuments of their times. Among other events, the biographies show the settling of the C Group in Nubia, first in three princedoms, and later in a single political unit, with which Egypt's relations gradually deteriorated. The town of Kerma, south of the third cataract, rose to importance in this period and may have been one of the centers with which Egypt traded. Sites in el-Dakhla Oasis demonstrate the importance of its region in this period.

The deterioration in relations was probably an aspect of Egypt's declining power during the more than fifty years of Pepy II's reign. The decline can be seen in nonroyal tombs in the Memphite area, whose decoration is much more modest than hitherto, and sometimes all underground, perhaps for reasons of security. But although details of this sort are significant, nothing prepares for the eclipse of royal power and the poverty that came after Pepy II. The numerous kings of the next 20 years (late 6th

and 7th–8th Dynasties) were accepted in the whole country, but central control was only nominal. Provincial notables had become hereditary office-holders and treated their nomes virtually as their own domains, whose interests they defended, often by force, against their neighbors. Famine was a common theme of inscriptions and may have contributed to the political collapse if there was a persistent sequence of disastrous low inundations. That could explain why there is relatively little earlier indication of decline, but the human elements of a line of weak kings and failing administration also probably played their part.

First Intermediate Period (c. 2125–1975) and 11th-Dynasty reunification

In the 1st Intermediate Period, rulers from Herakleopolis (Ihnasya el-Medina) claimed the kingship, extinguishing the Memphite lines that had ruled hitherto and forming the 9th dynasty. After a generation or two, during which the Herakleopolitans were acknowledged throughout the country even though they may have had little authority, a rival dynasty, the 11th, was proclaimed in Thebes and from that time the Herakleopolitan line is conventionally termed the 10th Dynasty. The power of the two dynasties gradually increased and there were frequent clashes at the border, which was mostly north of Abydos. Both sides seem to have used Nubian mercenaries in their armies, and a number of funerary stelae of Nubians have been found at Gebelein. Although the period was relatively poor and its artistic styles were diverse and provincial, quite large numbers of modest monuments, made for lower strata of society than hitherto, are preserved, biographical inscriptions of individuals are numerous and sometimes highly inventive, and many simple cemeteries are known.

The Herakleopolitan Dynasty suffered frequent changes of ruler and is little known because few monuments survive from it. The most important king of the more stable Theban Dynasty was the fourth, Nebhepetreʿ Mentuhotep (called I or II by different writers, c. 2010–1960), who defeated the northern dynasty and reunited the country. Mentuhotep began with a programmatic Horus name, "He who gives heart to the Two Lands," which was replaced first by "Divine of the White Crown" (the crown of Upper Egypt) and later by "Uniter of the Two Lands." These changes may correspond to stages in the reunification, the second indicating that he had united, or hoped to unite, all of Upper Egypt and the third – a traditional epithet to which Mentuhotep gave a new pictorial formulation – that he had conquered the entire country. During his reign there was also activity in Lower Nubia (possibly building on campaigns of his predecessors), and a landscaped mortuary complex of novel type was built at Deir el-Bahri. The artistic style of reliefs from the site is a refined version of 1st Intermediate Period work more than a resumption of Old Kingdom traditions, emphasizing, like the complex's Theban location, the local base of the king's power. Mentuhotep was later venerated as one of the founders of Egypt; part of this prestige may go back to his own self-glorification, for he was depicted in a form more nearly divine than that of most Egyptian kings. This presentation, which was probably intended also to enhance the status of the kingship

Kings of Egypt

These pages list the names and *approximate* dates of most of the important kings of Egypt, with female kings designated Q.

A king's full titulary consisted of five main elements, of which the first three were given in their order of origin. These are (1) Horus, (2) Two Ladies, (3) Golden Horus, all of which are epithets evoking how the king manifested a deity or deities; (4) the first cartouche, prefaced by two words for king that were identified with the two halves of the country, which contains a statement about the sun god Reʿ in relation to the king; (5) the second cartouche, which contains the king's own birth name preceded by "Son of Reʿ."

Since the pronunciation of names is uncertain, Greek forms from the history of Manetho (3rd century BCE) are used for some kings. In the list the birth name is generally placed first, followed by the first cartouche, which is in *italics*. 20th Dynasty kings used Ramesses as a dynastic name in their second cartouches; Ptolemaic kings were similarly called Ptolemy.

Overlapping dates within dynasties indicate coregencies. Where dynasties overlap, they were mostly accepted in different parts of the country.

The dates are calculated from ancient lists, especially the Turin royal papyrus, and from various other sources. The margin of error rises from a decade or so in the 3rd Intermediate Period and New Kingdom to perhaps 150 years for the 1st Dynasty; dates for the 3rd millennium are given for whole dynasties and are rounded, as are numerous later dates. From the 12th Dynasty on, possible sequences of dates can be calculated from astronomical evidence; presently accepted sequences are used here. Dates from 664 BCE on are precise to within a year. All native rulers mentioned in Part Two are listed, as well as Roman emperors whose names occur in hieroglyphic and demotic texts. Hieroglyphic inscriptions from after 300 CE are dated to the "era of Diocletian" which began in 283 and do not give the current emperor's name.

Dates that are fixed with precision are marked *.

Above A typical full titulary. "Horus: Mighty bull, perfect of glorious appearances; Two Ladies: Enduring of kingship like Atum (the aging form of the sun god); Golden Horus: Strong of arm, oppressor of the Nine Bows (traditional enemies); *Nisut* and *bity* (terms for king); Menkheprureʿ (the Enduring One of the manifestations of Reʿ); Son of Reʿ: Thutmose (IV), greatly appearing one; beloved of Amon-Reʿ, given life like Reʿ."

Right Typical hieroglyphic writings of selected kings' names; those in the first line are Horus names. Most of the rest are pairs of throne names, by which the kings' contemporaries knew them, and birth names, by which we now know them.

LATE PREDYNASTIC c. 3100

"Dynasty 0"
Several kings; Iryhor(?); Ka(?); Naʿrmer

EARLY DYNASTIC PERIOD c. 2950–2575

1st Dynasty c. 2950–2775
Menes (= ʿAha?); Djer; Wadj; Den; ʿAnedjib; Semerkhet; Qaʿa

2nd Dynasty c. 2775–2650
Hotepsekhemwy; Reʿneb; Ninetjer; Peribsen; Khaʿsekhem(wy)

3rd Dynasty c. 2650–2575
Djoser (Netjerykhet)
Sekhemkhet
Zanakht (= Nebka?)
Khaʿba
Huni(?)

OLD KINGDOM c. 2575–2150

4th Dynasty c. 2575–2450
Snofru
Khufu (Cheops)
Reʿdjedef
Khephren (Reʿkhaʿef)
Menkaureʿ (Mycerinus)
Shepseskaf

5th Dynasty c. 2450–2325
Userkaf
Sahureʿ
Neferirkareʿ Kakai
Shepseskareʿ Izi
Reʿneferef
Neuserreʿ Ini
Menkauhor
Djedkareʿ Izezi
Wenis

6th Dynasty c. 2325–2175
Teti
Pepy I (*Meryreʿ*)
Merenreʿ Nemtyemzaf
Pepy II (*Neferkareʿ*)

7th/8th Dynasty c. 2175–2125
Numerous ephemeral kings, including Neferkareʿ

1st INTERMEDIATE PERIOD c. 2125–1975

9th Dynasty (Herakleopolitan) c. 2125–2080

10th Dynasty (Herakleopolitan) c. 2080–1975
Several kings called Khety; Merykareʿ; Ity

11th Dynasty (Theban) c. 2080–1975
Inyotef I (Sehertawy)
Inyotef II (Wahʿankh)
Inyotef III (Naktnebtepnufer)
Nebhepetre Mentuhotep

MIDDLE KINGDOM c. 1975–1640

11th Dynasty (all Egypt) c. 1975–1940
Nebhepetreʿ Mentuhotep c. 2010–1960
Sʿankhkareʿ Mentuhotep c. 1960–1948
Nebtawyreʿ Mentuhotep c. 1948–?

12th Dynasty c. 1938–1755
Amenemhet I (*Sehetepibreʿ*) c. 1938–1908
Senwosret I (*Kheperkareʿ*) c. 1918–1875
Amenemhet II (*Nubkaureʿ*) c. 1876–1842
Senwosret II (*Khaʿkheperreʿ*) c. 1842–1837
Senwosret III (*Khaʿkaureʿ*) c. 1836–1818
Amenemhet III (*Nimaʿatreʿ*) c. 1818–1770
Amenemhet IV (*Maʿakherureʿ*) c. 1770–1760
Nefrusobk (*Sebekkareʿ*) c. 1760–1755

13th Dynasty c. 1755–1630
About 70 kings; better-known ones are listed (numbers are their approximate positions in a complete list)
Wegaf (*Khutawyreʿ*) 1;
Amenemhet V (*Sekhemkareʿ*) 4;
Harnedjheriotef (*Hetepibreʿ*) 9;
Amenyqemau 11b
Sebekhotep I (*Khaʿankhreʿ*) 12 c.1725
Hor (*Awibreʿ*) 14; Amenemhet VII (*Sedjefakareʿ*) 15; Sebekhotep II (*Sekhemreʿ-khutawy*) 16;
Khendjer (*Userkareʿ*) 17;
Sebekhotep III (*Sekhemreʿ-swadjtawy*) 21
Neferhotep I (*Khasekhemreʿ*) 22 c. 1710–1700
Sebekhotep IV (*Khaʿneferre*) 24 c. 1700–1690
Sebekhotep V (*Khaʿhotepreʿ*) 25 c. 1690–1685
Aya (*Merneferreʿ*) 27 c. 1685–1670
Mentuemzaf (*Djedʿankhreʿ*) 32c;
Dedumose II (*Djedneferreʿ*) 37;
Neferhotep III (*Sekhemreʿ-sʿankhtawy*) 41a

14th Dynasty
Minor kings who were probably all contemporaneous with the 13th or 15th Dynasties

2nd INTERMEDIATE PERIOD c. 1630–1520

15th Dynasty (Hyksos) c. 1630–1520
Salitis; Sheshi; Khian (*Swoserenreʿ*)
Apophis (*ʿAwoserreʿ* and others) c. 1570–1530
Khamudi c. 1530–1520

16th Dynasty
Minor Hyksos rulers, contemporaneous with the 15th Dynasty

17th Dynasty c. 1630–1540
Numerous Theban kings; numbers give positions in a complete list
Inyotef V (*Nubkheperreʿ*) 1;
Sebekemzaf I (*Sekhemreʿ-wadjkhaʿu*) 3; Nebireyeraw (*Swadjenreʿ*) 6; Sebekemzaf II (*Sekhemreʿ-shedtawy*) 10
Taʿo (or Djehutiʿo) I (*Senakhtenreʿ*) 13
Taʿo (or Djehutiʿo) II (*Seqenenreʿ*) 14
Kamose (*Wadjkheperreʿ*) 15 c. 1545–1539

NEW KINGDOM c. 1539–1075

18th Dynasty c. 1539–1292
ʿAhmose (*Nebpehtireʿ*) c. 1539–1514
Amenhotep I (*Djeserkareʿ*) c. 1514–1493
Thutmose I (*ʿAkheperkareʿ*) c. 1493–?
Thutmose II (*ʿAkheperenreʿ*) c. ?–1479
Thutmose III (*Menkheperreʿ*) c. 1479–1425
Hatshepsut (*Maʿatkareʿ*) Q c. 1473–1458
Amenhotep II (*ʿAkheprureʿ*) c. 1426–1400
Thutmose IV (*Menkheprureʿ*) c. 1400–1390
Amenhotep III (*Nebmaʿatreʿ*) c. 1390–1353
Amenhotep IV/Akhenaten (*Neferkheprureʿ waʿenreʿ*) c. 1353–1336
Smenkhkareʿ (*ʿAnkhkheprureʿ*) c. 1335–1332
Tutʿankhamun (*Nebkheprureʿ*) c. 1332–1322
Aya (*Kheperkheprureʿ*) c. 1322–1319
Haremhab (*Djeserkheprureʿ*) c. 1319–1292

19th Dynasty c. 1292–1190
Ramesses I (*Menpehtireʿ*) c. 1292–1290
Sety I (*Menmaʿatreʿ*) c. 1290–1279
Ramesses II (*Usermaʿatreʿ setepenreʿ*) c. 1279–1213
Merneptah (*Baenreʿ hotephirmaʿat*) c. 1213–1204
Sety II (*Userkheprureʿ setepenreʿ*) c. 1204–1198
Amenmesse (*Menmireʿ*), usurper during reign of Sety II
Siptah (*Akhenreʿ setepenreʿ*) c. 1198–1193
Twosre (*Sitreʿ meritamun*) Q c. 1198–1190

20th Dynasty c. 1190–1075
Sethnakhte (*Userkhaʿureʿ meryamun*) c. 1190–1187
Ramesses III (*Usermaʿatreʿ meryamun*) c. 1187–1156
Ramesses IV (*Heqamaʿatreʿ setepenamun*) c. 1156–1150
Ramesses V (*Usermaʿatreʿ sekheperenreʿ*) c. 1150–1145
Ramesses VI (*Nebmaʿatreʿ meryamun*) c. 1145–1137
Ramesses VII (*Usermaʿatreʿ setepenreʿ meryamun*) c. 1137–1129
Ramesses VIII (*Usermaʿatreʿ akhenamun*) c. 1129–1126
Ramesses IX (*Neferkareʿ setepenreʿ*) c. 1126–1108
Ramesses X (*Khepermaʿatreʿ setepenreʿ*) c. 1108–1104
Ramesses XI (*Menmaʿatreʿ setepenptah*) c. 1104–1075

3rd INTERMEDIATE PERIOD c. 1075–715

21st Dynasty c. 1075–945
Smendes (*Hedjkheperreʿ setepenreʿ*) c. 1075–1050

36

HIEROGLYPHIC WRITINGS OF SELECTED KINGS' NAMES

Na'rmer 'Aha Den Peribsen Kha'sekhemwy Djoser Snofru

Khufu Sahure' Wenis Pepy II Mentuhotep (Nebhepetre') Amenemhet I

Senwosret I Senwosret III Neferhotep I Apophis Ta'o II

'Ahmose Thutmose III Hatshepsut Amenhotep III Akhenaten (Amenhotep IV)

Sety I Ramesses II Ramesses III Ramesses IX Psusennes I

Shoshenq I Piye Taharqa Psammetichus I Amasis

Darius I–III Nectanebo II Ptolemy I Soter Ptolemy IV Philopator Ptolemy XII Auletes

Cleopatra VII Philopator Augustus Domitian Trajan Septimius Severus

Amenemnisu	c. 1050–1040
(Neferkare')	
Psusennes I	c. 1040–995
('Akheperre' setepenamun)	
Amenemope	c. 994–985
(Userma'atre' setepenamun)	
Osorkon I	c. 985–978
(Akheperre' setepenre')	
Siamun	c. 978–960
(Netjerkheperre' setepenamun)	
Psusennes II	c. 960–945
(Titkheprure' setepenre')	

22nd Dynasty c. 945–715
Shoshenq I	c. 945–925
(Hedjkheperre' setepenre')	
Osorkon II	c. 925–910
(Sekhemkheperre' setepenre')	
Takelot I	c. 910–?
(Userma'atre' setepenamun)	
Shoshenq II	?–c. 885
(Heqakheperre' setepenre')	
Osorkon III	c. 885–855
(Userma'atre' setepenamun)	
Takelot II	c. 860–835
(Hedjkheperre' setepenre')	
Shoshenq III	c. 835–785
(Userma'atre' setepenre'/amun)	
Pami	c. 785–775
(Userma'atre' setepenre'/amun)	
Shoshenq V	c. 775–735
('Akheperre')	
Osorkon V	c. 735–715
('Akheperre' setepenamun)	

23rd Dynasty c. 830–715
Various contemporary lines of kings recognized in Thebes, Hermopolis, Herakleopolis, Leontopolis, and Tanis; arrangement and order are disputed
Pedubaste I	c. 830–805
Osorkon IV	c. 775–750
Peftjau'awybast (Neferkare')	

24th Dynasty (Sais) c. 730–715
(Tefnakhte (Shepsesre'?))	
Bocchoris (Wahkare')	c. 722–715

25th Dynasty c. 770–715
(Nubia and Theban area)
Kashta (Nima'atre')	c. 770–750
Piye	c. 750–715
(Userma'atre' and others)	

LATE PERIOD c. 715–332

25th Dynasty c. 715–657
(Nubia and all Egypt)
Shabaka (Neferkare')	c. 715–700
Shebitku (Djedkaure')	c. 700–690
Taharqa	c. 690–664
(Khure'nefertem)	
Tantamani (Bakare')	c. 664–657
(possibly later in Upper Nubia)	

26th Dynasty *664–525
(Necho I	*672–664)
Psammetichus I	*664–610
(Wahibre')	
Necho II (Wehemibre')	*610–595
Psammetichus II	*595–589
(Neferibre')	
Apries (Ha'a'ibre')	*589–570
Amasis (Khnemibre')	*570–526
Psammetichus III	*526–525
('Ankhkaenre')	

27th Dynasty *525–404
(Persian)
Cambyses	*525–522
Darius I	*521–486
Xerxes I	*486–466
Artaxerxes I	*465–424
Darius II	*424–404

28th Dynasty *404–399
Amyrtaios	*404–399

29th Dynasty *399–380
Nepherites I	*399–393
(Baenre' merynetjeru)	
Psammuthis	*393
(Userre' setepenptah)	
Hakoris	*393–380
(Khnemma'atre')	
Nepherites II	*380

30th Dynasty *380–343
Nectanebo I	*380–362
(Kheperkare')	
Teos (Irma'atenre')	*365–360
Nectanebo II	*360–343
(Senedjemibre' setepenanhur)	

2nd Persian Period *343–332
Artaxerxes III Ochus	*343–338
Arses	*338–336
Darius III Codoman	*335–332
Period interrupted by an indigenous ruler Khababash (Senentanen setepenptah)	

GRECO-ROMAN PERIOD
*332 BCE–395 CE

Macedonian Dynasty *332–305
Alexander III the Great	*332–323
Philip Arrhidaeus	*323–316
Alexander IV	*316–305

Ptolemaic Dynasty *305–30
Ptolemy I Soter I	*305–284
Ptolemy II Philadelphus	*285–246
Ptolemy III Euergetes I	*246–221
Ptolemy IV Philopator	*221–205
Ptolemy V Epiphanes	*205–180
Ptolemy VI Philometor	*180–164, *163–145
Ptolemy VIII Euergetes II (Physkon)	*170–163, *145–116
Ptolemy VII Neos Philopator	*145
Cleopatra III Q and Ptolemy IX Soter II (Lathyros)	*116–107
Cleopatra III Q and Ptolemy X Alexander I	*107–88
Ptolemy IX Soter II	*88–81
Cleopatra Berenice Q	*81–80
Ptolemy XI Alexander II	*80
Ptolemy XII Neos Dionysos (Auletes)	*80–58, *55–51
Berenice IV Q	*58–55
Cleopatra VII Philopator Q	*51–30
Ptolemy XIII	*51–47
Ptolemy XIV	*47–44
Ptolemy XV Caesarion	*44–30

Further coregencies with queens called Arsinoe, Berenice, and Cleopatra, who had no independent reigns. Native usurpers: Harwennofre (205–199), 'Ankhwennofre (199–186), Harsiese (131)

Roman emperors *30 BCE–395 CE
(names attested in hieroglyphic and demotic texts, down to the tetrarchy of 284–305)
Augustus	*30 BCE–14 CE
Tiberius	*14–37
Gaius (Caligula)	*37–41
Claudius	*41–54
Nero	*54–68
Galba	*68–69
Otho	*69
Vespasian	*69–79
Titus	*79–81
Domitian	*81–96
Nerva	*96–98
Trajan	*98–117
Hadrian	*117–138
Antoninus Pius	*138–161
Marcus Aurelius	*161–180
Lucius Verus	*161–169
Commodus	*180–192
Septimius Severus	*193–211
Caracalla	*198–217
Geta	*209–212
Macrinus	*217–218
Diadumenianus	*218
Severus Alexander	*222–235
Gordian III	*238–244
Philip	*244–249
Decius	*249–251
Gallus and Volusianus	*251–253
Valerian	*253–260
Gallienus	*253–268
Macrianus and Quietus	*260–261
Aurelian	*270–275
Probus	*276–282
Diocletian	*284–305
Maximian	*286–305
Galerius	*293–311

Gallery of Kings

The image of an Egyptian king is more a statement of an ideal than a portrait. Of those shown, only Amenhotep IV and Ptolemy IV depart from the norm, one highly stylized, the other influenced by Hellenistic portraiture.

Faces may depict general qualities. Some early figures convey an impressive strength, which became greatly refined. Neferhotep I follows the 12th-Dynasty tradition of the "suffering king." The later heads are mostly rather blander.

Kings normally wear a crown, uraeus (cobra on the forehead), and false beard. The most important of the many crowns are the tall white crown, the primary early symbol of kingship associated with *nisut* (the normal word for king) and with Upper Egypt; and the squat blue crown – blue is the most prestigious color – from the 18th Dynasty on. Further crowns on these figures are the *nemes* headcloth, typical of the Old and Middle Kingdoms; a flat cap; and a skull cap. Pepy I (?) may be shown with natural hair.

Palette of Narmer, Dynasty 0 (c. 3000). Schist.

1st-Dynasty king, c. 2850. Ivory.

Kharsekhem, 2nd Dynasty (c. 2700). Limestone.

3rd-Dynasty king, c. 2600. Pink granite.

Shepseskaf, c. 2450. Diorite.

Pepy I or Merenrer Nemtyemzaf, c. 2250. Copper.

Neferhotep I, c. 1710–1700. Black basalt.

Amenhotep IV (Akhenaten), c. 1350. Sandstone.

Tutrankhamun, c. 1333–1323. Wood and gesso.

Ramesses II, c. 1279–1213.
Granodiorite.

Sety I, c. 1290–1279. Black basalt.

King of the 3rd Intermediate
Period, c. 1000–800. Quartzite.

Amasis, 570–526 (?). Quartzite.

Ptolemy IV Philopator,
221–205 (?). Schist.

at an important juncture, continued under his successor Sˤankhkareˤ Mentuhotep.

Middle Kingdom (c. 2000–1640)

The last two kings of the 11th Dynasty retained Thebes as their capital. Both kings built widely. Quarries were opened up, notably in the Wadi Hammamat, and the route to the Red Sea was revived. All this indicates that Egypt was strong, but the political order did not last. The second king, Nebtawyreˤ Mentuhotep, is absent from later lists, which record seven blank years at the relevant point, and he was probably viewed retrospectively as an illegitimate ruler. His vizier Amenemhet was also the first king of the 12th Dynasty; the mode of transfer of power between them is unknown.

The most important political act of Amenemhet I (c. 1938–1908) was to move the royal residence from Thebes to near Memphis where, perhaps late in his reign, he founded a place called Itjtawy, "(Amenemhet) who takes possession of the Two Lands." The site itself is likely to have consisted of an administrative complex and royal residence, together with the pyramids of Amenemhet I and Senwosret I and associated cemeteries; the main center of population remained at Memphis, so that the capital was located where it had been in the Old Kingdom. This move was thus both an innovation and a return to older traditions, which were also taken up in art. The nomarchs in Middle Egypt, who had been virtually independent local rulers, were left in office but made to display loyalty to the new regime, while the parallel central administration acquired increasing authority.

The 12th dynasty kings maintained a sizable standing army, whose organization was different from that of later times. In foreign policy Amenemhet I built on the work of Nebhepetreˤ Mentuhotep in Nubia, and in several campaigns late in his reign, in which he was not himself present, conquered as far as the second cataract. The leader of the campaigns was probably Senwosret I (c. 1918–1875), who is presented in slightly later literary sources as acting for his father and may have been his coregent for ten years, in a new development in patterns of rule. The same literary sources apparently allude to Amenemhet I's being murdered, but there seems to have been no resulting disorder; since the kings will have controlled the information disseminated about such events, these works may have served in part to legitimize the royal position.

Senwosret I built widely in Egypt and began the great series of forts in Lower Nubia. The literary works and the material and intellectual achievements of the dynasty made it classical in later Egyptian and in modern eyes. An instance of this is the relief carving of the "White Chapel" of Senwosret I at Karnak, which served as a model for early 18th-Dynasty artists. But despite these achievements of the first 12th-dynasty rulers, far more archaeological material is preserved from the reigns of Senwosret III (c. 1836–1818), Amenemhet III (c. 1818–1770), and later, than there is for the dynasty's first century.

The 12th-Dynasty king with the most lasting reputation was Senwosret III. He is noted especially for his Nubian campaigns, in which the frontier was moved south to Semna, at the southern end of the second cataract, for the establishment of new forts, and for the extension of others. In later times he was worshiped there as a god, and the temple of Thutmose III at Semna is dedicated to him and to Dedwen, a local deity. The main purpose of this military activity may have been to counter the increasing influence of the rulers of the Kerma state of Kush to the south. During his reign there was also a campaign to Palestine, which was apparently not intended to conquer the area – his grandfather Amenemhet II (c. 1876–1842) had also dispatched armies to the region – but marked a period of considerable Egyptian influence there. Palestine may have been seminomadic, becoming settled around the end of the 12th Dynasty.

Senwosret III made important reforms in internal administration, which seem to have completed the removal of power from nomarchs. The country was organized into four "regions," each of which corresponded to roughly half the Nile valley or the delta. Titularies of officials and documents of the late 12th and 13th Dynasties, notably from el-Lahun, give the impression of a pervasive bureaucracy that came to run the country under its own momentum.

Within Egypt the most striking visible legacy of Senwosret III is his royal statuary, which breaks earlier conventions in showing an aging, careworn face, perhaps symbolizing the burdens of kingship depicted in the period's literature. The same style was used in statues of his successor Amenemhet III (c. 1818–1770), whose long reign seems to have been peaceful. Amenemhet III was deified later in the Faiyum, where he built one of his two pyramid

Right: Egypt in the Middle Kingdom and Second Intermediate Period
The map includes:
    Sites with finds of the Palestinian Middle Bronze culture of the 18th–16th centuries BCE.
    Selected sites of the "Pangrave" culture of the Second Intermediate Period. These nomads of the eastern desert were often mercenaries in the service of various rulers. Pottery similar to theirs has been found in the Red Sea hills and eastern Sudan. By the New Kingdom they were assimilated in Egypt and their name, *Medjay*, designated the police force, with a very minor element of ethnicity.

Far right: The second cataract forts of the Middle Kingdom
The cataract is a largely unnavigable series of rapids more than 30 km long. The 12th-Dynasty frontier forts formed the largest surviving ancient group in the world until submerged in Lake Nasser in the 1970s. The northern forts were begun under Senwosret I; those south of Mirgissa were added by Senwosret III.

Below Reliefs in the "White Chapel" of Senwosret I at Karnak, reconstructed from blocks found in the 3rd pylon. The scene shows Atum leading the king before Amon-Reˤ Kamutef. The elaborate, refined style inspired artists of the early 18th Dynasty.

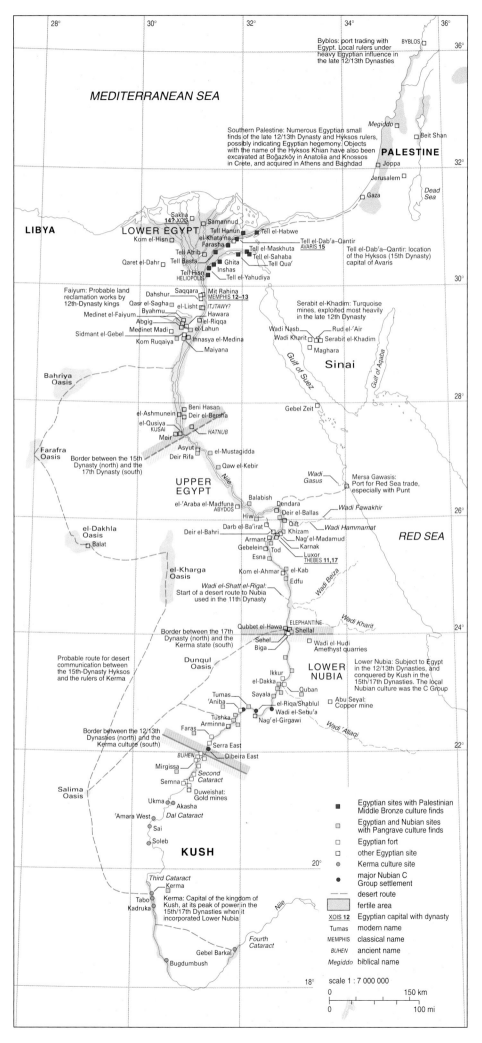

MEDITERRANEAN SEA

Byblos: port trading with Egypt. Local rulers under heavy Egyptian influence in the late 12/13th Dynasties

BYBLOS

Megiddo

Beit Shan

PALESTINE

Southern Palestine: Numerous Egyptian small finds of the late 12/13th Dynasty and Hyksos rulers, possibly indicating Egyptian hegemony. Objects with the name of the Hyksos Khian have also been excavated at Boğazköy in Anatolia and Knossos in Crete, and acquired in Athens and Baghdad

Joppa

Jerusalem

Gaza

Dead Sea

LIBYA

Sakha 14? XOIS

Samannud

LOWER EGYPT

Kom el-Hisn

Tell Hanun

el-Khata'na, Farasha

Tell el-Habwe

Tell el-Dab'a–Qantir

AVARIS 15

Tell el-Dab'a–Qantir: location of the Hyksos (15th Dynasty) capital of Avaris

Tell Atrib

Tell el-Maskhuta

Qaret el-Dahr

Tell Basta

Tell el-Sahaba

Ghita

Tell Qua'

Tell Hisn

Inshas

HELIOPOLIS

Tell el-Yahudiya

Faiyum: Probable land reclamation works by 12th-Dynasty kings

Dahshur

Saqqara

Mit Rahina

MEMPHIS 12–13

Qasr el-Sagha

el-Lisht

ITJTAWY?

Serabit el-Khadim: Turquoise mines, exploited most heavily in the late 12th Dynasty

Medinet el-Faiyum

Byahmu

Hawara

Abgig

el-Riqqa

Medinet Madi

el-Lahun

Wadi Nasb

Rud el-'Air

Sidmant el-Gebel

Ihnasya el-Medina

Wadi Kharit

Serabit el-Khadim

Kom Ruqaiya

Maiyana

Maghara

Sinai

Bahriya Oasis

Gulf of Suez

Gulf of Aqaba

Gebel Zeit

Beni Hasan

el-Ashmunein

Deir el-Bersha

el-Qusiya

KUSAI

HATNUB

Farafra Oasis

Meir

Border between the 15th Dynasty (north) and the 17th Dynasty (south)

Asyut

el-Mustagidda

Deir Rifa

Qaw el-Kebir

UPPER EGYPT

Wadi Gasus

Mersa Gawasis: Port for Red Sea trade, especially with Punt

Balabish

el-Dakhla Oasis

Balat

el-'Araba el-Madfuna

ABYDOS

Dendara

Deir el-Ballas

Wadi Fawakhir

RED SEA

Hiw

Qift

Darb el-Ba'irat

Khizam

Wadi Hammamat

Deir el-Bahri

Nag' el-Madamud

el-Kharga Oasis

Armant

Karnak

Gebelein

Tod

Esna

Luxor

THEBES 11,17

Kom el-Ahmar

el-Kab

Edfu

Wadi Beiza

Wadi el-Shatt el-Rigal: Start of a desert route to Nubia used in the 11th Dynasty

Qubbet el-Hawa

ELEPHANTINE

Shellal

Wadi Kharit

Border between the 17th Dynasty (north) and the Kerma state (south)

Sehel

Biga

Wadi el-Hudi Amethyst quarries

Probable route for desert communication between the 15th-Dynasty Hyksos and the rulers of Kerma

Dunqul Oasis

Ikkur

el-Dakka

LOWER NUBIA

Quban

Lower Nubia: Subject to Egypt in the 12/13th Dynasties, and conquered by Kush in the 15th/17th Dynasties. The local Nubian culture was the C Group

Tumas

Sayala

'Aniba

el-Riqa/Shablul

Abu Seyal: Copper mine

Tushka

Wadi el-Sebu'a

Arminna

Nag' el-Girgawi

Wadi 'Allaqi

Faras

Border between the 12/13th Dynasties (north) and the Kerma culture (south)

Serra East

Salima Oasis

BUHEN

Dibeira East

Mirgissa

Semna

Second Cataract

Duweishat: Gold mines

Ukma

Akasha

'Amara West

Dal Cataract

Sai

Soleb

KUSH

20°

18°

Third Cataract

Kerma

Tabo

Kadruka

Kerma: Capital of the kingdom of Kush, at its peak of power in the 15th/17th Dynasties when it incorporated Lower Nubia

Fourth Cataract

Gebel Barkal

Bugdumbush

Legend:

- ■ Egyptian sites with Palestinian Middle Bronze culture finds
- ▫ Egyptian and Nubian sites with Pangrave culture finds
- □ Egyptian fort
- □ other Egyptian site
- ● Kerma culture site
- ● major Nubian C Group settlement
- - - - desert route
- fertile area
- XOIS 12 Egyptian capital with dynasty
- Tumas modern name
- MEMPHIS classical name
- BUHEN ancient name
- Megiddo biblical name

scale 1 : 7 000 000

0 — 150 km
0 — 100 mi

complexes and a number of other monuments, and may have begun a land reclamation scheme, changing the area from a huntsman's marshy paradise into productive arable land.

Egypt remained prosperous under Amenemhet IV (c. 1770–1760) and the female king Nefrusobk (c. 1760–1755), but the presence of a woman on the throne suggests that the ruling family was dying out. The archaeological record shows no break between the 12th and 13th Dynasties, even though the character of the kingship changed considerably in practice.

In about 150 years some 70 kings of the 13th Dynasty came and went. While at times rivals no doubt claimed the throne, this was not the rule. The country seems to have remained stable, even though there was no acknowledged means of replacing kings in rapid succession, but many individual kings must have been of relatively little account. Stable authority seems instead to have rested with the viziers, the highest officials, of whom a family is known that spanned a large part of the 18th century BCE. Official titles of all ranks proliferated, possibly because of an increase in the size of the bureaucracy, a phenomenon with parallels in other societies and institutions during periods of slow decline.

As late as 1700 Egypt appears to have lost little power or prestige at home or abroad. If the number of nonroyal monuments is any guide, prosperity may even have increased, while the distribution of wealth became less unequal since there were few royal monuments. Many immigrants came from

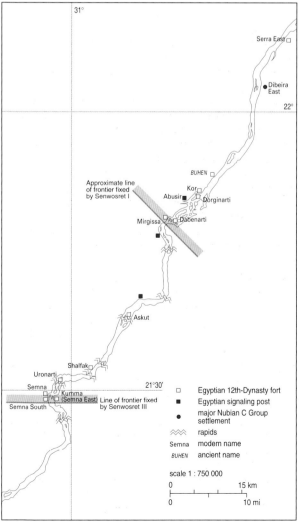

Serra East

Dibeira East

Approximate line of frontier fixed by Senwosret I

BUHEN

Abusir

Kor

Dorginarti

Mirgissa

Dabenarti

Askut

Shalfak

Uronarti

Semna

Kumma

Semna East

Semna South

Line of frontier fixed by Senwosret III

- □ Egyptian 12th-Dynasty fort
- ■ Egyptian signaling post
- ● major Nubian C Group settlement
- ∿∿ rapids
- Semna modern name
- BUHEN ancient name

scale 1 : 750 000

0 — 15 km
0 — 10 mi

Palestine, apparently peaceful arrivals who were absorbed into the lowest levels of Egyptian society, but at least one of whom, Khendjer, became king. They probably came as a result of shifts of population in the Near East after 1800, and were earlier members of the movement that was to bring foreign rule in the 2nd Intermediate Period. Areas of the eastern delta that had been Egyptian in the 12th Dynasty were heavily settled by Asiatics; notable among these was Tell el-Dabʿa–Qantir, which became the Hyksos capital of Avaris and much later the Ramessid capital Pi-Riʿamsese. Egypt retained control of Lower Nubia, probably until the later 13th Dynasty, but the local army contingents became increasingly independent, and some settled permanently, staying behind after the area was overrun by the Kerma state around the beginning of the 15th/17th Dynasties. At about the time of the loss of Nubia, the capital city of the 13th Dynasty may have moved from the Memphite area to Thebes; the latest kings of the dynasty are attested only from there.

Second Intermediate Period (c. 1630–1520)

Around 1630 kingship in Lower Egypt was taken over by a group conventionally called the Hyksos, a Greek form derived from an Egyptian phrase meaning "ruler of foreign lands"; it is uncertain how they achieved power. The Hyksos, the 15th Egyptian Dynasty, seem to have been recognized as the chief line of kings in the whole country, but they tolerated other dynasties. The 13th Dynasty may have continued in existence, as may also the 14th, a line of rulers in the northwestern delta (whose existence has been doubted). There were also other Hyksos rulers known as the 16th Dynasty, a term that may simply cover other Asiatic rulers who proclaimed themselves king, wherever they may have resided. The most important of the concurrent dynasties was the 17th, a line of native Egyptians who ruled from Thebes, holding the Nile valley from the first cataract north as far as Kusai (el-Qusiya). The area that had been held by the 12th–13th Dynasties was thus divided between the Kerma rulers in the south, the Theban 17th Dynasty, and the Hyksos in the north. For nearly a century they appear to have coexisted more or less peacefully.

Names of 15th-Dynasty kings have been found on small objects from widely separated sites in the Near East, showing that they had diplomatic or trading relations over a vast area. Contact abroad brought with it a number of primarily technical innovations that were important in later periods. Some novelties probably came with Asiatic immigrants, while specifically military ones may have been acquired during campaigns, in some cases in the early 18th Dynasty. Until this time Egypt had been technologically backward in comparison with the Near East; during the New Kingdom the two were roughly on a par. Among the new techniques were bronzeworking, which replaced the importation of ready-alloyed bronze and the use of arsenical

copper; an improved potter's wheel and the vertical loom; hump-backed cattle (zebu) and new vegetable and fruit crops; the horse and chariot, composite bows, and new shapes of scimitar and other weapons. On a different plane, new musical instruments were introduced, and 18th-Dynasty dances are different from those of earlier periods.

With Seqenenreʿ Taʿo II of the 17th Dynasty the Thebans began to campaign against the Hyksos. The first episode is known only from a New Kingdom tale, the "Quarrel of Apophis [the Hyksos king] and Seqenenreʿ", but Seqenenreʿ's mummy supports the reality of conflict since it shows that he died violently, possibly in battle. Two stelae of his successor Kamose describe extensive skirmishes between Thebes and the Hyksos, who were allied with the Nubian kings. Kamose nearly reached Avaris, the Hyksos capital, and campaigned in the south as far as Buhen and perhaps much further, but nothing is known of him after his third year.

New Kingdom (c. 1520–1075)

Kamose's successor ʿAhmose (c. 1539–1514) finally drove out the Hyksos rulers around 1520 – many years after Kamose's attempts. The course of the expulsion is presented very briefly in the biography of ʿAhmose, son of Ebana, a soldier from el-Kab. After his victory King ʿAhmose thrust into Palestine, where the Hyksos may have had allies or some measure of control, and campaigned there for some years. In Nubia he fought as far south as the island of Sai, near the third cataract; he also suppressed rebellions in Egypt or Lower Nubia. A number of inscriptions of his time survive from different parts of the country, including one showing family piety to his grandmother in Abydos; in this time there was a notable emphasis on the women of the royal family.

ʿAhmose left behind him a unified state with a strengthened economy that stretched from south of the second cataract to Palestine and was the chief power in the Near East. His son Amenhotep I (c. 1514–1493) may have extended Egyptian influence still farther south; nothing is known of Asian affairs during his reign. In the late 18th–20th Dynasties Amenhotep and his mother ʿAhmose-Nofretari were revered by the inhabitants of Deir el-Medina, possibly because he had founded the institutional complex to which they belonged, which built the royal tombs. The Valley of the Kings and the site of the village itself, however, appear not to have been used until rather later.

Thutmose I (from c. 1493) was a relative by marriage of his predecessor, who probably left no male heir. His campaigns extended farther than those of any Egyptian king. In the first years of his reign he reached the Euphrates in the north and Kurgus, far upstream of the fourth cataract of the Nile, in the south. Either Amenhotep I or he destroyed the powerful Kerma state in Upper Nubia. These feats define the limits of territory ever conquered by Egypt, but may not have been such a leap forward as they seem. In Syria-Palestine there may have been preparatory campaigns in the previous reigns, and the Egyptians seem not to have had another major power as an opponent. During the reign of Amenhotep I the kingdom of Mitanni, Egypt's chief northern rival for a century, formed in Syria; this new polity was Thutmose I's adversary on the Euphrates.

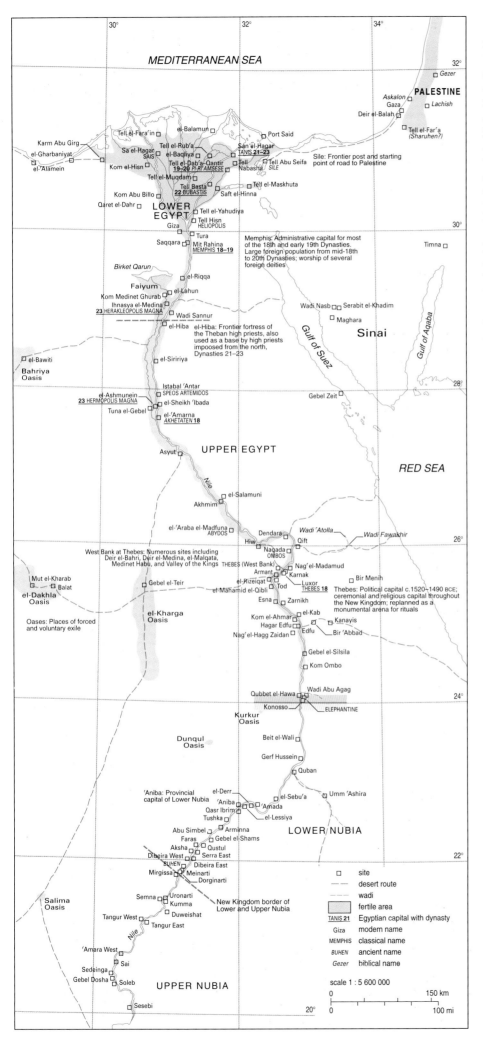

The rulers of the petty states of Palestine and Syria that formed the Egyptian "empire" were bound to the Egyptian king by oaths of allegiance and paid him tribute, but remained self-governing and pursued their own local political ends. Egyptian presence was maintained by relatively small army detachments and a few high officials. Nubia, in contrast, was treated as a colonial land and administered directly by Egyptians under a viceroy who was responsible to the king of Egypt. Both areas included territories that formed part of the endowment of Egyptian institutions such as temples, but the harsher Nubian system seems to have contributed to widespread depopulation in the 19th–20th Dynasties. Both in the Near East and in Nubia, a prime motive for Egyptian expansion – over and above an ideological drive – was to secure the routes for long-distance trade and access to raw materials; defense was probably a secondary consideration. Trade and gold, much of it from Nubia, enhanced the country's wealth and standing in international relations.

Within Egypt, the corollary of the continued wars of expansion was a reformed and enlarged standing army. In effect there were two new forces in internal politics, the priesthood and the army. These became ever more important in later times; in the 18th Dynasty the role of religion can be seen in royal donations to temples – particularly that of Amon-Reʿ at Karnak – in gratitude for success in war, and in the way some kings were presented as having been selected as rulers by a god in an oracle. On the military side several significant men in civil life were former army officers, while the army itself was drafted for construction projects.

Thutmose II, whose reign has left little trace, was succeeded by his young son by a minor wife, Thutmose III (c. 1479–1425), for whom Hatshepsut, Thutmose II's sister and widow, acted initially as regent. There seems to have been little military activity in the first 20 years of Thutmose III's reign and Egypt lost some ground in Asia. Around Thutmose III's seventh year Hatshepsut proclaimed herself "king" (there was no place in Egyptian ideology for a queen regnant), and ruled as the dominant partner in a coregency with her nephew until her death around his year 22. Thutmose III must have acquiesced in the arrangement to some extent, since for much of the time he was old enough to have organized resistance to his aunt if he had wished.

Under Hatshepsut there flourished one of Egypt's few great commoners, Senenmut, who was tutor and steward to her daughter Nefrureʿ. About 20 statues of Senenmut have been recovered from sites in the Theban area, and he was uniquely privileged in having himself depicted in some reliefs in Hatshepsut's funerary temple of Deir el-Bahri. His charge Nefrureʿ, who is also very prominent in the record, may have been intended to be the future coregent or wife of Thutmose III, but she died around the time he assumed sole rule.

No campaign to Asia is attested from the time of Hatshepsut. An inscription in the temple of Speos Artemidos near Beni Hasan details her hatred for the Hyksos, stating that she restored good order – a paradoxical assertion two generations after their expulsion. It is as if her rejection of the Hyksos, who seem not previously to have come in for such

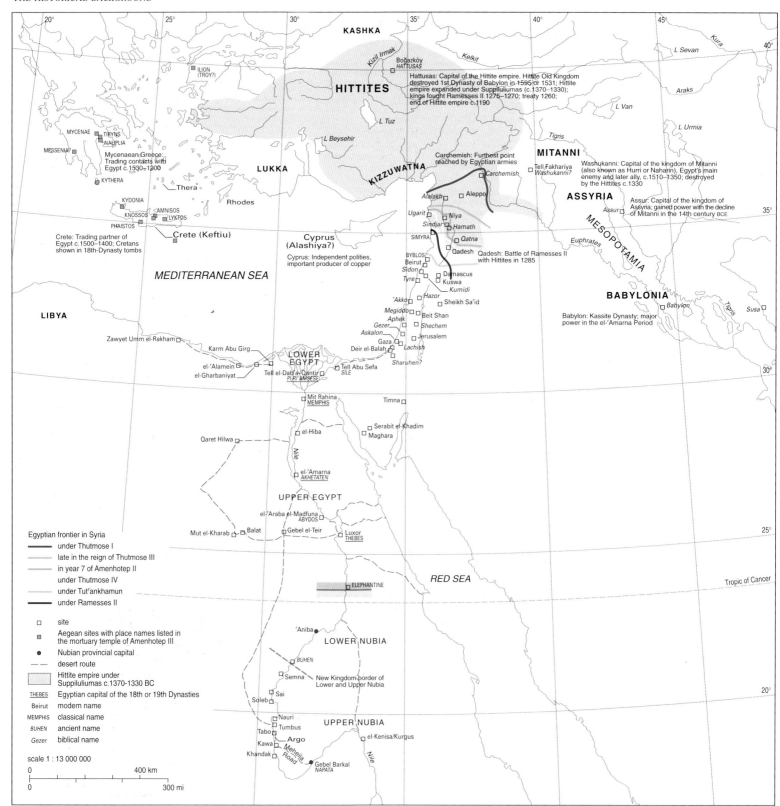

Egyptian frontier in Syria

———	under Thutmose I
———	late in the reign of Thutmose III
———	in year 7 of Amenhotep II
———	under Thutmose IV
··········	under Tut'ankhamun
———	under Ramesses II

☐ site

▣ Aegean sites with place names listed in the mortuary temple of Amenhotep III

● Nubian provincial capital

– – – desert route

▨ Hittite empire under Suppiluliumas c.1370–1330 BC

THEBES Egyptian capital of the 18th or 19th Dynasties

Beirut modern name

MEMPHIS classical name

BUHEN ancient name

Gezer biblical name

scale 1 : 13 000 000

0 ———————— 400 km

0 ———————— 300 mi

vilification, justified her not following her predecessors' policy in Asia. At her death Thutmose III launched a series of campaigns to the Near East, starting by reconquering territory in Palestine that had recently rejected allegiance to Egypt. In the next 20 years the Egyptians fought mainly in Syria, where the Mitanni resisted successfully, and Thutmose could not maintain his furthest points of expansion on the Euphrates. This conflict was to last for another generation. Thutmose III was also active in Nubia late in his reign, and established the provincial capital of Napata at the downstream end of the fourth cataract.

Thutmose III built at many sites and important

nonroyal tombs date to his reign. All this activity is a sign of the economic benefits of expansion. At some point he turned against the memory of Hatshepsut, ordering that her images in relief be erased and replaced with figures of his two predecessors and of himself and that statues of her be smashed. This change of heart may have been due as much to the politics of the time when it was done as to actions of Hatshepsut herself.

In the last years of his reign Thutmose took his son Amenhotep II (c. 1426–1400) as his coregent. Amenhotep fought campaigns both before and after his father's death, and, like other kings, was faced with the problem that vassal rulers owed allegiance

Egypt and the Near East (c.1520–1200 BCE)
The successive frontiers of Egyptian possessions in Syria-Palestine, from north to south and in chronological order, show the limits of Egyptian expansion under a series of rulers from Thutmose I to Ramesses II. A separate key marks places in the Aegean named in a list in the mortuary temple of Amenhotep III.

to and had respect for a king rather than for Egypt in general. New kings often needed to assert their authority afresh. His military exploits were parades of strength as far as Syria – he presented himself as a formidable athlete – not strategically significant campaigns. The parades had a message for foreign powers; in his year 9 Amenhotep received presentations of gifts (the normal mode of diplomatic contact) from the three major powers of the time, the Hittites, Mitanni, and Babylon. The Hittites and Babylon were emerging from periods of relative weakness, while Mitanni was at its peak of power.

Both abroad and at home the reigns of Thutmose IV (c. 1400–1390) and Amenhotep III (c. 1390–1353) form a single phase. Egypt lost more ground to Mitanni, but the two powers made peace before Thutmose IV's death, sealing their relationship with the gift of a Mitanni princess to the king as a minor wife. This one-way traffic in women shows either that Egypt was acknowledged to be the superior power or simply that, in the words of Amenhotep III to the king of Babylon, "since antiquity, a daughter of the king of Egypt has not been given to anyone." In his turn Amenhotep III married more than one Mitanni princess.

Peace brought a further upsurge in wealth. In the number and size of buildings erected, the reign of Amenhotep III can be compared only with the much longer one of Ramesses II, while royal and nonroyal statuary was produced on an unparalleled scale. Much of this work is of very high quality. New approaches were exploited in the planning of the whole Theban area (and probably Memphis), with processional ways lined with sphinxes linking the main temples. A vast artificial lake on the west bank, the Birket Habu, acted as the focus of a new quarter that included a royal palace at el-Malqata and the king's massive mortuary temple. In a significant ideological shift, Amenhotep III was deified in his own lifetime. The leading nonroyal private individual of the reign, Amenhotep son of Hapu, was a former military official who directed much building work and was honored with a mortuary temple of his own. In later periods he too was deified, his reputation in death building on his status in life.

Amenhotep IV (c. 1353–1336) became heir to the throne after the death of his elder brother Thutmose. At the start of his reign he gave himself the title of high priest of the sun god, a role that was traditional for Egyptian kings but was not incorporated into their titulary. He also formulated a new "dogmatic" name for the sun god, "Rec-Harakhty who rejoices on the horizon in his name of Shu [or: 'light'] which is the sun disk [Aten]." This was soon incorporated into a pair of cartouches, giving the god the character of a king, and the god was shown in a new iconography of a disk with rays ending in hands that hold out the hieroglyph for "life" to the king and queen. The development of this cult, which left almost no place for traditional deities except for the sun god, became the king's main purpose in life; he presented himself as the only person who comprehended the god, and also promoted his own godlike status. His queen, Nefertiti, was almost equally prominent in the changes. There was a vast building program at Karnak in the first six years of the reign, in addition to structures in a number of other cities. All were decorated with reliefs in a radically new artistic style and iconography. One of the

Karnak shrines seems to have been decorated principally with figures of Nefertiti; where temples are represented in nonroyal tombs at el-cAmarna from later in the reign, equal numbers of colossi of king and queen are present.

Probably in his fifth year Amenhotep IV changed his name to Akhenaten ("One Beneficial for the Disk") and began a new capital on a virgin site at el-cAmarna, naming it Akhetaten ("Horizon of Aten"). The remains of the city were very thoroughly dismantled in the following period, but are now vitally important as the only accessible major urban site. A great solar hymn was inscribed in the tomb of his most prominent official, Aya, and other reliefs and small objects demonstrate the development of his religion. Around year 9 the god's dogmatic name was changed to the more purist "Rec, horizon ruler, who rejoices on the horizon in his name of Rec the father(?), who has returned as the sun disk," but after this there was little further development, and the number of monuments from the latest years of the reign is small. Probably at the time when the second dogmatic name was introduced Akhenaten closed all temples for other gods and had the word Amun, as well as occasionally "gods" in the plural, hacked out wherever they occurred – a vast undertaking that must have required military participation. The survival of traditional religious practices in some areas of el-cAmarna suggests that there was little popular enthusiasm for these changes.

The end of Akhenaten's reign and its aftermath can only be conjecturally reconstructed. The king had six daughters but no son by Nefertiti; his second successor Tutcankhamun was perhaps the son of a secondary wife, Kiya, whose images were recaptioned in the name of other royal women late in the reign. Around the same time there appeared a few images of a coregent of uncertain identity. After

Above Cuneiform letter from Tushratta of Mitanni to Amenhotep III. At the bottom of the tablet is an Egyptian hieratic filing note of year 36 of Amenhotep, in ink. The letter accompanied a statue of Ishtar of Nineveh that was sent to Egypt perhaps as a healing deity. The statue had been in Egypt before in the time of Tushratta's predecessor Suttarna II. From el-cAmarna. London, British Museum.

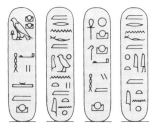

Above Cartouches of the sun god of Amenhotep IV/Akhenaten. The left pair is the early form and the right the late form; translations in the text.

Right Squatting statue of Amenhotep, son of Hapu, shown as a corpulent, elderly man (he lived more than 80 years); found by the 7th pylon at Karnak. The statue, which is in a learned form influenced by Middle Kingdom models, was later venerated, and its nose was recut in antiquity. Height 1·42 m. Reign of Amenhotep III. Cairo, Egyptian Museum.

Akhenaten's death in his year 17 a woman may have succeeded him briefly, perhaps his eldest daughter Meritaten. The next ruler, whose personal name Smenkhkareʿ was evidently not his birth name so that he cannot be identified among the royal family, may have reigned for about three years. Tutʿankh-aten, later Tutʿankhamun, a boy of about nine, then succeeded (c. 1332–1322). Early in his reign the new religion was abandoned, although it was not suppressed completely until later. Memphis, which had long been the chief city, became the capital.

While Tutʿankhamun was king, executive power was in the hands of Aya and the general Haremhab. Tutʿankhamun's inscriptions record the restoration of the temples, but no details of foreign policy; Egyptian possessions in the Near East were in disarray after the campaigns of the Hittite king Suppiluliumas. Aya (c. 1322–1319) occupied the throne briefly, and was succeeded by Haremhab (c. 1319–1292), who is normally placed in the 18th Dynasty, but was considered by Egyptians of the next century to be the first king of their era, which we call the 19th Dynasty.

Haremhab dismantled the temples of Amenhotep IV/Akhenaten at Karnak and built there extensively himself. He also annexed most of Tutʿankhamun's inscriptions, which may in part have recorded his own exploits. His second successor, Sety I (c. 1290–1279), continued his restoration work, repairing countless monuments and removing the names of Akhenaten and his successors down to Haremhab from the official record. He also built extensively himself. In the Near East he fought several campaigns, succeeding, during a period of Hittite weakness, in regaining temporarily some Egyptian possessions in Syria (Egypt's former adversary and later ally Mitanni had disappeared during the previous generation). The main surviving records of Sety's campaigns are impressive battle reliefs of a new, more "realistic" type.

Late in his reign Sety I nominated his son Ramesses II (c. 1279–1213) crown prince. The new king inherited his father's problems in Syria. After a success in year 4 he confronted the Hittite army for the first time in year 5 in an indecisive battle at Qadesh, which Ramesses presented as a great victory and recorded in many temple reliefs. After further engagements in the next few years there was a truce, followed by a formal treaty in year 21. The text of this is preserved in Egyptian in temple reliefs of Ramesses II, and in Akkadian on cuneiform tablets from the Hittite capital Hattusas (modern Boğazköy). Peace continued for more than 50 years, reinforced diplomatically by marriages between Ramesses II and Hittite princesses.

Ramesses II built more buildings and had more colossal statues than any other Egyptian king, as well as having his name or reliefs carved on many older monuments. Like Amenhotep III, he was deified in his own lifetime, and by his projection of his personality he made the name Ramesses synonymous with kingship for centuries. But the official building program was not accompanied by as many works for nonroyal individuals as that of Amenhotep III. Many projects date to early in his reign, while the later buildings show a fall-off in craftsmanship, perhaps during a time of economic decline.

One of the most important undertakings of Ramesses II was the removal of the capital city to a new site in the delta called Pi-Riʿamsese ("Domain of Ramesses"), modern Tell el-Dabʿa–Qantir. The royal family came from this area, but the main reason for the move was probably that the economic and international center of the country had shifted into the delta proper, where relatively few standing monuments are preserved. This development is one reason why less is known of the history of the Late Period than of the New Kingdom.

Ramesses II survived many of his enormous family, and was succeeded by his 13th son Merneptah (c. 1213–1204). Early in his reign Merneptah was confronted with Libyan aggression, which had already been resisted by Sety I and had led to Ramesses II's construction of forts westward along the Mediterranean coast. A battle was fought in the western delta against invading Libyans and "Sea Peoples" – groups with names that suggest origins around the Mediterranean seaboard. The invaders may have intended to settle, bringing their wives and children with them. The battle went against them, however, and some fled, while others were forcibly settled as prisoners of war.

After the death of Merneptah a period of dynastic struggles ended in the brief sole rule of a woman, Twosre (c. 1193–1190), the widow of Sety II (c. 1204–1198). During this time the power in the land seems to have been a high official, Bay, perhaps of Syrian origin, who may be mentioned under an alias in a later document that presents such a person as the period's evil genius.

The first king of the 20th Dynasty, Sethnakhte (c. 1190–1187), referred in an inscription to a period of civil war that lasted into the second year of his own reign, and ended with his defeat of the rebels. He implied that disorder was widespread in the country before his arrival, but some minor officials lived from the reign of Merneptah into that of Ramesses III, so the violence may have been limited to court and military circles. Ramesses III (c. 1187–1156) inherited a stable country, which he exploited in a number of building works, but was severely pressed from the west and north by two attempted Libyan invasions and by a renewed attack of the Sea Peoples that came in the interval between them. All of these were defeated, and Egypt also retained control of Sinai and southern Palestine.

Ramesses III's titulary was almost identical to that of Ramesses II, and his mortuary complex at Medinet Habu was modeled closely on Ramesses II's Ramesseum. He and later 20th-Dynasty kings were unusually conservative in their self-presentation, as if they did not have the confidence to innovate. But whereas the achievements of Ramesses III were considerable, this is not the case with his successors. In 90 years there were eight more kings called Ramesses, a name they adopted at accession in addition to their birth names. All were apparently descended from Ramesses III, but the throne was the center of rivalry, beginning with the death of Ramesses III himself, before which there was a conspiracy among his wives to place one of his sons on the throne. Abroad Egypt lost control of Palestine during the dynasty, while Nubia fell away at its end. The only major monuments of the period after Ramesses III are the royal tombs, the temple of Khons at Karnak, which was not finally completed until the Ptolemaic Period, and some nonroyal tombs.

Egypt in the late Third Intermediate Period
This map shows political divisions of Egypt around the time of the campaign of Piye (c. 730). It indicates the cities ruled by a king, with dynasty number if appropriate, as well as the cities listed with their rulers in the victory stela of Piye. Several further cities cannot be located. Compare Assurbanipal's list marked on the map on p. 49.
The limits of the areas ruled by Hermopolis Magna and Herakleopolis Magna are hypothetical.

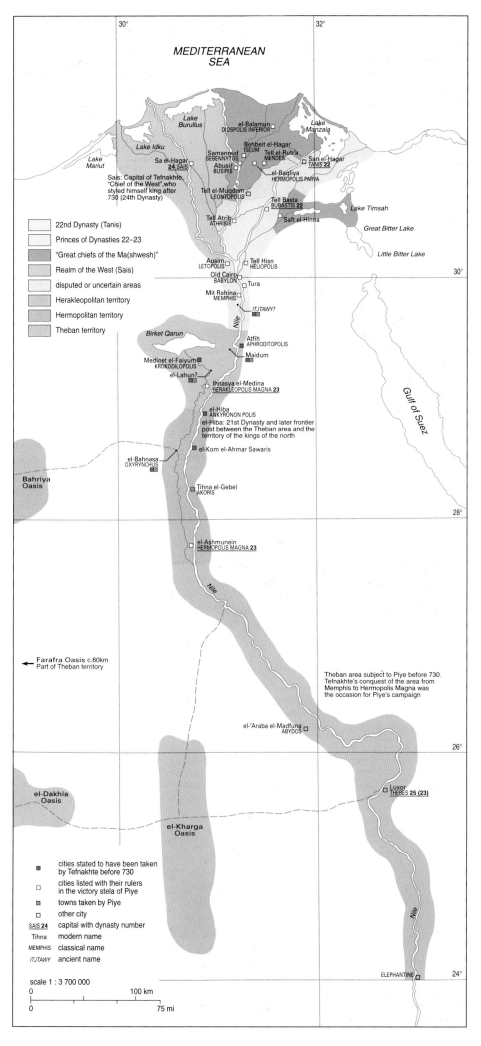

22nd Dynasty (Tanis)

Princes of Dynasties 22–23

"Great chiefs of the Ma(shwesh)"

Realm of the West (Sais)

disputed or uncertain areas

Herakleopolitan territory

Hermopolitan territory

Theban territory

Farafra Oasis c.60km
Part of Theban territory

Theban area subject to Piye before 730.
Tefnakhte's conquest of the area from
Memphis to Hermopolis Magna was
the occasion for Piye's campaign

cities stated to have been taken
by Tefnakhte before 730

cities listed with their rulers
in the victory stela of Piye

towns taken by Piye

other city

SAIS 24   capital with dynasty number

Tihna   modern name

MEMPHIS   classical name

ITJTAWY   ancient name

scale 1 : 3 700 000

0   100 km

0   75 mi

Administration of the 19th and especially the 20th Dynasty can be studied in numerous papyrus documents and ostraca (inscribed limestone flakes and potsherds), most of them discovered on the Theban West Bank. The most important long-term change was that a high proportion of land passed to temples, in particular that of Amon-Reʿ at Karnak. State and temple interacted to manage the land, but the temple of Amon-Reʿ eventually acquired virtual control of Upper Egypt. The major priestly offices became hereditary, and thus largely independent of the king, so that the high priests formed a succession that came to rival him.

Another significant practice was the settling of prisoners of war, especially Libyans, in military colonies. Although the Libyans were soon culturally Egyptian, they kept a separate identity, marked by the tribal name Meshwesh (often shortened to Ma), and in time became the main political force in the country.

These developments tended to divide Egypt gradually into a loose-knit, almost feudal society, whereas the movements of peoples in the Near East in this period brought profound social and technological change, conventionally termed the Iron Age. The east Mediterranean entered a twilight period, from which Egypt suffered less than other countries, but in the long term the Near East emerged renewed while Egypt definitively lost its preeminent position.

In the reign of Ramesses XI (c. 1104–1075) the viceroy of Nubia, Panehsy, fought a long battle for the Theban area which he ultimately lost, retiring to his residence of ʿAniba in Lower Nubia, where he was buried. After his intervention the previous line of high priests disappeared from office, and a military man called Herihor, who was probably an ethnic Libyan, replaced them in Ramesses' year 19. Priest and officer made a powerful combination, and Herihor enhanced his status beyond that of any of his predecessors, having himself portrayed as king in the Karnak temple complex and using an alternative dating system, which probably alludes to the presence of two "kings" in the country. After only five years he died. His successor Piʿankh also predeceased Ramesses XI, but by then the virtual partition of the country was established, although later high priests only occasionally claimed the titles of king. The pattern had been set for the next period.

From the reigns of Ramesses IX–XI comes a group of papyri recording investigations of tomb robberies on the West Bank at Thebes, including some of royal tombs. It is difficult to assess these documents, which were chance finds – and tomb robbery was a practice of all periods – but the highest local officials seem to have shown some complicity, and in the next two decades officials moved most royal mummies to new locations, while almost all their burial equipment was discarded or recycled.

Third Intermediate Period (c. 1075–715)

Ramesses XI was succeeded by Smendes (c. 1075–1050), the first king of the 21st Dynasty, and Piʿankh by Pinudjem I. The new dynasty, who may have been collateral descendants of the 20th-Dynasty royal family, ruled from Tanis in the northeastern delta and controlled the country as far south as el-Hiba. Tanis had not previously been an important center, and much in its monuments was transferred from other sites in the delta. It was not far from the Ramessid capital, and the move to it may have been dictated by the silting-up of waterways.

The Nile valley from el-Hiba to Aswan was controlled by the Theban high priests, who acknowledged the Tanite kings, dated by their regnal years, and intermarried with their family, but ruled a separate domain. The Thebans, many of whom were ethnically Libyan, harked back to their military origins. Libyans were also active in the north – their chief area of settlement – and Osorkon I (c. 985–978), the little known fifth king of the Tanite Dynasty, bore a Libyan name. The last king, Psusennes II (c. 960–945), probably also held the office of high priest of Amun, uniting the two realms in his person but not turning them into a single unit.

Shoshenq I (c. 945–925), the first king of the 22nd Dynasty, belonged to a Libyan family from Bubastis (Tell Basta) that had been prominent for some decades before he gained power. He exploited the simultaneous extinction of the line of high priests to install his son in Thebes, attempting to centralize Egypt, as did some of his successors. But although there was never a fully independent ruler of Thebes, the region was not integrated with the north for another 300 years.

Shoshenq fought a campaign in Palestine, which is recorded in reliefs at Karnak, where he began extensive building works. In Asia he may have taken up an initiative of Siamun (c. 978–960) on a more ambitious scale. He also revived relations with Byblos, Egypt's traditional Phoenician trading partner, and these were maintained for several generations. Shoshenq's reign brought an increase in prosperity that is visible in renewed building activity.

After nearly a century of internal peace, the 22nd Dynasty from the reign of Takelot II (c. 860–835) was a period of conflict and decline. The first major cause of unrest was the appointment of Takelot's son and heir, Osorkon, as high priest of Amun, an office which he combined with military functions. Osorkon was rejected by the Thebans, and a long civil war followed, which he recorded, after its apparently successful conclusion, in an enormous quasi-royal inscription at Karnak.

Beginning with the reign of Shoshenq III (c. 835–785), who may have usurped a throne that had been destined for his brother, the high priest Osorkon, the kingship became split. The first rival was Pedubaste I (c. 830–805) of what is conventionally termed the 23rd Dynasty, who was recognized alongside Shoshenq III. From this time on the way was open for powerful local rulers to call themselves kings and to be accepted wherever this suited the local elites. By the late 8th century there were numerous kings in the country, with the 22nd–25th Dynasties ruling simultaneously, apart from others who are absent from the later official lists. After 770 an important force joined the melee. A Nubian king Kashta (c. 770–750), whose capital was at Napata near the fourth cataract, was accepted as a ruler as far north as Thebes, marking the arrival of the 25th Dynasty in Egypt.

While kingship weakened, so also did the high priesthood of Amun. Osorkon IV of the 23rd Dynasty (c. 775–750) installed his daughter Shepenwepet in an old Theban office with the title "Divine Adoratrice of Amun". From this time on the adoratrice, who could not marry and passed on her office by "adoption," was a member of a royal family and the chief religious figure in the Theban area. In later periods the real power lay with nominally subordinate male officials, but in the case of Shepenwepet this is not clear. The 23rd-Dynasty control of the office was short-lived. Shepenwepet soon adopted Amenirdis I, a sister of Kashta, who had presumably been imposed on her by Kashta's brother and successor Piye (c. 750–715).

In the late 8th century the most important factions in Egypt were the ancestors of the 24th Dynasty, who were local rulers in Sais in the western delta, and the 25th Dynasty. Around 730 they came into conflict, perhaps because Saite influence had expanded into the Nile valley, which was the traditional Theban preserve and therefore part of the area to which the 25th Dynasty were the chief claimants. Piye set out from Napata on a campaign through Egypt as far as Memphis to extract submission from local rulers, in particular Tefnakhte of Sais. The episode was recorded at great length on a stela set up in the temple of Amon-Reʿ at Napata, which is of outstanding interest both for its text and for its scene showing four kings, whose names are written in cartouches, doing obeisance to Piye, as

Egypt in the Late Period, with the state of Napata–Meroe (712 BCE–4th century CE) The Egyptian sites shown include cities whose "kings" are listed in Assurbanipal's annals (several further Assyrian names cannot be identified with Egyptian places). Compare these with those of the campaign of Piye on the map on p. 47.

Texts in Aramaic, the official language of the Persian empire, have been found at several sites; they include papyri, ostraca, and rock graffiti.

The route of the Nubian campaign sent by Psammetichus II in 592 BCE is conjectural; its soldiers left Greek and Carian graffiti at Buhen and Abu Simbel, and probably at Gebel el-Silsila.

The canal from the Nile to the Red Sea appears on this map. This was begun by Necho II, completed by Darius I (who set up a series of stelae in c. 490 at the locations shown on the map), and which was later restored by Ptolemy II Philadelphus, Trajan and Hadrian, and Amr ibn el-ʿAs, the Muslim conqueror of Egypt. Its length from Tell el-Maskhuta to Suez was about 85 kilometers.

Block statue of the vizier Nespaqashuty from the Cachette north of the Seventh Pylon at Karnak. This form is characteristic of the Third Intermediate Period, when temple statues were the principal permanent semi-public display medium for the elite. Nespaqashuty holds a plant, perhaps the lettuce of Min, and proffers a sistrum of Hathor suspended from a cord around his neck. The front and sides are decorated with scenes of him offering to deities. Height: 72 cm. Limestone. 8th century BCE. Luxor Museum.

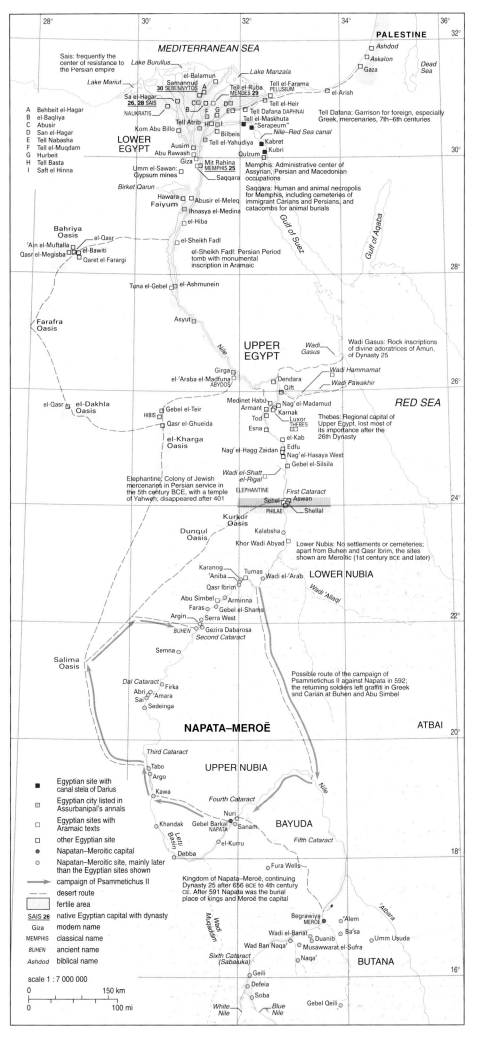

28°   30°   32°   34°   36°

PALESTINE

MEDITERRANEAN SEA

Ashdod

Askalon

Gaza

Dead Sea

Sais: frequently the center of resistance to the Persian empire

Lake Burullus

Lake Mariut

Lake Manzala

el-Balamun

Samannud
30 SEBENNYTOS

Tell el-Ruba
MENDES 29

Tell el-Farama
PELUSIUM

el-Arish

Sa el-Hagar
26, 28 SAIS

NAUKRATIS

Tell el-Heir

A Behbeit el-Hagar
B el-Baqliya
C Abusir
D San el-Hagar
E Tell Nabasha
F Tell el-Muqdam
G Hurbeit
H Tell Basta
I Saft el-Hinna

Tell el-Farama

Tell Dafana DAPHNAI

Tell Dafana: Garrison for foreign, especially Greek, mercenaries, 7th–6th centuries

Tell el-Maskhuta "Serapeum"

Nile–Red Sea canal

Kom Abu Billo

Tell Atrib

Bilbeis

Tell el-Yahudiya

Kabret

Kubri

LOWER EGYPT

Ausim

Abu Rawash

Giza

Mit Rahina
MEMPHIS 25

Saqqara

Qulzum

Memphis: Administrative center of Assyrian, Persian and Macedonian occupations

Umm el-Sawan: Gypsum mines

Birket Qarun

Saqqara: Human and animal necropolis for Memphis, including cemeteries of immigrant Carians and Persians, and catacombs for animal burials

Gulf of Suez

Gulf of Aqaba

Hawara

Faiyum

Abusir el-Meleq

Ihnasya el-Medina

el-Hiba

el-Sheikh Fadl

el-Sheikh Fadl: Persian Period tomb with monumental inscription in Aramaic

Bahriya Oasis

'Ain el-Muftalla
Qasr el-Megisba

el-Qasr
el-Bawiti
Qaret el-Farargi

Tuna el-Gebel

el-Ashmunein

Farafra Oasis

Asyut

UPPER EGYPT

Wadi Gasus

Wadi Gasus: Rock inscriptions of divine adoratrices of Amun, of Dynasty 25

Girga

el-'Araba el-Madfuna
ABYDOS

Dendara

Qift

Wadi Hammamat

Wadi Fawakhir

RED SEA

el-Qasr
el-Dakhla Oasis

HIBIS

Gebel el-Teir

Qasr el-Ghueida

Medinet Habu

Armant

Karnak
Luxor
THEBES

Nag' el-Madamud

el-Kharga Oasis

Tod

Esna

el-Kab

Thebes: Regional capital of Upper Egypt, lost most of its importance after the 26th Dynasty

Edfu

Nag' el-Hagg Zaidan

Nag' el-Hasaya West

Gebel el-Silsila

Wadi el-Shatt el-Rigal

Elephantine: Colony of Jewish mercenaries in Persian service in the 5th century BCE, with a temple of Yahweh; disappeared after 401

ELEPHANTINE

Sehel

PHILAE

First Cataract

Aswan

Shellal

Kurkur Oasis

Kalabsha

Dunqul Oasis

Khor Wadi Abyad

Lower Nubia: No settlements or cemeteries, apart from Buhen and Qasr Ibrim, the sites shown are Meroitic (1st century BCE and later)

Karanog

'Aniba

Tumas

Qasr Ibrim

Wadi el-'Arab

LOWER NUBIA

Wadi 'Allaqi

Abu Simbel

Arminna

Faras

Argin

Gebel el-Shams

Serra West

BUHEN

Gezira Dabarosa

Second Cataract

Semna

Salima Oasis

Dal Cataract

Firka

Abri

Amara

Sai

Sedeinga

Possible route of the campaign of Psammetichus II against Napata in 592; the returning soldiers left graffiti in Greek and Carian at Buhen and Abu Simbel

NAPATA–MEROË

ATBAI

Third Cataract

Tabo

Argo

UPPER NUBIA

Kawa

Fourth Cataract

Nuri

BAYUDA

Khandak

Gebel Barkal
NAPATA

Sanam

Letti Basin

el-Kurru

Fifth Cataract

Debba

Egyptian site with canal stela of Darius

Egyptian city listed in Assurbanipal's annals

Egyptian sites with Aramaic texts

other Egyptian site

Napatan–Meroitic capital

Napatan–Meroitic site, mainly later than the Egyptian sites shown

campaign of Psammetichus II

desert route

fertile area

SAIS 26   native Egyptian capital with dynasty

Giza   modern name

MEMPHIS   classical name

BUHEN   ancient name

Ashdod   biblical name

scale 1 : 7 000 000

0   150 km

0   100 mi

Kingdom of Napata–Meroë, continuing Dynasty 25 after 656 BCE to 4th century CE. After 591 Napata was the burial place of kings and Meroë the capital

Fura Wells

Wadi Muqaddim

Begrawiya
MEROË

'Alem

Wadi el-Banat

Ba'sa

Duanib

Umm Usuda

Sixth Cataract (Sabaluka)

Wad Ban Naqa'

Musawwarat el-Sufra

Naqa'

BUTANA

'Atbara

Geili

Defeia

Soba

Gebel Qeili

White Nile

Blue Nile

---

well as a number of other local leaders. Tefnakhte (who did not yet style himself king) was in theory forced to submit, but he did not come to Piye in person. The affair had little deep impact, because Piye established his supremacy but returned to Napata without making himself the sole king of Egypt. His inscription presents him as more Egyptian than the Egyptians and his campaign almost as a holy mission to right the evils of the land. Napata was an old center of the worship of Amon-Reʿ, so that this may be valid, but Piye could have been using a religious legitimation for a political act.

Late Period (c. 715–332)
At the beginning of the reign of Piye's successor Shabaka (c. 715–700), the conflict between Napata and Sais was renewed, and the 24th-Dynasty King Bocchoris (c. 722–715) was killed in battle between the two powers. Shabaka's action finally disposed of all the other kings in the country. From his reign on the Nubians took a far greater interest in Egypt as a whole, making Memphis their capital and residing in the country for some of the time. The elimination of other kings did not, however, alter the political structure greatly; local rulers remained largely independent, and were indeed called "kings" in the records of the Assyrian invasion of Egypt 40 years later. Nonetheless, the economic gains from the change were considerable. The half-century of Nubian rule produced as many monuments in Upper Egypt as the previous two centuries, and accelerated an existing artistic revival that looked to earlier periods for inspiration.

Under Shebitku (c. 700–690) and Taharqa (c. 690–664) the economic improvement continued. Taharqa left monuments over much of Egypt and Nubia, where his name has been found at the later capital of Meroe, upstream of the fifth cataract. Several inscriptions recount the beneficial effects of a high inundation in his year 6, which is also documented by water level records on the quay at Karnak. Average inundation levels may have increased at the time, and this would have contributed to prosperity.

In Thebes Shebitku's sister Shepenwepet II was adopted by Amenirdis I, and members of the Nubian royal family held high religious offices. Under Taharqa Shepenwepet II adopted Amenirdis II. Power in the area, however, lay with one or two local families. The most important person in Thebes was Montemhet, the fourth priest of Amun and "prince of the city," who was the effective ruler of much of Upper Egypt and survived well into the 26th Dynasty. His tomb, statues, and inscriptions are the first great nonroyal monuments of their period, on a grander scale than New Kingdom tombs and displaying much learning and technical accomplishment.

The unified Egyptian and Nubian state was a major power, whose only rival in the Near East was Assyria, which had been expanding since the 9th century. The furthest southwestern extension of the Assyrian empire was Palestine, whose small states looked to Egypt for assistance in their attempts to throw off Assyrian rule. Initially the Nubian kings did not respond to these approaches, but in 701 an Egyptian force fought the Assyrian King Sennacherib (704–681) in Palestine on the side of the kings of Judah. The engagement was incon-

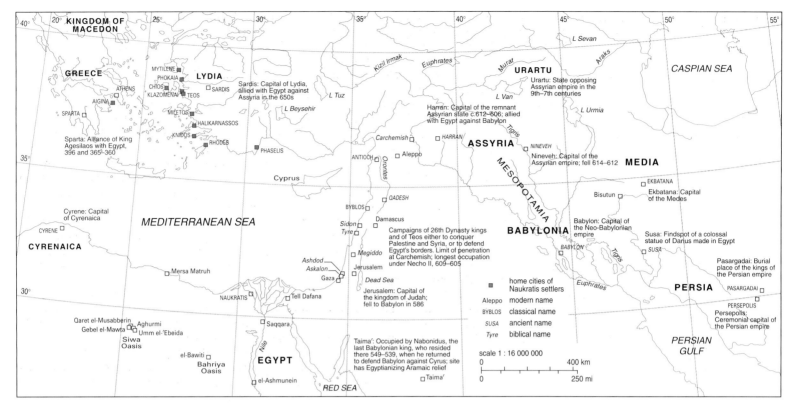

clusive, and for a generation the two main powers kept a buffer of minor polities between each other.

The Assyrian king Esarhaddon (681–669) attempted to conquer Egypt in 674, but was repulsed at the frontier post of Sile. A renewed attack in 671 was successful; Memphis was taken and the country forced to pay tribute. Taharqa fled south, but returned within two years to retake Memphis. Esarhaddon died on the way to Egypt for a counterattack, and the next campaign was sent by his son Assurbanipal (669–627) in about 667. Assurbanipal used the ruler of Sais, Necho I (before 672–664), who now styled himself king, and his son the later King Psammetichus I as his chief agents in reestablishing Assyrian rule. In 664 Tantamani (664–657 in Egypt, possibly later in Nubia) succeeded Taharqa and immediately mounted a campaign as far as the delta; his account of this does not even mention the Assyrians. The Nubians' main opponent was Necho I, who seems to have died in the fighting. The remaining local rulers accepted Tantamani fairly readily.

Sometime between 663 and 657 Assurbanipal led a campaign of reprisal in person, plundering as far south as Thebes while Tantamani fled to Nubia. This was the last phase of the Assyrian occupation; Assurbanipal had to turn his attention to a rebellion in Babylon, and Psammetichus I (664–610) was able to make himself completely independent before 653. These events mark the end of Egypt's relative isolation; it was involved with all the major empires of Mediterranean antiquity.

Between 664 and 657 Psammetichus I eliminated all the local rulers in Lower Egypt, and in 656 he had his daughter Nitocris adopted by Shepenwepet II as the future divine adoratrice in Thebes, bypassing Amenirdis II. Until the previous year dating in Thebes had been by Tantamani's years of reign.

Psammetichus I's campaigns of unification were significant in another way. He was the first king to employ Greek and Carian mercenaries, setting the pattern for more than 300 years. By the 4th century all major powers used Aegean troops, who were a prerequisite for engaging in international conflict and sometimes determined its course. Some of them settled in Egypt, building up a nucleus of foreigners in the country who played a disproportionate part in history because they specialized in trade and warfare. The Greeks also influence our view of history for this period, because native Egyptian sources are sparser than Classical ones.

In the Late Period the Egyptian economy was less self-sufficient than before, since the basic metal, iron, was imported, apparently from the Near East rather than Nubia. Egypt had exports such as grain and papyrus but, unlike Greece and Anatolia, did not have coinage, and continued to use older systems of exchange.

With the reunification of Egypt and the imposition of a central administration in place of local rulers the 25th-Dynasty increase in prosperity resumed, culminating in the later 26th Dynasty, but relatively little of this wealth is evident in the archaeological record, because it was concentrated in the delta. The chief exception is the small group of grandiose private tombs of the later 7th century in Thebes. The artistic revival also continued, and there is an archaizing or classicizing flavor in the use of some titles and religious texts. The kings may have wished to bypass the political and economic importance of temples and reach back toward earlier, more secular periods, but if so, they failed.

Policy of the 26th Dynasty toward the Near East had two main aims: to maintain a balance of power by supporting the rivals of whichever major power was dominant, and if possible to repeat New Kingdom conquests in Palestine and Syria. Thus Psammetichus I supported Lydia in Anatolia and later Babylon against Assyria until Assyria declined after 620, when he reversed his allegiance; in the 6th century Egypt continued to support the enemies of Babylon until Persia had become the main power. Necho II (610–595), Psammetichus II (595–589), and Apries (589–570) built on the work of Psam-

Right Figures of an Egyptian and a Persian, from the base of the statue of Darius I found at Susa. The base has 24 figures representing provinces of the Persian empire. They kneel with their hands raised in adoration of the king; their names are written in hieroglyphs in ovals beneath. The statue was made in Egypt, but the figures were carved according to a hybrid model. The statue as a whole seems to have been created in an international style that may have been planned for the whole empire. Tehran, Museum Iran Bastan.

Left: Egypt, the Aegean, and the Near East in the Late Period

Assyrian empire Expanded from the 9th century; occupied Syria and Palestine in the 8th; held Egypt 671–c. 660. Destroyed by the Medes and Babylonians 614–612.

Kingdom of Judah Principal local enemy of Assyria and Babylon in Palestine until the Babylonian captivity of 586; looked to Egypt for help, usually in vain.

Lydia Allied with Psammetichus I against the Assyrians; defeated by the Kimmerians c. 653.

Caria and Ionia Homelands of many of the foreign soldiers employed in Egypt from the reign of Psammetichus I on.

Neo-Babylonian empire (612–539) Defeated the Assyrian successor state by 605 and attacked Egypt 591 and 567; destroyed by Cyrus of Persia 539.

Persian empire Expanded in succession to the Medes from 549; at its maximum extent included Sind, Anatolia, Cyrenaica and Egypt. Destroyed 336–323 by Alexander the Great, who inherited the same area and held Macedonia and Greece in addition.

Athens Frequent ally of Egypt against the Persians; expedition of 200 ships to help Egyptian rebels in the western delta sent in 460, finally annihilated in 454. In 385–c. 375 and 360 the Athenian general Chabrias commanded Egyptian resistance to Persia. Egypt paid mainly in grain for Athenian help.

Cyrenaica Settled by Greek colonists who founded a local dynasty c. 630; internal war in 570 led to Amasis' seizure of the Egyptian throne. Subsequently allied with Egypt; incorporated in the Persian empire c. 515.

Cyprus Parts of the island held by Amasis c. 567–526. King Euagoras allied with Egypt against the Persian empire 389–380.

Naukratis Greek trading settlement founded late 7th century and made into the exclusive Greek community in Egypt by Amasis. The original Greek settlers came from the cities marked.

metichus I and moved over to attack. Necho II, probably continuing a campaign begun by Psammetichus immediately before his death, campaigned in Syria from 610 to 605, but had to withdraw. In 601 he repulsed an attack by the Babylonian King Nebuchadnezzar II (604–562) on Egypt. He fitted out Egyptian fleets with Greek-designed triremes in both the Mediterranean and the Red Sea, attempting also to link the Nile and the Red Sea with a canal. There is evidence for a later persecution of Necho's memory, and this may account in part for the small number of the monuments bearing his name.

Psammetichus II made a single expedition to Asia, with no apparent long-term effects. His most significant political act, however, was a major campaign to Nubia in 592, which brought an end to 60 years' peaceful relations. The invading army, which included Egyptians, Greeks, and Carians, apparently reached Napata, but no lasting conquest seems to have been intended. On the return journey the foreign soldiers left graffiti at Buhen and Abu Simbel in Lower Nubia; the course of the campaign has been reconstructed from these. After 592 the memory of the 25th-Dynasty kings was persecuted in Egypt.

In 595 the divine adoratrice of Amun, Nitocris, who must have been in her seventies, adopted Psammetichus II's daughter ʿAnkhnesneferibreʿ as her successor. ʿAnkhnesneferibreʿ took office in 586, and was still alive in 525. Thus for 130 years only two women were the representatives of the royal family in Thebes.

Like his predecessors, Apries supported Palestinian polities against Babylon. The Babylonian captivity of the Jews occurred in 586 during his reign, and many Jews fled to Egypt. From the next century records of a Jewish colony in Elephantine survive. Some Jews elsewhere in the country may have been ancestors of the Jewish population of Alexandria.

In 570 Apries sent an all-Egyptian army to support a local Libyan ruler in Cyrene in a struggle against Greek colonists. The army was defeated and then mutinied. Apries sent a general, Amasis, to quell the revolt, but Amasis joined it, declared himself king (570–526), and drove Apries into exile. Around 567 Apries returned with a Babylonian invading force sent by Nebuchadnezzar II, but was

defeated and killed. Amasis then buried him with royal honors and recorded the whole episode in a proclamation inscribed on stelae, in terms that pass over his seizure of power.

From the point of view of the Greeks, who are our sources, Amasis' most notable policy was his treatment of the Greeks, whose trading activities were confined to the delta town of Naukratis, while foreign soldiers were kept in garrisons in Memphis and in the eastern delta. The Greeks felt that the special status of Naukratis was a favor to them, yet the policy reduced the scope for friction between Egyptians and Greeks by restricting contact of any sort. Amasis, whose reign marked the high point of prosperity in the 26th Dynasty, was also remembered as a drinker and a philanderer; both Herodotus and later Egyptian sources tell stories illustrating these characteristics which could, however, belong to folklore.

Amasis' reign ended in the shadow of the growing power of Persia, but it was his short-lived successor Psammetichus III (526–525) who faced the Persian invasion, which was immediately successful. Cambyses (525–522), the first ruler of the 27th Dynasty, was also the first outsider whose main interest was not Egypt to become king. He undertook campaigns through Egypt to Nubia and to the western oasis of Siwa, but both failed. His rule was later resented bitterly, partly because of an attempt to reduce the incomes of the politically influential temples. Darius I (521–486) followed a more conciliatory line, commissioning buildings and decorating the temple of Hibis in el-Kharga oasis, the largest temple surviving from the period 1100–300. He also completed Necho II's Nile–Red Sea canal, adorning it with monumental stelae decorated in a mixed Egyptian–Near Eastern style. Until it silted up, the canal provided a direct sea link between Persia and Egypt. The mixed style, which was first used in royal statues, proclaimed the cosmopolitan character of Darius' empire.

Darius' reign was prosperous, but the Egyptians tolerated Persian rule only so long as there was no real chance of throwing it off. The Persian defeat at the battle of Marathon in Greece in 490 signaled the beginning of 80 years of resistance, in which Egyptian rebels traded grain with Greek states in return for military aid. The western delta was the center of revolts; Persian rule was more easily maintained in the Nile valley, which could be reached by the Red Sea or canal routes. Like other rulers, the Persians used foreign troops, for example employing the Jewish frontier garrison at Elephantine. Documents in Aramaic, the administrative language of the Persian empire, have been found there and at other sites. Few Egyptian documents or monuments survive from the period 480–400. This scarcity reflects insecurity, hatred of the Persians, and impoverishment.

In 404 Amyrtaios of Sais (404–399) freed the delta from Persian rule, and by 400 the entire country was in his hands. Like some earlier rebels against the Persians he styled himself king, but unlike them he became part of the official listing as the sole ruler of the 28th Dynasty. In 399 Nepherites I of Mendes (399–393) usurped the throne, founding the 29th Dynasty. He, Psammuthis (393), and Hakoris (393–380) built at numerous sites and with the help of Greek mercenaries warded off a Persian attack in

385–383. The 4th-century mercenaries had no intention of settling in Egypt and their loyalty was variable, as proved fatal more than once.

Nectanebo I (380–362), a general from Sebennytos in the delta, usurped the throne from Nepherites II (380) and founded the 30th Dynasty; one of his inscriptions is quite frank about his nonroyal origins. The dynasty was a time of great prosperity, with building all over the country; artistic traditions of the 26th Dynasty were resumed and developed. In 373 a Persian invasion was defeated, and in the 360s Nectanebo joined a defensive alliance of Persian provinces. His successor Teos (365–360 with a coregency) moved into the offensive in Palestine, but was betrayed by a rebellion in Egypt, in which a cousin, Nectanebo II (360–343), was placed on the throne, and by the defection of his Spartan ally to the new king.

Nectanebo II withstood an invasion by the Persian Artaxerxes III Ochus in 350, but the attack of 343 was successful. The ten-year Second Persian Period (also called the 31st Dynasty) was itself interrupted for about two years by a native king Khababash, whose memory lived on for many years; he appears to have controlled all of Lower Egypt. Renewed Persian rule was oppressive and predisposed the country toward almost any alternative.

Greco-Roman Period (332 BCE – 395 CE)

In 332 Alexander the Great took possession of Egypt, apparently without a struggle. During his brief stay he initiated plans to build Alexandria, sacrificed to the Egyptian gods, and consulted the oracle of Ammon (perhaps not the Egyptian Amun) in Siwa Oasis. At his death Ptolemy, son of Lagos, succeeded in acquiring Egypt as his satrapy, and buried his king in Memphis (the body was later moved to Alexandria). In 305–04 he followed the lead of other satraps and made himself the independent king of Egypt.

Greco-Egyptian terracotta statuettes. *Left*: the Egyptian protective dwarf god Bes holding a knife and a Roman shield. *Above*: a high relief of Herakles-Harpokrates (Horus the Child) holding a cornucopia and seated on a goose. The whole genre of terracotta is Greek rather than Egyptian; but while the Bes is close to Egyptian style, Herakles-Harpokrates is almost wholly Classical. Roman Period. Cairo, Egyptian Museum.

For the next 250 years Egypt was ruled by Macedonian Greeks, but as a separate country with its own interests to pursue, even if they were not always those of the indigenous population. Ptolemaic rule was oppressive in some ways – possibly no more so than its indigenous forerunners – and provoked nationalistic uprisings, but, unlike its predecessor and successor, it was centered on Egypt. An indication of this is that the Ptolemies sought to enlarge Egyptian possessions in a traditional way, by annexing Palestine and later moving a short distance into Lower Nubia, where control alternated between Egypt and the Meroitic state. In addition, Cyrene, Cyprus (already held briefly by Amasis), parts of Anatolia, and some Aegean islands came under Ptolemaic overlordship for a time.

The reigns of the first three Ptolemies were a period of development for Egypt, in which the country was brought into the Hellenistic world in terms of agriculture, commerce and, for the Greek population, education. New crops, such as wheat, were introduced, and by early Roman times the water wheel (*saqiya*) had become widespread, increasing the potential of irrigation, while the arrival of the camel opened up new possibilities for long-distance and desert transport. Many economic changes were managed by state monopolies; it is uncertain whether the Ptolemies followed earlier Egyptian kings in this. Foreign soldiers were allocated crown land, which they cultivated in return for a liability for military service. Greek settlements grew up in many areas, especially where there was land reclamation. This was particularly significant in the Faiyum, where new forms of irrigation made it possible to grow two crops per year. A gradual but fundamental change was the introduction of coinage, leading to a largely monetized economy in Roman times.

Although contact between native and Greek was

Left Over-life-size diorite head of an Egyptian, from Mit Rahina (Memphis), perhaps 1st century BCE. This commanding piece continues Late Period sculptural traditions; only the rendering of the hair shows Classical influence. Brooklyn Museum of Art.

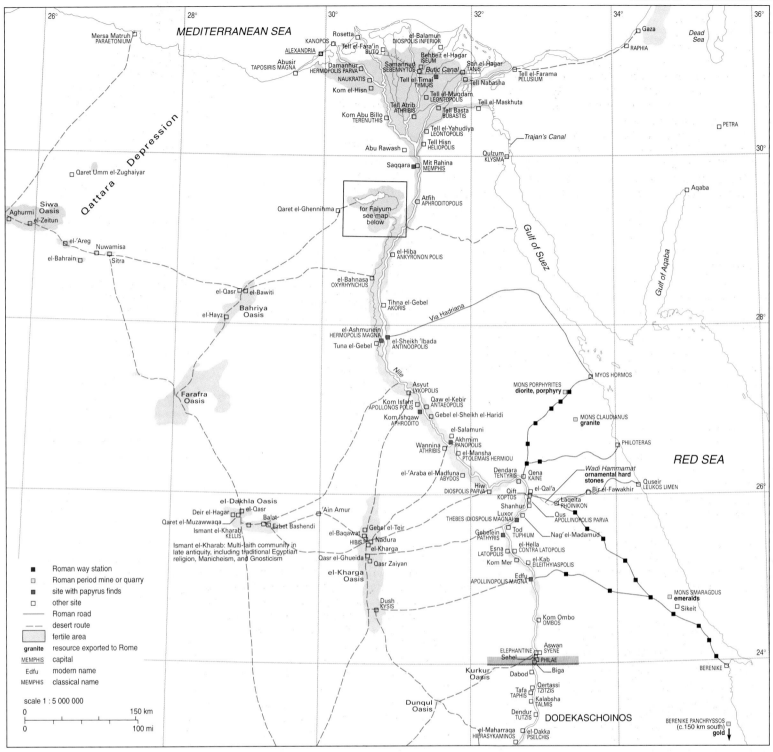

Legend (main map)

- ■ Roman way station
- ▫ Roman period mine or quarry
- ▪ site with papyrus finds
- □ other site
- —— Roman road
- - - - desert route
- ▨ fertile area
- **granite** resource exported to Rome
- MEMPHIS capital
- Edfu modern name
- MEMPHIS classical name

scale 1 : 5 000 000

0 — 150 km

0 — 100 mi

for Faiyum see map below

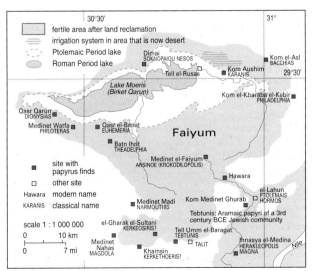

Legend (Faiyum map)

- ▨ fertile area after land reclamation
- irrigation system in area that is now desert
- Ptolemaic Period lake
- Roman Period lake
- ▪ site with papyrus finds
- □ other site
- Hawara modern name
- KARANIS classical name

scale 1 : 1 000 000

0 — 10 km

0 — 7 mi

Tebtunis: Aramaic papyri of a 3rd century BCE Jewish community

Above: Egypt in the Greco-Roman Period

Important finds of Greek papyri and ostraca are marked for relevant sites. The Roman way-stations identified in the eastern desert were built at regular intervals along roads, and normally had a well. The roads led to four Red Sea ports, which traded with East Africa and India throughout the period.

Right: The Faiyum in the Greco-Roman Period

Land reclamation from Lake Moeris and irrigation of the desert made the Faiyum (the Arsinoite nome) into the most prosperous area of Greek agricultural settlement.

Many towns of settlers are now in the desert, where papyrus preserves well.

relatively limited, all this new activity, as well as the increase in cultivated land, generated wealth for the whole country. The chief development was, however, foreign: the building of Alexandria, which became the leading city in the Greek world. In later parlance Alexandria was "adjoining," not "in" Egypt. By acting as a magnet for the country's wealth and as the kings' chief concern it restricted expansion in other areas, especially because of its location in the extreme northwest.

The 2nd century was a time of decline in the economy and of political strife. Within the ruling family there were conspiracies, while native revolts in Upper Egypt were common from the reign of Ptolemy IV Philopator (221–205) onward; as late as the 50s and 40s, whole areas of Upper Egypt were not always in government control. Egypt lost most of its foreign dependencies, and was conquered by

53

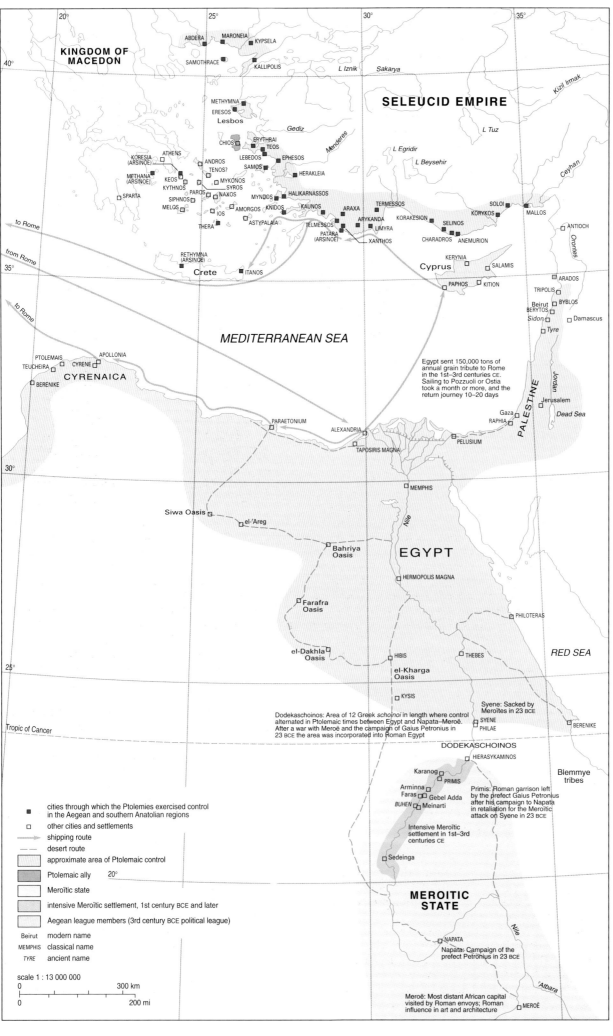

Egypt and the east Mediterranean in the Greco-Roman Period

In the 3rd century BCE the principal powers in the Near East were the kingdom of Macedon, the Seleucid empire, and the Ptolemaic kingdom. This map shows the approximate maximum extent of Ptolemaic possessions in the reigns of Ptolemy III Euergetes I and IV Philopator. Almost all were lost before 30 BCE, by which time the entire Mediterranean area shown was incorporated in the Roman empire.

In the Aegean and southern Anatolia the Ptolemies used cities to exercise control – in many of them only for brief periods. The kingdom was one of cities, not regions; the edge of the colored area indicates the approximate limit of their control, but is not a political frontier.

The map also shows islands belonging to the Aegean league of the 3rd century BCE; probable members are queried. This league was formed under Ptolemaic influence. Chios, an independent state, was a Ptolemaic ally.

Egypt sent 150,000 tons of annual grain tribute to Rome in the 1st–3rd centuries CE. Sailing to Pozzuoli or Ostia took a month or more, and the return journey 10–20 days.

Dodekaschoinos: Area of 12 Greek *schoinoi* in length where control alternated in Ptolemaic times between Egypt and Napata–Meroë. After a war with Meroë and the campaign of Gaius Petronius in 23 BCE the area was incorporated into Roman Egypt.

Syene: Sacked by Meroïtes in 23 BCE

Primis: Roman garrison left by the prefect Gaius Petronius after his campaign to Napata in retaliation for the Meroïtic attack on Syene in 23 BCE

Intensive Meroïtic settlement in 1st–3rd centuries CE

Napata: Campaign of the prefect Petronius in 23 BCE

Meroë: Most distant African capital visited by Roman envoys; Roman influence in art and architecture

■ cities through which the Ptolemies exercised control in the Aegean and southern Anatolian regions
□ other cities and settlements
→ shipping route
--- desert route
▨ approximate area of Ptolemaic control
▨ Ptolemaic ally
▨ Meroïtic state
▨ intensive Meroïtic settlement, 1st century BCE and later
▨ Aegean league members (3rd century BCE political league)

Beirut modern name
MEMPHIS classical name
TYRE ancient name

scale 1 : 13 000 000
0 ___ 300 km
0 ___ 200 mi

2ND CENTURY BCE—4TH CENTURY CE

the Seleucid Antiochus IV Epiphanes, who was briefly proclaimed king in 168. In the 1st century the weakness of government continued, working in some ways to the native population's advantage. But the overshadowing force of Rome doomed Ptolemaic and Egyptian independence.

Right Pair of over-life-size statues of Ptolemy II Philadelphus and his queen Arsinoe II Philadelphus, who holds a necklace counterpoise in her left hand. The style and iconography are wholly Egyptian; even the "smile" occurs in native works. Found in 1710 in the Villa Verospi in Rome; from the imperial pavilion in the Gardens of Sallust on the Monte Pincio, where they were set up under Domitian (81–96) or Hadrian (117–138); originally from Heliopolis. Highly polished pink granite. Rome, Città del Vaticano, Museo Gregoriano Egizio.

Below Relief-decorated cartonnage coffin of Artemidorus with portrait, from Hawara in the Faiyum. The coffin goes back to Late Period models. Top register: Anubis embalms the mummy; center: Horus and Thoth protect an emblem of Osiris; bottom: the resurrecting Osiris with Isis hovering over him in the form of a kite. The portrait is one of many hundreds, few of which are still with the mummies and coffins to which they related. They are the only substantial legacy of painted portraiture from the Classical world. 2nd century CE. London, British Museum.

The Ptolemies and the Roman emperors appeared on the native monuments as traditional Egyptian kings, and the earlier rulers set up inscriptions in Egyptian with accounts of such of their deeds as were intended to benefit the native population. Some public decrees were set up in three scripts, hieroglyphic Egyptian, demotic Egyptian, and Greek. The best known of these is the decree preserved on the Rosetta Stone, which was promulgated in 196 under Ptolemy V Epiphanes (205–180).

Throughout the Ptolemaic dynasty traditional Egyptian temples were built. It seems that the temple lands, which produced the everyday income of temples, were more or less unchanged in extent from earlier periods; the resources for building programs probably came from the kings. The benefactions for building temples were not greatly affected by the ebb and flow of the economy, or even by struggles in the royal house, and may have been a consistent policy aimed at attracting native support, as well as pleasing the native gods. Within the temples, however, the figure of the king who performed the traditional cult was artificial. In times of uncertainty images of kings continued to be carved in temple reliefs but the cartouches for their names were left blank.

Traditional nonroyal statuary developed richly, showing the continuing vitality and wealth of the native elite, even though their sphere of action was curtailed, as is exemplified in the pietism and resignation of many inscriptions. Native monuments show little clear evidence of receptiveness to Greek influence. The Greek population, by contrast, was influenced by Egyptian religion, in increasing measure as the period progressed. Ptolemaic times also saw the greatest development of Egyptian animal worship. The cults attracted both Egyptians and Greeks, creating mortuary towns for the mummification of animals, pilgrimage, and oracular consultations.

During the first century or so of Roman rule (after 30 BCE) prosperity increased. The improved administration was aimed at securing wealth for Rome more than developing Egypt for its own sake, and in the long term problems of excessive taxation and official coercion were serious. Some emperors, notably Hadrian (117–138 CE), showed a special regard for Egypt, but new policies were not directed toward the benefit of the local Greek population, let alone the Egyptian (the two groups were kept more sharply separate than in Ptolemaic times). The wealthy indigenous inner elite seem to have lost almost all their status, producing very few monuments after 100 CE. Unlike other provinces of the empire, Egypt was not granted significant local autonomy, but was administered by a prefect under the emperor's direct jurisdiction.

The Greco-Roman Period was crucial for Egypt's later fame. Egyptian cults spread into the Mediterranean world under the Ptolemies, but their greatest popularity was in early imperial times, when native Egyptian priests, as well as many Egyptian objects, came to Rome, while the cults developed throughout much of the empire. Prominent among them was that of Sarapis, a Greco-Egyptian god created as a deliberate hybrid under the first Ptolemies. Egypt was also the exotic land par excellence, whose landscape was shown in a fanciful form in Roman paintings and mosaics.

Native Egyptian temples continued to be built in the Roman Period, with the long reign of the first emperor Augustus (30 BCE – 14 CE) marking a peak of activity, while the native religion continued to function in other areas, notably in burial practices that the Greek population also adopted. Few new temples were constructed after the 1st century CE, perhaps in part because of economic difficulties, but the decoration of existing ones continued, even keeping up with the struggles for the imperial throne in the names used in cartouches. The latest inscription in hieroglyphs dates to 394 CE, while Egyptian demotic literary texts, as well as some documents, were common as late as the 3rd century.

The force that eventually destroyed traditional Egyptian culture and led to the mutilation of traditional monuments was not Roman rule but Christianity, whose success was due to some extent to its not being associated with Roman power. Native Egypt may, however, have contributed also to Christianity: the role of the Virgin Mary and the iconography of Virgin and Child resemble strikingly the myth and iconography of Isis and the infant Horus. The notional end of ancient Egyptian history in 395 CE is the date of the final separation of the Roman Empire, by then strongly Christian, into east (Byzantine) and west; Egypt belonged with the east.

ART AND ARCHITECTURE

Egyptian representational art forms – sculpture in the round, relief, and painting – acquired a distinctive appearance by the beginning of the Dynastic Period. At the same time the level of work in decorative and functional art forms, such as painted patterning, stone vase manufacture, ivory carving, furniture making, and metalwork, was very high, while architecture evolved rapidly from then on, continuing to develop as new materials were mastered and new forms introduced. From the beginning, works of art in a wide range of genres are the most important single legacy from ancient Egypt, and one that is remarkably consistent in character. Changes in art through different periods relate to changes in society and throw light on them, although art seeks its inspiration more in other art than in the world. Egyptian art is superficially approachable, yet also alien from western art.

Few Egyptian works were produced as "art for art's sake." They all had a function, either as everyday objects or, more commonly among those preserved, in a religious or funerary context. It has sometimes been said that they should not be called "art," but there is no necessary contradiction between an object's artistic character and its function. Rather, the artistic quality of an object is the aesthetic element that enhances its function or is additional to function. The status of Egyptian art as "art" in the minds of Egyptians was different in degree from that of western art for western viewers, but there is no fundamental difference in kind. Indeed, the ranges of Egyptian and western genres resemble each other strikingly. In Egypt as in many societies art was a crucial focus of prestige.

Relief and painting

Relief achieves its effect through modeling, light and shade, while painting works with line and color, but the techniques of representation in both are basically the same; both were also colored. Relief can be raised or sunk, the latter being a characteristically Egyptian form. In raised relief the surface surrounding the figures is removed to the depth of a few millimeters, so that they stand out against it; in sunk relief the outlines of the figures are incised in the surface, which is then left, and the figures are modeled within it. Raised relief was generally used indoors, and sunk relief, which shows up better in the sun, out of doors. There were, however, variations in fashion in different periods; sunk relief was also less labor-intensive. Major religious buildings and the finer private tombs were decorated in relief. Painting was used in tombs where poor rock made relief impossible, or in order to save expense, or where the work was not permanent and the surface to be covered was not suitable for relief, as in mud-brick royal palaces and private houses. Although painting was second best, magnificent works were created in the medium, whose techniques encouraged artists to work more freely than in relief.

A third, very rare type is representation in inlay. A small group of 4th-Dynasty tomb scenes at Maidum was made of colored paste set in the stone, while in later times glass and colored stones were used in the same way, chiefly on small objects, and to supply details in elaborate reliefs, a method typical of the ʿAmarna Period. In the later New Kingdom, pictorial faience tiles were used as another form of composite decoration.

Egyptian writing and pictorial representation are very closely linked. Hieroglyphic signs are themselves pictures, whose conventions, apart from the linguistic and ornamental ones that govern their arrangement, are not very different from those of representation. Most pictures contain hieroglyphic texts, which may comment on the scene, supplying non-pictorial information, or can dominate the visual component, as in some temple reliefs. In non-royal tomb scenes the main figure is in one sense a greatly magnified hieroglyph, acting as a sign that is omitted from the text caption, which supplies the person's name. Figure and text are mutually dependent.

Methods of representation

In contrast with western art and with the optical devices of photography and motion pictures, Egyptian representation is not based on either of the two main principles of perspective: the use of foreshortening; and the adoption of a single, unified viewpoint for an entire picture. Instead, figures are rather like diagrams of what they show, whose aim is to convey information rather than a view. The picture surface is mostly treated as a neutral element, not as an illusionistic space; spatial features are commonest in small groups of figures. These characteristics are universal in the world; perspective became the norm of representation only very slowly, and its adoption seems often to have been the result of direct or indirect Greek influence.

In order to understand Egyptian "diagrams," it is necessary to become familiar with their conventions, rather as we do when we learn to read a map.

Right Schist statue of Amenopemhat kneeling to present an emblem of Hathor to Ptah. His momentarily flexed calf muscle is visible; the forearm is also tensed. A comparable treatment occurs already in the Old Kingdom. c. 630 BCE. Height 64 cm. New York, Metropolitan Museum of Art.

Above Statue of Metjetjy, carved from a single block of high-quality wood. The medium is exploited in a subtle composition that departs from conventional standing statue types. Note the right hand holding the kilt. Height 61·5 cm. From Saqqara. 6th Dynasty. Brooklyn Museum of Art.

Left Inlay relief from the tomb of Itet at Maidum. Most of the inlay is restored, but the man's kilt and right leg retain substantial areas of the original paste. Early 4th Dynasty. Oxford, Ashmolean Museum.

Below Raised and sunk relief, after Schäfer. A Stages in carving raised relief. B Stages in carving sunk relief. C Sunk relief with beveled incisions. D Raised relief with two thicknesses and with one thickness.

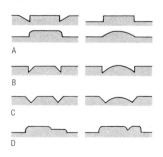

In theory the conventions could be as arbitrary as in a map, but in fact they are not, and their resemblance to perspective images often seduces the modern viewer into reading whole works in perspective. Among non-perspective representational systems the Egyptian is one of the closest to visual images. It allows precise depiction of idealized typical forms, as in the human figure, and it is relatively simple to transmit and to understand, unlike the highly elaborate conventions of early Chinese or Central American art. There must be further reasons for this visual character, but these have not so far been identified. It has been suggested that the Egyptians' belief in the recreative force of representation was its origin, but the strength of this belief has probably been exaggerated, and in its extreme form such an idea would imply that they were more literal-minded than is easily credible. On a different plane, the conventions of artistic representation are, as we shall see, a repository of Egyptian values.

The Egyptians typically depicted an object by means of an assembly of its most characteristic aspects, which was contained within an outline that conveyed much of the crucial information. The various aspects were shown without foreshortening, which means that rectilinear forms were rendered precisely. In such a scheme the front and side of a box, for example, might well be next to each other. For objects with curved surfaces the method is more paradoxical, and very occasional foreshortenings are found, although they are not significant for the system as a whole (in true perspective, too, such objects cause difficulty). Many further conventions stem from the basic principles. Thus, a part of an object that would not be visible in reality may be shown in a "false transparency," or the contents of something may be shown above it. The number of parts shown and the choice of them depend on the information that is to be conveyed rather than on narrowly visual considerations.

The representation of single objects is best exemplified by the human form, which is an elaborate composite. The description here is of the standing figure at rest; there are many variations of pose and of detail. The basic type faces to the right. The head is a profile, into which a half-mouth is set, which may be less than half the width of a mouth in full view. A full-view eye and eyebrow, very often of exaggerated size, are placed within the profile. The shoulders and chest are shown at full width, but on the forward side of the body the line from armpit to waist is a pseudo-profile that includes the nipple, which would be covered by a woman's dress. The expanse of the chest may show details of clothing, most commonly necklaces and broad dress straps, but, except in occasional figures that are turning or in other unusual poses, does not depict any specific part of the body. The line from the back armpit to the waist is similarly no more than a connecting line, but it gives some sense of the curve of a back. The waist is in profile, as are the legs and feet. The navel is placed near the front line of the waist, which often bulges slightly at that point (it could not be shown in the profile). The rendering of the feet is an instance of how the form is an assembly rather than a view. Until the mid-18th Dynasty, and often after that, both feet were shown from the inside, with a single toe and the arches indicated.

Since arches cannot otherwise be shown without indication of depth, the whole foot leaves the ground to form them. This feature acquires a life of its own, and the second foot may be seen through the gap of the arch, so that the drawing convention is interpreted visually within the image itself. This is one of countless self-generating elaborations of the system.

In the Egyptian language color, skin, and nature are related words. A colorless figure would not be quite complete, and color is rarely absent from completely finished works. The color is as diagrammatic as the figures to which it is applied. Since they do not render views, light and shade are irrelevant. The color is uniform over the whole figure. It may be a single tone, or a texture or pattern such as render wood grain or the skins of some animals. The basic repertory of colors is small: black, white, red, yellow, blue, green. From the 18th Dynasty on the range became wider, but remained simple and clear. Colors are not mixed, and there are few transitions from one to another. Despite the prevalence of color, it is dominated by line, and is never the only means of conveying information. Outlines are picked out in contrasting colors, chiefly black.

There are two main approaches to composing scenes and whole walls: arranging the elements on a neutral surface; or using the surface as a depicted flat area, as is done in western maps. The former is the ancient norm, the latter being used only for specialized purposes and during a few periods.

The basis of articulation according to the first approach is the register. The figures stand on horizontal lines called base lines, which may represent the ground but more often do not, and are spaced at intervals up the wall. Thematically related scenes may be next to one another in a single register, may be read in sequences up or down a wall, or may follow both principles. Two different versions of the same set of scenes – for example, a sequence from plowing to reaping – may be organized in opposite directions, showing that position on the wall does not in itself convey information.

Examples of the much less frequent "map" method of composition are plans of houses and areas of desert. In either case the outline that defines the map – which seldom shows a specific location – may also serve as a base line for figures depicted in registers. Very occasionally a group of figures in a "map" composition is rendered in vertical layers that coincide strikingly with images of recession in the optical field. This is, however, virtually the only feature that tends toward the assumption of a unifying viewpoint, as in perspective. Such an assumption is contradicted by many other features.

A vital characteristic of all Egyptian representation is the treatment of scale, which forms, together with iconography, the main means of ideological expression. Within a figure the parts are shown in their natural proportions, and this is often true also of whole scenes, but entire compositions are organized by scale around their chief figures. The larger the figure, the more important. In nonroyal tombs a single figure of the owner is often the height of the entire pictorial area of a wall, up to six or more registers of the scenes which he "views" as he faces them. He may also be several times the size of figures of his wife and children, who have their arms

Detail of hunting scene in the tomb of Qenamun at Thebes (TT 93). The speckled picture surface shows the desert, and is both ground and background. Blank areas adapt to the animals' forms and make lairs for some; the outlines are base lines and perhaps also paths. Reign of Amenhotep II.

False transparency. The man dips a ladle into a cooking cauldron. Ladle and contents are visible inside the cauldron, but could not be seen in reality. Tomb of Ramesses III.

Contents above an object. A man lifts a jewel box lid; within is another box in the form of two cartouches that is shown on the rim. Theban Tomb 181. Reign of Amenhotep III.

Internal elaboration of the system. The arches of the feet are shown as a curve above the base line. The dogs' paws are visible through the nonexistent "hole." 12th-Dynasty stela. Berlin, Ägyptisches Museum.

around his calves. The king towers similarly above his subjects. In New Kingdom battle reliefs an enormous figure of the king and his chariot may occupy almost half the area, the rest being filled with Egyptian soldiers, defeated enemies, and an enemy fort on a hilltop, containing tiny people whom the king reaches out to attack. The internal visual logic and the ideological message triumph over verisimilitude. The main reliefs to exhibit little variation in scale are in temples, where only the king and deities are normally shown, all being of comparable rank within the context. Scaling may also be adjusted for reasons of style. Thus, offering bearers of all periods often lead minute animals that overlap their legs, in an arrangement that economizes on space and produces a neat grouping. At the opposite extreme, 4th-century bearers sometimes carry strangely colossal geese around their shoulders; here the reason seems to be stylistic exuberance.

A further ideological feature of Egyptian art is not representational, but is almost as fundamental as if it were. Most works exhibit a pervasive idealization; things are shown as they should be, not as they are. The idealization is, however, as selective as the treatment of scale. Major figures are in ideal form, with men mostly in youthful maturity and all women young and slim. They are normally at rest. Subordinate figures, by contrast, may be depicted as wrinkled, balding, and deformed, and they may argue and fight. Details of this sort are commonest in the finest Old Kingdom tombs, where they may be present partly in order to give interest and individuality to the scenes. They are absent from temple reliefs, which show a timeless, abstract world.

Statuary

The obvious stylistic similarity between statuary and relief and painting is based in part on techniques that are common to both. There may be more fundamental reasons for the rigid axes that are seen in statuary, since this characteristic is nearly as widespread in the world as non-perspective representation in two dimensions, but it is not clear what they are. Whatever the answer to this broader question may be, the continuity and parallels in development between the two forms are evident, as they are in some other artistic traditions.

Almost all major statues show a figure that looks straight ahead in a line at right angles to the plane of the shoulders, with the limbs constrained within the same planes. Mostly it stands at rest or is seated, and is not engaged in any activity. The organic interplay of the parts of the body is scarcely indicated, so that statues resemble the two-dimensional "diagram" in being an assembly of discrete parts. This analogy suggests that this may be a basic feature of representation rather than an element of style. Part of the similarity between the genres is due to sculpture's dependence on drawings in a modified form of normal two-dimensional rendering.

The chief exceptions to rigid geometry are heads that look up slightly, perhaps in order to see the sun, or down, in scribe statues, to look at a papyrus unrolled across the lap. Kneeling figures sometimes have flexed calf muscles, presumably showing that their pose is a momentary gesture of deference. Details of this sort, and slight indications of the organic coherence of the body, are restricted to the finest works, in which the normal rigidity is taken

for granted and softened, probably in part for aesthetic reasons. Some small works, principally in wood and of the later 18th Dynasty, depart from the rule, showing turns and contrapposto and retaining no more than traces of the normal defining axes. These are important in showing that the strict forms were not the only ones the Egyptians had at their disposal. Because most examples are in perishable media, they may have been more frequent than now appears.

Techniques in painting, relief, and statuary

In two and in three dimensions, the basis of the artist's work was the preparatory drawing and the laying out of compositions on large surfaces. Squared grids or sets of guidelines were used in order to ensure accurate representation. For the human body the grids were founded, until the 26th Dynasty, on a square the size of the fist of the figure being drawn, which is related proportionally to all the other parts of the body. In theory the grid had to be redrawn for each figure of a different size, but in practice the less important ones were often drawn freehand. Preliminary drawings were made on grids, and were then turned into the finished product in several stages of correction and elaboration. Artists worked in groups and were probably specialized in the tasks they performed.

Paintings were produced by this process, using a prepared background of stone or mud plaster with a fine gypsum plaster wash. Reliefs were carved and then painted. This involved the initial drawing, carving, and often fresh drawings which served as the basis for painting.

Works of statuary started as squared blocks whose main sides served as surfaces for grids and preparatory drawings. The stone was then removed, with the drawing acting as a guide. As work progressed the drawings were renewed again and

Boxwood statuette of a servant girl carrying an unguent jar. The equilibrium of a body carrying a weight is rendered and the figure is almost free from the axial constraints of most Egyptian statuary. Height 15 cm. Reign of Amenhotep III. University of Durham, England, Oriental Museum.

Block statue of Petemihos. The sloping line of the arms balances the raised head. Gray granite. From Tell el-Muqdam. Height 46·3 cm. Late Period. Brooklyn Museum of Art.

Conventions and Representation

Egyptian representation is rooted in Egyptian culture. Unlike perspective, it is not based on scientific laws, but generally it aims as ease of recognition. Where what is shown is familiar to us, we have little difficulty in understanding it, although it is easy to be misled. Where the object or scene is unfamiliar, it may be impossible to identify it, or we may fail to apply a rule that explains a puzzling feature. On this page different methods of representation are illustrated, all of them operating within the same basic principles.

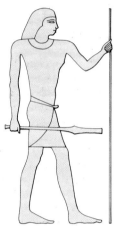

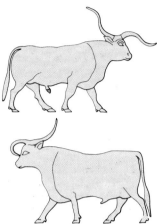

Orientation
Figures are designed to face right, and the relationship between right and left is symbolically important. Where a figure faces left, it sometimes retains the "correct" hands for the insignia it holds. Here the staff is held by a left hand, on what looks like a right arm, and the scepter is in a right hand. Probably because of the visual incongruity of this, there are several different solutions to this problem in left-facing figures.

Oxen with artificially deformed horns illustrate the same point. Their left horns are bent down, but where the ox faces left, the bent horn is the apparent "right" one. The effect is so natural that it is very easy to misunderstand the detail.

Assembly of parts: depiction of turns and occasional views
Statues of women show that they wore dresses whose shoulder straps covered their breasts.

In relief such figures show a bare breast, because the forward line of the body is a chest profile at this point. The shoulder straps are within the torso.

When a figure is turning, the normal scheme may be modified. Occasional nude figures show both breasts from the front and on the profile. These are often musicians, whose bodily attractions were important. Very rare figures in complex groups are shown full face, but they too are composites.

In the freest pictures, such as this sketch of a woman blowing into an oven, figures can be in almost pure profile (except for the eye). The indication of breath is an unusual detail. A broken hieratic text states that her "head is toward the chamber (opening?)," and she is "blowing into the oven."

Some statues of lions have crossed paws, with the head at 90° to the body. In a painting, the lion appears to face straight ahead; there is no means of deducing the form of the statue from the painting.

Relationship of parts; materials
Furniture is particularly difficult to depict clearly, because it is both three-dimensional and rectilinear.

This early painting shows two-legged couches whose surfaces slope to the ground. They are in a side profile both with and without indication of the surface, which ceases to be right-angled. There seem to be two couches, but these may be two pictures of the same one.

When two people sit on a chair, their ranking is shown. The man is ahead of the woman, who is on his left, inferior side. But in this position it is impossible to show her right arm around his shoulder, or her left arm over the chair arm. The apparent depth of the chair is probably its width, while the man is placed arbitrarily so that his body is not obscured by the chair's arm.

The material of which an object is made may be indicated in unexpected ways. This man's shelter is made of fresh reed matting (painted green) and his chair is on a mat. The thickness of the "walls" is enough to show that they are of matting; in reality they would have been no more than 2 cm thick.

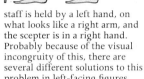

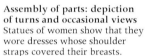

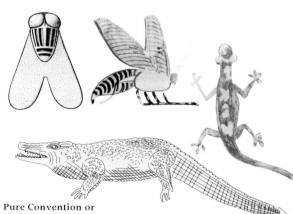

Pure Convention or characteristic views
In some cases arbitrary rules help to distinguish similar forms. Crocodiles are always in a side profile, while lizards are shown from above. This takes into account the size of the creatures, and hence the angle from which they are normally seen. But with flies and bees the difference is simply a convention.

The production of a relief

Reliefs and paintings depended heavily on preliminary drawings, which were prepared according to guidelines, or from the Middle Kingdom within squared grids. Grids were also drawn over existing works to facilitate copying.

In the early scheme six horizontal guidelines intersected with the vertical median lines of the body to define its proportions. The horizontal lines were often continued through long processions of figures. For the human figure both the guidelines and the grids worked according to the canon of proportion, which was closely related to normal Egyptian measures of length. When these changed in the Late Period, the canon was modified too. Existing lines are shown in red, conjectural ones in yellow.

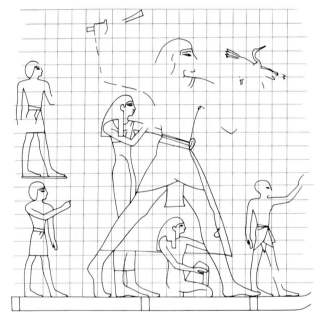

The earlier grid is based on 18 squares from the ground to the hair line (the part above is variable in size according to the type of headdress worn). Although the grid relates only to figures at one scale at a time, it sometimes covers the whole area that is to be filled with a scene; the design may then have been enlarged mechanically from a smaller draft. Occasionally the grid is subdivided.

The later grid has 21 squares up to a new, lower measuring point at the eyes. Differences in proportions between the two systems are very slight.

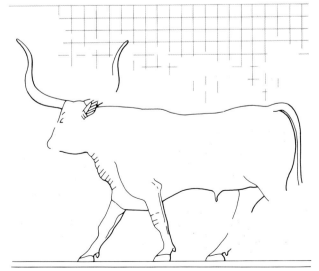

Grids were also used for animals. In this example the squares are preserved above the ox, but the figure itself has been modeled in the stone, removing the original surface and the drawing.

again; some almost completely finished works have the line of the vertical axis marked down the middle of the face. As in relief, the final stages involved smoothing the surface, obliterating tool marks, and applying paint.

The technical difficulty of carving varied greatly with the material, but the Egyptians mastered with the simplest tools even the hardest substances available to them. Unstinting labor was the chief component of success, but cannot account by itself for the artistry and sophistication of its products.

All the basic techniques had been acquired by the beginning of the Dynastic Period, so that artistic development was chiefly in the elaboration of representational forms and in iconography and composition. The main equipment consisted of hammers of very hard stone, copper (later bronze) chisels, drills, and saws, all the metal tools being used with wet sand as the abrasive that did most of the actual cutting. The hammers had various forms; an example from the Great Pyramid is about the size and shape of a tennis ball. For wooden statuary the tools and techniques were those of carpentry. Iron tools appeared around 650 BCE.

For large works of sculpture technical problems turned into ones of engineering. The first stages of work on a colossal statue had more in common with quarrying than with art. Such statues were probably roughed out before transport in order to make them as light as possible, and completed at their destination. Moving them involved specially constructed roads and ships, and extensive earthworks for the final siting.

Architecture

Religious buildings form the vast majority of surviving works of architecture. Virtually all of them were symbolic as well as narrowly functional. The precise nature of the symbolism in mortuary buildings – pyramids, mastabas, and rock-cut tombs – is not well established, but with temples the matter is relatively clear. The principles are, however, probably similar for both types: they recreate the cosmos or part of it. This cosmos is an ideal one, purified and set apart from the everyday world, and its relationship with the latter is one of analogy, not of direct representation. Its aim is to make the inhabitant of the temple (or tomb) partake symbolically in the process of creation itself or in the cosmic cycles, in particular that of the sun.

This symbolism is expressed in the siting and design of temples and in the decoration of walls and ceilings. All of this is most easily observed in the temples of the Greco-Roman Period, which are probably little different in meaning from their New Kingdom forerunners. The structure is set apart from the outside world by a massive mud-brick enclosure wall built in undulating courses that may mimic the watery state of the cosmos at creation. Within this is the main pylon or entrance wall, decorated on the outside with scenes of the king slaughtering enemies; these ensure magically that disorder should not enter the temple behind. The pylon is the largest element in the temple; viewed in section, it encloses the area behind it within its height. At the same time its two massifs with the gap between them resemble the hieroglyph for "horizon". The theoretical orientation of most temples is east–west (since this relates to the Nile and

Tomb Stelae

The tomb stela (gravestone) and the coffin with the mummy were the most important elements of Egyptian tombs (as opposed to simple graves).

The stela identified the deceased by their names and titles (the Egyptians said that it "made the name live"), and often showed the person seated at a table laden with offerings or receiving offerings from relatives. On tomb stelae from later periods, the deceased was represented in the company of deities, especially Osiris and various forms of the sun god. This was the ideal state of affairs which everyone wished for the *ka* and the stela helped to perpetuate eternally. In early periods a list or representations of the provisions the *ka* needed for its continued existence was an important element of the stela. The *hotep-di-nesu* formula, which was a constant feature, ensured that these commodities were forthcoming: "A boon which the king gives to Osiris, so that he may give invocation-offerings of bread, beer, oxen, fowl, alabaster, clothing, and all things good and pure on which a god lives, to the *ka* of the deceased." The ancient formula shows how the provisioning of the tomb was thought to have been done: the king presented offerings to Osiris, the ruler of the underworld (or another

deity), and it was through him that the *ka* of the deceased received its share. Visitors and passers-by were asked to recite the formula and thus make the wish contained in it come true.

Unlike the underground burial chamber which contained the coffin with the body of the deceased, the tomb stela was situated in the chapel above ground and usually publicly accessible. It was the focus of the funerary cult, and offerings were brought and placed in front of it on prescribed days.

The majority of tomb stelae were made of stone, especially limestone or sandstone, but more prestigious monuments were made of hard materials such as red granite (and limestone was sometimes painted to imitate granite). Rock-cut tombs contained stelae which were cut in the rock in the same way as the rest of the tomb and its sculptures. These were paralleled during the New Kingdom when in some tombs the stela was painted on the tomb's wall. Wood was occasionally used for the manufacture of stelae (perhaps more often than now appears but the chances of survival of such monuments are slim), especially from the Third Intermediate Period on.

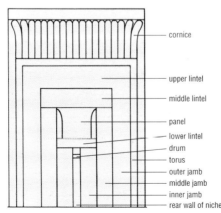

The false door (left) was the typical stela of the Old Kingdom, which developed from the earlier "palace facade" and its niche stela. While the stela can still be recognized in the false door's panel, the "palace facade" was transformed into a complex system of jambs and lintels designed along the lines of real doorways (*below*). This dummy "door" connected the world of the living with the world of the dead, and the *ka* was believed to pass freely through it. A person standing in front of the false door was facing west, and the stela usually formed part of the west wall of the tomb chapel. This orientation remained the ideal throughout Egyptian history.

- cornice
- upper lintel
- middle lintel
- panel
- lower lintel
- drum
- torus
- outer jamb
- middle jamb
- inner jamb
- rear wall of niche

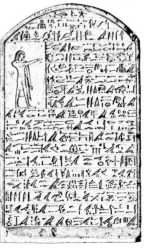

Royal stelae of the first two dynasties (above) are known from Abydos and Saqqara. It seems that at Abydos two of them, round topped, symmetrically designed and free standing, were set up at the east side of the tomb pit. They contained only the king's principal name.

Provincial stelae of the 1st Intermediate Period (left) gave up the elaborate design of the false door in favor of flat rectangular forms and simple decoration, as if looking back to the tradition of niche stelae. Their representations were often crude and the writing of their inscriptions poor, but these features enable us to ascribe stelae to specific areas of Egypt with considerable accuracy.

Stelae of the Middle Kingdom (left and *right*)* developed from those of the 1st Intermediate Period, and can be either rectangular or round-topped. They vary enormously in their subject matter and texts, but many criteria have been established by which they can be dated (e.g. the type of the *hotep-di-nesu* formula) and ascribed to a particular necropolis (e.g. the selection of deities invoked).

Brick-built superstructures of nonroyal tombs of the first three dynasties had a "palace facade," an elaborate design of recesses (niches) (*above*). In the rear wall of one of these, near the southeast corner of the mastaba, was a stone or wooden *niche stela* (*left*). The "palace facade" was occasionally used in the chapel inside the mastaba; the number of niche stelae might then be increased.

Slab stelae (*above*) were characteristic of the earliest mastabas with stone super- structures built at Giza during the 4th Dynasty. Positioned in the east face of the mastabas, they were, like the tombs them- selves, presented by the king, and made by the best craftsmen.

Despite the enormous variety in form and decoration, designers employed simple constructional procedures. These, rather than mysterious "systems," are responsible for the interplay of proportions, as shown here on a *Late Period stela*.

Apart from some new forms, the most striking feature of *New Kingdom stelae* (*above*) was the appearance of gods (in particular Osiris) in their main scenes.

not to the cardinal points there is considerable variation), so that the sun "rises" in the pylon gateway, sending its rays into the sanctuary, which is directly on the axis, and runs its course through the temple.

The most imposing part of the main temple is the hypostyle or columned hall, which conveniently summarizes the decorative scheme of the whole. The column capitals show aquatic plants, and the lowest register of the walls has similar plants in relief; symbolically the hall is the marsh of creation. The architraves and ceiling have reliefs of the sky, so that the decoration encompasses the whole world. What is shown on the walls is the activity of this world. Instead of marsh, the lowest register may contain offering bearers who do duty for the king in bringing the produce of the land to provide for the temple. Neither is part of the more abstract main scheme, which consists of several registers of scenes, arranged like a checkerboard, showing the king, who faces in toward the sanctuary, making offerings to and performing rituals for the god. The god, who takes up residence in the temple, faces outward; the deities shown in the reliefs are a wider range than that worshiped in any one temple. Many scenes show rituals performed in the temple, but others have a less specific meaning. In terms of the temple, the give and take between king and god is the focus of the world's activities. Most of the reliefs in the temple are of the same general character.

The inner areas have a raised floor level and lower ceiling than the hypostyle hall. They are therefore contained within the protection of the outer area, and are more sacred. A number of smaller rooms surround the sanctuary, whose outside wall mimics the outside of a temple, forming a structure within a structure. The sanctuary represents the mound of creation, and relates to the marsh of the hypostyle hall; in passing toward the sanctuary a procession went through the stages of creation and renewal.

Techniques

Egyptian stoneworking produced rock-cut structures with techniques akin to those of quarrying, solid mounds – the pyramids – and more conventional free-standing structures. Here work on the latter is described.

Little is known of how the planning and surveying of sites was done; most reconstructions of these processes are almost entirely speculative. However it was achieved, there was enormous expertise in maintaining an accurate plan and elevation for a large pyramid, or in constructing the slightly sloping walls of a pylon.

The foundations of Egyptian buildings were often surprisingly meager, consisting of a trench filled with sand and topped with a few courses of rough stonework (the sand may even have had a symbolic as much as a functional purpose). Only in the Greco-Roman Period were there regularly massive foundations of proper masonry, much of it constructed from earlier buildings demolished to make way for the new ones.

In masonry mortar was used very sparingly. The technique was to lay a course of blocks, level it along the top, coat the surface with a thin layer of mortar whose prime purpose was to act as a lubricant, and maneuver the next course into position. The under surfaces and probably the rising joints of the blocks were dressed before they were set in place. Each block was fitted individually to the next, since the rising joints were not always vertical, or at right angles to the surface. A single block could even form an internal corner, and the levels of the horizontal courses might be maintained only for a short distance. Wooden cramps were often set into the horizontal joints behind the surface in order to provide extra rigidity or to prevent slippage while the mortar was setting. The main purpose of the complex jointing techniques was probably to minimize waste and to use the largest practicable size of block. The edges of the blocks were cut to size when they were mounted, but the main surface was left rough.

The Egyptians probably worked without mechanical lifting devices; the basic method of raising weights was to bury the wall that was being built behind a rubble ramp. This was added to continually until the walls reached their full height. The stones were then dressed smooth, either from the ramps as they were dismantled, or from wooden scaffolding, which was probably used later for carving the relief decoration. Several stages of work proceeded at once, so that stonemasons, plasterers, draftsmen, relief carvers, and painters could all be employed together. Something of this can be seen, for example, in the nonroyal tombs at el-ʿAmarna and in the tomb of Haremhab (c. 1319–1292) in the Valley of the Kings. Since few Egyptian tombs or temples were ever completely finished, the attendant confusion may have seemed a natural state of affairs.

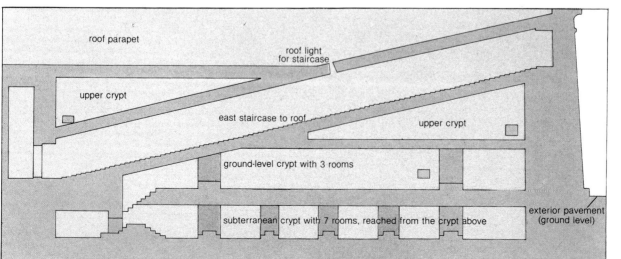

Temple of Dendara, section of east wall. The massive wall accommodates suites of rooms, called crypts, and a staircase within its thickness. The lowest set of crypts is below ground, contained within foundations about 6 meters deep. The roof area is similarly lavish; above the ceiling line on the left the outside wall forms a parapet about 4 meters high, within which was an open area for the performance of rituals, as well as a small separate kiosk. The blue squares in the ground-level and upper crypts are access holes from within the temple. Those in the upper crypts are 3 meters above ground level. All were concealed within the decoration of the rooms that contained them. 1st century BCE.

Labels within figure: roof parapet; roof light for staircase; upper crypt; east staircase to roof; upper crypt; ground-level crypt with 3 rooms; subterranean crypt with 7 rooms, reached from the crypt above; exterior pavement (ground level)

PART TWO
A JOURNEY DOWN THE NILE

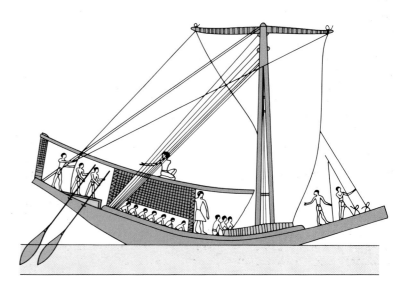

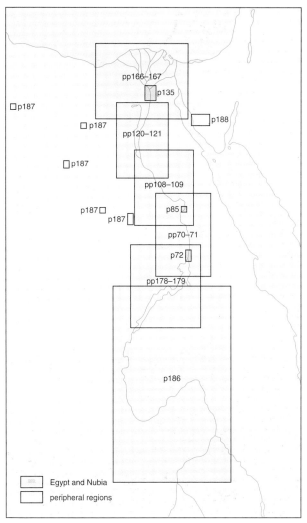

The land of Egypt has been likened to a lotus, with the heavy flower of the delta on the very long and thin stalk of the Nile valley, and the bud of the Faiyum nestling close to it. The surrounding areas, with the exception of the chain of oases running parallel to the river on the west, were arid and inhospitable, and thus unsuitable for settled habitation.

Two cities played key roles in Egyptian history until the scene shifted northward during the 19th Dynasty: Memphis, close to the apex of the delta, and Thebes, its counterbalance in the south. These provide two of the points at which we break our imaginary boat journey down the Nile through ancient Egypt. The first Nile cataract in the south is our logical point of departure.

Nubia, the oases, and Sinai, though never described as parts of Egypt, were colonized, in the case of the first two, and frequented, in the case of the third, to such an extent that their inclusion is essential. Going upstream into Nubia is, however, a different proposition from sailing gently down the Nile, and a donkey must replace our boat for the journeys into the oases and Sinai.

Boats on the Nile

The simple raft, made of bundles of papyrus stalks lashed together with ropes, was the earliest boat on the Nile. It was of limited life and use, but cheap and easily replaceable, a necessity for some, such as herdsmen who had to cross crocodile-infested

waters while grazing cattle in the delta, and a means of pleasure for hunters fowling in the swamps.

The word *sepy*, "to lash," was later also used for the building of wooden boats.

Geographically, it is hard to imagine a more extreme form than that of ancient Egypt: long and narrow, it reminds one of a sprawling town bestriding a highway. The advantage of this distribution was ease of communication, because the Nile connected all important localities. The boat was the most important means of transport.

The construction of the hull of smaller boats reflected the lack of good quality local wood. The shipbuilder had to use fairly short planks which were tenoned and mortised or secured to each other by binding; wood for larger craft and seagoing boats was imported. At least until the New Kingdom the most

conspicuous constructional feature of Egyptian boats was the absence of the keel.

Northerly winds, favorable to sailing up the river, prevailed in the Nile valley, but downstream traffic depended on oars. This was reflected in hieroglyphic writing to such an extent that in the words for "to travel northward" ("to fare downstream") and "to travel southward" ("to sail upstream") the appropriate sign of a boat was used even when describing an overland journey.

A simple but effective stepping of the mast was required by the frequent changes from sailing to rowing.

The main element of the steering gear was a massive rudder oar attached to a rudder post and the boat's stern. The boat was steered by moving the tiller sideways and thus rotating the stock of the rudder oar and its blade.

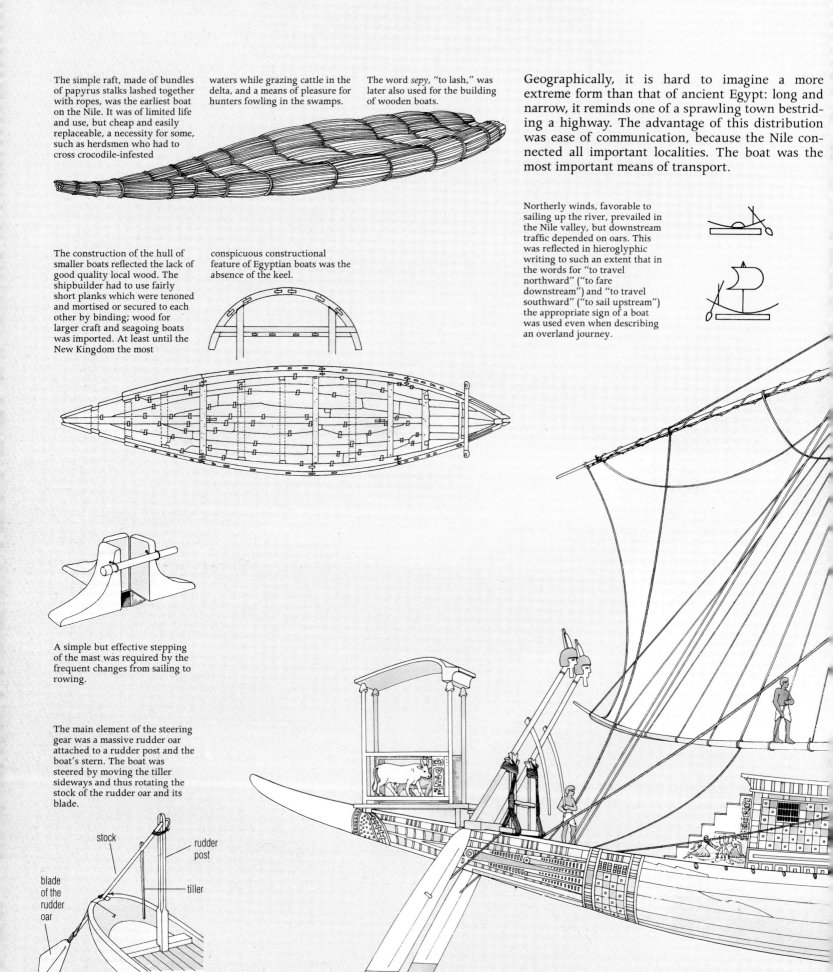

stock

rudder post

tiller

blade of the rudder oar

Much of our knowledge of ancient Egyptian shipping derives from representational evidence (reliefs and paintings), model boats found in tombs, and isolated discoveries of buried funerary boats (at Abydos, Giza and Dahshur). Texts provide a variety of nautical terms, and even the names of boats, but little specific information about boat construction. Nile boats varied greatly according to their purpose (traveling boats, cargo boats, ceremonial barks etc.), but a fairly reliable guide to their dating is provided by (1) the appearance of the hull, (2) the method of steering, (3) the type of the mast and sail, (4) the vessel's paddles or oars, (5) the disposition of the deckhouses, and (6) unusual features.

Predynastic Period: (1) sometimes, though not always, sharply upturned prow and stern (even large Nile craft were made mostly of papyrus or similar material); (2) one or more large steering oars; (3) rectangular sail; (4) and (5) paddles in two groups (interrupted by central deckhouse); (6) prow decoration of tree branches (?); standard close to deckhouse.

Old Kingdom: (1) "classical" Egyptian hull shape (wood now the main building material), often with animal-head prow; (2) several large steering oars, but from 6th Dynasty special steering gear; (3) usually bipod mast; probably trapezoidal sail, usually more tall than wide; (4) oars (from 5th Dynasty).

Middle Kingdom: (1) higher stern; (2) steering gear operated by a helmsman standing between the massive rudder post and the usually single large rudder oar; (3) single mast, lowered and supported on a forked stanchion when sailing downstream; (5) deckhouse forward of the rudder post.

New Kingdom (large range of specialized types): (2) steering gear with usually two rudder oars, operated by a helmsman standing in front of the rudder post; (3) sail more wide than tall; (5) castles forward and aft, with centrally placed deckhouse.

Late Period: (1) tendency toward a higher stern.

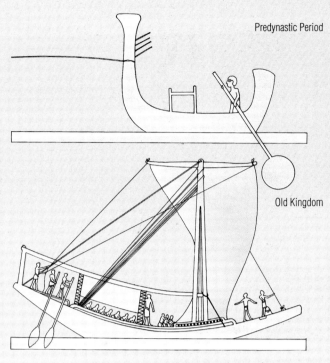

Predynastic Period

Old Kingdom

Middle Kingdom

Late Period

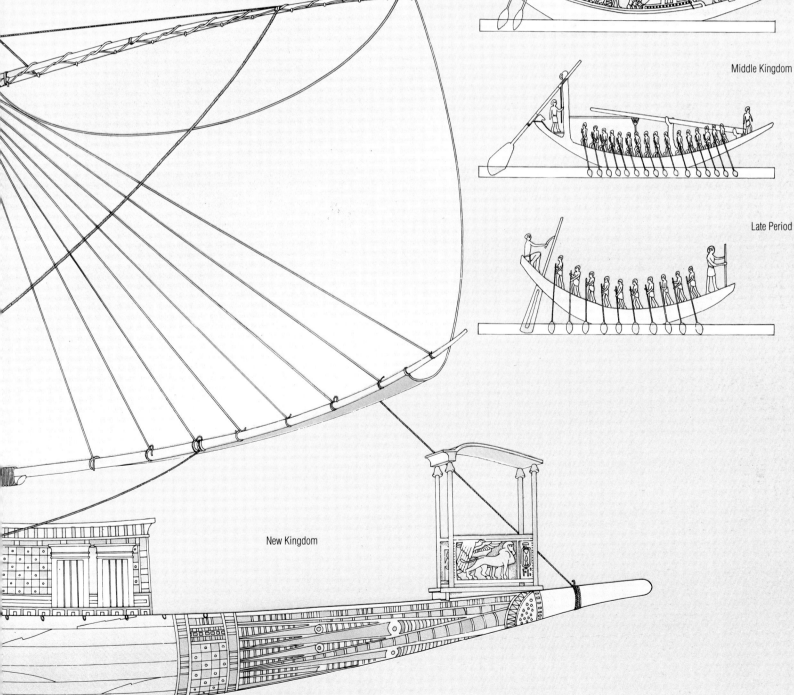

New Kingdom

SOUTHERN UPPER EGYPT

Because the Egyptians oriented toward the south, Aswan was the "first" town in the country north of the frontier at Biga island in the first cataract.

The southernmost part of the country falls into the natural divisions of the 1st Upper Egyptian nome, from Biga to north of Gebel el-Silsila, and the 2nd–4th nomes as far as Thebes. The two are roughly equal in length along the river, but the former belongs to the sandstone belt of Nubia, and is forbidding, infertile country, dominated by the desert and rich in minerals. To this day its character is strongly Nubian.

Kom el-Ahmar was one of the earliest urban centers, but declined in importance during the historical period. Probably because of the dominant position of Thebes, the districts to the south were included in the Viceroy of Nubia's territory during the New Kingdom. In this stretch of the river the

valley is relatively narrow, and could not support as large a population as the Theban area. There are, however, desert routes for trade and mining expeditions to east and west that were significant in most periods.

As befits its early importance, Southern Upper Egypt has numerous Predynastic and Early Dynastic sites. The best-represented later periods are the late Old Kingdom and 1st Intermediate Period, early New Kingdom, and Greco-Roman Period. These were all times when government was not very strongly centralized, so that an outlying area could benefit. Apart from the magnificent landscape, best seen from the river, the most impressive monuments are now probably the chapels and shrines of Gebel el-Silsila, with their reminder of the importance of the inundation for Egypt, and the major Greco-Roman temples, Philae, Kom Ombo, Edfu, and Esna.

Top left Elephantine Island and Qubbet el-Hawa from the east Nile bank. In the foreground are restored Roman walls near the Nilometer.

Above left Kiosk of Trajan at Philae, with foundations of a small chapel in the foreground; photographed in 1964 before the building of the High Dam.

Top right Colossal gray granite hawk at the entrance to the hypostyle hall of the temple of Edfu; probably Ptolemaic.

Above right Tomb complex of Pepynakht and others at Qubbet el-Hawa, north of Aswan; late 6th Dynasty. The entrance court, columns, and stairways are cut in the sandstone cliff.

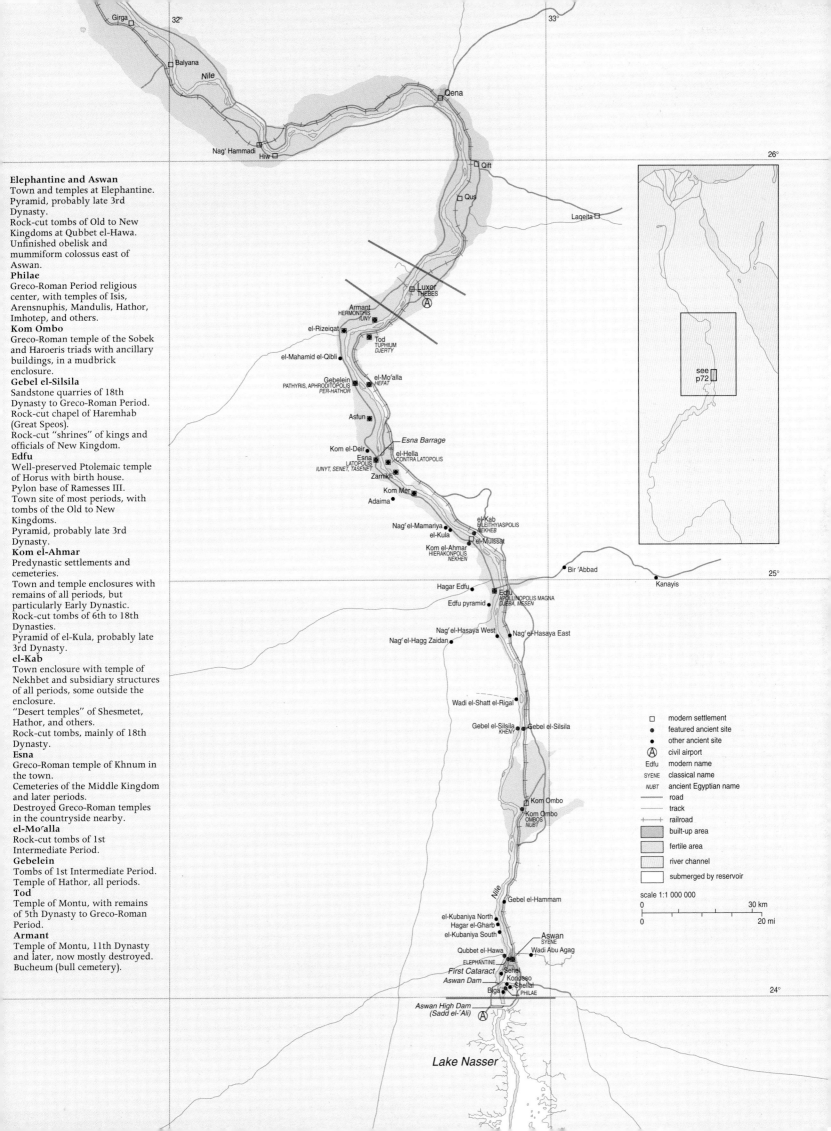

Elephantine and Aswan
Town and temples at Elephantine.
Pyramid, probably late 3rd
Dynasty.
Rock-cut tombs of Old to New
Kingdoms at Qubbet el-Hawa.
Unfinished obelisk and
mummiform colossus east of
Aswan.

Philae
Greco-Roman Period religious
center, with temples of Isis,
Arensnuphis, Mandulis, Hathor,
Imhotep, and others.

Kom Ombo
Greco-Roman temple of the Sobek
and Haroeris triads with ancillary
buildings, in a mudbrick
enclosure.

Gebel el-Silsila
Sandstone quarries of 18th
Dynasty to Greco-Roman Period.
Rock-cut chapel of Haremhab
(Great Speos).
Rock-cut "shrines" of kings and
officials of New Kingdom.

Edfu
Well-preserved Ptolemaic temple
of Horus with birth house.
Pylon base of Ramesses III.
Town site of most periods, with
tombs of the Old to New
Kingdoms.
Pyramid, probably late 3rd
Dynasty.

Kom el-Ahmar
Predynastic settlements and
cemeteries.
Town and temple enclosures with
remains of all periods, but
particularly Early Dynastic.
Rock-cut tombs of 6th to 18th
Dynasties.
Pyramid of el-Kula, probably late
3rd Dynasty.

el-Kab
Town enclosure with temple of
Nekhbet and subsidiary structures
of all periods, some outside the
enclosure.
"Desert temples" of Shesmetet,
Hathor, and others.
Rock-cut tombs, mainly of 18th
Dynasty.

Esna
Greco-Roman temple of Khnum in
the town.
Cemeteries of the Middle Kingdom
and later periods.
Destroyed Greco-Roman temples
in the countryside nearby.

el-Moʿalla
Rock-cut tombs of 1st
Intermediate Period.

Gebelein
Tombs of 1st Intermediate Period.
Temple of Hathor, all periods.

Tod
Temple of Montu, with remains
of 5th Dynasty to Greco-Roman
Period.

Armant
Temple of Montu, 11th Dynasty
and later, now mostly destroyed.
Bucheum (bull cemetery).

□ modern settlement
● featured ancient site
● other ancient site
Ⓐ civil airport
Edfu modern name
SYENE classical name
NUBT ancient Egyptian name
—— road
—— track
+−+−+ railroad
built-up area
fertile area
river channel
submerged by reservoir

scale 1:1 000 000
0   30 km
0   20 mi

see
p72

Elephantine and Aswan

Elephantine was the capital of the 1st Upper Egyptian nome and a significant frontier post. The site is strategically located at the north end of the first cataract, near numerous mineral deposits. The area is almost barren and may have relied on supplies from

further north, making its living as a garrison and by trade. The common meaning of the ancient word *swenet* from which the name Aswan derives is "trade."

Elephantine Island, which was inhabited at least from late Predynastic times, coalesced from two smaller islets during the third millennium. The ancient town at the south end has been studied systematically since 1969 and is one of the best known sites in Egypt. The core may have been an Early Dynastic fortress near a temple of the goddess Satis that was set in the space between two granite boulders, where an important deposit of early votive offerings was found. The temple was replaced by ever-larger buildings, culminating in one of the reign of Hatshepsut that has been reerected from discarded blocks. A small colonnaded temple of Amenhotep III of similar design was virtually intact around 1820, as was a building of Thutmose III; both have since disappeared. Most later periods down to the Roman have produced fragments of relief from the temples of Khnum, Satis, and Anukis, the local triad of deities. Only the main terrace of the 30th Dynasty temple of Khnum, together with a monumental granite gateway to its inner areas, remain in situ. Greco-Roman period burials of sacred rams of Khnum were excavated in the area of a temple of Alexander IV. The mummies had elaborate gilt cartonnage headpieces, some of which are in the nearby museum, and were placed in stone sarcophagi that are still in situ.

Above left Remains of the sacred area on Elephantine Island, looking northwest, with the modern village in the background. The stone walls that are visible date to many different periods (the standing gateway is restored).

Left Mummiform colossus abandoned in the granite quarries east of Aswan; possibly 19th Dynasty. The rock outcrops are characteristic of the cataract area, while the boulder by the statue shows clear marks of quarrying. The figure itself has been much eroded, and its face polished by generations of visitors.

Above Decorated pillar in the tomb of Setka at Qubbet el-Hawa; late 6th Dynasty. This is perhaps the finest Old Kingdom relief work at Aswan. The figure of the deceased has the leopard skin, full kilt, and cropped hairstyle of an elderly priest; he is described as the "Count, Overseer of the Phyles [groups of priests] of Upper Egypt." Setka confronts visitors to the tomb; just visible on the left face of the pillar are registers of animals and offering figures moving toward him.

North of the temples is a small nonfunerary pyramid, probably of the Third Dynasty, one of a number scattered through the country that may have related to a cult of the king. From the entrance to a memorial chapel for a 6th Dynasty notable comes unique wooden relief paneling that reminds us how many ancient artistic genres are almost completely lost. The cult of these men within the town continued in the Middle Kingdom, when the shrine of Heqaib, a 6th Dynasty official, was filled with stelae and statuary of the local elite; some kings also dedicated statues there.

The best-known monument on Elephantine is the Nilometer, a staircase with cubit markings beside it for measuring the height of the inundation, on the east. The levels inscribed on it are of the Roman Period and later.

On the west bank, to the north at Qubbet el-Hawa, are rock-cut tombs of Old Kingdom notables and leaders of expeditions to Nubia, Middle Kingdom nomarchs, and some New Kingdom officials. The 6th-Dynasty tombs, some of which form linked family complexes, contain important biographical texts, but the decoration is sparse. The 12th Dynasty tomb of Sarenput the Elder is more impressive in architecture; it too has only limited decoration.

The granite rocks south of Aswan and for some 6 kilometers to the east bear signs of quarrying in many places. The most striking remains are an abandoned obelisk and a mummiform colossus. The obelisk developed faults, but it is not clear why the colossus was never moved. Rock outcrops in the river and on land bear numerous ancient graffiti, either commemorating quarrying expeditions or having more general content. The greatest single body of them is on Sehel Island, 3 kilometers south of Elephantine.

Few remains survive in Aswan town, no doubt because it has been continuously built over. The two small Greco-Roman Period temples probably formed only a fraction of the original sacred area.

Philae

In its grandiose setting in the first cataract, the island of Philae was the most romantic tourist attraction in 19th century Egypt, but with the raising of the first Aswan dam it became submerged for most of each year. In the 1970s, after the building of the High Dam, the temples were dismantled and reerected on the nearby island of Agilkia.

The earliest monuments on the site are of the reign of Nectanebo I, but blocks discovered in foundations take the island's history back to the reign of Taharqa; New Kingdom blocks also found there may have come from elsewhere. Philae is the site of the latest hieroglyphic inscription (394 CE) and still later demotic graffiti (the latest of 452 CE).

The Egyptians gave an etymology to the name of Philae, "island of the time [of Reʿ]," which implies that the place recreated the primeval world when the sun god ruled on earth. On the neighboring island of Biga was the Abaton or "pure mound," one of many tombs of Osiris in the country. This was approached by way of the small temple of Biga, which faces Philae. The temple of Isis was the architectural climax of Philae, so that the most

Top The temple area at Philae, seen from nearby Biga; watercolor by David Roberts (published 1846). The temple of Biga, partly converted into a church, is visible in the foreground. The rear wall of the west colonnade forms the edge of Philae; to the left it continues into a landing stage and the entrance to the gate of Hadrian. Behind can be seen (right to left): the 1st east colonnade: kiosk of Trajan; 1st pylon; birth house and 2nd east colonnade; 2nd pylon and temple of Isis. There are remains of modern houses on the roof of the Isis temple (removed in the 19th century).

Above Sistrum figure of the reign of Ptolemy VI Philometor in the entrance to the main hall of the temple of Hathor at Philae. The motif, often a column capital, comprises a Hathor head on the sign for gold (the metal of Hathor), flanked by a pair of uraei, with a naos shape above (the actual sistrum).

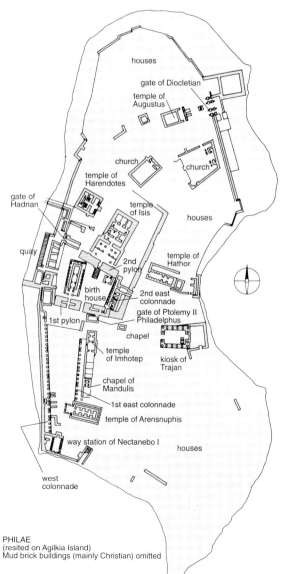

houses

gate of Diocletian

temple of Augustus

church

church

temple of Harendotes

gate of Hadrian

temple of Isis

houses

quay

temple of Hathor

2nd pylon

birth house

2nd east colonnade

gate of Ptolemy II Philadelphus

1st pylon

chapel

temple of Imhotep

kiosk of Trajan

chapel of Mandulis

1st east colonnade

temple of Arensnuphis

way station of Nectanebo I

houses

west colonnade

PHILAE
(resited on Agilkia Island)
Mud brick buildings (mainly Christian) omitted

Below Gate of Hadrian at Philae: relief showing Isis (with a cow's head) pouring milk over the sacred grove of trees on Biga, with the resurrected "soul" (*ba*) of Osiris above. Behind is the rocky "landscape" of Biga with a figure of the inundation in the cave from which it emerges, and a hawk and a vulture above.

Right Temple of Sobek and Haroeris at Kom Ombo, from the east. The mud brick outer wall is in the foreground, with the outer and inner enclosure walls beyond; the colossal relief figures are Roman.

important pair of deities of the Late Period had an island each. Isis was much the more popular, and had devotees to north and south. Ptolemaic Period rivalry over Philae between Egypt and Meroe has left traces in the decoration of the temple of Arensnuphis, which was done in the names of Ptolemy IV Philopator and of the Meroitic Arqamani (c. 220–200 BCE); there are also Meroitic graffiti dating from the 3rd century BCE to the 3rd century CE. Nonetheless, the buildings are completely Egyptian, and were presumably built with Egyptian resources.

The southeast portions of the island probably contained dwelling quarters. Pilgrims landed in the south near the way station of Nectanebo I (which was probably moved to there from another location) and proceeded into the open space bounded by the monumental west colonnade and first east colonnade. These structures were probably added to round off the group of buildings; they may be inspired by the planning of public spaces in the Classical world. The decoration of the west colonnade is mainly of Roman date.

On the east were temples dedicated to the Nubian gods Arensnuphis and Mandulis, and a temple of Imhotep, the deified official of the reign of Djoser, who is also mentioned in a Ptolemaic rock stela on Sehel Island to the north. In the gap north of the first east colonnade is a gate of Ptolemy II Philadelphus, leading to a small chapel and to the much later kiosk of Trajan by the eastern shore of the island.

The first part of the temple of Isis is composed of isolated elements. Behind the first pylon a courtyard is formed by the birth house, which is unconventionally placed parallel with the temple axis, and the second east colonnade with a set of rooms leading off it. The decoration of these areas is late Ptolemaic and early Roman. The main temple behind, whose earliest decoration dates to Ptolemy II Philadelphus, contains an abbreviated version of the full pylon, court and hypostyle hall, and is on a smaller scale than the other great temples of the period. On the roof are chapels dedicated to Osiris.

The most notable of the remaining temples is

that of Hathor, the angry goddess of myth who went south into Nubia spreading devastation and had to be pacified by Thoth before she would return. The columns of the temple's entrance courtyard contain figures of musicians, including the god Bes, who held performances in order to placate the goddess.

At the north end of the island were a temple of Augustus and a gate known as the "Gate of Diocletian" (284–305 CE). Between these and the temple of Isis were two churches; from the mid–4th century CE these coexisted with the pagan cults, which were finally suppressed under the Byzantine Emperor Justinian (527–565 CE). The hypostyle hall of the temple of Isis was turned into a church, and, as on many other sites, the flesh areas of all accessible figures of kings and gods in the temple were defaced.

Kom Ombo

Kom Ombo stands on a promontory at a bend in the Nile, at the north end of the largest area of agricultural land south of Gebel el-Silsila. Changes in agricultural techniques brought it to prominence in the Ptolemaic Period, to which almost all the visible monuments date. An 18th Dynasty gateway was, however, seen by Champollion in the south enclosure wall, and scattered New Kingdom blocks have been found on the site. Part of the temple forecourt has been eroded by the river, which may also have carried off other

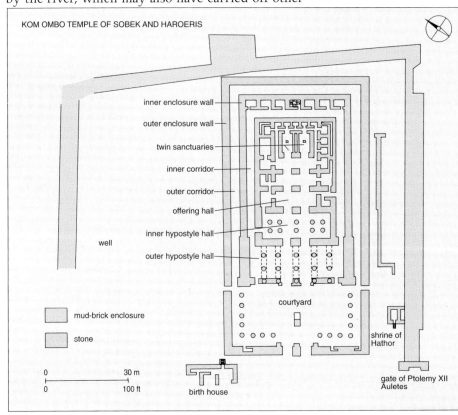

KOM OMBO TEMPLE OF SOBEK AND HAROERIS

inner enclosure wall
outer enclosure wall
twin sanctuaries
inner corridor
outer corridor
offering hall
inner hypostyle hall
outer hypostyle hall
well

courtyard

shrine of Hathor

mud-brick enclosure
stone

0   30 m
0   100 ft

birth house

gate of Ptolemy XII Auletes

Seated figure of a god with offerings in front, including a tall box of possibly surgical instruments that is placed on a stand; outer corridor, Roman Period.

contains a number of small chambers at the back. This is enclosed in turn by a second wall and corridor that take in the courtyard. Thus the double axis goes together with other dual features. Numerous reliefs in the inner corridor and its small rooms are unfinished, giving valuable insight into artists' methods in the Greco-Roman period. On the inner face of the outer corridor are some unique scenes, including a representation of a set of instruments that have generally been assumed to be those of a surgeon.

Some reliefs in the first hypostyle hall use the ancient technique of inlaying the eyes of the most important figures. The inlays, which must have given a special opulence and liveliness to the figure, are now lost, as they are on almost all ancient works that had this detail.

The small Roman Period shrine of Hathor south of the courtyard long stored the mummies of sacred crocodiles from a nearby necropolis. The well north of the temple is complex in design and, because of the temple's elevation above the river, very deep. Like other wells in temple enclosures, it allowed pure water, in theory from the primeval waters themselves, to be drawn within the sacred area, avoiding pollution from the outside world.

Gebel el-Silsila

Some 65 kilometers north of Aswan, at Gebel el-Silsila, steep sandstone cliffs narrow the stream and present a natural barrier to river traffic. The ancient Egyptian name of the place, *Kheny* (or *Khenu*), which has been translated as "The Place of Rowing," seems to reflect this fact. Local quarries, particularly those on the east bank, were exploited from the 18th Dynasty until the Greco-Roman Period.

On the west bank is the Great Speos (rock-cut chapel) of Haremhab. The seven deities to whom the chapel was dedicated were represented as seated statues in the niche at the back of the sanctuary, with the local crocodile god Sobek and King

Formerly well-preserved colored detail of the king on a column in the forecourt; reign of Tiberius. The crown relates the king to Onuris-Shu; the sign behind him symbolizes protection.

features. The mound behind the enclosure contains sherds of the First Intermediate Period, showing that the site is far more ancient than the sacred enclosure, which is all that has been explored.

The earliest king named in the temple is Ptolemy VI Philometor; most of the decoration was completed by Ptolemy XII Auletes. In the early Roman Period the forecourt was decorated and the outer corridor added. The temple is dedicated to two triads of deities: Sobek, Hathor, and Khons; and Haroeris (Horus the Elder), Tasenetnofret (the Perfect Companion), and Panebtawy (the Lord of the Two Lands). The last two have artificial names that express the goddess's function in such a group as a "consort," and the young god's to be kingly. Sobek and his triad are the primary deities, as is shown by his occupying the southern part: the Egyptians gave south priority over north.

The birth house, nearest to the river, has lost its western half. It abuts closely on the pylon of the main temple, perhaps because space was short in antiquity (the temple's rear is similarly cramped against the enclosure wall). The pylon has a double gateway that is the first sign of a complex plan with an axis for each main gateway and an unusually large number of intermediate rooms, culminating in two sanctuaries. From the first hypostyle hall runs a corridor that encloses the entire inner part of the temple and

Harembab himself among them. Numerous rock-cut "shrines" (chambers), functioning as cenotaphs, were made south of the Speos by kings (Sety I, Ramesses II, Merneptah) as well as high officials, particularly the 18th Dynasty.

The rock faces on both sides of the river abound in rock stelae and graffiti.

Edfu

The site of Edfu, near the river but raised above the broad valley, is an ideal position for settlement, since it is safe from the inundation but not isolated near the desert. The Ptolemaic temple of Horus was part of a larger area extending east and south under the modern town; this must have balanced the extensive remains to the west. The western side has an inner and outer enclosure wall dating to the Old Kingdom. A later wall, perhaps of the 1st Intermediate Period, runs outside the outer one. Within and on top of the walls are remains of the Old Kingdom and Greco-Roman Period town. The later wall overlaps an area of late Old Kingdom and 1st Intermediate Period tombs, including quite large mastabas, that extends to the west. Scattered finds have been made of 2nd Intermediate Period and New Kingdom stelae, statues, and offering tables.

Only the pylon base of a temple of Ramesses III is preserved. It is oriented, conventionally, toward the Nile, and formed part of a much smaller structure than its successor.

The major standing temple of the Ptolemaic period alludes to this forerunner by aligning a gateway in its first court with that between the two massifs of the earlier pylon. The temple complex has a gateway to the south with the birth house, which faces east, a little to its north. Blocks excavated from the pavement of the main temple courtyard come from other earlier structures dating from the 2nd Intermediate Period to early Ptolemaic times.

The temple is the most completely preserved in Egypt and a perfect example of Egyptian temple design. The building inscriptions, written in horizontal bands in the outer areas, give numerous details of construction. Building began in 237 BCE (Ptolemy III Euergetes I). The inner part was finished in 212 BCE (Ptolemy IV Philopator) and decorated by 142 BCE (Ptolemy VIII Euergetes II). The outer hypostyle was built separately, being completed, still under Ptolemy VIII, in 124 BCE. Decoration of this and the other outer parts was finished in 57 BCE. Mostly work continued regardless of the political situation, but it ceased for more than 20 years during disturbances in Upper Egypt under Ptolemy IV and Ptolemy V Epiphanes.

The unusual orientation of the temple toward the south may be due to constraints of the site. Behind the pylon the courtyard, the only large one preserved, has columns of distinctive capital design paired

across the axis, as in other buildings of the period, giving variety – and no doubt enhanced meaning – to otherwise uniform shapes. Gates lead beside the temple into an area bounded by the stone enclosure wall that continues the courtyard's outer wall. The scenes and inscriptions here and on the outer face of the enclosure wall include a list of donations of land to the temple, probably taken from a demotic original, a narrative of its mythical foundation, and grandiose reliefs with a "dramatic" text of a ritual in which Horus defeated his enemy Seth.

A striking feature of the inner parts is the subtle exploitation of scarce light. Some rooms are completely dark, while elsewhere the light comes from the openings between the columns of the hypostyle hall and from apertures in the roof or at the angle between roof and wall. The general progress is from light to dark, with the sanctuary receiving illumination only from the axis. The effect of all this must have been incomparably richer when the reliefs retained their original colors.

The monolithic naos of highly polished pink granite in the sanctuary will have contained a wooden

Top Aerial view of Edfu from the north, taken in 1932. Both the temple's domination of the site and much of the town mound can be clearly seen.

Above Set of column capitals in the forecourt. Two are composite forms, one with multiple papyrus umbels (?) and the other the shape of a single umbel with stem decoration. The palm frond capital is an ancient type with solar associations, but is also aquatic, since date palms often grow by pools. The architraves are decorated with solar scenes.

Right View east across the hypostyle hall at Edfu. The height and close spacing of the columns restrict the feeling of space; the result reflects the room's marsh or thicket symbolism. The columns have plant forms at the bottom, with several bands of emblematic motifs above and below central offering scenes.

shrine with the cult image of the god – probably about 60 centimeters high and made of wood, overlaid with gold and semiprecious stones – inside it. It is the oldest object in the temple, dating to Nectanebo II.

The outer areas of the birth house are much ruined, but the sanctuary and ambulatory are well preserved. In the south ambulatory some reliefs that are sheltered from the prevailing north wind preserve their color, giving an idea of the effect over large areas of the tones used in this period.

Like other late temples, Edfu was emptied of furniture and equipment when it fell out of use. A fortunate survival is the pair of colossal statues of hawks flanking the entrance and a single one by the door into the hypostyle hall. A group of over-lifesize hardstone statues of nude boys – probably the young gods Ihy or Harsomtus – that lay in the courtyard must also have formed part of the temple's decoration, relieving its present austere appearance.

Kom el-Ahmar

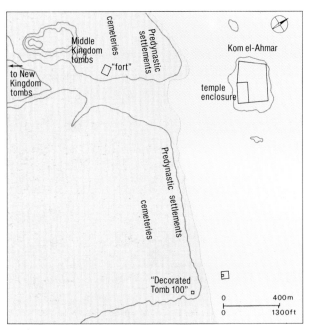

Kom el-Ahmar ("The Red Mound"), ancient *Nekhen*, Greek Hierakonpolis, lies a little over 1 kilometer southwest of the village of el-Muissat, on the west bank of the Nile.

Nekhen played an important part in Egyptian ideology: together with *Nekheb* (el-Kab) on the opposite bank, it constituted the Upper Egyptian counterpart of the twin towns *Pe* and *Dep* (modern Tell el-Fara'in) in the delta. The jackal-headed figures known as "The Souls of Nekhen" might be personifications of the early rulers of Nekhen. The chief god of the town, a falcon with two tall plumes on its head (*Nekheny*, "The Nekhenite"), was assimilated very early with Horus ("Horus the Nekhenite"). Nekhen was the

early center of the 3rd Upper Egyptian nome. In the New Kingdom it was replaced in this role by el-Kab, and belonged to the territory administered by the viceroy of Kush.

Extensive remains of Predynastic settlements and cemeteries are discernible for some 3 kilometers along the edge of the desert to the south and southwest of el-Muissat, and are particularly dense east of the wadi opposite which Kom el-Ahmar is situated. A mud brick structure known as "The Fort" stands some 500 meters into the wadi. Fragments of a granite doorway of Kha'sekhem of the 2nd Dynasty come from here, suggesting that it was constructed for his funerary cult.

The famous "Decorated Tomb 100" (now lost) was found in the easternmost part of the settlement/cemetery area at the end of the 19th century. This relatively small subterranean mud brick tomb (4·5 by 2 by 1·5 meters) had its west wall decorated with a remarkable painting showing boats, animals, and men. It probably belonged to a local chief of the Predynastic Naqada II Period, and is important as an indicator of the growing social stratification, as well as displaying the conventions and motifs of Egyptian art in process of formation.

At the beginning of the 1st Dynasty the irregularly shaped town enclosure known as Kom el-Ahmar replaced the earlier settlement on the edge of the

Above Small ivory and faience votive statuettes of the Early Dynastic Period, from the "Main Deposit" of the temple at Kom el-Ahmar. Oxford, Ashmolean Museum.

Left Seated lion, pottery with a shiny red slip, probably of the 3rd Dynasty. Several features of this sculpture are unusual, in particular the schematic treatment of the ears and the mane falling down on the chest of the animal like a bib in imitation of a headcloth. Height: 42·5 cm. Found in the temple. Oxford, Ashmolean Museum.

Limestone ceremonial mace head of king "Scorpion" (from the sign of a scorpion near the face of the king), perhaps identical with Naʿrmer. The main scene of the relief decoration shows a temple-founding ceremony with the king digging the first trench. Height: 25 cm. From the "Main Deposit." Oxford, Ashmolean Museum.

desert. In its south corner, occupying about one sixth of the total area, was the temple complex. This was partially uncovered in 1897–99 by J. E. Quibell and F. W. Green. In its earliest form the mud brick temple apparently enclosed a mound of sand revetted with stones, with a diameter of some 46 meters, perhaps the prototype of the hieroglyphic sign ⊙ with which the name of Nekhen was written. King Naʿrmer was the main benefactor, together with Khaʿsekhem/Khaʿsekhemwy. At an uncertain date, many votive objects that had been presented to the temple were brought together and deposited in a cache (the "Main Deposit"). Many objects in the Main Deposit, which included palettes, mace heads, stone vessels, and ivory figures, date between the Naqada III period and the 1st Dynasty. Monuments of most later periods were found, but they were not very numerous or spectacular. The exceptions are

two large copper statues representing Pepy I and perhaps his son Merenreʿ, which were restored in the 1990s, a granite stela showing a king Pepy in the company of Horus and Hathor, and a statue base of Pepy II. The gold head of a falcon, which belonged to a composite statue that had been altered over several centuries, may be one of the few cult images of a deity preserved from ancient Egypt.

Excavations in the Hierakonpolis area since the late 1960s, directed by M. A. Hoffman, R. Friedman, and B. Adams, have revealed a host of Predynastic remains, including very large, perhaps royal tombs of the Naqada III period, a late Predynastic sacred area, and one of the oldest mass brewing installations known in the world.

Decorated and inscribed rock-cut tombs ranging from the 6th to the 18th Dynasties have been found in the wadi of the "Fort" and its subsidiary branches.

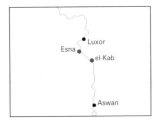

el-Kab

The earliest traces of human activities in the area of el-Kab go back to about 6000 BCE: the"Kabian"is a microlithic industry that predates the known Neolithic cultures of Upper Egypt. Ancient *Nekheb*, on the east bank of the Nile, and *Nekhen* (Kom el-Ahmar), on the opposite side of the river, were important settlements in the Predynastic and Early Dynastic Periods. Nekhbet, the vulture goddess of Nekheb, was the tutelary goddess of Egyptian kings (together with the cobra goddess Wadjit of Lower Egypt) and regarded as the Upper Egyptian goddess *par excellence*. Also known as "The White One of Nekhen," she was equated with the Greek Eileithyia in the Greco-Roman Period, when the town was called Eileithyiaspolis. From at least the beginning of the 18th Dynasty *Nekheb* served

as the capital of the 3rd Upper Egyptian nome, though it later relinquished this role in favor of Esna.

el-Kab's town enclosure measures about 550 by 550 meters and is surrounded by massive mud brick walls. It contains the main temple of Nekhbet with several subsidiary structures, including a birth house, as well as smaller temples, a sacred lake and an extensive Predynastic cemetery.

A granite block bearing the name of the 2nd Dynasty king Kharsekhemwy shows that temple structures were erected at el-Kab from an early date. During the Middle Kingdom Nebhepetrer Mentuhotep, Sebekhotep III (*sed*-festival chapel) and Neferhotep III (Sekhemrer-srankhtawy) turned their attentions to the site. Major building activities in the temple of Nekhbet started in the 18th Dynasty. Almost all the kings of the period contributed in smaller or larger measure, but Thutmose III and Amenhotep II seem to have been the most prominent among them. After the rAmarna Period the Ramessids continued to honor Nekhbet by adding to her temple. Taharqa of the 25th Dynasty, Psammetichus I of the 26th Dynasty, and Darius I of the 27th Dynasty are also attested, but the shape in which the now much-dilapidated temple presented itself to archaeologists was mainly due to the kings of the 29th and 30th Dynasties (Hakoris and Nectanebo I and II).

Two chapels, now destroyed, used to stand outside the enclosure. The first, about 750 meters northwest of it, was built by Thutmose III; the other, outside the northeast enclosure wall, was the

Left One of the desert temples at el-Kab, the Ptolemaic rock-cut sanctuary of the goddess Shesmetet, seen from the south.

"At a Place called *Caab* . . . we discover'd something that look'd like a Piece of Antiquity. . . we came to the Remains of an antient Temple, consisting of Six Pillars in Two Rows, with their Roofs intire. A little to the North of these are the fragments of many other broken Pillars, and considerable other Ruins, and curiously wrought with Hieroglyphics, &c." (C. Perry, *A View of the Levant*, 1743, p. 361, describing the columns of the hypostyle hall of Hakoris in the temple of Nekhbet).

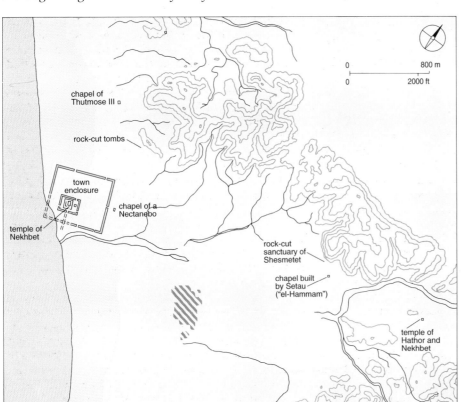

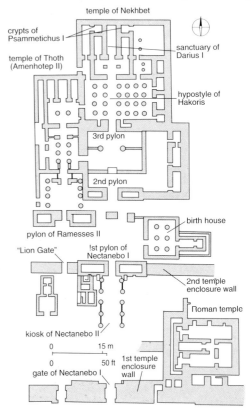

Temple of Khnum at Kom el-Deir,
northwest of Esna, now
destroyed; engraving made by
Napoleon's expedition of
1798–1800.

ʿAhmose Pennekhbet (No. 2) and of ʿAhmose, son
of Ebana (No. 5), are renowned for their biographical texts. The capture of the Hyksos capital Avaris,
the siege of Sharuhen in Palestine by King ʿAhmose, and Syrian and Nubian campaigns of the
kings of the early 18th Dynasty are among the historical events mentioned in them. Another tomb, of
the mayor of Nekheb Pahery, is remarkable for its
reliefs. There is a decorated tomb of the reign of
Ptolemy III Euergetes I northwest of the others,
nearer the river. It contains scenes which are
unusual in Ptolemaic tombs, such as agriculture,
boats, horses and chariots, and female mourners.

Esna

Esna, ancient Egyptian *Iunyt* or (*Ta*)*senet*, was called
in Greek Latopolis, after the Lates fish, which was
held sacred and buried in a cemetery west of the
town. The same area contains human burials of the
Middle Kingdom to Late Period.

The temple of Esna is about 200 meters from the
river, in the middle of the modern town. Because of
the accumulation of occupation debris and silt, it is
now about 9 meters below street level. The ceremonial way, which probably linked the quay with the
temple, has disappeared. The quay has cartouches of
Marcus Aurelius, and is still in use. Texts in the temple relate it to four others in the area, three to the
north and one on the east bank, all of which have
now disappeared completely, although parts of them
were visible in the 19th century. Another temple of
the same period has been identified at Kom Mer, 12
kilometers to the south, but cannot be excavated
because a modern village is built over it.

The temple is dedicated to Khnum with several
other deities, of whom the most prominent are Neith
and Heka "Magical Power," who is here a child deity.
As it stands, it consists only of a completely preserved
hypostyle hall. Its west wall formed the beginning of
the undecorated inner temple, which had been
demolished in antiquity, probably in preparation for
a grand rebuilding. This west wall is the earliest part,
with reliefs of Ptolemy VI Philometor and VIII Euergetes II. The rest of the hypostyle has the latest preserved major temple decoration inside and out,
dating from the 1st to 3rd centuries CE. Some scenes,
notably that of gods and the king netting birds, are
most imposing.

The most significant feature of the decoration is
the series of texts written on the columns. These give
a full and rich picture of some of the festivals of the
sacred year at Esna, which is set out in schematic form
in a calendar, also inscribed on a column. There is in
addition a remarkable pair of cryptographic hymns
to Khnum, one written almost entirely with hieroglyphs of rams, and the other with crocodiles.

Facade of the temple of Khnum at
Esna; 1st century CE. The side
doorways into the hypostyle hall
have important mythological
texts, and were the normal
entrances for priests.

work of one of the Nectanebos. Some 2·2 kilometers
northeast of the enclosure, at the entrance to Wadi
Hellal, is the first of the "desert temples," the
partly free-standing and partly rock-cut sanctuary
of the goddess Shesmetet (Smithis). This was built
chiefly by Ptolemy VIII Euergetes II and Ptolemy
IX Soter II. About 70 meters to the southeast is the
well-preserved chapel (known as "el-Hammam")
built by the viceroy of Kush Setau during the reign
of Ramesses II, and restored under the Ptolemies,
which was probably dedicated to Reʿ-Harakhty,
Hathor, Amun, Nekhbet, and Ramesses II himself.
Further away, about 3·4 kilometers from the town
enclosure, Thutmose IV and Amenhotep III built a
temple for Hathor "Mistress of the Entrance to the
Valley" and Nekhbet.

Tombs, mostly rock-cut, of the first half of the
18th Dynasty, but also of the Old and Middle Kingdoms and the Ramessid Period, are some 400 meters
north of the town enclosure. Two of them, those of

el-Moʿalla

Two decorated rock-cut tombs of the early 1st Intermediate Period, belonging to ʿAnkhtifi and Sebekhotep, are the most important monuments at el-Moʿalla (probably ancient Egyptian *Hefat*). Apart from its unconventional and lively paintings, the tomb of ʿAnkhtifi contains the most extensive biographical texts of its period, exalting his status and describing the situation in the southern nomes after the end of the Old Kingdom.

Gebelein

The name of this place means the same in Arabic as in ancient Egyptian: "The Two Hills," and derives from the most conspicuous landmark visible on the west bank of the Nile at the point where the 3rd and 4th Upper Egyptian nomes meet.

Gebelein has produced predynastic finds, notably fragments of linen with the oldest known large painting. Tombs, mainly of the 1st Intermediate Period, were found on the west hill, while on the east hill stood a temple of Hathor, from which came the Greek name Pathyris, from *Per-Hathor*, "Domain of Hathor," or Aphroditopolis. The temple existed as early as the 3rd Dynasty. Reliefs, stelae, or inscriptions of Nebhepetreʿ Mentuhotep, and several kings of the 13th and 15th Dynasties have also been discovered. The temple continued to function in the Greco-Roman

Far left top Tomb of ʿAnkhtifi at el-Moʿalla: the deceased spearing fish from a papyrus boat. The figures of his wife and daughters standing behind him were destroyed by tomb robbers. Painting. 1st Intermediate Period.

Above and far left below Tomb of Iti at Gebelein. Three kneeling nude youths, perhaps engaged in gymnastics, and a scene of transport and storing grain in granaries. Painting. 1st Intermediate Period. Turin, Museo Egizio.

Left The Ptolemaic temple at Tod.

Black granite statue of the herald Sebekemzauf, the brother-in-law of one of the kings of the 2nd Intermediate Period. The sculpture, seen by John Gardner Wilkinson at Armant in the first half of the last century, is now in two parts. The base (a cast is shown on this photograph) belongs to the National Museum of Ireland in Dublin, and is on loan to the Kunsthistorisches Museum in Vienna, which owns the rest of the statue. Height: 1·50m.

sacred lake in front of the temple of Senwosret I, and a Roman Period kiosk was located nearby.

The site is currently being explored by an expedition of the Musée du Louvre in Paris.

Armant

Ancient *Iuny*, on the west bank of the Nile in the 4th Upper Egyptian nome, was one of the most important places of worship of the war god Montu. The modern name Armant derives from *Iunu-Montu*, Coptic Ermont, Greek Hermonthis.

A temple dedicated to Montu existed at Armant as early as the 11th Dynasty, which perhaps originated there, and Nebhepetre⸗ Mentuhotep is the earliest builder known with certainty. Important additions were made during the 12th Dynasty and the New Kingdom; of these only the remains of the pylon of Thutmose III are still visible. The temple was destroyed some time during the Late Period. In the reign of Nectanebo II a new temple was probably started, being continued by the Ptolemies. The most important contribution to the appearance of the site was made by Cleopatra VII Philopator and Ptolemy XV Caesarion, who built a birth house with a sacred lake. The building still existed in the first half of the 19th century, but is now destroyed. Two gates, one of them erected by Antoninus Pius, have also been found. The Bucheum (from ancient Egyptian *Bekh*), the burial place of the sacred Buchis bulls of Armant, is on the desert edge north of Armant. The earliest bull burial dates to Nectanebo II, and the complex was in use for some 650 years, until the mid 4th century CE. The burial place of the "Mother of Buchis" cows has also been located. In the neighborhood of Armant are extensive cemeteries from all periods.

Period, and demotic and Greek papyri have been found in the area. The town was sited below the east hill.

The site has been excavated by Italian expeditions (Ernesto Schiaparelli and Giulio Farina) between 1910 and 1937, and by the Museo Egizio of Turin and the University of Rome since the mid-1990s.

Tod

Apparently in the reign of Userkaf of the 5th Dynasty there already stood a mud brick chapel at ancient Egyptian *Djerty* (Tuphium of the Greco-Roman Period), on the east bank of the Nile. Major building activities connected with the local cult of the god Montu started in the Middle Kingdom, during the reigns of Nebhepetre⸗ Mentuhotep, S⸗ankhkare⸗ Mentuhotep, and Senwosret I, and the base of the latter's temple wall was incorporated into the Ptolemaic structure. In the New Kingdom, Thutmose III erected a shrine, still partly preserved, for the bark of Montu, and Amenhotep II, Sety I, Amenmesse, and Ramesses III and IV carried out restoration work. Ptolemy VIII Euergetes II added his temple with a

THEBES

Ancient Egyptian *Waset* was called Thebai by the Greeks, but we are at a loss when searching for a reason for this. It has been suggested that the pronunciation of the Egyptian names *Ta-ipet* (*Ipet-resyt* was the Luxor temple and *Ipet-isut* Karnak) or *Djeme* (Medinet Habu) sounded similar to that of their Boeotian city, but the argument lacks conviction.

Waset was in the 4th Upper Egyptian nome, deep in the south. Its geographical position contributed greatly to the town's importance in history: it was close to Nubia and the eastern desert with their valuable mineral resources and trade routes, and distant from the restricting power centers in the north. Theban local rulers of the earlier part of Egyptian history pursued active expansionist policies, particularly during the 1st and 2nd Intermediate Periods; in the latter this was disguised as an Egyptian reaction against foreign invaders (the Hyksos). Monuments earlier than the end of the Old Kingdom are scarce, and *Waset* was little more than a provincial town. Its rise to prominence occurred during the 11th Dynasty; although the capital was moved to Itjtawy at the beginning of the 12th Dynasty, Thebes with its god Amun was established as the administrative center of southern Upper Egypt and the foundations were laid for its role as Egypt's religious capital. The peak came during the 18th Dynasty when for some time it was the administrative capital of the country. Its temples were the most important and the wealthiest in the land, and the tombs prepared for the elite among its inhabitants on the west bank were the most luxurious Egypt ever saw. Even when the center of royal activities moved to the north (el-ʿAmarna, Memphis and Pi-Riʿamsese), Theban temples continued to flourish, monarchs were still buried in the Valley of the Kings, and the town retained some importance in the administrative life of the country. During the 3rd Intermediate Period Thebes, with the High Priest of Amun at its head, formed a counterbalance to the realm of the 21st- and 22nd-Dynasty kings, who ruled from the delta. Theban political influence receded only in the Late Period.

The main part of the town and the principal temples were on the east bank. Across the river, on the west bank, was the necropolis with tombs and mortuary temples, but also the west part of the town; Amenhotep III had his palace at el-Malqata and in the Ramessid Period Thebes itself centered north of there, at Medinet Habu.

"The Pyramids, the Catacombs, and some other Things to be seen in Lower Egypt, are look'd upon as great Wonders; and are justly held in Preference to whatever the rest of the World can boast of. But if these challenge the Preeminence to all the extra Egyptian World, on the one hand, they must yield the Glory of Superiority to the many ancient Temples, &c. of Saaide [Upper Egypt] on the other" (C. Perry, *A View of the Levant*, 1743, Preface).

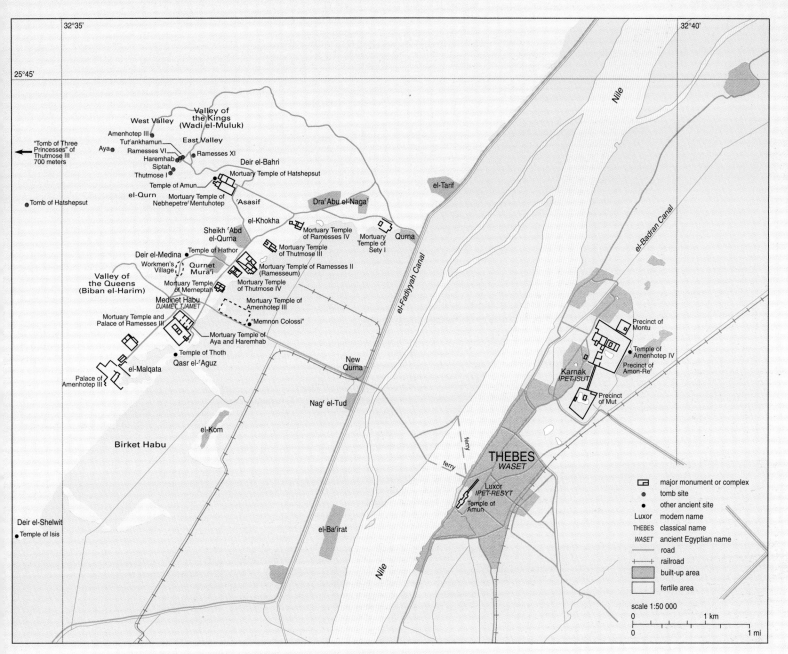

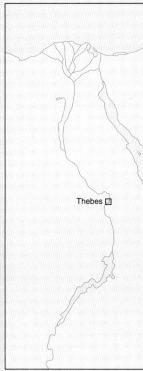

Luxor
Temple of Amun, chiefly of
Amenhotep III, Ramesses II, and
Alexander the Great.
Karnak
Precincts of Amon-Reᶜ, Montu,
and Mut, with temple of Khons
and numerous smaller temples
and chapels, 12th Dynasty to
Greco-Roman Period.
The West Bank: Temples
Deir el-Bahri: mortuary temples
of Nebhepetreᶜ Mentuhotep and
Hatshepsut, and temple of Amun
by Thutmose III.
Ramesseum: mortuary temple of
Ramesses II.
Medinet Habu: temple of Amun
of the 18th Dynasty and later,
and mortuary temple of
Ramesses III.
Other mortuary temples,
particularly those of Sety I at
Qurna and Amenhotep III with
"Memnon Colossi."

Royal Tombs
el-Tarif: 11th Dynasty.
Draᶜ Abu el-Nagaᶜ: 17th
Dynasty.
Valley of the Kings: 18th to 20th
Dynasties, including tomb of
Tutᶜankhamun.
Deir el-Medina: workmen's
village, 18th to 20th Dynasties.
Nonroyal Tombs
Tombs dating from Early
Dynastic Period to Greco-Roman
Period.

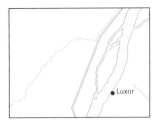

Luxor

A sanctuary stood on the site of the Luxor temple or in its vicinity at the beginning of the 18th Dynasty, or even earlier, but the temple we see today was built essentially by two kings, Amenhotep III (the inner part) and Ramesses II (the outer part). Several other rulers contributed to its relief decoration and inscriptions, added minor structures, or made alterations, chiefly Tutʿankhamun, Haremhab, and Alexander the Great. The overall length of the temple between the pylon and the rear wall is nearly 260 meters.

The temple was dedicated to the ithyphallic Amun (Amenemope) and linked to ideas about the royal *ka* (the generative principle that carried down the generations) and the annual renewal of the king's divine powers. Once a year, during the second and third months of the inundation season, a long religious festival was held at Luxor during which the image of Amun of Karnak visited his *Ipet-resyt*, "Southern Ipet," as the temple was called.

At the end of the reign of the Roman Emperor Diocletian, just after 300 CE, the first antechamber in the inner part of the temple was converted into a sanctuary of the imperial cult serving the local military garrison and town. It was decorated with exquisite paintings which were still visible in the 19th century but are now almost completely lost. A small mosque of Abu el-Haggag was built in the court of Ramesses II in the Fatimid Period (11th century CE).

An alley of human-headed sphinxes of Nectanebo I linked Karnak, some 3 kilometers to the north, with Luxor, and brought the visitor to a mud brick enclosure wall. Several later structures stood in the forecourt in front of the temple itself, including a colonnade of Shabaka (later dismantled) and chapels of Hathor, built by Taharqa, and of Sarapis, built by Hadrian. The burned brick walls visible to the east and west of the temple are remains of the late Roman town, contemporary with the imperial sanctuary.

The temple is fronted by a pylon of Ramesses II, with reliefs and texts on its outside relating the story of the famous battle against the Hittites at Qadesh in Syria in c. 1274 BCE. Two red granite obelisks originally stood in front of the pylon but only one, approximately 25 meters high, now remains: the other

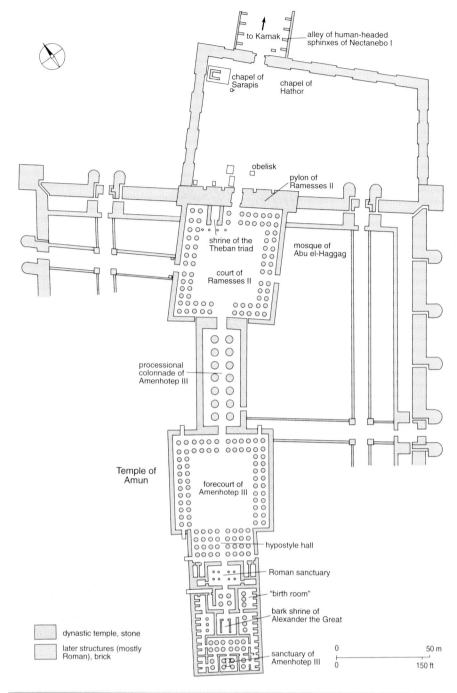

to Karnak

alley of human-headed sphinxes of Nectanebo I

chapel of Sarapis

chapel of Hathor

obelisk

pylon of Ramesses II

shrine of the Theban triad

mosque of Abu el-Haggag

court of Ramesses II

processional colonnade of Amenhotep III

Temple of Amun

forecourt of Amenhotep III

hypostyle hall

Roman sanctuary

"birth room"

bark shrine of Alexander the Great

sanctuary of Amenhotep III

dynastic temple, stone

later structures (mostly Roman), brick

0   50 m
0   150 ft

Far left The colonnade of
Amenhotep III from southwest,
with the pylon of Ramesses II
visible behind, and the mosque
of Abu el-Haggag on the right.

Left The pylon from the north,
with the remains of standing
colossal statues of Ramesses II
outside the side doorway to the
court, and the massive
papyriform columns of the
processional colonnade of
Amenhotep III on the right.

Right The pylon in 1838, shortly
after the removal of the northern
obelisk, as seen by the Scottish
artist David Roberts (1796–
1864). The colossal seated statues
of Ramesses II outside the pylon
were still half-buried in debris.

Far right top Columns of the
hypostyle hall, with capitals in
the form of unopened papyrus
umbels, and abaci and
architraves with names and texts
of Amenhotep III.

Above and far right bottom
Paintings on the walls of the
Roman sacellum: section of the
east wall, and part of the
representations left of the apse (a
semicircular recess created by
conversion of the doorway
between the 1st and 2nd
antechambers of the older
temple). Recorded by Sir John
Gardner Wilkinson in or before
1856 (earlier than the date
quoted in specialized studies).
Now almost completely lost.

Overleaf Detail of a granite
statue, probably of Amenhotep
III, with an added cartouche of
Merneptah. From Luxor.
"Kingship is a perfect office; it
has no son, it has no brother,
who can make its monuments
endure: it is one individual who
restores another's. A man should
act for his predecessor for the
sake of his achievements' being
restored by another succeeding
him." (Instruction for Merikareʿ
E 116–18).

was removed to Place de la Concorde in Paris in
1835–36. Several colossal statues of Ramesses II, two
of them seated, flank the entrance. The central gateway of the pylon was partly decorated by Shabaka.

The peristyle court of Ramesses II which opens
behind the pylon has 74 papyrus columns with
scenes of the king before various deities. The
columns are arranged in a double row around its
sides, and are interrupted by a shrine consisting of
three chapels (or bark stations) of Amun (center),
Mut (left) and Khons (right), built by Hatshepsut
and Thutmose III and redecorated by Ramesses II. It
was the existence of this shrine which probably
caused the considerable deviation of the axis of the
buildings of Ramesses II from that of the earlier temple of Amenhotep III. Colossal standing statues of
the king (some usurped from Amenhotep III) are
placed in the gaps between the front row of columns
at the south end of the court.

The entrance to the processional colonnade of
Amenhotep III, with seven columns on either side,
has two seated colossi of Ramesses II with Queen
Nefertari by his right leg on the north side, while

two seated double statues of Amun and Mut are on
the south side. The walls behind the columns were
decorated by Tutʿankhamun and Haremhab with
reliefs depicting the Festival of Opet: those on the
west wall show a procession of barks from Karnak to
Luxor, while the east wall shows their homeward
journey.

A peristyle forecourt of Amenhotep III is fused
with the hypostyle hall, which is the first room in the
inner, originally roofed, part of the temple. This
leads to a series of four antechambers with subsidiary rooms. The so-called "Birth Room," east of
the second antechamber, is decorated with reliefs
showing the symbolic "divine birth" of Amenhotep
III resulting from the union of his mother Mutemwia
and the god Amun. Alexander the Great built a bark
shrine in the third of the antechambers. The sanctuary of Amenhotep III is the last room on the central
axis of the temple.

In 1988, a major cache of 21 royal and divine statues was discovered in the court of Amenhotep III.
The sculptures had been deposited there during one
of the late renovations of the temple.

Karnak

The name Karnak, from that of a modern village nearby (el-Karnak), describes a vast conglomeration of ruined temples, chapels and other buildings of various dates, measuring some 1·5 by at least 0·8 kilometers. This was ancient Egyptian *Ipet-isut*, perhaps "The Most Select of Places," the main place of worship of the Theban triad with the god Amun (often, especially during the New Kingdom, described as Amon-Reᶜ) at its head, and also the home of various "guest" deities. No site in Egypt makes a more overwhelming and lasting impression than this apparent chaos of walls, obelisks, columns, statues, stelae, and decorated blocks. Theban kings and the god Amun came to prominence at the beginning of the Middle Kingdom. From that time, the temples of Karnak were built, enlarged, torn down, added to, and restored for more than 2,000 years. The temple of Amun was ideologically and economically the most important temple establishment in the whole of Egypt.

The site is divided into three groups delimited by the remains of mud-brick walls enclosing the temple precincts. The largest and most important is the central enclosure, the temple of Amun proper. It is also the best preserved. The northern enclosure belongs to Montu, the original local god of the Theban area, while the enclosure of Mut lies to the south and is connected with Amun's precinct by an alley of ram-headed sphinxes. An avenue bordered by sphinxes linked Karnak with the Luxor temple, and canals connected the temples of Amun and Montu with the Nile.

Amenhotep IV (Akhenaten) erected several temples for his new state deity, the Aten, to the east of the central enclosure of Amun. The most conspicuous features of these temples were open courts surrounded by pillars and colossal statues of the king. The temples were dismantled in the post-ᶜAmarna period and the stone blocks reused in later structures, especially the pylons built by Haremhab.

The precinct of Amon-Reᶜ

The trapezoidal central enclosure contains the Great Temple of Amon-Reᶜ, built along two axes (east–west and north–south), a number of smaller temples and chapels, and a sacred lake. The layout of the Great Temple consists of a series of pylons of various dates, with courts or halls between them, leading to the main sanctuary. The earliest are Pylons IV and V, by Thutmose I; from then on the temple was enlarged by building in a westerly and southerly direction.

Pylon I is preceded by a quay (probably reconstructed in its present form during the 25th Dynasty), and an avenue of ram-headed sphinxes protecting the king, most of which bear the name of the high priest of Amun, Pinudjem I of the 21st Dynasty. South of the avenue are several smaller structures, including a bark shrine of Psammuthis

and Hakoris, and parapets of the 25th–26th Dynasties with texts connected with the ceremony of refilling the water jars of the Theban triad. The pylon is probably of the 30th Dynasty or Ptolemaic. The court which opens behind it contains a triple bark shrine of Sety II consisting of three contiguous chapels dedicated to Amun, Mut, and Khons. In the center of the forecourt there are remains of a colonnaded entrance of Taharqa, one of the columns of which has been re-erected. A small temple (bark station) of Ramesses III faces into the forecourt from the south.

Pylon II, probably a work of Haremhab, is preceded by colossal statues of Ramesses II, including one (on the north) showing him with Princess Bentᶜanta. Behind the pylon, the now lost roof of the hypostyle hall, the most impressive part of the whole temple complex, was borne by 134 papyrus columns, of which the 12 in the central aisle are larger and have capitals of a different type. The relief decora-

Top Ram-headed sphinxes ("criosphinxes") outside Pylon 1. The ram was the sacred animal of Amun; the motif of an animal, bird or serpent "protecting" a king or even a nonroyal individual was common in Egyptian statuary and relief.

Above left Headless statue of Sety II kneeling with an offering table, now restored and set up north of the 4th column on the north side of the central axis of the hypostyle hall.

Above Senwosret I led by the god Atum to the ithyphallic Amun Karmutef. In the waystation constructed after the king's *sed*-festival and now re-erected north of the hypostyle hall.

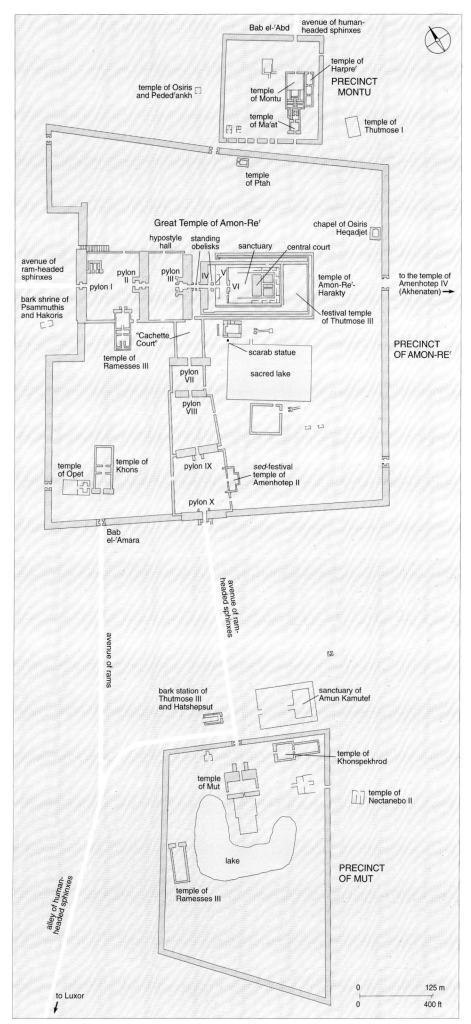

The small temple of Ramesses III
between Pylons I and II: Osirid
pillars on the west side of the
court seen from the temple
entrance. Reliefs on the sides of
the pillars show the king before
various gods.

tion of the hypostyle hall is the work of Sety I and
Ramesses II. The exterior walls depict military campaigns of these kings in Palestine and Syria, including Ramesses II's battle at Qadesh.

Pylon III was built by Amenhotep III, but the
porch in front of it was decorated by Sety I and
Ramesses II. Numerous blocks from earlier buildings
were found reused in the pylon: a *sed*-festival
waystation of Senwosret I (the "White Chapel"),
shrines of Amenhotep I and II, Hatshepsut (the "Red
Chapel," so called for its red quartzite stone) and
Thutmose IV, and a pillared portico of the same king
(a number of these have been reerected to the north
of the hypostyle hall). The four obelisks which stood
behind the pylon were erected by Thutmose I and
III to mark the entrance to the original temple; only
one obelisk of Thutmose I is still standing.

Between Pylons IV and V, both of Thutmose I, is
the earliest part of the temple still standing, with 14
papyrus columns, originally gilded, and two
obelisks of Hatshepsut (one standing, one fallen).

Pylon VI and the court which precedes it were
built by Thutmose III. Behind them is a vestibule
with two magnificent granite pillars with the
emblems of Upper and Lower Egypt. The bark shrine
(sanctuary) dates to Philip Arrhidaeus and stands on
the site of earlier shrines built by Hatshepsut and
Thutmose III. The earliest known temple of Amun,
built under Senwosret I and now completely
destroyed, was situated in the area behind it.

Further east is the Festival Temple of Thutmose
III. One room in this temple is known as the "Botan-
ical Garden," because of its representations of exotic
plants, birds and animals. It may have contained the
core sanctuary of the temple.

Another four pylons were added along a new axis
which extended the Great Temple of Amon-Reʿ in a
southerly direction. The court north of Pylon VII is
known as the "Cachette Court": here a deposit of
thousands of statues which originally stood in the
temple was found at the beginning of the 20th century. Remains of earlier buildings uncovered in this
court include pillars of Senwosret I and several
chapels of Amenhotep I. Pylons VII and VIII were
built by Hatshepsut and Thutmose III, and the court
between them contains the latter's bark station.

Pylons IX and X were decorated under Haremhab; Pylon X may have been built, at least in part, by Amenhotep III. Many "talatat," blocks from buildings of Amenhotep IV (Akhenaten), mostly dating before his move to el-ʿAmarna, were found reused in these pylons. A *sed*-festival temple of Amenhotep II stands in the court between them.

Near the northwest corner of the temple's sacred lake is a colossal statue of the sacred scarab beetle on a tall plinth, dating to Amenhotep III.

The temple of Khons stands in the southwest corner of the enclosure. Its propylon in the main enclosure wall, built by Ptolemy III Euergetes I and known as Bab el-ʿAmara, is approached from the south by an avenue of ram-sphinxes protecting Amenhotep III. The pylon was decorated by Pinudjem I, the forecourt by Herihor, and the inner part by various Ramessids (at least part of the temple was built by Ramesses III); there is also some Ptolemaic relief work.

The temple of the hippopotamus goddess Opet, close to that of Khons, was built chiefly by Ptolemy VIII Euergetes II. The decoration was completed by several later rulers, including Augustus. There is a symbolic "Crypt of Osiris" below the sanctuary at the back of the temple.

Nearly 20 other small chapels and temples are within the precinct of Amon-Reʿ, including a temple of Ptah built by Thutmose III, Shabaka, several Ptolemies, and Tiberius (north of the Great Temple, close to the enclosure wall), and a chapel of Osiris Heqadjet "Ruler of Time" of Osorkon IV and Shebitku (northeast of the Great Temple, close to the enclosure wall).

The precinct of Montu
The square northern enclosure is the smallest of the three precincts and its monuments are poorly preserved. It contains the main temple of Montu (although this area may have at first been associated with other deities), several smaller structures (particularly the temples of Harpreʿ and Maʿat), and a sacred lake. In 1970 a structure which is interpreted as a temple treasury built by Thutmose I was discovered outside the east enclosure wall.

The temple of Montu is fronted by a quay and an avenue of human-headed sphinxes which approaches the temple from the north. The propy-

lon, known as Bab el-ʿAbd, was built by Ptolemy III Euergetes I and IV Philopator, and the temple by Amenhotep III; later kings, particularly Taharqa, modified the original plan.

The precinct of Mut
The southern enclosure contains the temple of Mut, surrounded by a crescent-shaped lake, and subsidiary structures, especially the temple of Khonspekhrod, originally of the 18th Dynasty, and a temple of Ramesses III.

The temple of Mut was built by Amenhotep III, but here too the propylon in the enclosure wall is Ptolemaic (Ptolemy II Philadelphus and III Euergetes I), and there are later additions to the temple by Taharqa and Nectanebo I, among others. Hundreds of granodiorite statues of the lioness goddess Sakhmet inscribed for Amenhotep III from the temple are in museums around the world and some are still on site. These are thought to have been moved to this temple from the king's mortuary temple on the West Bank.

"The Northernmost, said to be the statue of Memnon, is cover'd with a great Number of Greek and Latin Inscriptions; being so many testimonies of Persons who pretend to have heard it utter a Sound at Sun-rise" (C. Perry, *A View of the Levant*, 1743, p. 348).

The West Bank

The temples

Across the Nile from the temples of Karnak and Luxor, the remains of temples occupy a stretch of some 7·5 kilometers. Most of these were royal mortuary temples of the New Kingdom, and their main function was to maintain the cult of the deceased kings buried in their tombs cut in the cliffs further to the west, though gods were also worshiped there, particularly Amun and Re ͨ-Harakhty. The most important of these temples are those of Deir el-Bahri, the Ramesseum, and Medinet Habu. The mortuary temple of Sety I stands at Qurna, while only huge seated statues, the "Memnon Colossi," and other fragmentary statuary now mark the site of the enormous temple of Amenhotep III. Several of the temples on the west bank were not mortuary, such as those of Hathor (Deir el-Medina), Thoth (Qasr el-ͨAguz), and Isis (Deir el-Shelwit), all of the Greco-Roman Period.

Deir el-Bahri
Deir el-Bahri was traditionally connected with the goddess Hathor, the chief deity of the Theban necropolis. It is situated almost directly opposite the temples at Karnak and was chosen by Nebhepetre ͨ Mentuhotep of the 11th Dynasty and Queen Hatshepsut of the 18th Dynasty for the site of their mortuary temples. In the case of Mentuhotep the temple was directly connected with the burial, while Hatshepsut had two tombs prepared for her elsewhere, one in a remote valley behind, the Wadi Sikket Taqet Zaid, the other in the Valley of the Kings. Thutmose III built a temple complex for the god Amun (*Djeser-akhet*) and a chapel for Hathor between the two earlier structures, and a kiosk (*Djeser-menu*) in the court of Mentuhotep's temple.
The mortuary temple of Nebhepetre ͨ Mentuhotep *(Akh-isut)*. Although the architects of Old Kingdom pyramid complexes must already have

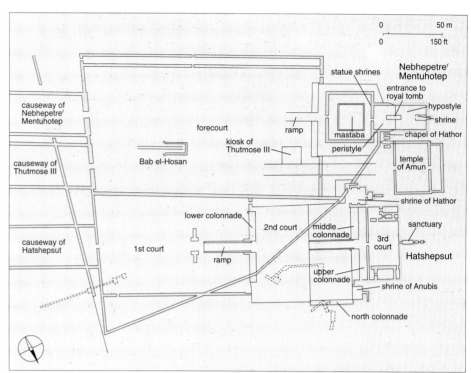

formulated the basic conception of a design that placed different parts of a temple on terraces of varying height, such a plan had not been executed in Egypt until Nebhepetreᶜ Mentuhotep built his temple at Deir el-Bahri. Another new element introduced there, the colonnaded porticoes, may have derived from the appearance of the *saff*-tombs of the earlier 11th Dynasty kings.

The upper part of the temple is approached by a causeway (1,200 meters long and 46 meters wide), originally lined with statues, which started at the now lost valley temple. The front, free-standing, part of the upper temple consists of a forecourt, enclosed by walls on its three sides, and a terrace with a now ruined mastaba-shaped structure, probably associated with the cult of the sun god. In the east part of the forecourt is the opening known as "Bab el-Hosan," which is connected by a long underground passage with a probably symbolic royal tomb, left unfinished. The west part of the forecourt originally contained a grove of tamarisk and sycamore trees on either side of an ascending ramp leading on to the terrace. Behind the colonnades at the west end of the forecourt and on the terrace were reliefs showing boat processions, foreign campaigns, hunting scenes, and other subjects; large numbers of small fragments of these are preserved in museums. The mastaba-shaped structure, which was the dominant feature of the temple, is surrounded by a pillared roofed ambulatory on all sides. In its west wall are six statue-shrines (and, further west, tombs) of royal ladies of the reign of Nebhepetreᶜ (from the north: Myt, ᶜAshayt, Zadeh, Kawit, Kemsyt, and Henhenet).

The inner part of the temple, cut into the cliff, consists of peristyle and hypostyle courts located east and west of the entrance to an underground passage, which after some 150 meters leads to the tomb proper. Little of the royal burial and funerary equipment was found. The rock-cut shrine at the back of the inner part of the building was the main cult place of the deceased king in the temple.

The mortuary temple of Hatshepsut *(Djeser-djeseru)*. The temple is a partly rock-cut and partly freestanding terraced structure. Its builders took up and developed, in more than one stage, the remarkable architectural ideas of its 550-year-old predecessor to

the south. Even now, in its incompletely preserved state, the temple conveys a unique harmony between human creation and the natural environment. The effect of its original appearance, with trees, flowerbeds and numerous sphinxes and statues, must have been even more overwhelming. The temple was built chiefly between years 7 and 22 of the reign of Hatshepsut and Thutmose III, and a number of high officials were involved in its construction, including the influential "Chief Steward of Amun" Senenmut.

The valley temple of the complex is attested by its foundation deposits, but the building itself has disappeared, at least partly as a result of the proximity of the later temple of Ramesses IV. The monumental causeway, some 37 meters wide, lined by sphinxes and provided with a bark chapel, led on to a series of three courts at different levels, approached by ramps and separated by colonnades (porticoes) protecting the now famous reliefs. These show huge barges specially constructed to bring obelisks from Aswan for the temple of Amun at Karnak (the lower colonnade), scenes of the divine birth and coronation of Hatshepsut (the north half of the middle colonnade), and a trade expedition by sea to the exotic African land

Top left Soldiers taking part in a bark procession: relief on the north wall of the hypostyle hall of the shrine of Hathor, in the south part of Hatshepsut's temple.

Above The temples at Deir el-Bahri from the cliff to the north.

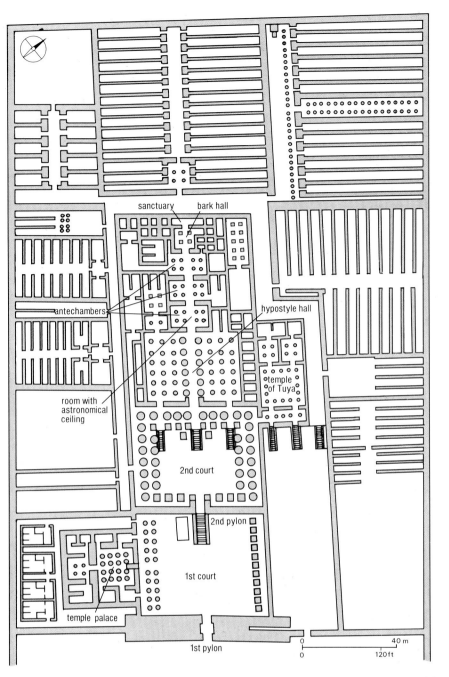

sanctuary   bark hall

antechambers

hypostyle hall

room with
astronomical
ceiling

temple
of Tuya

2nd court

2nd pylon

1st court

temple palace

1st pylon

0   40 m
0   120 ft

Top right The hypostyle hall of the Ramesseum from the southwest.

Above right The east wall of the hypostyle hall of the Ramesseum, south of the entrance, bottom register: detail of relief showing the assault on the fort of Dapur, "the town which His Majesty sacked in the land of Amor," in year 8 of the reign of Ramesses II. The exact location of this northern Syrian town, perhaps in the region of Aleppo, is not known.

of Punt (the south half of the middle colonnade). The upper colonnade, formed by pillars showing the Queen in the *sed*-festival cloak, with crossed arms holding a scepter and a flagellum, preceded the upper court. Vaulted rooms on the north and south sides of this court were dedicated to Hatshepsut and her father Thutmose I, and the gods Reʿ-Harakhty and Amun. Theirs were the main cults maintained in the temple. A series of niches at the back (the west side) of the hall contained statues of the queen, and an entrance in the same wall led to the sanctuary proper. The innermost room of the present sanctuary was cut by Ptolemy VIII Euergetes II; otherwise, the temple's architecture is remarkably free from later interference. Special shrines of Anubis and Hathor were approached from the second court.

The mortuary temple of Ramesses II *(Khnemtwaset)* **or Ramesseum.** The mortuary complex of Ramesses II, somewhat misleadingly described by the Greek writer Diodorus Siculus as "the tomb of Osymandyas" (from Usermaʿatreʿ, part of the praenomen of Ramesses II), nowadays known as the Ramesseum, consists of the temple proper and the surrounding mud brick magazines and other buildings (Ramesses

II's tomb is KV 7 in the Valley of the Kings).

The interior disposition of the stone temple is fairly orthodox, though somewhat more elaborate than usual: two courts, a hypostyle hall, a series of antechambers and subsidiary rooms, the bark hall, and the sanctuary. The temple's overall plan is, unusually, a parallelogram rather than a rectangle. This was probably caused by retaining the orientation of an earlier small temple to the north of the Ramesseum's hypostyle hall, dedicated to Tuya, the mother of Ramesses II, while making the pylons face the Luxor Temple on the east bank.

The 1st and 2nd pylons of the Ramesseum are decorated with reliefs depicting, among other things, the battle of Qadesh (also known from Karnak, Luxor, Abydos, and Abu Simbel). Two granite colossi of Ramesses II originally stood before a platform preceding the hypostyle hall: the upper part of the southern statue is now in the British Museum, but the head of the companion piece can still be seen in the Ramesseum. Diodorus' description of the sculpture provided inspiration for the poem "Ozymandias" by the English Romantic poet Percy Bysshe Shelley. The bases of the rear walls of the hypostyle hall are decorated with long processions showing sons of Ramesses II (their tomb is KV 5 in the Valley of the Kings). The first room behind the hypostyle hall has an astronomical ceiling and might have served as the temple's library. The usual temple palace stood south of the first court.

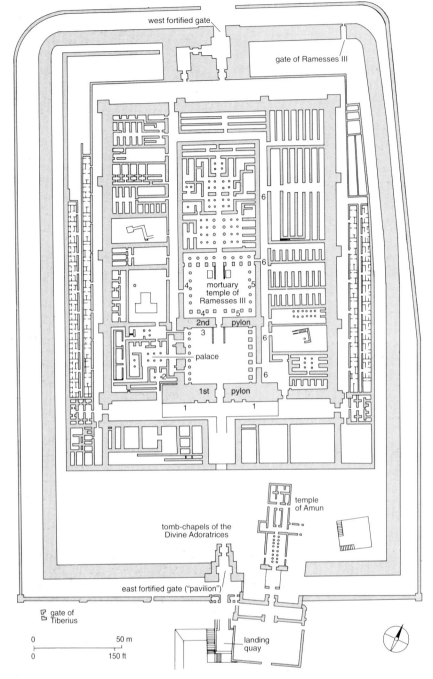

Right Plan of the mortuary temple complex of Ramesses III and temple of Amun at Medinet Habu. The key shows the location of the principal cycles of reliefs.

Medinet Habu

Situated opposite Luxor, ancient Egyptian *Tjamet* (or *Djamet*), Coptic *Djeme* (or *Djemi*), was one of the earliest places in the Theban area to be associated closely with Amun as a creator god. Hatshepsut and Thutmose III built a temple for him there on the site of an 11th dynasty precursor. Next to it, Ramesses III erected his mortuary temple, enclosing both structures within a massive mud brick enclosure that also encompassed magazines, workshops, administrative buildings, and dwellings of priests and officials. Medinet Habu became the focus of the administrative and economic life of the whole of Thebes, performing this role for the next several hundred years. Even tombs and tomb chapels started to be built there, in particular those of the Divine Adoratrices of the 25th and 26th Dynasties. The site continued to be inhabited well into the Middle Ages (9th century CE).

The temple of Amun *(Djeser-iset)*. The temple, built by Hatshepsut and Thutmose III, underwent many alterations in the course of the following 1,500 years, mainly during Dynasties 20 (Ramesses III), 25 (Shabaka and Taharqa), 26, 29 (Hakoris), 30 (Nectanebo I), and the Greco-Roman Period (Ptolemy VIII Euergetes II, X Alexander I, and Antoninus Pius). These considerably extended its plan by adding a columned hall, two pylons, and a court at the front.

The mortuary temple of Ramesses III *(Khnemt-neheh)*. The temple used to be connected with the Nile by a canal, and a landing quay was built outside the enclosure. The entrance to the temple enclosure was through one of the two fortified gates in the east and west; only the former, sometimes called the "Pavilion," now remains.

The temple, some 150 meters long, is of orthodox

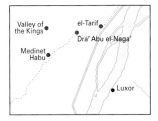

Above The kneeling Ramesses III being crowned and receiving a symbolic *sed*-festival emblem from the Theban triad: the enthroned Amon-Reʿ accompanied by Khons and Mut (behind the king, not shown on the photograph). East part of the south wall of the 1st hypostyle hall, temple of Ramesses III at Medinet Habu, lower register.

Above right The Valley of the Kings.

Left The temple of Ramesses III: from the right, the 1st pylon, the wall of the 1st court with three doorways and a "window of appearances" connecting the court with the palace south of it, the 2nd pylon, and the south wall of the 2nd court and the inner part of the temple.

Note. We refer to tombs on the Theban West Bank with standard abbreviations for number sequences: KV = tomb in the Valley of the Kings; TT = nonroyal Theban Tomb elsewhere in the necropolis.

design, and resembles closely the mortuary temple of Ramesses II (the Ramesseum), which it probably imitates. South of the 1st court stood the mud brick palace, now badly damaged, which was used by the king during religious festivals held at Medinet Habu. Two building phases of the structure have been recognized. The palace's interior walls were originally decorated with exquisite faience tiles, similar to those known from palaces of the period in the delta (Tell el-Yahudiya and Qantir). The "window of appearances" connected the palace with the temple.

Some of the reliefs at Medinet Habu are not only artistically but also historically important, recording events of the reign of Ramesses III:

1st pylon: On the outside, the king is shown smiting foreign captives before Amun and Reʿ-Harakhty in symbolic scenes of triumph. The subjugated foreign lands and towns are represented by their names inscribed in rings surmounted by human heads. Hunting scenes are on the short outside west face of the south massif.

2nd pylon: On the outside (east face) of the south massif, the king presents captives to Amun and Mut. On the inside, and also on the south and north walls of the 2nd court, are representations of the festivals of Sokar and Min.

The exterior of the temple: Campaigns against the Libyans, Asiatics, and "Sea Peoples" are shown on the north wall.

Scenes of the king offering to deities are on other parts of the exterior wall and in the rooms of the inner part of the temple.

Royal tombs

el-Tarif

The ambitious rulers of the early Theban 11th Dynasty, who vied with the northern Herakleopolitan (9th/10th) Dynasty for supremacy over Egypt, built their tombs at el-Tarif, in river terms the northernmost part of the Theban necropolis. Although the tombs are comparable in type to contemporary provincial tombs elsewhere, their majestic size and truly monumental architecture connect them with the mortuary temple and tomb of the king who finally gained control over the whole of Egypt, Nebhepetreʿ Mentuhotep, at Deir el-Bahri.

The tombs consist of an open excavation running into the rock that forms a huge court (as much as 300 meters long and 60 meters wide). At the back of the court a series of door-like openings creates the impression of a pillared facade. This gave the tombs the name *saff*-tombs (from *saff*, "row" in Arabic). The fairly modest burial chamber and other rooms are cut in the rock behind the facade, and a mud brick valley temple completes the complex. Little of the decoration of the tombs is preserved.

Three *saff*-tombs are known:
Inyotef I (Horus Sehertawy): Saff el-Dawaba
Inyotef II (Horus Wahʿankh): Saff el-Kisasiya
Inyotef III (Horus Nakhtnebtepnufer): Saff el-Baqar.

Draʿ Abu el-Nagaʿ

Theban rulers of the 17th Dynasty and their families were buried in modest tombs at Draʿ Abu el-Nagaʿ, between el-Tarif and Deir el-Bahri. The relative position of these tombs and their ownership are known from a papyrus recording an inspection of them in about 1080 BCE (the Abbott Papyrus). A number of inscribed objects, including the so-called *rishi* coffins, decorated weapons, and jewelry, were found during excavations conducted by A. Mariette before 1860. The architecture of the tombs, which may have had small mud brick pyramids, is little known.

The Valley of the Kings ("Wadi el-Muluk")

After the defeat of the Hyksos, the Theban rulers of the 18th Dynasty began to build themselves tombs in a style befitting kings of all Egypt. The tomb of Amenhotep I was probably at Draʿ Abu el-Nagaʿ. The esteem in which that king was held by the community of specialized workmen who constructed royal tombs suggests that his was the earliest tomb of the new type. Thutmose I was the first to have his tomb cut in the cliffs of a desolate wadi behind Deir el-Bahri, now known as the Valley of the Kings. The area is dominated by the peak of el-Qurn ("the Horn"), and the wadi consists of two main branches, the East Valley, with most of the tombs, and the West Valley, with the tombs of Amenhotep III and Aya. The total number of tombs is 62 (tomb KV 62 is that of Tutʿankhamun, discovered last), but some are not royal tombs, while the ownership of others is still disputed. The tombs were separated from the corresponding mortuary temples, which were built at the

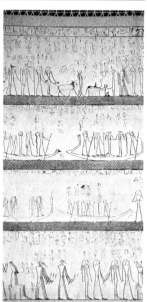

edge of the cultivation. The motivation for separating temple and tomb was not just security: there were also religious and architectural reasons.

The plan of the royal tombs of the 18th to 20th Dynasties (the last is the tomb of Ramesses XI) in the Valley of the Kings consists of a long inclined rock-cut corridor with one or more halls (sometimes pillared), terminating in the burial chamber. In the earlier tombs the corridor turns right or left, usually at a right angle, after some distance, but from the end of the 18th Dynasty it was straight. Its length could be considerable: Haremhab's is 105 meters long, Siptah's 88 meters and Ramesses VI's 83 meters. The decoration of the tombs is almost exclusively religious. There are numerous scenes of the king in the presence of gods, but the most striking elements are the texts and accompanying illustrations of various religious compositions ("books"), such as the Book of *Amduat* ("that which is in the netherworld"), of Gates, of Caverns, the Litany of Reʿ, and others. Early examples of these texts were made in such a way as to create the impression of huge funerary papyri unrolled on the tomb walls. From the end of the 18th Dynasty the decoration was carved in relief.

It is not easy to imagine the original wealth and beauty of the contents of these royal sepulchers. The only one which has been found largely intact and which provides a tantalizing glimpse of what is lost, that of Tutʿankhamun, may well not be typical.

The Valley of the Kings may still have some surprises left. In 1989, a remarkable discovery was made when the entrance to the long-lost tomb KV 5 was rediscovered by an American expedition led by Kent R. Weeks. The tomb, which had been plundered in antiquity, proved to be an enormous communal family burial of the sons of Ramesses II.

The workmen's village at Deir el-Medina
The everyday life of the community of workmen ("Servants in the Place of Truth") employed in the

construction of royal tombs in the Valley of the Kings can be reconstructed in considerable detail from ostraca, papyri, and other evidence. The ruins of the walled settlement (some 70 houses), in which workmen and their families lived from the reign of Thutmose I, can be seen in a small wadi behind the hill of Qurnet Muraʿi, at Deir el-Medina; the visible remains are mainly of the Ramessid Period. The workmen's own tombs and the chapels of their local gods are nearby.

The "gang" of workmen, numbering some 60 men or more, was divided into two "sides," each with a foreman, his deputy, and one or more scribes. Their superior was the vizier, who occasionally came, or sent one of the royal "butlers," to visit the site and inspect the progress of work. The workmen's wages were paid in goods, mainly grain, received at the end of each month. Other commodities, such as fish and vegetables, and occasionally meat, wine, salt etc., were also supplied. It is symptomatic of the 20th Dynasty that in that period the rations were often overdue, and on several occasions the workmen resorted to demonstrations. The earliest recorded "industrial action" took place in the 29th year of Ramesses III. The workmen normally stayed at the site of the tomb in the Valley of the Kings during the working "week" of 10 days, returning to the village for rest days or for religious festivals which were also holidays.

Valley of the Kings.
Above left Tomb of Haremhab (KV 57): the king offers jars of wine to the hawk-headed Harsiese, "great god, king of the gods, lord of heaven," and stands in adoration before Hathor, "foremost in Thebes, lady of all gods, mistress of heaven" (painted relief on east wall of the room preceding the sarcophagus chamber).

Above Tomb of Thutmose III (KV 34): scenes and texts of the 3rd "hour" (division) of the Book of *Amduat* (wall painting in the oval-shaped sarcophagus chamber).

Left Workmen's village at Deir el-Medina.

Tut'ankhamun:
A Story not yet Fully Told

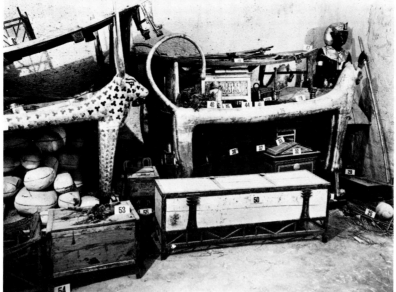

"At last have made wonderful discovery in Valley; a magnificent tomb with seals intact; re-covered same for your arrival; congratulations" (Cable sent by Carter to Lord Carnarvon on the morning of 6 November 1922).

The tomb of Tut'ankhamun (KV 62 in the Valley of the Kings) was discovered in 1922 by the English Egyptologist Howard Carter, whose work was financed by the Earl of Carnarvon. It is the only royal tomb of the New Kingdom found largely intact, and will probably stay unique in this respect forever. Although it is the most widely publicized discovery made in Egypt in the 20th century, and despite all the public interest generated by the traveling exhibitions all over the world, the majority of Tut'ankhamun's treasures have not yet been evaluated in detail by Egyptologists, so that this exceptional find has not yet made its full contribution to our knowledge of ancient Egypt. Most of the material is kept in the Egyptian Museum in Cairo; the detailed notes taken by Carter and his collaborators during the years of painstaking clearing of the tomb are in the Archive of the Griffith Institute in Oxford.

Some of the objects found in the tomb are:

Connected with the mummy
four wooden shrines
quartzite sarcophagus
outer and middle wooden coffins
inner solid gold coffin
gold mask and trappings
gold diadem
gold dagger
canopic canopy
canopic chest

Funerary equipment
statuettes of the king
dismantled chariots
couches and beds
headrests
throne of gilded wood (*right*)
chairs and stools
boxes
vases and lamps
bows, bow cases, and shields
sticks, whips, and scepters
garments
writing palettes
gaming boards
jewelry
fans
musical instruments
model boats
shrines of wood and gold
statuettes of gods
shawabtis

(Carter's documentation of the tomb of Tut'ankhamun can be found on: www.ashmol.ox.ac.uk/Griffith.html)

Far left Tomb of the Vizier
Ra'mose at Sheikh 'Abd el-Qurna
(TT 55), of the early part of the
reign of Amenhotep IV. Relief.

Left Coffin base-board of Soter,
early 2nd century CE, with a
representation of the goddess
Nut surrounded by signs of the

zodiac. From a communal tomb at
Sheikh 'Abd el-Qurna. London,
British Museum.

Below Tomb of the God's Father
Amenemone at Qurnet Mura'i
(TT 277), of the early 19th
Dynasty: episode from the
funeral of the deceased. Painting.

Nonroyal tombs

The larger Theban tombs are concentrated in several areas of the west bank. Starting from the river north, these are: Dra' Abu el-Naga', Deir el-Bahri, el-Khokha, 'Asasif, Sheikh 'Abd el-Qurna, Deir el-Medina, and Qurnet Mura'i. When the list of tombs was revised in 1960, altogether 409 tombs received numbers recognized by the Egyptian Antiquities Service (now the Supreme Council of Antiquities), but others have been added since and close to fifty tombs were seen in the past but are now lost or destroyed. For each decorated tomb there were hundreds, if not thousands, of simple graves. The large tombs range from the Early Dynastic Period to the Greco-Roman Period, but the majority are of the New Kingdom. There are further tombs in the Valley of the Queens, south of Deir el-Medina, which have their own numbering, and in smaller valleys nearby, including the "Tomb of Three Princesses" of the reign of Thutmose III in Wadi Qubbanet el-Qirud ("Valley of the Tombs of the Monkeys") with a treasure of gold and silver vessels, now in the Metropolitan Museum in New York.

Many of the lesser tombs and burials at el-Tarif and Dra' Abu el-Naga' are contemporary with the royal tombs of the 11th and 17th Dynasties, but the latter area in particular continued to be used well into the Late Period. An important discovery of a cemetery of small New-Kingdom tombs with free-standing chapels was made at Dra' Abu el-Naga' in 1991 by a German team led by D. Polz. The cemeteries at 'Asasif and el-Khokha around the causeways leading to the temples of the 11th and 18th Dynasties at Deir el-Bahri, and at Deir el-Bahri itself, were used for smaller tombs throughout the rest of Pharaonic history.

In 1891 E. Grébaut and G. Daressy found a large cache of coffins of priests of Amun of the 3rd Intermediate Period at Deir el-Bahri. It was the second find of this type; in 1858 Mariette had found a cache of coffins of priests of Montu. The most spectacular of these secret hideaways was that found in tomb TT 320, in the first of the wadis south of Deir el-Bahri, in 1881. This contained coffins and mummies of the most renowned Egyptian kings of the 17th to 20th Dynasties, assembled there for security during the 21st Dynasty.

Below Tomb of Amenemone at Qurnet Mura'i (TT 277), of the early 19th Dynasty: two anthropoid coffins of the deceased set up outside the tomb entrance during the funeral. Painting.

Right Tomb of the Servant in the Place of Truth Pashed at Deir el-Medina (TT 3), of the reign of Sety I: the painted burial chamber.

As the name suggests, the Valley of the Queens ("Biban el-Harim") contains tombs of queens and other members of the royal family, particularly Ramessid princes. Although on a much smaller scale, the design of these tombs is reminiscent of that of royal tombs because it consists of a complex burial chamber without a chapel.

Most of the larger Theban tombs were rock-cut, and relatively few had any free-standing superstructure. Their plans vary greatly; the following are only very general characteristics.

Late Old Kingdom. One or two rooms of an irregular shape, sometimes with pillars. Sloping shafts lead to one or more burial chambers.

Middle Kingdom. The rear wall of an open forecourt forms the facade. A long corridor is followed by a chapel connected with the burial chamber by a sloping passage.

New Kingdom. An open forecourt, often with stelae, precedes the facade, which has a row of pottery "funerary cones" above the doorway. A transverse ("broad") hall, sometimes with stelae on its end walls, is followed by a "long" hall on the central axis. The sanctuary has a statue niche or a false door. All inner rooms can have pillars. The shaft of the burial chamber is usually cut in the forecourt.

Ramessid tombs at Deir el-Medina combine a completely, or partly, free-standing superstructure (pylon, open court, portico, and vaulted chapel with statue niche and mud brick pyramid above) with rock-cut chambers approached by a shaft.

Late Period. Some of these tombs are enormous and their plans very complex. Mud brick pylons and open sunk courts precede a series of underground rooms, usually with pillars, leading to the burial chamber.

Painting is the usual method of decoration of Theban tombs, but relief is not uncommon. The subject matter includes both scenes of everyday life and religious themes, which predominate from the Ramessid Period on.

John Gardner Wilkinson at Thebes

Modern Egyptologists stand on the shoulders of the scholars who, often under extraordinarily hard conditions, pioneered the discipline in the first half of the nineteenth century. It was a period during which Egyptology was assembling its basic corpus of material for study, a time of intensive recording and copying of Egyptian inscriptions, reliefs and paintings. Some of the works published at that time remain indispensable for a good Egyptological library even now, more than 150 years later.

John Gardner Wilkinson came to Egypt as a young man of 24 in 1821, a year before Jean François Champollion rediscovered the principles of the Egyptian script. For the next 12 years he stayed there continuously, and there was hardly an ancient Egyptian site which the skillful and compulsive copyist did not visit and record in his notebooks. His interest was almost an obsession: no inscription, however small or incomplete, was too insignificant for him. He was one of the first who mastered the conventions of Egyptian representation to such an extent that he was able to produce completely faithful copies. Thanks to this, his papers, now kept in the Bodleian Library in Oxford, contain a wealth of information on the most varied aspects of ancient Egypt. Much of this archive is still awaiting evaluation by Egyptologists. Wilkinson published the theoretical results of his work in a number of books, but not all of his copies; those which appeared in books were often badly disfigured by inadequate reproduction. His most important work was entitled *Manners and Customs of the Ancient Egyptians including their private life, government, laws, arts, manufactures, religion, agriculture, and early history, derived from a comparison of the paintings, sculptures, and monuments still existing, with the accounts of ancient authors.* It was published in three volumes in 1837, and remained the best general treat-

ment of ancient Egypt for almost 50 years. It brought to its author a knighthood in 1839.

Many a difficult problem has been solved by consulting Wilkinson's copies, because they show monuments as they were between 1821 and 1856 (the date of his last visit to Egypt). His work in Theban nonroyal tombs is a case in point: many of the scenes copied by Wilkinson have since been damaged or even completely destroyed, while others, including entire tombs, still await publication or are now inaccessible.

Top Craftsmen at work; relief from Theban Tomb 36 of the chief Steward of the Divine Adoratrice, Ibi, of the reign of Psammetichus I (the scene partly imitates a relief of the 6th Dynasty at Deir el-Gabrawi). The following crafts are represented (from left): 1st register from top, leather workers making sandals, makers of stone vessels, shawabtis and canopic jars, metal workers; 2nd register, chariot makers, sculptors, joiners, and makers of stone vessels; 3rd register, joiners, sculptors, jewelers; 4th register, metal workers, men carrying a wooden plank, boat builders; 5th register, boat builders and scribes. Now badly damaged.

Center left Two bearded men plucking geese: painting in Theban Tomb 88 of the Standard-Bearer of the Lord of the Two Lands, Pehsukher Tjenenu, dated to Amenhotep II. The scene takes place in a hut, and the birds already dealt with are hung from its rafters. There are three other slaughtered geese on the ground. Now damaged, the figure of the man on the left is completely lost.

Bottom left Two scribes and an overseer, from a scene of the counting of cattle: painting in Theban Tomb 76 of the Fan-Bearer on the Right of the King, Tjenuna, of the reign of Thutmose IV. The men are squatting in the typical posture of Egyptian scribes, with their feet tucked under their thighs, holding an unrolled papyrus (writing tables were not used in ancient Egypt). Containers for papyri are placed nearby. Now badly damaged.

Center right The Vizier Paser and his wife, followed by relatives, assist at the purification of offerings by censing and libation: relief in Theban Tomb 106 of Paser, Vizier of Sety I and Ramesses II. The tomb is only now being prepared for publication and this scene is almost completely destroyed.

Bottom right A Nubian dancing-girl accompanied by female and male musicians playing the lyre, double flute, and harp: painting in Theban Tomb 113 of the Priest, Keeper of Secrets of the Domain of Amun, Keynebu, dated to the reign of Ramesses VIII. This Nubian dance, perhaps called *keskes*, is shown on several other monuments. Apart from the Nubian girl, the participants are Keynebu's sons and daughters; this may indicate the popularity of the dance in the Ramessid Period. Now completely destroyed.

NORTHERN UPPER EGYPT

Northern Upper Egypt extends between Thebes and Asyut. It was the heart of ancient Egypt, the cradle and forge of her earliest dynasties, the hinterland which remained Egyptian in times of crisis and from which, with Thebes at the head, movements for new political unity were launched. Economically, control of access to the gold and minerals of the eastern desert was always of paramount importance, while politically Thebes in the south dictated the course of events from the 11th Dynasty.

Naqada, Qift, and Abydos dominated the scene in the Predynastic and Early Dynastic Periods, with Dendara gaining in importance during the Old Kingdom. Abydos became something of a religious center for the whole country in the Middle Kingdom. The rise of Thebes stifled its northerly neighbors in the New Kingdom, though Abydos held its position, and Qift continued to be favored by royal building activities. The temple of Dendara is easily the most impressive structure of late antiquity in the area.

Left The name of this basalt statuette in the Ashmolean Museum in Oxford, "MacGregor man," derives from the Revd. William MacGregor, from whom it was acquired at Sotheby's in 1922. The well-known collector had bought it, together with a group of ivory figurines, from a dealer. All the objects were claimed to have been found at Naqada, a site which produced large numbers of Predynastic (probably Naqada III) and Early Dynastic artefacts. Height: 39 cm.

Far left Typical landscape of limestone cliffs west of the Nile near Nagʿ Hammadi, with a very narrow flat strip by the river. A geologist can read the history of the rock formations and the ice ages from the layering and terracing of the cliffs.

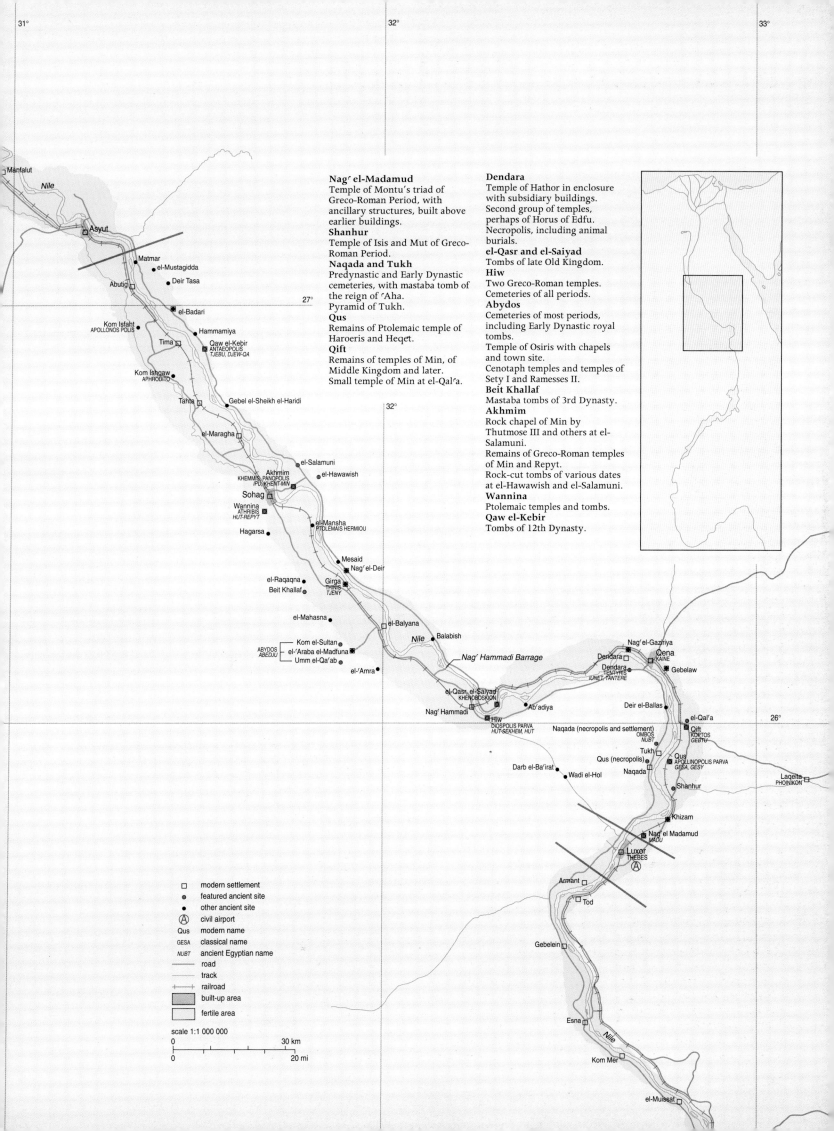

Nag' el-Madamud
Temple of Montu's triad of Greco-Roman Period, with ancillary structures, built above earlier buildings.
Shanhur
Temple of Isis and Mut of Greco-Roman Period.
Naqada and Tukh
Predynastic and Early Dynastic cemeteries, with mastaba tomb of the reign of 'Aha.
Pyramid of Tukh.
Qus
Remains of Ptolemaic temple of Haroeris and Heqet.
Qift
Remains of temples of Min, of Middle Kingdom and later.
Small temple of Min at el-Qal'a.

Dendara
Temple of Hathor in enclosure with subsidiary buildings.
Second group of temples, perhaps of Horus of Edfu.
Necropolis, including animal burials.
el-Qasr and el-Saiyad
Tombs of late Old Kingdom.
Hiw
Two Greco-Roman temples.
Cemeteries of all periods.
Abydos
Cemeteries of most periods, including Early Dynastic royal tombs.
Temple of Osiris with chapels and town site.
Cenotaph temples and temples of Sety I and Ramesses II.
Beit Khallaf
Mastaba tombs of 3rd Dynasty.
Akhmim
Rock chapel of Min by Thutmose III and others at el-Salamuni.
Remains of Greco-Roman temples of Min and Repyt.
Rock-cut tombs of various dates at el-Hawawish and el-Salamuni.
Wannina
Ptolemaic temples and tombs.
Qaw el-Kebir
Tombs of 12th Dynasty.

31° 32° 33°

Manfalut
Nile
Asyut
Matmar
el-Mustagidda
Abutig
Deir Tasa
el-Badari
Kom Isfaht
APOLLONOS POLIS
Hammamiya
Tima
Qaw el-Kebir
ANTAEOPOLIS
TJEBU, DJEW-QA
Kom Ishgaw
APHRODITO
Tahta
Gebel el-Sheikh el-Haridi
el-Maragha
el-Salamuni
Akhmim
KHEMMIS, PANOPOLIS
IPU, KHENT-MIN
el-Hawawish
Sohag
Wannina
ATHRIBIS
HUT-REPYT
el-Mansha
PTOLEMAIS HERMIOU
Hagarsa
Mesaid
Nag' el-Deir
el-Raqaqna
Girga
THINIS
TJENY
Beit Khallaf
el-Mahasna
el-Balyana
Nile
Balabish
Kom el-Sultan
el-'Araba el-Madfuna
ABYDOS
ABEDJU
Umm el-Qa'ab
el-'Amra
Nag' Hammadi Barrage
Nag' el-Gazriya
Dendara
Qena
KAINE
Gebelaw
Dendara
TENTYRIS
IUNET, TANTERE
Deir el-Ballas
el-Qasr, el-Saiyad
KHENOBOSKION
Ab'adiya
el-Qal'a
Nag' Hammadi
Hiw
DIOSPOLIS PARVA
HUT-SEKHEM, HUT
Naqada (necropolis and settlement)
OMBOS
NUBT
Qift
KORTOS
GEBTU
Darb el-Ba'irat
Wadi el-Hol
Tukh
Qus (necropolis)
Qus
APOLLINOPOLIS PARVA
GESA, GESY
Naqada
Laqeita
PHOINIKON
Shanhur
Khizam
Nag' el Madamud
MADU
Luxor
THEBES
Armant
Tod
Gebelein
Esna
Nile
Kom Mer
el-Muissat

27° 32° 26°

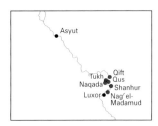

Nagꜥ el-Madamud

Ancient Egyptian *Madu* was an important place of worship of the falcon-headed god Montu. The early temple, now destroyed, dated to the Middle Kingdom (Senwosret III), but stood on the site of a shrine of the Old Kingdom or the 1st Intermediate Period. Kings of the late Middle Kingdom and the 2nd Intermediate Period continued to build there and there are also scattered monuments of the New Kingdom and the Late Period.

The temple of Montu, Raꜥttawy, and Harpokrates, which is still partly standing, is of the Greco-Roman Period. A quay and remains of an avenue of sphinxes precede a gate in the mud brick enclosure wall of Tiberius. The facade of the temple is formed by three kiosks of Ptolemy XII Auletes, and from there one proceeds through the court of Antoninus Pius. From the outer hypostyle hall of Ptolemy VIII Euergetes II the temple is conventional in plan. Immediately behind is a second temple, dedicated to the sacred bull of Montu. The exterior walls of the temples were decorated by Domitian and Trajan.

There was a sacred lake south of the temple of Montu, and an early Ptolemaic temple (Ptolemy II Philadelphus, III Euergetes I, and IV Philopator) once stood in the southwest corner of the enclosure.

Shanhur

Shanhur is the site of a temple of Isis and Mut built during the Greco-Roman Period. The temple contains scenes showing Emperors Augustus and Tiberius before various Egyptian deities and a remarkable astronomical ceiling.

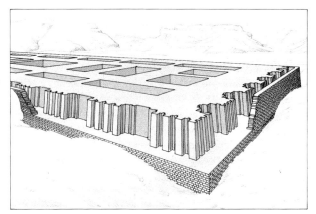

Naqada and Tukh

Archaeologists often use the names of important sites as descriptive terms for whole archaeological cultures. Naqada I–III are Predynastic cultures named after the cemeteries excavated by W. M. Flinders Petrie in 1895. In this case the term is something of a misnomer: although Naqada is the largest modern settlement in the area, the cemeteries are about 7 kilometers north of it, between Tukh and el-Ballas.

About 3 kilometers northwest of the village of Naqada, on the edge of the desert, an Early Dynastic mastaba tomb was found by J. de Morgan in 1897. It was a large (54 by 27 meters) mud brick structure with a "palace facade" on all sides. The tomb contained ivory tablets, vase fragments, and clay sealings bearing the names of King ꜥAha as well as Neithotep, perhaps his wife and subsequently a queen regnant. It was most probably built for a local administrator of the beginning of the 1st Dynasty. The nearby cemeteries have also produced a number of stelae of the end of the Old Kingdom and the 1st Intermediate Period. The necropolis belonged to the town of Qus, on the east bank of the Nile.

The size of the cemeteries and settlement sites excavated by Petrie ("Naqada") shows that ancient *Nubt* (Greek Ombos), usually connected with mod-

Above Red granite colossal head of a Roman emperor, probably Caracalla, found at the 2nd pylon of the Northern Temple of Min and Isis at Qift. Height: 51 cm. Philadelphia (PA), University of Pennsylvania Museum.

Below Qus at the time of Napoleon's expedition to Egypt: the west pylon of the temple of Haroeris and Heqet and the modern town.

ern Tukh, some 4 kilometers to the southeast, must have been a very important town in the later Predynastic Period. The name probably derives from ancient Egyptian *nub*, "gold," on account of the proximity of gold mines in the eastern desert accessible from the Wadi Hammamat, and this could also explain the town's rise to prominence. The local god was Seth (*Nubty*, "The Ombite"), later regarded as the Upper Egyptian god *par excellence*. A New Kingdom temple dedicated to him has been located to which various kings of the 18th Dynasty (Thutmose I and III, Amenhotep II) and several Ramessids contributed.

The small step pyramid of Ombos (or Tukh or Naqada) is built of undressed stone and probably dates to the end of the 3rd Dynasty. It is one of a series of such monuments which provided focus points for the cult of the king in the provinces.

Qus

To judge by its cemeteries, Qus, northwest of Naqada, ancient Egyptian *Gesa* or *Gesy* (Apollinopolis Parva of the Greco-Roman Period), on the opposite bank of the Nile, must have been an

important town in the early part of Egyptian history. This was probably because at that time it served as the point of departure for expeditions to Wadi Hammamat quarries and the Red Sea. Nowadays only two pylons of the Ptolemaic temple of Haroeris and Heqet remain.

Qift

The town of *Gebtu* (Coptic *Kebto* or *Keft*, Greek Koptos [not connected with the word "Coptic"]), modern Qift, was the capital of the 5th Upper Egyptian nome. The town's prominence was due to its geographical position: it was here (or at Qus, a little to the south) that trading expeditions heading for the Red Sea coast and many mining expeditions into the eastern desert left the Nile valley. *Gebtu* soon became the most important religious center of the area, and its local god Min was also regarded as the god of the desert region to the east. Isis and Horus were the deities connected with Qift during the Greco-Roman Period; one of the reasons for this was a reinterpretation of the two falcons of the nome standard as Horus and Min. As one would expect, monuments discovered at Qift span the whole of Egyptian history, though only temple structures of the Late and Greco-Roman Periods were found *in situ*.

Remains of three temple groups surrounded by an enclosure wall were located during the excavations of W. M. Flinders Petrie (1893–94) and Raymond Weill and Adolphe Joseph Reinach (1910–11).

The largely undecorated Northern Temple of Min and Isis, which still stands, was the work of an official called Sennuu on behalf of Ptolemy II Philadelphus, with some later additions of Ptolemy IV Philopator, Caligula, and Nero (particularly the three pylons). The temple stands on the site of earlier structures of Amenemhet I, Senwosret I, and Thutmose III, the last ruler being attested by a large number of foundation deposits. Remains of a chapel of Osiris erected by Amasis were found south of the 3rd pylon of the Northern Temple.

The site of the Middle Temple also had a long history: blocks of Senwosret I and a gate of Thutmose III with additions made by an Osorkon (probably II) were found, and also a set of stelae ("Koptos Decrees"), dating to the 6th and 7th Dynasties, with copies of royal decrees concerning the temple and its personnel. The Middle Temple itself was built by Ptolemy II Philadelphus, with minor additions by Caligula, Claudius and Trajan.

Gates of Nectanebo II, Caligula and Claudius, and a chapel of Cleopatra VII Philopator and Ptolemy XV Caesarion were found at the site of the Southern Temple.

Claudius built a small temple (approximately 24 by 16 meters) dedicated to Min, Isis and Horus northeast of Qift, at el-Qalʿa.

Below Dendara: central area of
the main temple enclosure.

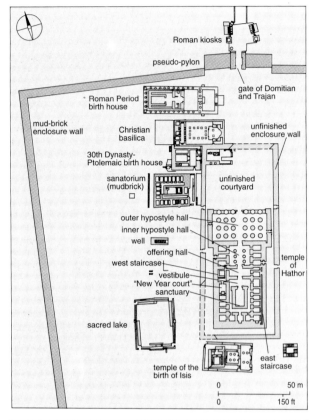

Above Temple of Hathor from
the southwest, with reliefs of
Ptolemy XV Caesarion and
Cleopatra VII Philopator. The
mutilated colossal sistrum
originally had a wooden canopy.
The characteristic lion gargoyles
remove rain water from the roof.

Left Gateway of the Roman
Period east of the main
enclosure. This and a few
remaining wall bases formed
part of a complex perhaps
dedicated to Horus of Edfu.

Dendara

Dendara, ancient Egyptian *Iunet* or *Tantere*, Greek
Tentyris, was the capital of the 6th nome of Upper
Egypt and a town of some importance; since antiquity the center of population in the area has moved
to Qena on the east bank. The temple complex now
stands isolated on the desert edge.

The necropolis of Dendara included tombs of the
Early Dynastic Period, but the most important phase
that has been identified was the end of the Old Kingdom and the 1st Intermediate Period. The provinces
were virtually autonomous at that time and, although Dendara was not a leading political force in
Upper Egypt, its notables built a number of mastabas
of some size, only one of which has any decoration
apart from stelae and false doors. On the west of the
site are brick-vaulted catacombs of Late Period animal burials, primarily of birds and dogs, while cow
burials have been found at various points in the
necropolis – one of Hathor's forms being as a cow.

A small chapel of Nebhepetre Mentuhotep was
recovered from the site and has been reerected in the
Cairo Museum. The building, which has secondary
inscriptions of Merneptah, was as much for the cult
of the king as for the goddess, and was probably
ancillary to the lost main temple of its time.

The main temple complex is oriented, as usual,
toward the Nile, which here flows east–west, so that
the temple faces north, although this was symboli-

cally "east." In this description the points of the com-
pass are used.

The monumental gateway of Domitian and Trajan
is set in the massive mud-brick enclosure wall, and
leads to an open area with the Roman Period birth
house on the west. This is the latest preserved temple of its type; it was the ritual location where Hathor
gave birth to the young Ihy or Harsomtus, two alternative youthful deities who stand for the youthful
phase of creator gods in general. The temple was built
when the earlier structure, begun by Nectanebo I
and decorated in the Ptolemaic Period, was cut
through by the foundations of the unfinished first
court of the main temple of Hathor. Both birth houses
are now accessible; they differ considerably in plan
and decoration. South of the earlier birth house is a
mud-brick "sanatorium," where visitors could
receive the sacred waters or "incubate" – spend the
night in the hope of having a healing dream of the
goddess.

The main temple is the grandest and most elaborately decorated of its period; the massive foundations probably contain many blocks from the earlier
structure it replaced. Fragments of earlier periods
have been found on the site, but no buildings; Pepy
I and Thutmose III in particular were recalled in the
temple inscriptions.

The rear part of the temple was built first, probably in the early 1st century BCE. The earliest king
named is Ptolemy XII Auletes, but mostly the cartouches are blank, probably because of dynastic
struggles in the mid 1st century. The outer hypostyle
hall was decorated from Augustus to Nero; on the

cornice thickness above the entrance is a dedicatory inscription in Greek of 34–35 CE.

The temple follows the classic plan. The columns of the two hypostyle halls and the "new year court" have capitals in the form of a sistrum, a musical instrument sacred to Hathor. Their use evokes the image of Hathor as a cow appearing between the plants in the marsh of creation. At the center of the south outside wall was a relief of a sistrum that was gilded, both to show its importance and to evoke Hathor, the "gold of the gods." All sistrum figures were severely mutilated in the early Christian Period.

Within the temple the most distinctive parts are the decorated "crypts." These are suites of rooms on three stories, set in the thickness of the outside wall; unlike other crypts, those at Dendara are decorated in relief. Their main use was for keeping cult equipment, archives, and magical emblems for the temple's protection. Their decoration conforms to the temple's axis; the most important reliefs, among which sistra are prominent, were on the axis itself. Also within the wall thickness are the staircases, which lead up to and return from the roof. On the roof is a kiosk, in which the ritual of the goddess's union with the sun disk was performed. There is also a pair of shrines of Osiris, from one of which came the famous Dendara zodiac, now in the Louvre in Paris. Dendara was one of Osiris' many tombs, and the shrines, which have no link with Hathor, were used to celebrate his resurrection. His death may have been reenacted in the sacred lake to the west of the temple.

Immediately south of the Hathor temple is the temple of Isis, which used foundation blocks from a destroyed Ptolemaic building and was decorated under Augustus. The east gateway, also Roman in date, leads to this temple, which is almost unique in having a dual orientation with the outer rooms facing east and the inner ones north toward the temple of Hathor. The central high relief in the sanctuary, which showed Isis giving birth, has been mutilated.

East of the temple lay part of the town, which the temple texts mention as having a temple of Horus of Edfu in its midst. This may be the same as some remains of the Roman Period about 500 meters from the main enclosure.

The triads of deities worshiped at Edfu and at Dendara were similar, consisting of Horus, Hathor (or Isis), and Ihy or Harsomtus. Hathor of Dendara and Horus of Edfu met at a sacred "marriage" ceremony, when she made a progress to the south.

el-Qasr and el-Saiyad

The rock-cut tombs at Gebel el-Tarif, near the modern villages of el-Qasr, el-Saiyad, and Hamra Dom, northeast of Hiw, on the right bank of the Nile in the 7th Upper Egyptian nome, date to the end of the Old Kingdom. Two of them, of the "Great Overlords of the Nome" Idu Seneni and Tjauti, from the reign of Pepy II, deserve special attention because of their preserved relief decoration.

Hiw

Hiw was a major settlement in Predynastic times. During the reign of Senwosret I a royal estate named "Kheperkareʿ (Senwosret I) the Justified is Mighty" was founded on the west bank of the Nile in the 7th Upper Egyptian nome. The locality soon became more important than the original nome capital, and its long-winded name started being abbreviated to *Hut-sekhem* or *Hut. Hut-sekhem* was reinterpreted as "The Mansion of the Sistrum," alluding to the local goddess Bat, who was worshiped as a sistrum-shaped object with human head and bovine ears and horns, and was assimilated to Hathor of the neighboring Dendara during the New Kingdom. In the Greco-Roman Period Hiw was known as Diospolis Mikra or Diospolis Parva. The Coptic version of the name, *Ho* (or *Hou*), led to the name by which the place is now known.

Temples of the Dynastic Period at Hiw are mentioned in such documents as Papyrus Harris I, which records a donation in the reign of Ramesses III, but none has been identified on site. The two principal surviving structures date to the Greco-Roman Period: one was probably built by Ptolemy VI Philometor, the other by Nerva and Hadrian. In 1990 an inscribed Ptolemaic chapel to a local deified deceased woman was identified in the town of Hiw still standing and in use as a store for animal fodder.

About 1·5 kilometers south of the temples was the

now destroyed Ptolemaic tomb of a certain Harsiese Dionysius. Fortunately, early Egyptologists recorded its details in the first half of the 19th century.

East of the town are extensive cemeteries of all periods, and burials of sacred animals (dogs, ibises, and falcons) of the Greco-Roman Period.

Abydos

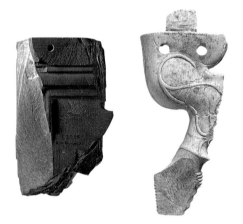

Ancient *Abedju* (Greek Abydos, Coptic *Ebot* or *Abot*) was the most important burial ground in Egypt at the beginning of the Dynastic Period and its cemeteries contain graves going back to Predynastic Naqada I times. The political role of the town of Abydos and its relationship with the nome capital *Tjeny* (Greek Thinis; perhaps modern Girga) are less clear.

The temple of the local necropolis god Khentamentiu ("Foremost of the Westerners": ruler of the dead) was an important early religious center. During the 5th and 6th Dynasties the god became identified with the originally Lower Egyptian Osiris, and in the Middle Kingdom Abydos was for officials the chief religious center of Egypt. The annual ritual that included a ritual enactment of the god's death and resurrection attracted pilgrims from all over Egypt. Many wished to share in the ceremonies in the next life, as a token of sharing in Osiris' resurrection, and they built small brick cenotaphs and set up stelae in the area between the temple of Osiris and the cemeteries. The cemeteries themselves, which extend north and west from Kom el-Sultan, are far larger than other local burial grounds; cemeteries of other periods run south toward the temple of Sety I. In the Late Period a distinctive type of nonroyal tomb appeared with a brick pyramid and stone pyramidion (capstone).

Late and Greco-Roman Period burials of dogs or jackals, ibises, and falcons have been found at Abydos.

The early funerary areas
From the late Naqada I period a cemetery developed about 2 kilometers from the cultivation, running

Left Fragments of furniture from the Early Dynastic royal tombs at Abydos. Left: piece of schist of unknown use, carved with extraordinary accuracy and skill. Right: leg of a bed, in the form of a bull's hind leg, with tenon for insertion in the frame and holes for leather lashings; ivory. Oxford, Ashmolean Museum.

Bottom left Baying hippopotamus made of pottery, from an early Naqada II grave at Hiw. Animal sculpture of the Predynastic and Early Dynastic Periods is often superior in quality to human figures of the time. Oxford, Ashmolean Museum.

Below Clapper in the form of a forearm (a common musical instrument), made of bone and inscribed for the Female Servant of the Goddess Heqet, Sithathor. 2nd Intermediate Period. From Hiw. London, British Museum.

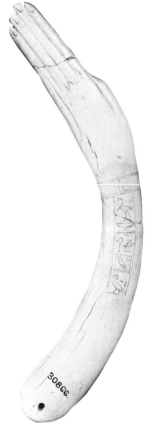

Temple of Sety I, relief in the king's chapel showing the Iunmutef priest or deity before the mummified king, who is seated on a throne on top of the hieroglyph for "festival." The text is an elaborate version of a censing formula.

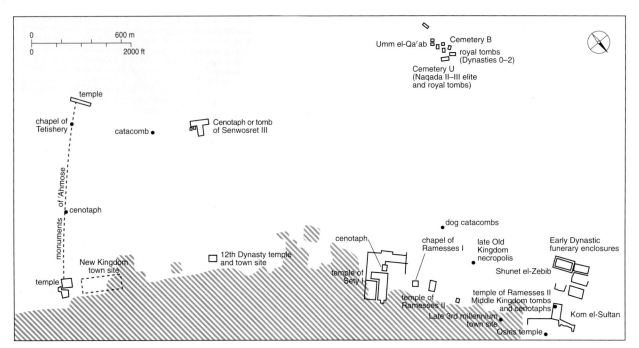

Left Map of the area with ancient remains, stretching along the edge of the cultivation for some 5 kilometers. The ancient city, which may have extended onto the floodplain, was concentrated at the northern end, with royal and private funerary monuments toward the south.

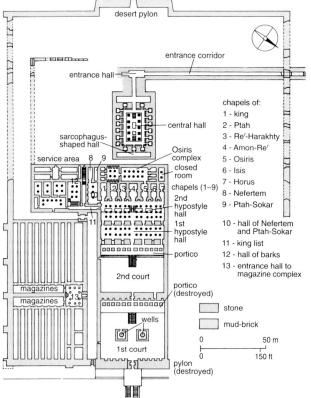

Far left Temple of Ramesses II from northwest. Most of the structure is preserved up to about 3 meters. In the foreground is the inner suite of rooms with mortuary scenes; beyond are the two hypostyle halls, with square pillars instead of columns, and the portico. Outside the modern entrance was a further court with a side chapel, and a pylon.

Structural supports are in sandstone, which the Egyptians believed could span considerable widths, but the relief surfaces are in limestone; the two gateways are of gray granite. Similar composite techniques are found in the temple of Sety I.

Left Plan of the temple of Sety I at Abydos, together with the subterranean cenotaph behind, the mud brick enclosure wall, and the magazines north of the temple's outer part.

toward a prominent cleft in the desert escarpment. This developed into Cemetery U, a large elite burial ground of late Naqada II–III, and thence into Cemetery B and Umm el-Qaᶜab, the royal cemeteries of Dynasty 0 and the 1st Dynasty. Tomb U-j is the oldest known royal tomb, dating to perhaps 3200 BCE and containing the earliest writing so far found in Egypt.

The tomb complex of ᶜAha, perhaps the first king of the 1st Dynasty, in Cemetery B is on an altogether larger scale and contained evidence for the burial of sacrificed retainers, as well as the king's young lions. In Umm el-Qaᶜab were heavily plundered tombs for all the kings of the 1st Dynasty – that of Den being the largest and having the richest grave goods – and Peribsen and Khaᶜsekhemwy of the 2nd. They had hardly any surface structure, although they were marked with name stelae for the kings, for whom they were evidently a stage on an otherworldly journey rather than a dwelling for the hereafter.

Near the cultivation, west of the temple of Osiris, were large mudbrick enclosures for the funerary cult of the kings buried at Umm el-Qaᶜab; the earlier enclosures were surrounded by elite burials in small graves. Each enclosure may have been destroyed when the next was built. The only one now visible is the massive Shunet el-Zebib, which belonged to Khaᶜsekhemwy and is perhaps the largest mud brick building of its age in the world, retaining most of its original height at about 10 meters. Inside this enclosure are traces of buildings, including a structure with a sloping side that may

be a forerunner of pyramids. In front were buried a number of funerary boats relating either to all the enclosures or to the Shunet el-Zebib only. A Christian village to the north is built on the probable remnants of a 1st Dynasty enclosure.

The town and temple of Osiris

The ancient walled town is in the area called Kom el-Sultan, which is enclosed by massive mud-brick walls of the 30th Dynasty. Its most important feature must have been the temple, at first of Khentamentiu and from the 12th Dynasty of Osiris. The temple was built in brick, with only a few elements, such as door jambs and lintels, in stone, and is almost completely

Above Temple of Ramesses II, courtyard: fattened ox with drover, from a procession of festival offerings. The ox is identified as being from the estate of this temple. On the right is another drover and the head of an oryx.

Above right Temple of Ramesses II, 1st hypostyle hall, north wall. Personification of Dendara, from a series carrying food offerings and libations. The figure's fatness symbolizes abundance, and its blue flesh and green wig are part of a patterning scheme, also symbolic. The text identifies him with the king: "Ramesses has come, bringing food offerings" (the right band relates to the next figure). Above is part of a scene with priests carrying a divine bark in procession.

destroyed. The earliest objects found are of the beginning of the 1st Dynasty: a vase fragment of King ʿAha, and a number of small stone and faience figures of men, animals, and reptiles. Starting with Khufu of the 4th Dynasty (an ivory statuette, the only preserved likeness of him), most kings of the Old Kingdom down to Pepy II are attested from finds. In the Middle Kingdom Nebhepetreʿ Mentuhotep probably added a small shrine to the existing temple, and from then on many kings down to the 17th Dynasty dedicated objects. In the 18th Dynasty Amenhotep I, Thutmose III, and Amenhotep III did rebuilding work, and all the major Ramessids are represented, Ramesses II by a complete temple that was built over the Middle Kingdom cenotaphs, while for the Late Period Apries, Amasis, and Nectanebo I are prominent. The temple probably continued to function in the Greco-Roman Period.

Royal cenotaphs and temples

At Abydos South the oldest known monument is the small 3rd Dynasty pyramid of Sinki, which may have been a focus for a royal cult. Some Middle and early New Kingdom kings built cenotaphs — secondary mortuary complexes — a little further north; the earliest identifiable one is of Senwosret III. The other excavated buildings in this area are connected with ʿAhmose, including one he built for his grandmother Tetisheri; his own temple had many reliefs, including battle scenes with the oldest known representations of the horse in Egypt. Several 18th Dynasty temples are mentioned in texts but have not been located.

The large temple of Sety I has a very unusual L-shaped plan, but its internal arrangements are a variation of the norm. It has two largely destroyed pylons with courts and pillared porticoes, followed by two hypostyle halls and seven chapels side by side. From the south, the chapels were dedicated to: Sety I, Ptah,

Reʿ-Harakhty, Amon-Reʿ, Osiris, Isis, and Horus. The Osiris chapel leads into a transverse area devoted to the Osiris cult that includes two halls and two sets of three chapels for Osiris, Isis, and Horus; adjacent is a room with two pillars that was designed to be inaccessible. The temple's southern extension contains rooms for the cult of the Memphite gods Nefertem and Ptah-Sokar and a gallery with one of Egypt's few king lists, here serving the cult of the royal ancestors. The gallery leads southward to a set of storerooms and westward to a stairway opening onto the desert behind. In front of this extension is a mud brick area of magazines with a stone-lined central hall.

The reliefs of the reign of Sety I in the inner parts of the temple are exceptionally fine. The outer areas, including the first hypostyle hall, were completed by Ramesses II, often overlaying work of his father.

Behind the temple and on the same axis is the cenotaph of Sety I. Both in its plan and in its decoration (mainly executed by Merneptah) this resembles a royal tomb. It is approached from the north through a long, sloping corridor. The main rooms are a hall in the form of an island and another resembling a sarcophagus, with an astronomical ceiling. The massive granite architraves roofed only part of the island hall, the center remaining open. It recreated the waters of creation — the island being surrounded by groundwater — within their midst the solid primeval mound on which barley may have been germinated to symbolize Osiris' resurrection.

Ramesses II built himself a smaller temple northwest of his father's. This is noteworthy for the excellent color preservation on its reliefs, which may be seen in full sunlight; only the lower parts of the walls survive. The plan is comparable to that of the temple of Medinet Habu. Magnetometer survey of the unexcavated area behind the temple suggests that it too may have had a cenotaph attached.

Beit Khallaf

Five very large mud brick mastabas with clay sealings bearing the names of the 3rd Dynasty kings Netjerykhet (Djoser) and Zanakht were found near the village of Beit Khallaf, some 20 kilometers northwest of Abydos. The tombs were probably made for administrators of the Thinite area of the early 3rd Dynasty.

Akhmim

Akhmim (ancient Egyptian *Ipu* or *Khent-min*, Coptic *Khmin* or *Shmin*, hence Greek Khemmis and the modern name), on the east bank of the Nile, was once the flourishing center of the important 9th Upper Egyptian nome. Very little of its past glory remains nowadays: nothing is left of the town, the temples were almost completely dismantled and their material reused in the later Middle Ages, and the extensive cemeteries of ancient Akhmim have not yet been fully explored. However, the destroyed corner of a Greco-Roman period temple with colossal statues of Ramesses II and Queen Merytamun that had fallen across it were discovered in the northeast part of Akhmim in 1981.

Northeast of Akhmim, at el-Salamuni, is a rock chapel dedicated to the local god Min. The Greeks equated Min with Pan, also using the name Panopolis for the town. The chapel was created during the reign of Aya by the "First Priest of Min," Nakhtmin. The reliefs show Aya and his wife Teye before local gods; some 1,000 years later the "Chief Priest of Min" Harmaʿkheru added representations of his own king Ptolemy II Philadelphus, depicted in a similar fashion.

Left Lid of the outer anthropoid coffin of Espamai, a priest at Akhmim in the 26th or 27th Dynasty. The Pyramid Texts on the lid were compiled some 2,000 years earlier. Wood. Height: 2·10 m. Berlin, Ägyptisches Museum.

Below Colossal statue of Merytamun, a daughter and queen of Ramesses II, restored and re-erected at Akhmim. The sculpture had probably been moved in front of Roman Period temple, presumably of the local god Min. Limestone. Height: about 8·5 m.

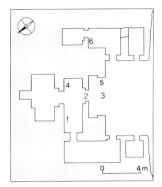

1 two registers: *Ptolemy II
Philadelphus before Min
and other deities*

2 above doorway: *Aya
and Queen Teye before Min
and other deities*

3 above doorway: *Aya and
Queen Teye before Min and Hathor
and before Horus and Mehyt*

4 *Thutmose III before Min*

5 *Thutmose III before Amon-Re*

6 *Thutmose III
before deities*

Above Rock-cut chapel of Min
near Akhmim.

Right Limestone sarcophagus lid
of the Priest Shepen-min, the son
of Heprenpu and Tashentmin,
probably of the Ptolemaic
Period. Theophoric names (those
containing names of deities) are
good evidence for the
monument's provenance: in this
case the names of the owner and
his mother relate them to the
local god Min. Height: 1·80 m.
Copenhagen, Ny Carlsberg
Glyptotek.

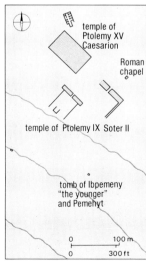

Above Wannina.

Far right Head of a statue of Ibu,
probably a contemporary of
Senwosret III, from his tomb at
Qaw el-Kebir. Painted limestone.
Height: 25 cm. Turin, Museo
Egizio.

The two temples which once stood west of the
modern town of Akhmim were built for Min (Pan)
and the goddess Triphis (Repyt), who was regarded
as his companion. Both apparently dated to the
Greco-Roman Period; although some earlier blocks
were also found, it is not clear whether they
belonged to these temples or whether they had
been reused.

Three groups of cemeteries and rock-cut tombs of
various dates are known in the area, especially at el-
Hawawish, northeast of Akhmim, and at el-Salamuni, some 5 kilometers further north-west. The
tombs at el-Hawawish (or Beit el-Medina) were
made for officials of the Panopolite nome during the
late Old Kingdom and the 1st Intermediate Period
and were thoroughly explored in the 1980s by an
expedition of Macquarie University led by N.
Kanawati. The ceilings of the tombs of the Greco-
Roman Period at el-Salamuni are decorated with
painted circular zodiacs.

Wannina

Wannina, some 10 kilometers southwest of Akhmim,
is the site of a temple (ancient *Hut-Repyt*, Greek
Athribis) built for the goddess Triphis (Repyt) by
Ptolemy XV Caesarion and several Roman Emperors.
South of it was an earlier temple of Ptolemy IX Soter
II. One of the tombs nearby, belonging to the broth-
ers Ibpemeny "the younger" and Pemehyt of the late
2nd century CE, has two zodiacs on its ceiling.

Qaw el-Kebir

Several large terraced funerary complexes built by
officials of the 10th Upper Egyptian nome in the area
of the modern village Qaw el-Kebir (ancient *Tjebu*,
later *Djew-qa*, Antaeopolis of the Greco-Roman
Period) during the 12th and 13th Dynasties represent the peak of nonroyal funerary architecture of
the Middle Kingdom. A causeway approached a
series of courts and halls, partly cut in the rock, from
the valley. The innermost room of the chapel was
connected by a shaft with the burial chamber.

Cemeteries of other dates have been found nearby.
A Ptolemaic temple (probably of Ptolemy IV Philopator, enlarged and restored under Ptolemy VI
Philometor and Marcus Aurelius), which stood near
the river, was destroyed in the first half of the 19th
century.

MIDDLE EGYPT

The term Middle Egypt describes the area between Asyut and Memphis, that is, rather confusingly, the northern part of Upper Egypt of the traditional terminology; both limits are geographically well defined and historically significant. Asyut became the southernmost area of the Herakleopolitan kingdom during the 1st Intermediate Period. The boundary between the southern and northern administrative regions remained in its vicinity until the end of the New Kingdom.

The area is characterized by the provincial tombs of the late Old Kingdom and 1st Intermediate Period cut in the desert escarpment. Ihnasya el-Medina was the residence of the Herakleopolitans, while in the 12th Dynasty the royal residence was further north, at Itjtawy, somewhere near el-Lisht. During the Middle Kingdom the Faiyum gained importance. El-ʿAmarna became the royal residence for a few years in the 18th Dynasty. During the 3rd Intermediate and Late Periods Middle Egypt was the meeting ground of the delta and the south. In late antiquity it prospered and traded extensively with the oases: although smaller and less spectacular than their southern contemporaries, many temples testify to the renewed vitality of Middle Egyptian towns in those times.

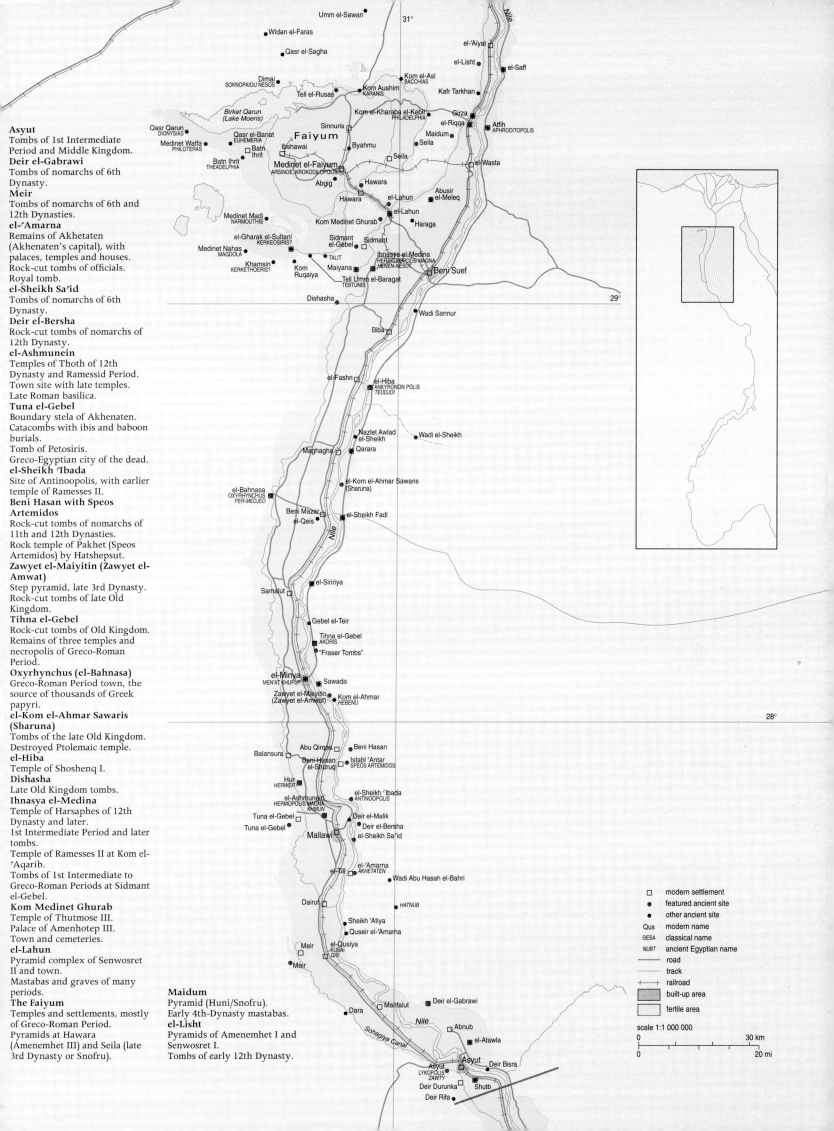

Asyut
Tombs of 1st Intermediate Period and Middle Kingdom.

Deir el-Gabrawi
Tombs of nomarchs of 6th Dynasty.

Meir
Tombs of nomarchs of 6th and 12th Dynasties.

el-ʿAmarna
Remains of Akhetaten (Akhenaten's capital), with palaces, temples and houses. Rock-cut tombs of officials. Royal tomb.

el-Sheikh Saʿid
Tombs of nomarchs of 6th Dynasty.

Deir el-Bersha
Rock-cut tombs of nomarchs of 12th Dynasty.

el-Ashmunein
Temples of Thoth of 12th Dynasty and Ramessid Period. Town site with late temples. Late Roman basilica.

Tuna el-Gebel
Boundary stela of Akhenaten. Catacombs with ibis and baboon burials. Tomb of Petosiris. Greco-Egyptian city of the dead.

el-Sheikh ʿIbada
Site of Antinoopolis, with earlier temple of Ramesses II.

Beni Hasan with Speos Artemidos
Rock-cut tombs of nomarchs of 11th and 12th Dynasties. Rock temple of Pakhet (Speos Artemidos) by Hatshepsut.

Zawyet el-Maiyitin (Zawyet el-Amwat)
Step pyramid, late 3rd Dynasty. Rock-cut tombs of late Old Kingdom.

Tihna el-Gebel
Rock-cut tombs of Old Kingdom. Remains of three temples and necropolis of Greco-Roman Period.

Oxyrhynchus (el-Bahnasa)
Greco-Roman Period town, the source of thousands of Greek papyri.

el-Kom el-Ahmar Sawaris (Sharuna)
Tombs of the late Old Kingdom. Destroyed Ptolemaic temple.

el-Hiba
Temple of Shoshenq I.

Dishasha
Late Old Kingdom tombs.

Ihnasya el-Medina
Temple of Harsaphes of 12th Dynasty and later. 1st Intermediate Period and later tombs. Temple of Ramesses II at Kom el-ʿAqarib. Tombs of 1st Intermediate to Greco-Roman Periods at Sidmant el-Gebel.

Kom Medinet Ghurab
Temple of Thutmose III. Palace of Amenhotep III. Town and cemeteries.

el-Lahun
Pyramid complex of Senwosret II and town. Mastabas and graves of many periods.

The Faiyum
Temples and settlements, mostly of Greco-Roman Period. Pyramids at Hawara (Amenemhet III) and Seila (late 3rd Dynasty or Snofru).

Maidum
Pyramid (Huni/Snofru). Early 4th-Dynasty mastabas.

el-Lisht
Pyramids of Amenemhet I and Senwosret I. Tombs of early 12th Dynasty.

modern settlement
featured ancient site
other ancient site
Qus modern name
GESA classical name
NUBT ancient Egyptian name
road
track
railroad
built-up area
fertile area

scale 1:1 000 000

0   30 km
0   20 mi

Asyut

Asyut (ancient Egyptian *Zawty*) was the capital of the 13th nome of Upper Egypt. Its place in Egyptian history was ensured by its strategic position at a point where the Libyan desert encroaches on the cultivated land and narrows the Nile valley, and where the Darb el-Arba'in caravan route departs for el-Kharga oasis and further south.

Although the town of Asyut and its shrines (particularly the temple of the local jackal god Wepwawet) are often mentioned in Egyptian texts, the remains so far discovered are almost exclusively connected with the Asyut necropolis, west of the modern town. The most important tombs date to Dynasties 9/10 and 12, but the Ramessid tombs of Siese and Amenhotep have also been found.

During the 1st Intermediate Period, the "Great Overlords of the Lycopolite Nome," Khety I, Itefibi and Khety II, were staunch supporters of the Herakleopolitan kings, of whose domain the nome formed the southern limit. The city was a major center of artistic production of the period. Biographical inscriptions at Asyut provide valuable information on the history of the Herakleopolitan conflict with "the southern nomes" (i.e. the 11th Dynasty). The ultimate victory of Thebes adversely affected the status of Djefaiha'py I–III, the nome officials of the 12th Dynasty, but their tombs retained the high artistic standards of the earlier period.

Deir el-Gabrawi

During the 6th Dynasty, the powerful nomarchs of the 12th Upper Egyptian nome were buried in two groups of rock-cut tombs near the modern village of Deir el-Gabrawi. Some of these local rulers also held the title of the "Great Overlord of the Abydene Nome," and so controlled a large area extending from the 8th nome (Abydos) in the south as far north as the 12th (or 13th) nome.

It is remarkable that some scenes in the tomb of one of them, Ibi, occur again in the Theban tomb (TT 36) of a man of the same name from the reign of Psammetichus I, about 1,600 years later.

Meir

There is nothing at el-Qusiya, on the west bank of the Nile, to suggest that this is the site of ancient *Qis* (Kusai), once the center of the 14th Upper Egyptian nome. Some 7 kilometers west of el-

Qusiya is the village of Meir, which gave its name to several groups of tombs further west, in a low slope leading on to the desert plateau.

The most important of these rock-cut tombs belong to the men who were in charge of the nome during the 6th and 12th Dynasties. For both these periods the sequence of tombs is unbroken and the hereditary office passed from one man to his son or younger brother.

Most tombs were decorated in relief. Some astonishingly lively scenes were created by the craftsmen of the 12th Dynasty, such as the desert-

"William," the blue faience hippopotamus decorated with aquatic plants, in the Metropolitan Museum of Art in New York. It was found at Meir in tomb B.3 of Senbi, dating to Senwosret I – Amenemhet II. Height: 11·5 cm.

hunt scene in tomb B.1 of Senbi, dating to Amen-emhet I. In the latest of the tombs, that of Wekh-hotep (C.1), the walls were only painted.

In the past, Meir suffered much from illicit digging. The most prominent among the archaeologists who worked there in the first half of the 20th century was Aylward M. Blackman.

el-ʿAmarna

El-ʿAmarna (less correctly Tell el-ʿAmarna), ancient Egyptian *Akhetaten* ("The Horizon of the Sun Disk"), was the short-lived capital of Egypt during much of the reign of King Akhenaten, and the center of the new state religion introduced at that time. It is one of the very few Egyptian cities that it has been possible to excavate to any significant extent. The site was almost completely abandoned early in the reign of Tutʿankhamun, some 15 years after it had been founded. Akhenaten built it on virgin soil, not sullied by an earlier presence of people and their gods. The exact reasons for his choice of the large bay on the east bank of the Nile, north of the massif of Gebel Abu Feda, are not known, but it has been suggested that the appearance of the landscape, resembling a large "horizon"

hieroglyph, was one of them. The boundaries of the city of Akhetaten were marked by a chain of stelae surrounding the area on both banks of the river. On the west bank, the northernmost of these (Stela A) is at Tuna el-Gebel, while on the east bank Akhetaten extended close to the tombs of el-Sheikh Saʿid (Stela X).

Although it has produced a number of famous works of art, for the visitor el-ʿAmarna is confusing because hardly any buildings remain standing. The spoliation started with the removal of stone to building sites nearby, notably to el-Ashmunein.

Except for the side facing the river, the plain of el-ʿAmarna is entirely enclosed by a rock escarpment, occasionally broken by wadis. The bay is some 10 kilometers long and about 5 kilometers deep, but the town occupied only the area closest

Left Wekh-hotep (the owner of tomb C.1 at Meir) with his two wives Khnemhotep and Nebkau, and a small daughter. Granite. Height: 37 cm. Reign of Senwosret II or III. Boston (MA), Museum of Fine Arts.

Below left Blind singers, one of the smaller groups below a large scene of Akhenaten and family offering to the Aten. Tomb of Meryreʿ I (No. 4) at el-ʿAmarna, south wall of the pillared hall, east side.

Below Map of the site el-ʿAmarna.

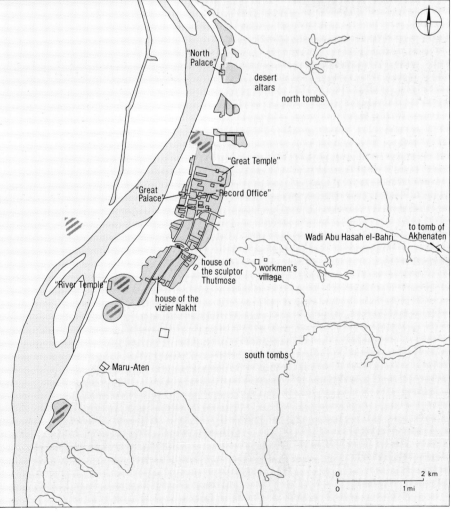

to the river. Its most important central part contained the *Per-Aten-em-Akhetaten* ("The Temple of the Aten in Akhetaten"), known as "The Great Temple," several other temples of the Aten, and the official state building, "The Great Palace." The main features of the last were (1) the "State Apartments," formed by a series of courts and columned halls and built of stone, (2) the "Harim," with adjacent servants' quarters, and (3) the so-called "Coronation Hall." Akhenaten's private residence was across the road from "The Great Palace" and was connected with it by a bridge. Close to it was the "Record Office," which in 1887 produced the cuneiform diplomatic correspondence (ʿAmarna Letters) exchanged between Amenhotep III, Akhenaten, Tutʿankhamun, and rulers and vassals of Palestine, Syria, Mesopotamia, and Anatolia. This conglomeration of official buildings was surrounded by private houses, workshops, sculptors' studios etc., on the north and south sides. The names of the owners of many of the houses are known (the sculptor Thutmose, the vizier Nakht, and others). A workmen's village was situated to the east of the central city.

Near the southern extremity of the ʿAmarna bay was the *Maru-Aten*, a group of buildings which also included an artificial lake, a kiosk on an island, and flower beds, and was adorned with painted pavements. The north part of Akhetaten contained the "North Palace".

ʿAmarna officials had their tombs in the escarpment encircling the plain. The tombs form two large groups, and their plan is similar to that of the Theban tombs of the 18th Dynasty: (1) an outer court, (2) and (3) a long hall and a broad hall, both sometimes with columns, (4) a statue niche. The decoration was in sunk relief. The date is betrayed by their novel subject-matter and the unusual artistic conventions of ʿAmarna art. How many of these tombs were put to use is not clear; some of their owners had other tombs made elsewhere, either before the move to el-ʿAmarna or afterwards.

Left Painted limestone bust of Nefertiti wearing her characteristic crown with the uraeus. It was found with many other pieces in the studio of the sculptor Thutmose during the German excavations at el-ʿAmarna in 1912. Height: 48 cm. Berlin, Ägyptisches Museum.

Above Painting from the king's private residence, showing two small daughters of Akhenaten, Neferneferuaten-tasherit and Neferneferureʿ. This is part of a much larger composition which included the whole royal family (the heel of a foot of the seated Nefertiti is next to the head of the princess on the right). Oxford, Ashmolean Museum.

Below "Talatat," the typical building blocks of Akhenaten, originally from a temple at el-ʿAmarna and reused in the pylon of a temple of Ramesses II at el-Ashmunein: two chariots and charioteers, and attendants kissing the ground in obeisance. New York, Metropolitan Museum of Art.

Tomb No. 25 of the south group was prepared for Aya, who later became the penultimate king of the 18th Dynasty and was buried in a tomb in the Valley of the Kings at Thebes (KV 23).

For his own family tomb Akhenaten chose a ravine about 6 kilometers from the mouth of the large Wadi Abu Hasah el-Bahri, which it joins. The tomb contains unique decoration, scenes of the royal family mourning the death of a daughter (or granddaughter). Akhenaten and Nefertiti, together with their daughters, courtiers, and even animals of the desert, are also shown greeting the sun rising on the eastern horizon. Fragments of Akhenaten's granite sarcophagus and calcite canopic chest were found in the tomb.

el-Sheikh Saʿid

The tombs of the men governing the Hare nome (15th Upper Egyptian nome) during the 6th Dynasty were cut in steep cliffs later named after a Muslim saint buried in the area. Their importance is greatly enhanced by the absence of contemporary evidence from el-Ashmunein, the capital of the nome.

Deir el-Bersha

Almost opposite the town of Mallawi, on the east bank of the Nile, a desert valley called the Wadi el-Nakhla breaks through the cliffs and runs in a southeasterly direction. Apart from limestone quarries of various periods it contains a number of rock-cut tombs. Some of them belong to the nomarchs of the 15th Upper Egyptian nome and date to the 11th and 12th Dynasties. The name Deir el-Bersha, by which the site is known, is from that of the village west of the wadi.

The most spectacular of the tombs was made for the "Great Overlord of the Hare nome" called Djehutihotep, who lived during the reigns of Amenemhet II, Senwosret II, and Senwosret III. The west wall of the inner room of the chapel bears the famous scene of the transport of a colossal statue from the calcite quarries at Hatnub.

The tombs were excavated by the Egypt Exploration Fund (P. E. Newberry and others) between 1891 and 1893, Harvard University and the Boston Museum of Fine Arts in 1915 (G. A. Reisner and others), and a Dutch–American expedition in the 1990s.

el-Ashmunein

El-Ashmunein, ancient Egyptian *Khmun* ("8-town"), named for the group of eight deities (ogdoad) who represented the world before creation, was called in Greek Hermopolis after Hermes (Egyptian Thoth). It was the capital of the 15th Upper Egyptian nome and the main cult center of Thoth, the god of healing and of wisdom, and the patron of scribes.

The site is in a broad and rich area of the Nile valley. It is now badly ruined, with small parts of temples standing above the general rubble. Only the Roman Period agora with its restored basilica is well preserved. No early remains have been found there, probably because they now lie beneath the water table.

The central sacred area of the town was surrounded by massive mud-brick enclosure walls of the Ramessid period and the 30th Dynasty. The temple of Thoth was rebuilt on many occasions. Only traces remain of the late extension that was standing until its destruction in 1826. It was a portico consisting of two rows of columns inscribed with the names of Alexander the Great and Philip

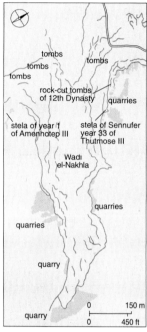

Above Wadi el-Nakhla.

Below Scene in the tomb of Djehutihotep at Deir el-Bersha (copied by John Gardner Wilkinson before 1856).

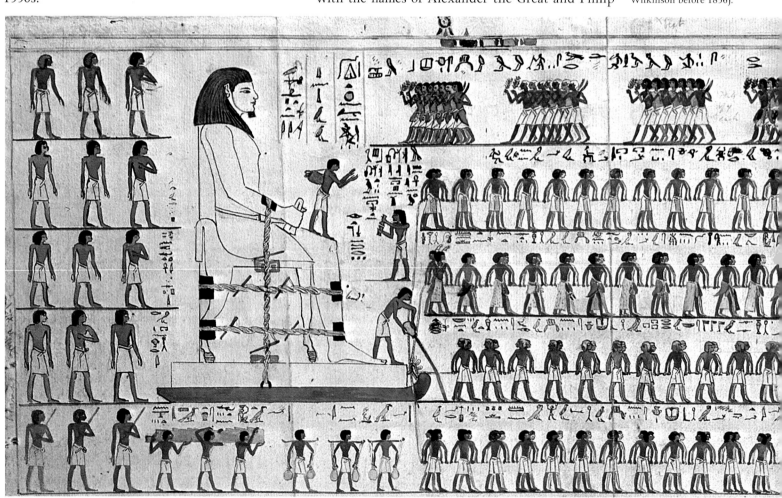

Below Granite columns of the late Roman basilica at el-Ashmunein, the only surviving large building of its kind in Egypt.

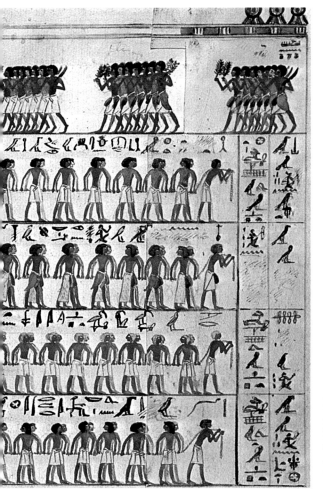

Above Ramessid calcite statuette of a priest with leopard-skin garment and a baboon squatting around his neck. The man probably dedicated a baboon in the temple of Thoth at el-Ashmunein. Oxford, Ashmolean Museum.

Arrhidaeus, but perhaps built earlier, during the 30th Dynasty. About 300 meters to the south is the pylon of Ramesses II in whose foundations more than 1,500 decorated blocks from dismantled temples of Akhenaten at el-ʿAmarna were discovered in the 1930s. An earlier pylon built by Haremhab is completely destroyed. The entrance to a temple of Amenemhet II is nearby.

A pylon and part of the hypostyle of the temple of Amun with reliefs of Merneptah and Sety II are visible to the west of the temple of Thoth. Another temple, built by Domitian and dedicated to the goddess Nehemetʿawai, lies to the east.

Several colossal statues of baboons were erected by Amenhotep III; two have been restored on site. A small temple of Ramesses II re-built by Nero is in the southern area. Roads laid out in the Greco-Roman Period were adorned with monumental objects up to 1500 years old at the time, including an altar of Amenhotep III.

The prosperity of the Greco-Roman Period was due to agriculture and to the prestige of Thoth, who was worshiped as Hermes Trismegistos ("thrice-great Hermes") by Greek and Egyptian alike, and had the Greco-Egyptian Hermetic Corpus of mystical–philosophical writings ascribed to him. Hermopolis and Tuna el-Gebel became centers of pilgrimage for Greeks and Egyptians.

Tuna el-Gebel

The monuments of Tuna el-Gebel are scattered for about 3 kilometers along the desert 7 kilometers west of el-Ashmunein. A boundary stela of Akhenaten, the earliest monument, consists of a rock-cut "shrine" a little way up the escarpment. The stela with its much-eroded text is on the north side.

To the south is the late necropolis of el-Ashmunein. Apart from material of Ramesses II that may have been out of context, the earliest objects found here are Aramaic administrative papyri of the 5th century Persian occupation discovered in a jar in the catacombs of ibis and baboon burials, which are the largest feature of the site and include a baboon sarcophagus dated to Darius I. A temple of the Macedonian period (Alexander IV) was incorporated into the catacombs. Most animal burials were Greco-Roman. A selection of pottery, bronze statuettes, and mummies is shown in the museum in nearby Mallawi. Ibis and baboon are the two chief sacred animals of Thoth, the god of el-Ashmunein.

The site also contains the almost unique tomb of the family of Petosiris, which probably dates to the early Greco-Roman period. It is in the form of a temple, with an entrance portico and a cult chapel behind; the burials are in underground chambers. In the portico there are scenes of daily life and of

offering bearers in a mixed Egyptian–Greek style. The chapel contains traditional religious scenes and important texts, including an extensive description of works in the temples of Hermopolis.

South of the tomb of Petosiris is a Greco-Egyptian city of the dead of the first centuries CE, with tombs and mortuary houses decorated in a complex mixture of Greek and Egyptian styles. Both the galleries and part of the city of the dead were excavated by the Egyptian scholar Sami Gabra between the two world wars. Egyptian, British, German, and Italian expeditions have worked there since the 1970s.

el-Sheikh ʿIbada

This is the site of the ancient Antinoopolis, founded by Emperor Hadrian in 130 CE to commemorate his favorite Antinous who had drowned here. Among the earlier monuments the largest is the temple of Ramesses II, dedicated to the gods of el-Ashmunein and Heliopolis. A large temple of the Greco-Roman Period was destroyed in the 19th century.

Beni Hasan with Speos Artemidos

Beni Hasan, some 23 kilometers south of el-Minya, on the east bank of the Nile, is the most important Middle Kingdom provincial necropolis between Asyut and Memphis. It contains 39 large rock-cut tombs, at least eight of them belonging to the "Great Overlords of the Oryx nome" (the 16th nome of Upper Egypt) of the end of the 11th and the early 12th Dynasties.

The biographical text in the tomb (No. 2) of the last of the holders of the title, Amenemhet, is dated "Year 43, month 2 of the inundation season, day 15" of the reign of Senwosret I. Although the tombs of his two successors, Khnumhotep II (No. 13) and Khnumhotep III (No. 3), do not show an appreciable diminution of material resources, the gradual centralization of the first half of the 12th Dynasty ultimately broke the string of the families of nomarchs in the whole of Middle Egypt, and large rock-cut tombs ceased to be built. The plan of the latest tombs consists of (1) an outer court with a portico formed by two pillars, (2) a rectangular main room with four polygonal pillars, and (3) a statue niche. The decoration is painted, and military activities, such as siege scenes, figure very prominently. Below these tombs there are others, more modest, some of which go back to the 6th Dynasty.

South of Beni Hasan is Speos Artemidos (locally known as Istabl ʿAntar), a rock temple dedicated to the local lioness goddess Pakhet, built by Queen Hatshepsut. The architrave bears a long dedicatory text with her famous denunciation of the Hyksos.

Zawyet el-Maiyitin

This site (also known as Zawyet el-Amwat) contains a step pyramid, of the late 3rd Dynasty, and a necropolis of rock-cut tombs, mainly of the end of the Old Kingdom, which belonged to ancient *Hebenu* (modern Kom el-Ahmar), the early capital of the 16th Upper Egyptian nome.

Tihna el-Gebel

The rock-cut tombs ("Fraser Tombs") at Tihna date to the Old Kingdom. About 2 kilometers north of them, near the modern village, are remains of the ancient town of Akoris, as well as three small temples and a necropolis of the Greco-Roman Period.

Left Greco-Egyptian painting in mortuary "house" 21 at Tuna el-Gebel, c. 2nd century CE. Apart from the decorative panel at the bottom, the motifs are Egyptian, and the hieroglyphs are intelligible. Above: Horus and Thoth pour libations over the deceased, shown in Greek style: to the right is her "shadow," shown as a symbolically black, emaciated corpse. Below: adoring figures of the "Mistress of the West," Atum, and two further deities face into an opening.

Right Gold statuette of the god Harsaphes, with an inscription on the lower side of its base naming Neferkareʿ Peftjauʿawybast, the local king at Herakleopolis contemporary with Piye of the 25th Dynasty. Height: about 6 cm. From the hypostyle hall of the temple at Ihnasya el-Medina. Boston (MA), Museum of Fine Arts.

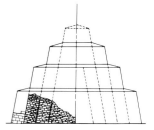

Section of the step pyramid at Zawyet el-Maiyitin.

The detective side of Egyptology: a keen eye, retentive memory and sense of detail can often help to identify errant monuments. The tomb relief on the right, now in the collection of the Museo Arqueológico Nacional in Madrid, was found during the excavation of a 1st Intermediate Period cemetery south of the temple of Harsaphes at Ihnasya el-Medina in 1968. The fragment on the left was, in disguise, on the New York art market already in 1964, incorrectly dated and with a misleading indication of its provenance.

Oxyrhynchus

Little is known about *Per-medjed* (Coptic *Pemdje*), the capital of the 19th Upper Egyptian nome, from the Dynastic Period. Its pharaonic remains are unknown. The modern name of the locality is el-Bahnasa.

The town came to prominence during the Greco-Roman Period when it was called Oxyrhynchus, after the local cult of the *Mormyrus* fish. Its rubbish heaps have produced tens of thousands of Greek papyri (Grenfell and Hunt, 1896–1907), approached in numbers only by those found in the towns of the Faiyum.

el-Hiba

This is a town site (ancient Egyptian *Teudjoi*) with a much-destroyed temple built by Shoshenq I. It was the northern limit of the Thebaid during the 21st–25th Dynasties.

Dishasha

Dishasha is known for its late Old Kingdom tombs, including some belonging to the chief officials of the 20th Upper Egyptian nome. The rock-cut tomb of Inti contains a rare scene of the siege of a fortified town.

Ihnasya el-Medina

About 15 kilometers west of Beni Suef, on the right bank of the Bahr Yusuf, is the modern village of Ihnasya el-Medina. The village derives its name from ancient Egyptian *Henen-nesut* (Coptic *Hnes*), the capital of the 20th Upper Egyptian nome. The chief god of the ancient town, the ram-headed Harsaphes (Egyptian Herishef, "He who is on his Lake"), later identified with Greek Herakles, gave the place its Classical name Herakleopolis Magna.

The remains of the temple of Harsaphes lie southwest of the village, and were excavated by Edouard Naville (1891–92), W. M. Flinders Petrie (1904), and Jesus López and others in the 1970s. The earliest monuments date to the 12th Dynasty. During the 18th Dynasty the temple was enlarged, but the major rebuilding program was due to Ramesses II. The temple continued to be used during the 3rd Intermediate and Late Periods.

During the 1st Intermediate Period Herakleopolis was the seat of the rulers of the 9th/10th (Herakleopolitan) Dynasty. No temples of this or earlier periods have yet been located, but contemporary and later tombs are nearby. In 1984, the excavation of these cemeteries was resumed by a Spanish expedition led by María del Carmen Pérez Die.

Southeast of the temple of Harsaphes, at Kom el-ʿAqarib, was another temple built by Ramesses II. Sidmant el-Gebel, about 7 kilometers to the west, was probably the main necropolis serving the town, with graves and rock-cut tombs ranging from the 1st Intermediate to the Greco-Roman Periods.

Above Wooden statue of the Lector-Priest Meryreʿ-haishtef as a naked youth. This type of wooden statue is characteristic of the end of the Old Kingdom, and similar pieces are known from Memphite as well as provincial cemeteries. Height: 51 cm. 6th Dynasty. From Sidmant el-Gebel. London, British Museum.

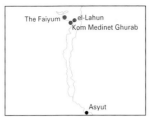

Kom Medinet Ghurab

At the south side of the entrance to the Faiyum, on the edge of the desert some 3 kilometers southwest of el-Lahun, are scanty remains of one or two temples and adjacent palace and town quarters and cemeteries. The larger temple was built by Thutmose III, and the settlement thrived during the second half of the 18th and the 19th Dynasty. A number of objects found there represent or are connected with Amenhotep III and Queen Teye, and one of the buildings is often described as a palace of his reign.

el-Lahun

The pyramid of el-Lahun, some 3 kilometers north of the modern town of that name, was built by Senwosret. II. It is on the right side of the opening through which the Bahr Yusuf enters the Faiyum, opposite Kom Medinet Ghurab, and overlooks the lakeside region to which the kings of the 12th Dynasty devoted much attention. The pyramid builders used a natural knoll of rock to site the monument, and employed the well-established Middle Kingdom method of core construction. This was based on stone retaining walls radiating from the center, and the filling of chambers formed between

them with mud bricks. The stone outer casing produced an effect comparable to that of pyramids completely built of stone, but nowadays, with the revetment gone, the structure is little more than a large mound of earth. The entrance to the interior of the pyramid was through two shafts near the south face; this is very unusual (normally the entrance is in the north face) and presented W. M. Flinders Petrie, the excavator, with considerable problems.

Beautiful Middle Kingdom jewelry, comparable to that discovered at Dahshur, was found south of the pyramid, in the shaft tomb of Princess Sithathoriunet.

There are mastabas and graves dating from the Middle Kingdom to Roman times in the neighborhood of the pyramid.

The valley temple lies about 1 kilometer to the east, near the line of cultivation. Close to it is the walled settlement of el-Lahun (also known as Kahun), excavated by Petrie. Most of the town was planned and laid out at the same time, with streets and houses arranged in neat geometrical rows. At least three town districts, separated by walls, can be distinguished: (1) the "acropolis," perhaps intended for the king himself, (2) the east quarter, with large mansions (about 40 by 60 m) centered around a court and consisting of as many as 70 or 80 rooms, (3) the west quarter of smaller uniform dwellings (about 10 by 10 m) with 4 to 12 rooms. The town housed priests and officials connected with the pyramid; although it is the only such settlement to have been excavated, it must have been one of many built near pyramid complexes. The town is known for the hundreds of Middle Kingdom hieratic papyri ("Kahun Papyri") found there. These contained a wide variety of texts, including belles lettres, mathematical, medical and veterinary works, and also administrative pieces such as legal and temple documents, accounts, and letters.

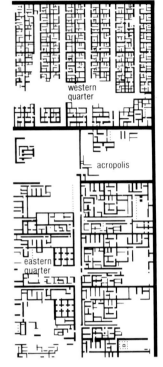

Above Plan of the northern part of the town of el-Lahun.

Top left Head of a queen, probably Teye, the wife of Amenhotep III, from Medinet Ghurab. The shrewd expression makes this head perhaps the most individually conceived female portrait known from ancient Egypt. Yew wood, glass, gesso, cloth etc. Height (without crown): 9·5 cm. Berlin, Ägyptisches Museum.

Below The pyramid of Senwosret II at el-Lahun.

Top right The temple at Qasr el-Sagha.

Far right Black granite colossal statue of a king (almost certainly Amenemhet III) dressed as a priest, wearing an unusual heavy wig, and carrying two hawk-headed standards (long staves sacred to the local god). Height as preserved: 1 m. 12th Dynasty. From Mit Faris in the Faiyum. Cairo, Egyptian Museum.

The following are the most important places of interest in the Faiyum:

Kom Aushim (Karanis)
Town site of the Greco-Roman Period with temples including one dedicated to the local gods Petesuchos and Pnepheros.

Dimai (Soknopaiou Nesos)
Ptolemaic temple of Soknopaios (a form of the crocodile god Sobek).

Qasr el-Sagha
Unfinished Middle Kingdom temple.

Qasr Qarun (Dionysias)
Late Ptolemaic temple.

Batn Ihrit (Theadelphia)
Ptolemaic temple of Pnepheros.

Byahmu
Masonry bases of a pair of colossal seated statues of Amenemhet III.

Medinet el-Faiyum, also el-Medina (Krokodilopolis or Arsinoe)
12th-Dynasty temple of Sobek, rebuilt or enlarged in later times.

Abgig
A large freestanding stela (formerly called an obelisk) of Senwosret I, now reerected in Medinet el-Faiyum.

Hawara
A pyramid of Amenemhet III (another pyramid of the same king stands at Dahshur), together with a large mortuary temple to its south (known as "The Labyrinth" to Classical authors).
Cemeteries of rock-cut tombs and graves (Middle Kingdom and Late and Greco-Roman Periods).

Seila
A small step pyramid, perhaps originally of the late 3rd Dynasty, with stelae of Snofru.

Medinet Madi (Narmouthis)
Temple complex of the cobra goddess Renenutet (Termuthis), initially built by Amenemhet III and IV, with Ptolemaic additions.

Tell Umm el-Baragat (Tebtunis)
Ptolemaic temple and town.

Kom Ruqaiya
Rock-cut tombs, probably of the 12th Dynasty.

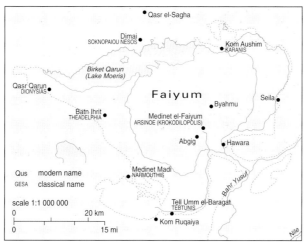

The Faiyum

Although usually described as an oasis, the Faiyum is connected with the Nile by a river arm known as the Bahr Yusuf (Arabic: "The River of Joseph"). The Faiyum (ancient Egyptian *She-resy*, "The Southern Lake," later divided into *She-resy* and *Mer-wer*, "The Great Lake," Greek Moeris) is a large, extremely fertile depression some 65 kilometers from east to west, with a lake (Birket Qarun, Lake Moeris of Classical writers) in its northwestern part. Nowadays the lake occupies only about one fifth of the Faiyum and is some 44 meters below sea level, but in the past it was much larger, teeming with wild life, and with abundant vegetation on its shores. Crocodiles must have been very common in the region, hence the role of the species as the chief deity of the area (Sobek, Greek Suchos). The name Faiyum derives from the collo-quial Egyptian term for "the Lake", Coptic *Peiom*.

Two periods were very significant for the area. When during the 12th Dynasty the capital of Egypt was moved to near el-Lisht, measures were taken to enhance the economic importance of the nearby Faiyum, probably by reducing or redirecting the inflow of water into the lake and reclaiming land. The majority of temples and settlements uncovered so far date to the Greco-Roman Period, when the area once again became the focus of royal attention. The lake was artificially reduced to win further arable land, and new settlers, especially Greco-Macedonian veterans, were introduced there under Ptolemy II Philadelphus in particular. Thousands of Egyptian (demotic) and Greek papyri have been found in Faiyum town sites of this period.

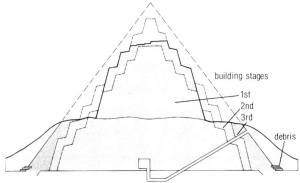

building stages
1st
2nd
3rd
debris

Maidum

Maidum presents the unmistakable appearance of a huge tower-shaped structure appearing above a hill formed by stone debris. These are the remains of one of the earliest true pyramids ever attempted in Egypt and, with the "Bent Pyramid" at Dahshur, one of the oldest pyramid complexes.

The monument started as a seven-stepped pyramid, but was subsequently altered to have eight steps; finally the steps were filled and an outer casing was applied to complete its conversion into a smooth pyramidal form. This need not have happened as a continuous process. Egyptologists still argue whether the king for whom the pyramid was begun was Huni, the last ruler of the 3rd Dynasty, or Snofru, the first king of the 4th Dynasty. New Kingdom graffiti tell us that the Egyptians themselves later connected it with Snofru and current opinion favours him as the original builder who returned to complete the structure as a true pyramid toward the end of his reign. However, the smooth dressing of the walls which had originally been intended to be exposed as outer faces of the step pyramid (some can still be seen on the pyramid) did not provide sufficient bonding to the later

Top left External masonry of the buttress walls of the Maidum pyramid and the less carefully built interior.

Above Aerial view of the Maidum pyramid from the east, showing the causeway, the mortuary temple, and the vast amount of material now surrounding the remains of the pyramid core following the partial collapse of the structure.

Above left Section of the Maidum pyramid looking west.

Left Statues of the Greatest of Seers (i.e. High Priest) of Heliopolis and King's Son of his Body (of Snofru) Re'hotep and his wife Nofret. Limestone with remarkably well preserved original coloring. Height: 1·20 and 1·18 m. Cairo, Egyptian Museum.

fill leaning against them. Furthermore, the outer casing did not rest on sound foundations, and the method employed in laying its blocks was not well chosen. As a result of these constructional deficiencies, the bases of the four outer buttress walls gave way and the walls slid down and collapsed, creating the tower that we see today. The date at which this happened is still hotly disputed; attempts have been made to connect this "building disaster" with the change of the angle of the "Bent Pyramid" at Dahshur, but the presence of an extensive contemporary necropolis speaks against such an early date. It is possible that the quarrying activities of later stone-robbers looking for building material were what mainly created the pyramid's present appearance.

Cemeteries of large mud brick mastabas of the beginning of the 4th Dynasty lie to the north and east of the pyramid. The best-known among them are the twin mastabas of Reʿhotep and his wife Nofret, and of Nefermaʿat and his wife Itet.

Although the site has not been by any means systematically explored, a number of excavators have worked at it, the most distinguished being A. Mariette, W. M. Flinders Petrie, and Alan Rowe.

el-Lisht

Amenemhet I, the first king of the 12th Dynasty, moved the administrative capital of Egypt and the royal residence from Thebes to Itjtawy, a newly founded walled town between the Faiyum and Memphis. The town has not been located, but the pyramid field of el-Lisht was its main necropolis, and Itjtawy was probably in the cultivated area to the east of it. The town retained its importance for at least 300 years, only to relinquish it to the Hyksos center Avaris in the northeastern delta and to Thebes during the 2nd Intermediate Period.

The main features of el-Lisht are the two dilapidated pyramids of Amenemhet I and his son Senwosret I, some 1·5 kilometers apart, surrounded by smaller pyramids and mastabas of members of the royal family and officials, and cemeteries of ordinary graves. The nearby Memphite necropolis provided Amenemhet I with a source of conveniently prepared building material, and many decorated blocks originating in earlier pyramids and temples have been recovered from the core of the pyramid. These can be traced to Saqqara, Abusir, and Giza.

The most interesting among the 12th-Dynasty mastabas near the north pyramid of Amenemhet I belong to the Vizier Inyotefoqer, the Chief Steward Nakht, the Overseer of Sealers Rehuerdjersen, and the Mistress of the House Senebtisy, while close to the south pyramid of Senwosret I are the tombs of the Vizier Mentuhotep, the High Priest of Heliopolis Imhotep with its walls covered with Pyramid Texts, the Steward Sehetepibre-ʿankh, the High Priest of Memphis Senwosret-ʿankh, again with Pyramid Texts, and others. The monuments of el-Lisht have been explored by the expeditions of the Institut Français d'Archéologie Orientale (1894–95) and the Metropolitan Museum of Art in New York (1906–34 and again since 1984).

Below Limestone relief of archers: one of the many Memphite blocks of the Old Kingdom reused at el-Lisht by Amenemhet I. Most of these reliefs come from royal monuments and are of superb quality. New York, Metropolitan Museum of Art.

Below right The goddess Seshat records foreign captives and booty: limestone relief of the 12th Dynasty which continues an Old Kingdom tradition of similar scenes in royal temples. From the mortuary temple of Senwosret I at el-Lisht. New York, Metropolitan Museum of Art.

MEMPHIS

The city of Memphis was the royal residence and capital of Egypt during the Early Dynastic Period and the Old Kingdom. The city's temples were among the most important in the land. Memphis always remained one of the most populous and renowned places of Egypt and, indeed, of the whole ancient world, inhabited by a cosmopolitan community. Its harbor and local workshops played an important part in Egypt's foreign trade.

A reflection of the size and importance of Memphis is the more than 30 kilometers covered by its cemeteries, on the edge of the desert on the west bank of the Nile, together with Helwan on the east. These form the Memphite necropolis: (1) Dahshur, (2) Saqqara, (3) Abusir, (4) Zawyet el-ʿAryan, (5) Giza, (6) Abu Rawash. When early in the 12th Dynasty Amenemhet I moved his residence to Itjtawy (el-Lisht), this was probably an attempt to return to the traditional Memphite area which, however, was not at that time suitable for establishing a new large settlement.

The names by which the various parts of the Memphite necropolis are now known derive from the names of modern villages nearby. Egyptians themselves had no special term for the whole necropolis, but its most conspicuous features, the royal pyramids, sometimes lent their names to the adjacent quarters of the city which had grown out of the original "pyramid towns" of priests and pyramid officials. One of these terms, the name of the pyramid of Pepy I at Saqqara, *Mennufer*, Memphis in its Grecized form, Coptic *Menfe*, was adopted as early as the 18th Dynasty to describe the whole city.

The town itself lies in the cultivated area to the east of the necropolis, buried under the deposits of silt left behind by Nile inundations and covered by modern settlements, fields, and vegetation. So far only small parts have been revealed at Mit Rahina and at Saqqara (east of the pyramid of Teti). From the beginning, the religious center of Memphis with the temple of the god Ptah was in the area of the modern village of Mit Rahina, although initially it may have been physically separated from the settlement around the royal palace further north. The extent of the city did not remain stable throughout Egyptian history, new thriving areas gaining in importance to the detriment of others whose popularity had waned. Our modern concept of the city of Memphis and of its shadowy counterpart, the Memphite necropolis, is therefore very artificial, because neither of them was ever active over its entire extent at any one time.

Classical sources as well as archaeological discoveries show that Memphis became one of the most important administrative centers of the country at the very beginning of Egyptian history, after 2950 BCE. Environmental considerations played a decisive role in the city's development, especially the need to protect it from the waters of the inundation and the effects of the gradual eastward

movement of the river. Herodotus says that it was Menes, the traditional first king of Egypt, who raised a dike to protect the city from the inundations of the Nile. According to Manetho the successor of Menes, called Athothis, was the builder of the earliest of the palaces of Memphis. The oldest name of the city and the district was *Ineb-hedj*, "The White Wall," possibly reflecting the appearance of its fortified residence. This was probably situated somewhere in the area of the modern town of Abusir, in the valley to the east of the northernmost section of the Saqqara necropolis. Perhaps the most apt name was *ʿAnkh-tawy*, "That which Binds the Two Lands," stressing the strategic position of the town at the tip of the economically important delta, between Lower and Upper Egypt of the traditional terminology. This, indeed, was probably the reason why the rulers of the 1st Dynasty chose the area as the site of the capital.

Only Thebes in the south was comparable in religious, political, and economic importance to Memphis, yet our knowledge of the remains of this truly national shrine of Egypt is altogether smaller. For foreigners Memphis represented Egypt. The name of one of its temples, *Hikuptah* ("The Temple of the *ka* of Ptah"), gave rise to the name of the whole country, Greek Aigyptos, our Egypt. This is also the etymology of the word "Coptic."

The city of Memphis did not survive the gradual eclipse of ancient Egyptian civilization in the early centuries of the Common Era. Economically, it suffered even earlier from the growth of Alexandria. Its religious importance was lost when Theodosius I (379–95 CE) decreed that Christianity should be the religion of the whole of the Roman Empire. The final *coup de grâce* was delivered in 641 CE, when the Muslim conqueror ʿAmr ibn el-ʿAs founded a new capital of Egypt, el-Fustat, on the east bank of the Nile at the south end of modern Cairo.

One of the most familiar faces of Memphis: the calcite sphinx at Mit Rahina.

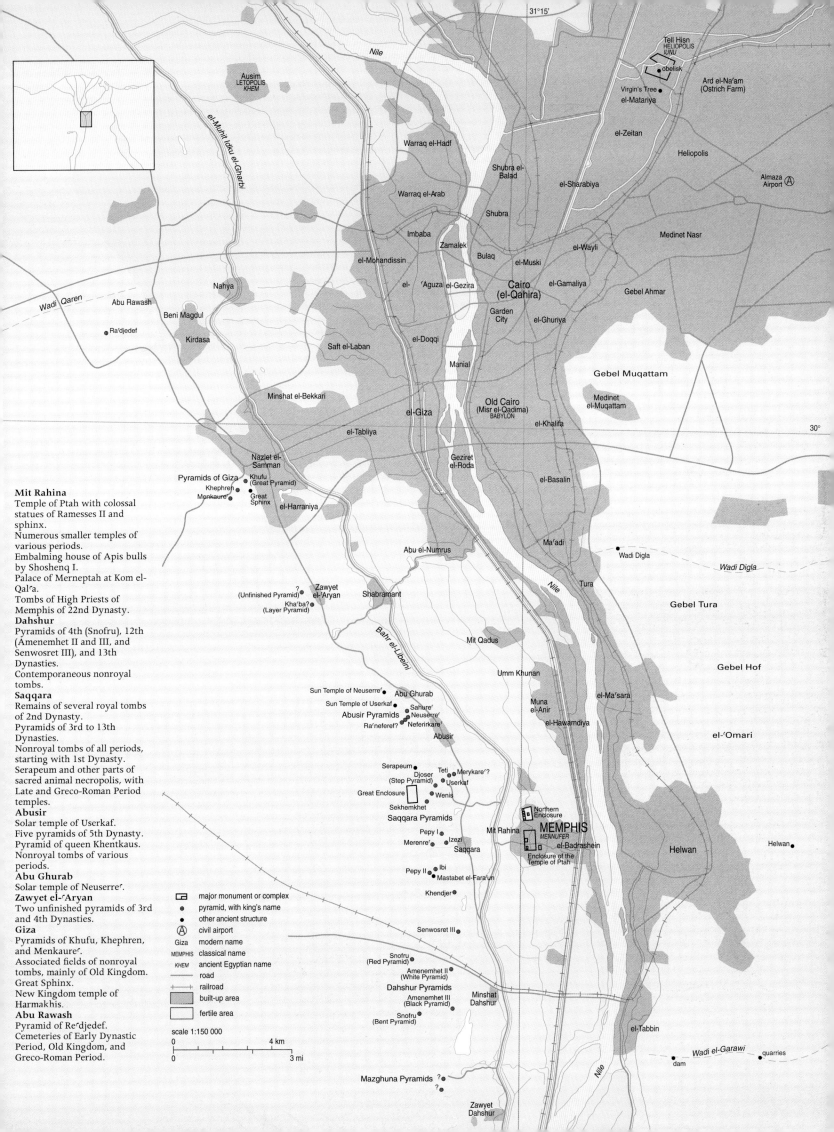

Mit Rahina
Temple of Ptah with colossal statues of Ramesses II and sphinx.
Numerous smaller temples of various periods.
Embalming house of Apis bulls by Shoshenq I.
Palace of Merneptah at Kom el-Qal'a.
Tombs of High Priests of Memphis of 22nd Dynasty.

Dahshur
Pyramids of 4th (Snofru), 12th (Amenemhet II and III, and Senwosret III), and 13th Dynasties.
Contemporaneous nonroyal tombs.

Saqqara
Remains of several royal tombs of 2nd Dynasty.
Pyramids of 3rd to 13th Dynasties.
Nonroyal tombs of all periods, starting with 1st Dynasty.
Serapeum and other parts of sacred animal necropolis, with Late and Greco-Roman Period temples.

Abusir
Solar temple of Userkaf.
Five pyramids of 5th Dynasty.
Pyramid of queen Khentkaus.
Nonroyal tombs of various periods.

Abu Ghurab
Solar temple of Neuserre'.

Zawyet el-'Aryan
Two unfinished pyramids of 3rd and 4th Dynasties.

Giza
Pyramids of Khufu, Khephren, and Menkaure'.
Associated fields of nonroyal tombs, mainly of Old Kingdom.
Great Sphinx.
New Kingdom temple of Harmakhis.

Abu Rawash
Pyramid of Re'djedef.
Cemeteries of Early Dynastic Period, Old Kingdom, and Greco-Roman Period.

major monument or complex
pyramid, with king's name
other ancient structure
civil airport
Giza   modern name
MEMPHIS   classical name
KHEM   ancient Egyptian name
road
railroad
built-up area
fertile area

scale 1:150 000
0   4 km
0   3 mi

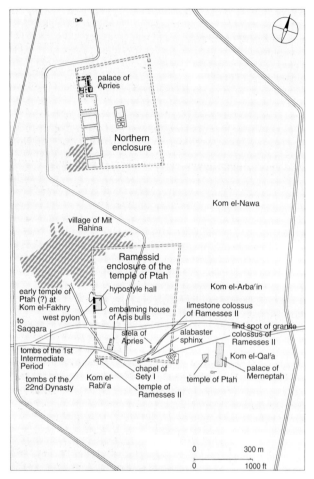

Colossus of Ramesses II, probably usurped from Amenhotep III, found near the south gate of the Ramessid enclosure of the temple of Ptah at Mit Rahina; now re-erected in the garden near the small museum which houses the famous limestone colossal statue of the same king. The original colors on the colossus are still partly preserved. Red granite. Height: 7·5 m.

Mit Rahina

Extensive remains of ancient Memphis can be seen in a picturesque setting of palm groves close to the modern village of Mit Rahina.

The most conspicuous remaining monument is the Ramessid enclosure (partly renewed during the Late or Ptolemaic Periods) with the temple of Ptah. It was built to mark one of the early *sed*-festivals celebrated by Ramesses II, perhaps that of his year 30 (c. 1250 BCE). The Apis Bull probably was the original deity of the area, but Ptah became the chief Memphite god at the beginning of the Dynastic Period if not earlier, and in Classical antiquity was identified with Hephaistos and Vulcan. Only the west section of the temple complex, once one of the largest in Egypt, has been excavated (mainly by W. M. Flinders Petrie, 1908–13) and epigraphically explored (by the Egypt Exploration Society, 1981–94). It consists of a massive pylon and a columned hypostyle hall.

One of the colossal statues near the enclosure's south gate is known as Abu 'l-Hol and is housed recumbent in a small museum on the site. There is also a large calcite sphinx as well as another two colossi of Ramesses II (probably usurped from earlier kings) which have been re-erected in the museum's garden. Other, smaller sanctuaries and shrines were along the southern approach and in its vicinity, including those dedicated to Ptah, Hathor, and probably the deified Ramesses II himself. Later kings continued to build within the enclosure, especially Shoshenq I, who added an embalming house for Apis Bulls.

Foundation deposits discovered west of the Ptah enclosure indicate the existence of a temple built by Thutmose IV. But the earliest temple of Ptah, of the Early Dynastic Period or Old Kingdom, is almost certainly still hidden under the mound of Kom el-Fakhry, further to the west of the enclosure of Ramesses II.

Another enclosure, with remains of the palace of King Apries, is visible north of the precinct of Ptah.

A number of mounds formed by continuous habitation are situated around the Ramessid Ptah enclosure. One of these is Kom el-Qalʿa, to the east, with a smaller temple dedicated to Ptah and a palace of Merneptah. These were excavated by Clarence S. Fisher and the expedition of the University Museum in Philadelphia in the 1920s. A small temple of the Aten, built during the reign of Akhenaten, was probably in the same area.

There are few tombs at Mit Rahina. The most important among them date to the 1st Intermediate Period or early Middle Kingdom, at Kom el-Fakhry, and to the 22nd Dynasty (tombs of the High Priests of Memphis called Shoshenq, Tjekerti, Peteese, and Harsiese), close to the southwest corner of the Ptah enclosure.

Dahshur

The pyramid field of Dahshur forms the southernmost extension of the Memphite necropolis. The site is some 3·5 kilometers long, and the pyramid variously called "Bent," "Blunted," "Rhomboidal" or "False," the only one of its shape in Egypt, is the most conspicuous landmark of Dahshur.

For royal tombs, the change from the 3rd to the 4th Dynasty is signaled by the transition from step pyramid to true pyramid, and the pyramids in which the process can be observed are at Maidum and Dahshur. The southern pyramid at Dahshur, of Snofru, was the earliest to be planned as a true pyramid from its inception (although it is possible that this was the second pyramidal tomb constructed by this ruler). However, when the structure reached more than half of its intended height, the slope of its outer faces was sharply reduced

(from 55°00′30″ to 43°01′30″), creating the characteristic "bent" silhouette, and the method of laying the casing and packing blocks was improved. This change of design was probably caused by the appearance of constructional flaws. The Bent Pyramid is unique in having two separate entrances, one in its north face and another in its west face. Large areas of the pyramid have retained their original smooth exterior casing. South of the pyramid is the usual subsidiary ritual pyramid. The valley temple is situated about 700 meters northeast of the pyramid, and has provided a series of remarkable reliefs, some of them showing processions of female figures personifying Snofru's estates in Upper and Lower Egypt.

Later in his reign, Snofru had the "Red" or "Pink Pyramid" (from the color of its reddish limestone) erected some 2 kilometers to the north. The incline of the faces of this pyramid was from the beginning similar to that of the upper part of the Bent Pyramid. The dimensions of its base (220 by 220 m) are surpassed only by those of the Great Pyramid of Khufu at Giza.

Three of the remaining pyramids at Dahshur, at some distance from each other and not forming any group, belong to the kings of the 12th Dynasty, Amenemhet II (the "White Pyramid"), Senwosret III, and Amenemhet III (the "Black Pyramid"). The last two are mostly brick built. A remarkable discovery of at least six wooden boats was made near the pyramid of Senwosret III, comparable to the find of a dismantled boat of Khufu at Giza. Other pyramids on the site are inconspicuous or invisible to the visitor. Near the pyramid of Amenemhet III is the tomb of the ephemeral king Awibreʿ Hor, and a small pyramidal structure of Amenyqemau, both of the 13th Dynasty. Three other pyramids at Dahshur are probably of the same date, although one of them, north-east of the Red Pyramid, may date from the Old Kingdom.

There are two groups of Old-Kingdom nonroyal tombs at Dahshur. Near the pyramids of Amenemhet II and Senwosret III, but still within the pyramid enclosure walls, are the mastabas of princesses (Iti, Khnemt, Itiwert, and Sitmerhut, all daughters of Amenemhet II, and Ment and Sentsenebtisi, daughters of Senwosret III) and queens. These tombs contained some superb examples of jewelry (bracelets, pectorals, collars, necklaces etc.), now in the Egyptian Museum in Cairo. New Kingdom tomb chapels were discovered by a Japanese expedition in the 1990s.

Among archaeologists who have excavated at Dahshur, several names are prominent: Jacques de Morgan, to whom we owe knowledge of the Middle Kingdom pyramids and tombs (1894–95), Ahmed Fakhry, who explored the Bent Pyramid (1951–55), and Rainer Stadelmann and Dieter Arnold, who have directed continuing excavations on behalf of the German Archaeological Institute and the Metropolitan Museum of Art in New York.

The "Bent Pyramid" and the "Red Pyramid" of Dahshur seen behind the landmarks of south Saqqara, the "Mastabet el-Faraʿun" and the pyramid of Pepy II, and showing how artificial the dividing line between Saqqara and Dahshur is.

Right Ka-statue, with the uplifted arms of the hieroglyphic sign *ka* on its head, from the tomb of King Awibreʿ Hor. Wood, remains of paint, and gilt. Height: 1·75 m. Cairo, Egyptian Museum.

Left Granite pyramidion (capstone) of Amenemhet III from Dahshur. Height: 1·40 m. Cairo, Egyptian Museum.

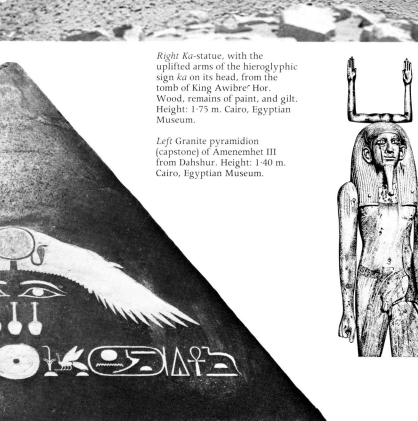

The Pyramids: Types and Construction

Between c. 2650 and 1630 BCE, Egyptian kings built for themselves tombs in the form of pyramids. Architectural as well as religious considerations played a part in the pyramid's introduction and development; although united by their purpose, pyramids differ in their form, size, interior design, and other details. There are two basic types: the step pyramid, and the true pyramid.

THE STEP PYRAMID

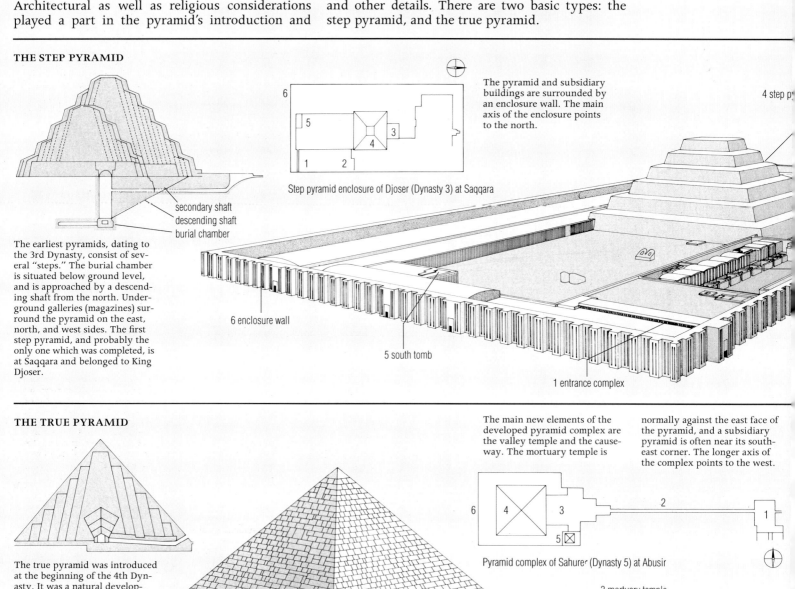

The pyramid and subsidiary buildings are surrounded by an enclosure wall. The main axis of the enclosure points to the north.

4 step p...

Step pyramid enclosure of Djoser (Dynasty 3) at Saqqara

secondary shaft
descending shaft
burial chamber

The earliest pyramids, dating to the 3rd Dynasty, consist of several "steps." The burial chamber is situated below ground level, and is approached by a descending shaft from the north. Underground galleries (magazines) surround the pyramid on the east, north, and west sides. The first step pyramid, and probably the only one which was completed, is at Saqqara and belonged to King Djoser.

6 enclosure wall

5 south tomb

1 entrance complex

THE TRUE PYRAMID

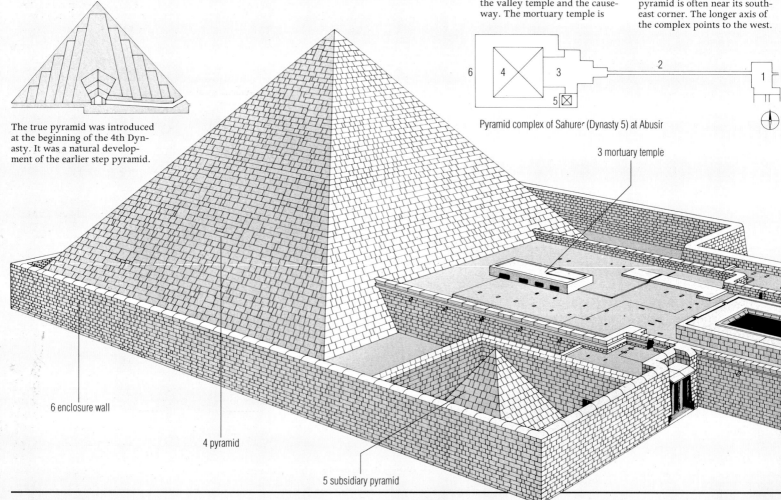

The main new elements of the developed pyramid complex are the valley temple and the causeway. The mortuary temple is normally against the east face of the pyramid, and a subsidiary pyramid is often near its southeast corner. The longer axis of the complex points to the west.

Pyramid complex of Sahureʿ (Dynasty 5) at Abusir

The true pyramid was introduced at the beginning of the 4th Dynasty. It was a natural development of the earlier step pyramid.

3 mortuary temple

6 enclosure wall

4 pyramid

5 subsidiary pyramid

Internal construction

In most true pyramids, the structure consists of a series of buttress walls (coatings of masonry) surrounding the central core. The buttress walls decrease in height from the center outwards; in other words, there is a step pyramid within most true pyramids. This clever internal arrangement

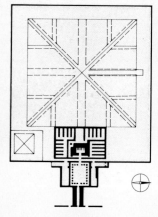

added stability to the structure but evolved historically, together with the pyramid itself. Packing blocks were used to fill the "steps" formed by the faces of the outermost buttress walls, and casing blocks (often of better-quality Tura limestone) completed the transformation into a true pyramid.

A different method of construction was employed in the pyramids of the 12th and 13th Dynasties. The main reason for its introduction was economy: it was suitable for relatively modest structures in inferior materials. Solid stone walls ran from the center of the pyramid, while shorter cross walls created a series of internal chambers filled with stone blocks, rubble or mud bricks. The whole structure then received the usual outer casing. Although quite effective in the short term, this could not compare with the earlier constructional methods, and all pyramids built in this way are now very dilapidated.

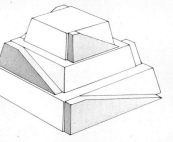

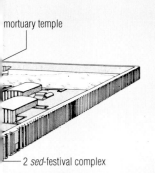

mortuary temple

2 sed-festival complex

The subsidiary buildings, in particular the south tomb and the mortuary temple, ensured the deceased king's well-being in his new existence, and served to maintain his cult. Djoser's *sed*-festival complex is a special feature not attested elsewhere.

The funerary monument of Sahure' at Abusir is a good example of the pyramid complex. The landing stages of the valley temple show that it could be approached by boat. The ascending causeway connects it with the mortuary temple. This consists of the outer part, with an entrance passage and a columned court, and the inner part, with five niches for statues, magazines to the north and south, and a sanctuary. In most pyramids the interior is reached by a descending passage starting in the north face. The roof of the burial chamber is formed by the largest and heaviest blocks in the whole structure.

Building ramps

A major problem facing the pyramid builders was how to lift the heavy stone blocks to the required height. The only method proved to have been used by the ancient Egyptians is based on ramps. These were inclined planes, built of mud brick and rubble, along which the blocks were dragged on sledges (wheeled transport was not used in the pyramid age). As the pyramid grew in height, the length of the ramp and the width of its base were increased in order to maintain a constant gradient (about 1 in 10) and to prevent the ramp from collapsing. Several ramps approaching the pyramid from different sides were probably used.

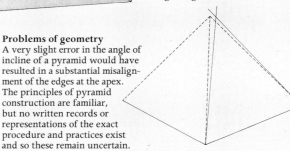

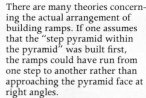

There are many theories concerning the actual arrangement of building ramps. If one assumes that the "step pyramid within the pyramid" was built first, the ramps could have run from one step to another rather than approaching the pyramid face at right angles.

Other methods of lifting

The size of the ramps and the volume of material required to build them have prompted alternative suggestions as to how the problem of raising the building blocks was solved. One, proposed by L. Croon, uses the principle of the *shaduf*. The Egyptians of the New Kingdom knew the *shaduf* for raising water, but there is no evidence that they used a similar

2 causeway

device for lifting weights. This is the main objection to this and similar ideas.

Models of "rockers," wooden cradle-like appliances, are known, and it has been thought that these were used to lift stone blocks. The rocker, with the stone placed on it, would have been raised by positioning wedges below its sides and rocking it up onto them. Stones might have been handled this way at some stage, but as a main lifting method this does not seem adequate.

Problems of geometry

A very slight error in the angle of incline of a pyramid would have resulted in a substantial misalignment of the edges at the apex. The principles of pyramid construction are familiar, but no written records or representations of the exact procedure and practices exist and so these remain uncertain.

Some of the pyramid measurements show an accurate use of π (e.g. height of Khufu's pyramid $= \dfrac{\text{perimeter of the base}}{2\pi}$).

This could have been produced "accidentally," for example through measuring distances by counting revolutions of a drum.

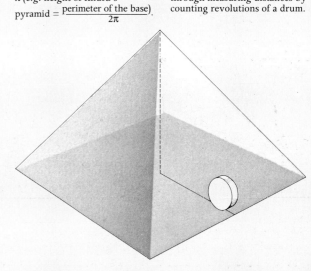

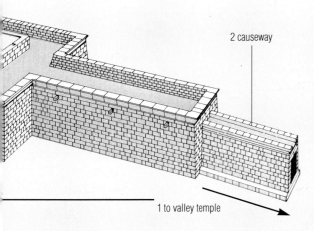

1 to valley temple

The Pyramids: Checklist

This list contains all the royal pyramids known from Egypt to date including provincial step pyramids for the maintenance of the royal cult. The pyramids tend to form pyramid fields which are referred to by the names of the modern villages situated nearby. There are various reasons for these groupings but, broadly speaking, the Old Kingdom pyramids were concentrated near Memphis while those of the Middle Kingdom were built close to Itjtawy (near modern el-Lisht), the capital of the land at that time. At the beginning of the 4th Dynasty the pyramids, together with the buildings associated with them, started to be given names.

△ true pyramid

⬜ step pyramid

△ bent pyramid

⬜ sarcophagus-shaped tomb

Each entry in the table lists the following information (if available): king's name and dynasty; ancient name of pyramid in hieroglyphs and English; modern name; dimensions (α = angle of incline); associated pyramids (△).

Abu Rawash

△ Re'djedef/Dyn 4
"The Pyramid which is the *Sehedu*-star"
105m sq; α = 60°; planned ht 92m
Subsidiary △
Unfinished; remains of granite casing

Giza

△ Khufu/Dyn 4
"The Pyramid which is the Place of Sunrise and Sunset"
Modern name: "The Great Pyramid" or "The First Pyramid of Giza"
230m sq; α = 51°30'35"; original ht 146m
Subsidiary △; queens △△△
5 boat pits, one containing a dismantled wooden boat, one as yet unopened

△ Khephren/Dyn 4
"The Great Pyramid"
Modern name: "The Second Pyramid of Giza"
214·5m sq; α = 53°7'48"; ht 143·5m
Subsidiary △
Lowest course of casing in granite; remains of original limestone casing near summit; 5 boat pits

△ Menkaure'/Dyn 4
"The Divine Pyramid"
Modern name: "The Third Pyramid of Giza"
105m sq; α = 51°20'25"; original ht 65·5m
queens △△△
Pyramid refurbished during Dyn 26; bottom 16 courses of casing in granite

Zawyet el-'Aryan

△ Owner unknown (probably the successor of Khephren)
Name unknown
Modern name: "The Unfinished Pyramid"
200m sq
Only the underground part begun; sarcophagus of unusual form found embedded in floor of burial chamber

⬜ Probably Kha'ba/Dyn 3
Modern name: "The Layer Pyramid" or "el-Medowwara"
84m sq
Ownership inferred from inscribed calcite vessels found nearby; unfinished

Abusir

△ Perhaps Shepseskare'/Dyn 5
115m sq
Hardly begun

△ Sahure'/Dyn 5
"The Pyramid where the *Ba*-spirit rises"
78·5m sq; α = 50°11'40"; original ht 47m
Subsidiary △

△ Neuserre'/Dyn 5
"The Pyramid which is Established of Places"
79m sq; α = 51°50'35"; original ht 51·5m
Subsidiary △; queens (?) △△
Valley Temple and part of causeway originally built for Neferirkare' and usurped

△ Neferirkare'/Dyn 5
"The Pyramid of the *Ba*-spirit"
105m sq; α = 53°7'48"; original ht 70m
Valley Temple and causeway unfinished at time of king's death and later usurped by Neuserre'

△ Re'neferef/Dyn 5
"The Pyramid which is Divine of the *Ba*-spirits"
65m sq
Hardly begun

Saqqara

△ Teti/Dyn 6
"The Pyramid which is Enduring of Places"
78·5m sq; α = 53°7'48"; original ht 52·5m
Subsidiary △; queens △ (Iput I), △ (Khuit)
Pyramid Texts

△ Probably Merykare'/Dyn 9 or 10
"The Pyramid which is Flourishing of Places"
Estimated 50m sq

No evidence for ownership except for titles of priests buried nearby; not yet fully excavated

△ Userkaf/Dyn 5
"The Pyramid which is Pure of Places"
Modern name: "el-Haram el-Makharbish"
73·5m sq; α = 53°7'48"; original ht 49m
Subsidiary △
Mortuary Temple placed, unusually, south of Pyramid

⬜ Netjerykhet (Djoser)/Dyn 3
Modern name: "The Step Pyramid" or "el-Haram el-Mudarrag"
121 × 109m; ht 60m
Begun as a mastaba tomb; plan modified 6 times; final form of superstructure a pyramid in 6 steps, the earliest pyramid built in Egypt

△ Wenis/Dyn 5
"The Pyramid which is Beautiful of Places"
57·5m sq; α = 56°18'35"; original ht 43m
Subsidiary △
Pyramid Texts
Causeway decorated by series of remarkable reliefs; 2 boat pits

⬜ Sekhemkhet/Dyn 3
Modern name: "The Buried Pyramid"
120m sq
Unfinished; raised to ht of only c.7m; sealed but empty sarcophagus found in burial chamber

△ Pepy I/Dyn 6
"The Established and Beautiful Pyramid"
78·5m sq; α = 53°7'48"; original ht 52·5m
Subsidiary △; queens △ (Inti), △ (Nubwent), △ (Mertiotes), △△
Pyramid Texts
Pyramid complex lent its name to city of Memphis

△ Izezi/Dyn 5
"The Beautiful Pyramid"

Modern name: "el-Shawwaf"
78·5m sq; α = 53°7'48"; original ht 52·5m
Subsidiary △; queen △

△ Merenre'/Dyn 6
"The Shining and Beautiful Pyramid"
78·5m sq; α = 53°7'48"; original ht 52·5m
Pyramid Texts

△ Ibi/Dyn 8
Name unknown
31·5m sq; α = ?; original ht ?
Pyramid too damaged to provide accurate measurements; Mortuary Temple only mud brick; apparently no Valley Temple or causeway; Pyramid Texts

△ Pepy II/Dyn 6
"The Established and Living Pyramid"
78·5m sq; α = 53°7'48"; original ht 52·5m
Subsidiary △; queens △ (Neit), △ (Iput II), △ (Wedjebten); Pyramid Texts

⬜ Shepseskaf/Dyn 4
"The Purified Pyramid"
99·5 × 74·5m
Not really a pyramid but a sarcophagus-shaped structure, though even the Egyptians sometimes wrote its name with the sign of a pyramid

△ Khendjer/Dyn 13
Name unknown
52·5m sq; α = 55°; original ht 37m
queen (?) △
Mainly mud brick

△ Owner unknown/Dyn 13
Name unknown
80m sq; α = ?; original ht ?
Too damaged to provide accurate measurements; mainly mud brick; at present only c. 3m high

Dahshur

△ Senwosret III/Dyn 12
Name not certain
105m sq; α = 56°18'35"; original ht 78·5
queens △△△△△△
Mud brick; 6 wooden boats buried near Pyramid

△ Owner unknown, possibly Old Kingdom or Dyn 13

△ Snofru/Dyn 4
"The Shining Pyramid"
Modern names: "The Red Pyramid" etc.
220m sq; α = 43°22'; original ht 105m

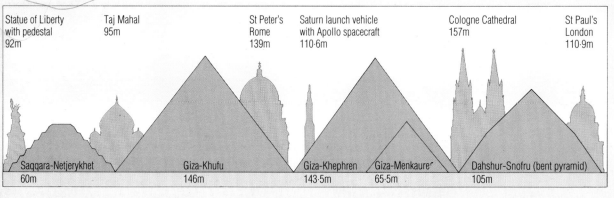

| Statue of Liberty with pedestal 92m | Taj Mahal 95m | St Peter's Rome 139m | Saturn launch vehicle with Apollo spacecraft 110·6m | Cologne Cathedral 157m | St Paul's London 110·9m |

| Saqqara-Netjerykhet 60m | Giza-Khufu 146m | Giza-Khephren 143·5m | Giza-Menkaure' 65·5m | Dahshur-Snofru (bent pyramid) 105m |

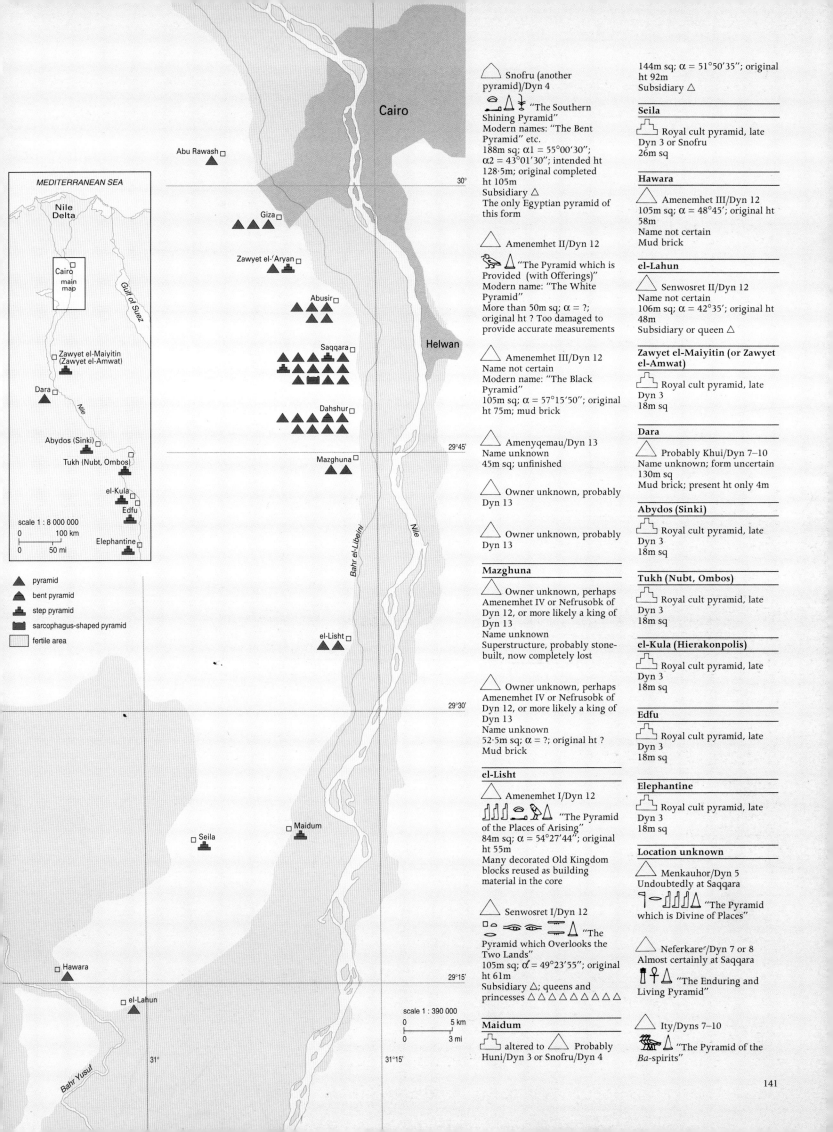

MEDITERRANEAN SEA

Nile Delta

Cairo main map

Gulf of Suez

Zawyet el-Maiyitin (Zawyet el-Amwat)

Dara

Nile

Abydos (Sinki)

Tukh (Nubt, Ombos)

el-Kula

Edfu

Elephantine

scale 1 : 8 000 000

0   100 km

0   50 mi

△ pyramid

▲ bent pyramid

⬛ step pyramid

⬛ sarcophagus-shaped pyramid

☐ fertile area

Cairo

Abu Rawash ☐

30°

Giza ☐

Zawyet el-'Aryan ☐

Abusir ☐

Saqqara ☐

Helwan

Dahshur ☐

29°45'

Mazghuna ☐

Bahr el-Libeini

Nile

29°30'

el-Lisht ☐

29°15'

Maidum ☐

Seila ☐

scale 1 : 390 000

0   5 km

0   3 mi

Hawara ☐

el-Lahun ☐

31°

Bahr Yusuf

31°15'

△ Snofru (another pyramid)/Dyn 4

"The Southern Shining Pyramid"
Modern names: "The Bent Pyramid" etc.
188m sq; α1 = 55°00'30";
α2 = 43°01'30"; intended ht 128·5m; original completed ht 105m
Subsidiary △
The only Egyptian pyramid of this form

△ Amenemhet II/Dyn 12

"The Pyramid which is Provided (with Offerings)"
Modern name: "The White Pyramid"
More than 50m sq; α = ?; original ht ? Too damaged to provide accurate measurements

△ Amenemhet III/Dyn 12
Name not certain
Modern name: "The Black Pyramid"
105m sq; α = 57°15'50"; original ht 75m; mud brick

△ Amenyqemau/Dyn 13
Name unknown
45m sq; unfinished

△ Owner unknown, probably Dyn 13

△ Owner unknown, probably Dyn 13

Mazghuna

△ Owner unknown, perhaps Amenemhet IV or Nefrusobk of Dyn 12, or more likely a king of Dyn 13
Name unknown
Superstructure, probably stone-built, now completely lost

△ Owner unknown, perhaps Amenemhet IV or Nefrusobk of Dyn 12, or more likely a king of Dyn 13
Name unknown
52·5m sq; α = ?; original ht ?
Mud brick

el-Lisht

△ Amenemhet I/Dyn 12

"The Pyramid of the Places of Arising"
84m sq; α = 54°27'44"; original ht 55m
Many decorated Old Kingdom blocks reused as building material in the core

△ Senwosret I/Dyn 12

"The Pyramid which Overlooks the Two Lands"
105m sq; α = 49°23'55"; original ht 61m
Subsidiary △; queens and princesses △ △ △ △ △ △ △ △

Maidum

⬛ altered to △ Probably Huni/Dyn 3 or Snofru/Dyn 4

144m sq; α = 51°50'35"; original ht 92m
Subsidiary △

Seila

⬛ Royal cult pyramid, late Dyn 3 or Snofru
26m sq

Hawara

△ Amenemhet III/Dyn 12
105m sq; α = 48°45'; original ht 58m
Name not certain
Mud brick

el-Lahun

△ Senwosret II/Dyn 12
Name not certain
106m sq; α = 42°35'; original ht 48m
Subsidiary or queen △

Zawyet el-Maiyitin (or Zawyet el-Amwat)

⬛ Royal cult pyramid, late Dyn 3
18m sq

Dara

△ Probably Khui/Dyn 7–10
Name unknown; form uncertain
130m sq
Mud brick; present ht only 4m

Abydos (Sinki)

⬛ Royal cult pyramid, late Dyn 3
18m sq

Tukh (Nubt, Ombos)

⬛ Royal cult pyramid, late Dyn 3
18m sq

el-Kula (Hierakonpolis)

⬛ Royal cult pyramid, late Dyn 3
18m sq

Edfu

⬛ Royal cult pyramid, late Dyn 3
18m sq

Elephantine

⬛ Royal cult pyramid, late Dyn 3
18m sq

Location unknown

△ Menkauhor/Dyn 5
Undoubtedly at Saqqara

"The Pyramid which is Divine of Places"

△ Neferkare'/Dyn 7 or 8
Almost certainly at Saqqara

"The Enduring and Living Pyramid"

△ Ity/Dyns 7–10

"The Pyramid of the Ba-spirits"

141

Below left Limestone gaming disk with calcite-inlaid black paste border and two owls with outstretched wings. Found with 44 others in the tomb of Hemaka, an official of King Den. Diameter: 9·7 cm. Cairo, Egyptian Museum.

Right "The Scribe ʿAhmose, son of Yeptah, came to see the Temple of Djoser. He found it as though heaven were within it, Reʿ rising in it." (Hieratic graffito of the 18th Dynasty.)

Saqqara

Saqqara

Saqqara is the most important link in the chain of cemeteries belonging to the ancient city of Memphis. It covers an area over 6 kilometers long, measuring more than 1·5 kilometers at its widest. However, the dividing lines between Memphite cemeteries, especially Abusir and Saqqara, are rather arbitrary and their definition is heavily influenced by modern topography. In antiquity, these probably were not felt to be separate sites.

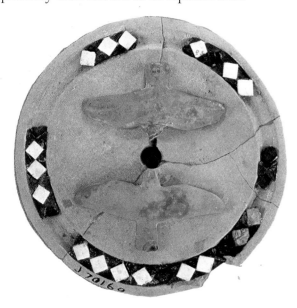

Nonroyal tombs of Dynasties 1 and 2

The earliest royal name found at Saqqara is that of the late Predynastic ruler Naʿrmer. It is engraved on a porphyry bowl which, together with thousands of other complete and fragmentary vessels of magnificent craftsmanship, was discovered in one of the subterranean magazines under the Step Pyramid of Djoser. The first mastaba tomb at Saqqara is only a little later, dating to the reign of King ʿAha who was perhaps the same as Menes, the legendary founder of Memphis.

Mastabas of the 1st Dynasty form an almost continuous line along the eastern edge of the desert plateau (*gebel*) north of the Step Pyramid of Djoser, above the modern village of Abusir. The earliest are near the northern extremity of the plateau. These tombs looked over the city of Memphis in the valley below and belonged to high officials and members of the royal family who lived there. The mastabas' superstructures were built of sun-dried bricks and had paneled "palace facades." They were of considerable size: tomb S 3504, for example, from the reign of King Wadj, measured 56·45 by 25·45 m. Chambers for funerary equipment were situated in the core of the brick mastaba, while the substruc-

ture cut into the rock consisted of a centrally placed burial chamber and subsidiary rooms. The most important mastabas were excavated by W. B. Emery between 1936 and 1956. An Early Dynastic cemetery with graves of more ordinary people was below the plateau in the north. Large Early Dynastic tombs occur sporadically along the desert edge as far north as Abu Rawash.

At the end of the 1st Dynasty the "palace-facade" paneling was reduced to two niches in the east face, of which that near the southeast corner became the focus of the cult of the deceased. The generally smaller mastabas of the 2nd Dynasty continued to be built in an apparently haphazard way in the area west of the large tombs of the 1st Dynasty.

Royal tombs of the 2nd Dynasty

A large complex of underground rock-cut galleries is concealed under the east side of the pyramid of Wenis, and another about 140 meters east of it. Nothing has survived of the mud brick superstructures, but the names on clay sealings, originally on jars and other articles of burial equipment, suggest that these galleries are the substructures of the tombs of two kings of the early 2nd Dynasty, Reʿneb and Ninetjer. A stela of Reʿneb was reused in a modern village nearby.

The huge enclosed area west of the pyramid of Sekhemkhet, known as *Qisr el-Mudir* (or "Great Enclosure" on early maps), probably represents the remains of a royal tomb complex of one of Djoser's predecessors (perhaps of Khaʿsekhemwy, the last king of the 2nd Dynasty, although in king-lists Djoser is preceded by the king called Nebka). The project, apparently, did not get beyond the initial delineation of the area.

The pyramids of Dynasties 3–13

At least 14 royal pyramids, treated here in chronological order, are known from Saqqara. Most of them have now lost their original, strictly geometrical, forms and are reduced to artificial hills. Amazing though it may seem, other pyramids almost certainly await discovery.

1. The Step Pyramid of Djoser was built some time after 2650 BCE. It was the first pyramid in Egyptian history, and the earliest stone structure of its size in the world. The pioneering character of the project is shown by the hesitation about its form, probably largely influenced by the new building material. Altogether six different plans were adopted in the course of construction: the monument was started as a large mastaba tomb, but ended up as a pyramid of six steps. The design of the Step Pyramid was traditionally credited to Imuthes (Imhotep), described by Manetho some 2,400 years later as "the inventor of the art of building with hewn stone." During the excavation of the entrance complex of the Step Pyramid in 1925–26 the name of Imhotep was, indeed, found inscribed on the

1	Netjerykhet Djoser	6	Wenis	11	Ibi
2	Sekhemkhet	7	Teti	12	Merykare' (?)
3	Shepseskaf	8	Pepy I	13	Khendjer
4	Userkaf	9	Merenre'	14	unknown king of 13th Dynasty
5	Izezi	10	Pepy II		

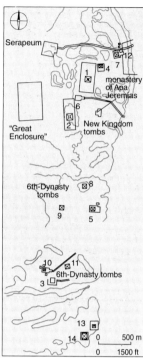

pedestal of a statue of Djoser, providing fascinating contemporary evidence for the correctness of Manetho's statement.

The complex of buildings near the southeast corner of the pyramid represents a stone replica of the chapels and pavilions built for the celebration of the *sed*-festival which was held to mark the beginning of a new phase in the reign of the king. The presence of these buildings in lasting stone guaranteed that Djoser would not be unprepared for the many celebrations of the *sed*-festival he hoped to enjoy in his existence after death. A closed room (*serdab*) near the northeast corner of the pyramid

contained his seated statue, the earliest large stone royal statue so far identified from Egypt.

The exploration and restoration of the Step Pyramid are especially associated with the name of the French Egyptologist Jean-Philippe Lauer. The most striking examples of his remarkable work are the chapels restored in the *sed*-festival court.

2. King Sekhemkhet intended to build an even larger step structure southwest of his predecessor's, but the pyramid remained unfinished and gradually disappeared under the sand. It was only in 1950 that it was discovered by the Egyptian Egyptologist M. Zakaria Goneim, who aptly called it "The Buried

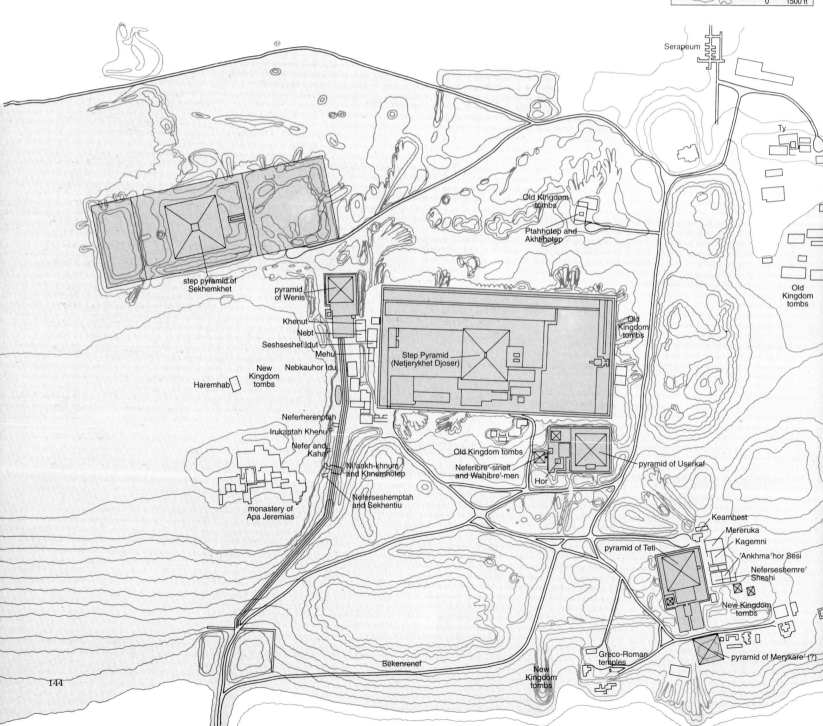

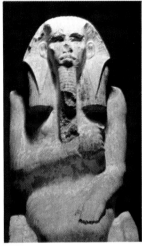

Hetepka

"Iseum"
(gallery of "Mother
of the Apis" cows)

temple of
Nectanebo II

galleries of ibises,
falcons and baboons

Hezyre'

Hemaka

tombs of the 2nd
and 3rd Dynasties

tombs of the
1st Dynasty

tomb
S 3504

tombs of the
1st Dynasty

| 0 | | 300 m |
| 0 | | 1000 ft |

Top left Step Pyramid of
Netjerykhet (Djoser): entrance
near the southeast corner of the
recessed enclosure wall; *top right*
colonnade with engaged ribbed
columns (partly attached to the
wall behind), linking the
entrance with the court south of
the pyramid; *above left* "South
Building" in the *sed*-festival
complex. All much restored.

Above Upper part of the
limestone seated statue of Djoser
found in the *serdab*. The king is
clad in a ceremonial robe, and
wears an unusual headdress. The
pose, with the right arm bent and
the hand clenched against the
chest, is typically archaic. Most
of the paint, a rare yellow for the
skin and black for the hair and
beard, has been lost; the
mutilation of the face is the
result of the gouging out of the
inlaid eyes. Height: 1·40m.
Cairo, Egyptian Museum.

Above right Pyramid complex of
Wenis: two boat pits, some 39 m
long, by the south side of the
causeway, about 180 m east of
the pyramid.

Pyramid." The still sealed calcite sarcophagus in the
burial chamber was, however, empty.

3. The burial complex at South Saqqara of Shepseskaf, one of the last kings of the 4th Dynasty, is
not a pyramid but a structure resembling a huge
sarcophagus. It is known as *Mastabet el-Fara῾un*
("The Mastaba of the Pharaoh"). The only parallel is
the Giza tomb of Khentkaus, the mother of two
early kings of the 5th Dynasty.

4. Userkaf, the first king of the 5th Dynasty, built
his pyramid near the northeast corner of Djoser's
enclosure, but his successors abandoned Saqqara
for Abusir, further north.

5. The pyramid of Izezi, the penultimate king of the
5th Dynasty, is at South Saqqara.

6. The pyramid of Wenis, the last king of the 5th
Dynasty, stands near the southwest corner of the
step pyramid enclosure of Djoser. The walls of the
interior of this pyramid are inscribed with the
Pyramid Texts, a collection of spells designed to
help the deceased king in the netherworld, which
may have been used during the burial ceremony.
The pyramid of Wenis was the first to contain such
texts, which are found in all later Old Kingdom
pyramids.

On the south face of the pyramid is a hieroglyphic inscription of Kha῾emwese, one of the sons
of Ramesses II and High Priest of Ptah in Memphis.
It records restoration work carried out by the
prince, who was known for his interest in
ancient monuments. He carved similar inscriptions
on other Old Kingdom monuments in the Memphite
area.

The causeway, linking Wenis' mortuary temple
against the east face of the pyramid with the valley

Left The causeway of Wenis, with the remains of the mortuary temple and the pyramid.

Below Wooden panel showing the Chief of Dentists and Physicians Hezyreꜥ of the 3rd Dynasty. Originally in a niche in his tomb at North Saqqara. Cairo, Egyptian Museum.

temple, was decorated with reliefs. These depict, among other scenes, boats transporting granite columns and architraves from the quarries near Aswan to the building site of Wenis' pyramid.

7. The pyramid of Teti, the first king of the 6th Dynasty, is the northernmost royal pyramid of Saqqara. The other rulers of the dynasty, Pepy I (8), Merenreꜥ (9) and Pepy II (10), followed Izezi's example and moved to South Saqqara. This change was almost certainly influenced by a southward transfer of the city center in the Nile valley to the east. The name of the pyramid of Pepy I and the settlement near its valley temple, *Pepy-mennufer*, was eventually adopted for the whole Egyptian capital, Mennufer (Memphis). Since 1965, the pyramids of the 6th Dynasty at South Saqqara have been systematically explored, and the Pyramid Texts inscribed on their walls copied and studied by French scholars of the *Mission archéologique française de Saqqara*. A spectacular result of their work has been the identification and excavation of five small pyramids of queens of Pepy I. Modern electromagnetic techniques were used during this work.

11. The small brick pyramid of the little-known King Ibi of the 8th Dynasty is in the same area.

12. The, as yet, unexcavated remains of a pyramid discernible to the east of the pyramid of Teti, at North Saqqara, might belong to King Merykareꜥ, of the Herakleopolitan Period (9th/10th Dynasty). Other possible owners of this structure have been proposed, especially Menkauhor of the 5th Dynasty.

13 and 14. The two southernmost Saqqara pyramids belong to kings of the 13th Dynasty and, characteristically for the period, are built of sundried bricks. One of these pyramids belonged to Khendjer, while the owner of the other remains unknown.

Nonroyal tombs of the Old and Middle Kingdoms

The largest conglomeration of nonroyal tombs of the Old Kingdom occupies the area north of the Step Pyramid of Djoser, and is a natural development of the cemeteries of Dynasties 1 and 2. Many of these tombs were partly excavated in the mid 19th century under the direction of the French archaeologist Auguste Mariette. Archaeological techniques and practices used during the excavation were those of the period. Before long the tombs were sanded up again and almost all are now inaccessible.

From the beginning of the 4th Dynasty, pyramids began to be surrounded by cemeteries of nonroyal tombs. However, only Userkaf, the first king of the 5th Dynasty, and Wenis, the last, were buried at North Saqqara during this period. The tombs south of the pyramid of Userkaf were in the way when the pyramid of Wenis was begun and some of them were literally covered by Wenis' causeway, avoiding the destruction and plundering of later times. Several of these were partly rock-cut, an uncommon technique at Saqqara, where the rock is not very suitable for this form of tomb. Late 5th and 6th Dynasty tombs occupy the space between Wenis' causeway and the south wall of the enclosure of Djoser.

Tombs of the 6th Dynasty and the 1st Intermediate Period are mainly in the vicinity of the pyramid of Teti (and possibly Merykareꜥ) and around the pyramids at South Saqqara.

The series of tombs at Saqqara is uninterrupted for at least the first ten Egyptian dynasties (c.2950–1975 BCE), and possibly even longer. The cult niche in the east face of the mastaba of the 1st and 2nd Dynasties was withdrawn into the body of the mastaba during the 3rd or early 4th Dynasty, probably in order to protect its decorated parts

Right Sheikh el-Beled, "the headman of the village," was the name given to this statue by the local workmen who discovered it in 1860. It is made of wood (the arms were carved as separate pieces and joined to the body) and was originally covered with plaster coating and painted, with the eyes inlaid. The feet and lower parts of the legs and the stick are modern. The statue is uninscribed, but the tomb in which it was found belonged to the Chief Lector-Priest Kaꜥaper of the early 5th Dynasty. It is an apparently realistic portrait of a corpulent aging man, and one of the finest of its type. Height. 1·10 m. Cairo, Egyptian Museum.

Far right Reliefs from Old Kingdom tombs. From the top: fowl-yard with men force-feeding geese and cranes (from an unknown tomb of the 5th Dynasty, in Berlin, Ägyptisches Museum); group of butchers felling an ox (Mereruka, reign of Teti); members of the household approaching the deceased with offerings for his tomb, partly unfinished (Akhtihotep, end of the 5th Dynasty); cattle crossing a canal, with a hippopotamus and fish (Kagemni, reign of Teti); shrine with a statue of the deceased dragged on a sled to the tomb (Hetepka, late 5th or early 6th Dynasty).

more effectively against the elements. It was connected with the outside by means of a passage, thus creating the classical Saqqara cruciform chapel. This, the simplest tomb chapel form, developed further during the 5th and 6th Dynasties through the addition of more rooms. These finally filled practically the whole body of the mastaba, originally a solid mass of mud brick or stone, and provided large areas suitable for relief decoration. The most famous Saqqara mastabas are of this type, for example that of Ty at the western edge of the cemetery north of the Step Pyramid, which has a portico, a pillared court, and another four rooms, and the tombs of Mereruka and Kagemni, north of the pyramid of Teti.

The few tombs of the Middle Kingdom at Saqqara are in areas popular during the late Old Kingdom and the 1st Intermediate Period, especially around the pyramid of Teti (the large tombs of Hetep and Ihy), north of the causeway of Wenis, and at South Saqqara.

Nonroyal tombs of the New Kingdom

Tombs of the New Kingdom are concentrated in two parts of Saqqara. The first is a wadi running in a westerly direction some 300 meters south-east of the pyramid of Teti. The steep northern face of the wadi is honeycombed with rock-cut tombs dating from the mid-18th Dynasty to the Ramessid Period. Some are decorated with carved or painted scenes which provide a remarkable counterpart for contemporaneous tombs in the Theban area. The most spectacular tomb belongs to the vizier ꜥAperia (ꜥAper-El) who probably lived late in the reign of Amenhotep III. It was excavated, in very difficult working conditions, by the French Egyptologist Alain-Pierre Zivie. Somewhat later freestanding tombs were built on the plateau between the wadi and the pyramid of Teti.

The second and more extensive area with New Kingdom tombs is south of the causeway of Wenis. These are freestanding tomb chapels. The two main groups explored so far consist of Ramessid tombs, such as that of Neferronpet, the vizier of Ramesses II, close to the causeway of Wenis (excavated by the Faculty of Archaeology of Cairo University under the direction of Sayed Tawfik in 1984–88), and tombs in the vicinity of the tomb of Haremhab in the southern section of the plateau. There are also some rock-cut tombs, little explored, in the rock face above the valley temple of Wenis.

Although large freestanding tombs of the New Kingdom appeared at Saqqara in the reign of Amenhotep III, the majority of those excavated so far are somewhat later. When Tutꜥankhamun abandoned el-ꜥAmarna and the royal residence moved to Memphis, the Saqqara cemetery experienced a period of remarkable activity. The best craftsmen and artists in the land accompanied the court and worked on the tombs. These artists successfully retained some elements of ꜥAmarna art during this period, which

was otherwise characterized by a return to pre-ꜥAmarna styles and beliefs. Saqqara remained important even when royal attention began to focus on the northeast delta during the reign of Ramesses II. At least one freestanding tomb near the pyramid of Teti, of the royal butler Heqamaꜥatreꜥ-neheh, dates to the reign of Ramesses IV.

The finest Saqqara tombs of the New Kingdom date between the reigns of Tutꜥankhamun and Ramesses II. Because they were fairly close to the surface, sometimes overlaying Old Kingdom tombs, they became easy prey for early 19th century collectors of antiquities, for whom the situation was made even easier by the proximity of Saqqara to Cairo. It was quite simple to dismantle the tombs and remove parts of their decorated walls and their statues.

A spectacular discovery that settled an Egyptological dispute of long standing was made by the Anglo-Dutch expedition of the Egypt Exploration Society and the National Museum of Antiquities, Leiden, led by G. T. Martin. Since the early 19th century, many major museums, notably those of Berlin, Bologna, Leiden, St Petersburg, London,

Opposite above The Overseer of Craftsmen Amenemone, followed by his wife Tahesyt and sons, offers papyrus and lotus flowers to Sakhmet, the lioness-headed Memphite goddess. End of the 18th Dynasty. Cairo, Egyptian Museum.

Opposite below Hoisting the mast of a sailing boat on the Nile, on the east wall, and (*above*) part of the west wall, with a series of false doors of various members of the family, in the tomb chapel of the Director of Singers, Nufer. Mid to late 5th Dynasty.

Center left The Inspector of Hairdressers, Hetepka, represented on the jambs and the rear wall of the niche of his false door (now destroyed). Late 5th or early 6th Dynasty.

Left Painted limestone statue of a scribe reading from a papyrus, his eyes fixed on his listener. A roll of papyrus is placed on the flat surface formed by his kilt stretched over his knees and while his left hand presses the beginning of the papyrus roll against it, his right hand is ready to unroll it as required. The papyrus still bears traces of a text in ink, but the statue itself is uninscribed and the exact circumstances of its discovery are not known, so that the owner remains anonymous. This type of sculpture was introduced in the 4th Dynasty and remained popular. Height: 49 cm. 5th Dynasty. Cairo, Egyptian Museum.

The Memphite tomb of
Haremhab, east wall of the 2nd
columned court. A group of
courtiers dressed in long pleated
costumes billowing at the front,
fashionable at the end of the 18th
Dynasty, and sporting long
walking sticks with ornamental
knobs, take part in a social
occasion. Their individual tastes
are shown by the different types
of wig they wear. The event is a
review of African and Asiatic
captives brought from military
campaigns abroad by the
"General of the Generals"
Haremhab. The captives are
dragged into his presence
unwillingly and subjected to
various indignities by Egyptian
soldiers escorting them. The
scene is surprisingly
unconventional, and the harsh
treatment meted out to the
foreigners contrasts markedly
with the effeminate finery of the
courtiers. The relief is very fine,
with beautifully modeled details
such as the hands of the men,
and is in many respects a
continuation of the best ʿAmarna
tradition. Some of the relief
fragments which have been
known for a long time have been
located on this wall and casts of
a few of them have been set in
their correct positions (a block
with southern captives in the
Museo Civico in Bologna, and
another which used to be in the
Zizinia collection in Alexandria).

and Vienna, have proudly displayed reliefs and stelae from the tomb of the Great Commander of the
Army, Haremhab. Haremhab was the military
power behind the throne in the post-ʿAmarna
period, during the reigns of Tutʿankhamun and
Aya, and himself became the last king of the 18th
Dynasty. His royal tomb is in the Valley of the Kings
at Thebes (KV 57), but the monuments in museums
came from an earlier tomb which he had built
before ascending the throne. Its position was
nowhere precisely recorded and both Thebes and
Memphis were initially considered until the Belgian

Egyptologist Jean Capart advanced strong argu-
ments in favor of a Memphite location in 1921.
However, it was not until 54 years later, in January
1975, that he was proved right.

The standard features of the New-Kingdom free-
standing tomb chapel at Saqqara were an open
court, sometimes with round columns or square pillars on one or more of its sides, and the cult room
situated at the back of the mastaba. The main element of the cult room was a stela on the central
east–west axis of the tomb, while there were often
further stelae and statues in other parts of the

Those allowed to enter the underground parts of the animal necropolis during an animal funeral used to leave behind small votive stelae as tokens of their piety. Nowadays only their emplacements are sometimes left.

chapel. A small pyramid was usually built above or behind the cult room. The mouth of the shaft leading to the underground burial chamber opened into the court.

Other important tombs close to Haremhab's monument include those of two treasury officials, Maya, who served Tut῾ankhamun and Haremhab, and Tia (and his wife of the same name, a daughter of Sety I), a contemporary of Ramesses II.

New Kingdom tombs of Apis bulls
The cult of the Apis bull was closely connected with that of the chief Memphite god Ptah. From the reign of Amenhotep III onwards the tombs of the mummified Apis bulls are known from the Serapeum at Saqqara.

Nonroyal tombs of the Late and Greco-Roman Periods
During the 26th Dynasty the designers of Egyptian tombs apparently achieved what they had vainly attempted for the previous two millennia: they designed an almost completely robber-proof tomb. In many Saqqara tombs of this period a vaulted burial chamber was built at the bottom of a very large and deep shaft which was subsequently filled with sand. Somewhat paradoxically, removing the enormous mass of this unstable material from the shaft presented the tomb robbers with much greater technical difficulties than cutting through or around the stone blocking of the shafts of earlier periods. The other type of tomb known from this period is the more conventional rock-cut tomb.

The majority of the tombs of the Late and Greco-Roman Periods are near the Step Pyramid enclosure: 1. to the north, along the avenue of sphinxes linking the temples on the eastern edge of the plateau with the Serapeum (mainly 30th Dynasty and later); 2. to the east, particularly shaft tombs in the area of the pyramid of Userkaf, with rock-cut tombs further east, in the escarpment (mainly 26th Dynasty); 3. to the west and continuing northward toward Abusir (apparently mainly Greco-Roman); 4. to the south, and close to the pyramid of Wenis (mainly 26th and 27th Dynasties, but also a large Ptolemaic tomb).

The Serapeum and other parts of the sacred animal necropolis in the Late and Greco-Roman Periods
The Apis bulls were by far the most important cult animals buried at Saqqara. Ramesses II abandoned the earlier individual tombs and started an underground gallery (the "Lesser Vaults") in which the mummified bodies of Apis bulls were deposited in large niches on either side. Since there was only one of these animals at a time, an Apis bull burial occurred about once every 14 years. The gallery of Ramesses II ultimately reached a length of 68 m. A second gallery (the "Greater Vaults"), cut at right angles to the earlier one, was inaugurated during

the 26th Dynasty, and the first Apis bull laid to rest there died in year 52 of Psammetichus I. This gallery, of a total length of 198 m, remained in use until the Greco-Roman Period. Visitors can admire huge stone sarcophagi of the buried Apis bulls as well as graffiti made by priests and workmen associated with the cult of Ptah "great of strength".

A complex of chapels and smaller temples grew up in the neighborhood of the catacombs of Apis bulls, together forming the Serapeum (from *Usir-Hapy*, the deceased Apis bull, Greek Osorapis, later linked to the artificially introduced god Sarapis of the Ptolemies). Nectanebo I and II of the 30th Dynasty were the two most distinguished contributors, the former probably also setting up the alley of human-headed sphinxes that approached the Serapeum from the city of Memphis, in the east, below the Saqqara plateau. In 1850 one of these sphinxes, which was visible above the sand, gave Auguste Mariette the idea that the Serapeum mentioned by Classical authors should be sought at Saqqara. Several years earlier the English antiquarian A. C. Harris had come independently to the same conclusion.

At the east end of the alley of sphinxes there were temples, among them the Anubieion and the Asklepieion, most of which were built by the Ptolemies. These temples were associated with animal cults and in their vicinity are communal burials of mummified jackals and cats. The excavations conducted since the 1960s by the Egypt Exploration Society revealed other parts of the sacred animal necropolis, with galleries of the mummified "Mother of the Apis" cows, falcons, ibises, and baboons, near the northwest edge of the Saqqara necropolis.

Below Abusir from the northeast: the pyramid of Sahureʿ in the foreground, followed by those of Neuserreʿ and Neferirkareʿ, with the remains of Reʿneferef's structure at the back. This aerial view was taken before the excavations of the Czech Institute of Egyptology (still in progress).

Abusir

The solar temple

The northernmost monument at Abusir, halfway between Abu Ghurab and the Abusir pyramids, is the solar temple built by King Userkaf at the beginning of the 5th Dynasty. This is the earliest preserved solar temple in Egypt, so its simplicity and lack of relief decoration come as no surprise; but Userkaf's short reign did not allow him to complete the temple. Some Egyptian texts write its name with a hieroglyphic sign of an obelisk base surrounded by an enclosure wall. This seems to indicate that the obelisk was a later feature, and the excavation and architectural study of the temple undertaken by Herbert Ricke and Gerhard Haeny between 1954 and 1957 showed that this was indeed the case.

Siegfried Schott and Ricke suggested that the lower part of the temple was connected with the cult of the goddess Neith, whose standard Memphite epithet during the Old Kingdom was "North-of-the-Wall" (indicating that her sanctuary was situated north of Memphis). Absence of any inscriptional evidence from Abusir referring to Neith, however, demands that the problem be approached with caution.

The pyramids

Userkaf built his pyramid at Saqqara, but the next five kings of the 5th Dynasty (and possibly also Menkauhor) moved to Abusir.

The pyramid complex of Sahureʿ was a magnificent structure both in size and decoration. Its plan can serve as a typical example of Egyptian royal funerary architecture of the 5th Dynasty. Fragments of the reliefs which decorated the causeway linking the king's valley and pyramid temples were discov-

ered in the early 1990s. They show the transport of Sahureʿ's pyramid capstone (pyramidion), men at military training (archery target practice, wrestling, fighting with staves), dancers, rows of officials, emaciated desert tribesmen, and other topics. The basic building material throughout the complex was local limestone, with finer limestone from the quarries at Tura (ferried across the river from the east bank) employed for reliefs, red granite from Aswan used for columns, door jambs and lintels, and black basalt for pavements. The core masonry of the pyramid, which was of poor quality, was originally concealed behind the outer casing. The casing was subsequently stripped away, so that the structure is now little more than a huge pile of rubble.

Only about one hundredth of the original 10,000 square meters of the temple decoration is preserved, but the fragmentary scenes, now mostly in museums, are spectacular. The theme of the reliefs is the king himself and his worldly activities, as well as scenes characterizing his relationship to the gods. Perhaps the most remarkable are the large wall compositions showing Sahureʿ shooting desert animals with a bow and arrows and Egyptian seagoing boats returning from an Asiatic expedition. It is, however, uncertain how historically accurate such scenes were. The carving technique is the best "low" raised relief (painted, as was always the practice) in which figures and texts project only a few millimeters above the surface of the stone.

The pyramid complexes of Neferirkareʿ and Neuserreʿ have suffered even more than that of their predecessor. Neferirkareʿ designed his funerary complex on a larger scale than Sahureʿ, but did not complete it; its unfinished lower part was later appropriated by Neuserreʿ, who diverted the causeway to his own pyramid temple. Neferirkareʿ's temple produced a large group of papyri which provide the most important source of information on Old

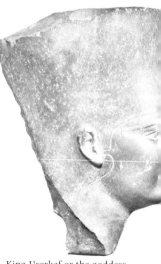

King Userkaf or the goddess Neith? An almost perfectly preserved head of a graywacke statue wearing the Egyptian red crown, found near the solar temple. This type of headdress was worn by the king, but also by the goddess Neith; the former seems a more likely identification. Cairo, Egyptian Museum.

Below Czech and Egyptian archaeologists preparing to open the sarcophagus containing the mummified body of Iuf'a, a priest of the 27th Dynasty, at south-west Abusir. This area is relatively little explored and may hold further surprises.

Kingdom temple administration. Similar documents were found in the small temple attached to the pyramid of queen Khentkaus, south of the pyramid of Neferirkare'. The southernmost pyramid at Abusir, which was hardly begun, belonged to Re'neferef; more papyri were found in its vicinity. The early stage of the building of yet another pyramid, perhaps belonging to the shadowy king Shepseskare', is at north Abusir.

The exploration of the pyramids and tombs at Abusir was carried out by Ludwig Borchardt at the beginning of the 20th century. The continuing excavations by the Czechoslovak (now Czech) Institute of Egyptology, which started in the mid-1960s, have transformed our understanding of the site through the discovery of important new monuments.

The nonroyal tombs

Among the nonroyal tombs at Abusir, the most important is the family mastaba of Ptahshepses, the vizier (the highest state official) and son-in-law of Neuserre'. It is situated north-east of the pyramid of Neuserre' and was restored in the 1970s and 1980s. It is one of the largest nonroyal tombs of the Old Kingdom, so much so that in the 1840s Carl Richard Lepsius numbered it as his nineteenth Egyptian pyramid. Other mastaba tombs, including several tombs of princesses, are to the south-east of Neuserre's pyramid and in the south part of Abusir.

Several shaft tombs of the 26th–27th Dynasties have been identified and excavated at Abusir since 1980, including the tomb of the Egyptian administrator under the Persian 27th Dynasty, Udjahorresnet. The contemporary tomb of Iuf'a, a priest connected with the temple of Neith at Sais, is among the few Egyptian tombs to have escaped the attention of ancient tomb robbers.

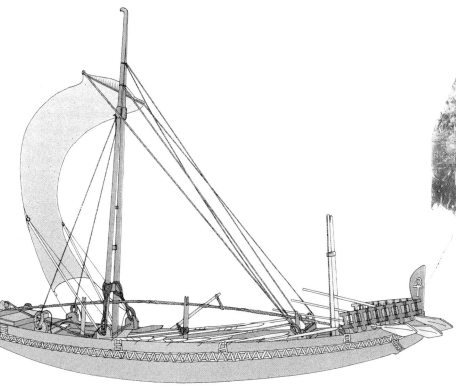

Although the mortuary temple of Sahure' produced the earliest pictorial record of Egyptian seagoing boats, their sophisticated features point to a long period of maritime activities before that (their appearance is shown here in a reconstruction). In particular, in the absence of a keel, Egyptian boats had to rely on a hogging truss (a cable connecting the prow and the stern of the vessel) for longitudinal rigidity. Old Kingdom representations of seagoing boats are rare: in addition to these only reliefs from the causeway of Wenis and another reused at el-Lisht are known. Berlin, Ägyptisches Museum.

Abu Ghurab

The rulers of the 5th Dynasty, with the exception of Shepseskareʿ, Izezi, and Wenis, hoped to ensure the continuation of their relationship with the Heliopolitan sun god Reʿ in the afterlife by building special temples for this purpose. Each king built only one such structure. Unlike temples of other deities, they were situated on the desert margin, not far from the royal pyramids. The names of six of these solar temples are known from Egyptian texts but only two have so far been located by archaeologists.

The solar temple built by King Neuserreʿ at Abu Ghurab is the finest example of this type of building, and is unlikely to be surpassed even if the four as yet undiscovered are found in the future. In its general features it owes much to the typical pyramid complex of the same period. Its main axis is east–west and it consists of:
1. the valley temple (close to a canal, so that it could be approached by boat);
2. the causeway (linking the valley temple with the upper part of the complex);
3. the upper temple.

The dominant feature of the upper temple was a large open court with an altar and a masonry-built (not monolithic) obelisk, the symbol of the sun god. A corridor around the temple and the chapel south of the obelisk were decorated with scenes showing the king taking part in the ceremonies of the *sed*-festival. Much more unusual, however, were scenes in the "Chamber of the Seasons." The creative influence which the sun god exerted on nature was expressed there by scenes characteristic of the Egyptian countryside in the *akhet* season (the inundation) and the *shemu* season (the harvest). Depictions of animals and plants

Left Open court of the upper temple at Abu Ghurab from the east, with the obelisk base and the altar, and (*right*) the latter seen from the west. The unusually shaped calcite altar consists of four *hetep* signs, each representing a simple offering mat with a loaf of bread placed on it; its diameter is some 6 m.

Below Reconstruction of the solar temple complex of Neuserreʿ at Abu Ghurab.

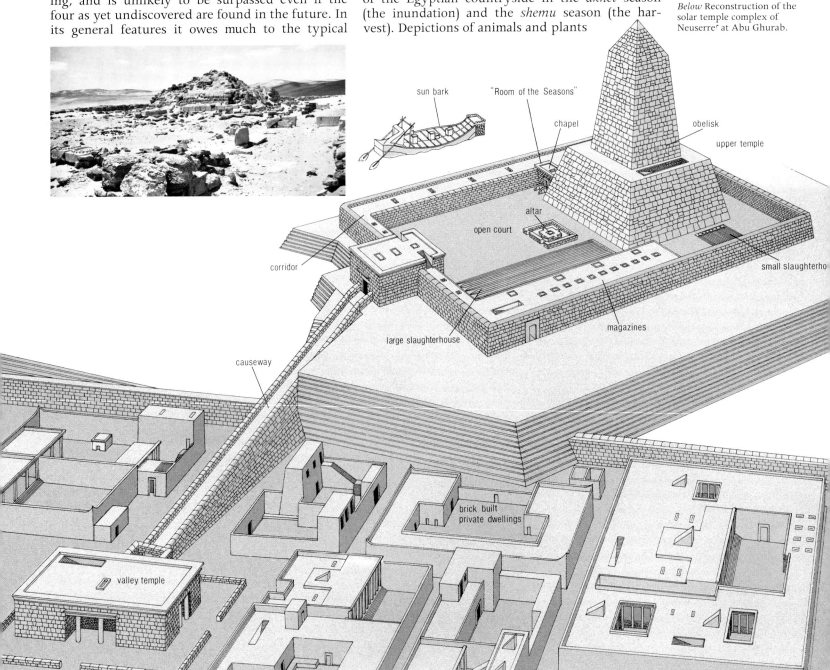

dominate these reliefs; human beings play only a limited role. Representations of this type are only partly paralleled in the pyramid complexes of Neuserre⸗ at Abusir and of Wenis at Saqqara.

South of the upper temple was a mud brick imitation of the bark of the sun god, about 30 m long.

The temple was uncovered by the German archaeologists Ludwig Borchardt, Heinrich Schäfer, and Friedrich W. von Bissing in 1898–1901, and its relief fragments were scattered among many museums and collections, mainly in Germany. Many of them perished during World War II.

Zawyet el-ʿAryan

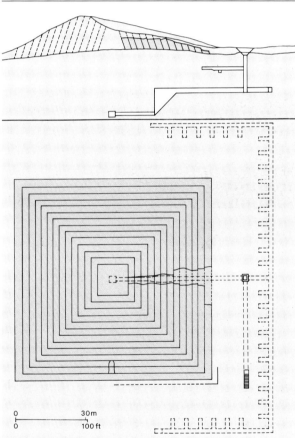

Plan and section of the "Layer Pyramid."

Neither of the two pyramids at Zawyet el-ʿAryan was completed. The earlier one, the "Layer Pyramid," which was started as a step pyramid, is tentatively attributed to King Khaʿba of the 3rd Dynasty, while the other, the "Unfinished Pyramid," is dated to the 4th Dynasty by its more advanced architectural features and the method of recording its owner's name in builders' graffiti.

One of the tombs near the pyramid of Khaʿba contained clay sealings and a pottery fragment with the name of the Dynasty 0 ruler Naʿrmer.

Below Egyptian countryside in summer (*shemu*), on a relief from the west wall of the "Chamber of the Seasons" at Abu Ghurab: mullet in water, and two registers of animals, some of them giving birth, including addax (upper register, 5th from left), oryx (upper register, 4th from left, also below), gazelle, with an ostrich (upper register); the hounds on the left of the lower register belong with the figure of a hunter, of which all that remains is a basket for carrying young captured animals that was slung over the shoulder. Berlin, Ägyptisches Museum.

Giza

The three Giza pyramids of the 4th Dynasty start looming on the horizon as soon as one has passed through the Cairo suburb which lent them its name and proceeds in a southwesterly direction along Shariaᶜ al-Ahram (Avenue of the Pyramids). The history of the site, however, goes back much further, at least to the reign of King Ninetjer of the 2nd Dynasty, whose name occurs on some jar sealings found in a tomb in the south part of the site. An even earlier tomb of the reign of King Wadj of the 1st Dynasty was located to the south of the area usually described as the Giza necropolis.

The site falls naturally into two well-defined groups situated on higher ground. The first unit, which is much the larger and more important, consists of the pyramids and the surrounding fields of nonroyal mastabas. The valley temples belonging to the pyramids, and the Great Sphinx with the adjacent temples, are situated below this elevated plateau. There is little doubt that the Giza pyramids are mutually related on the ground, but this is probably due to the techniques employed when the sites for each of them were surveyed. A relationship based on astronomical considerations, such as imitation of the positions of the stars of Orion's Belt, has not been proved and is unlikely.

The smaller and less important south group, containing only nonroyal tombs, is on a ridge to the southeast.

The systematic study of Giza started in the first half of the 19th century. Among early explorers the most prominent were Giovanni Battista Caviglia, Giovanni Battista Belzoni, R. W. Howard Vyse and J. S. Perring. C. R. Lepsius and the Prussian Expedition worked there in the early 1840s. Auguste Mariette and W. M. Flinders Petrie were active at the site in the second half of the 19th century and at the beginning of the 20th. George Andrew Reisner, Hermann Junker, and Selim Hassan, however, contributed more than anyone else to our knowledge of Giza. Although probably more systematically excavated than any other Egyptian site, recent discoveries by the Egyptian Supreme Council of Antiquities and other excavators show that its exploration cannot even now be regarded as complete.

The pyramid complex of Khufu

Khufu's pyramid, usually called the "Great Pyramid," is one of the most famous monuments in the world. Its majestic size and perfection of construction have made it the focus of attention of visitors to the Memphite area since time immemorial. The pyramid was almost certainly robbed of its original contents during the period of political instability and social unrest which followed the collapse of the central royal power after the end of the Old

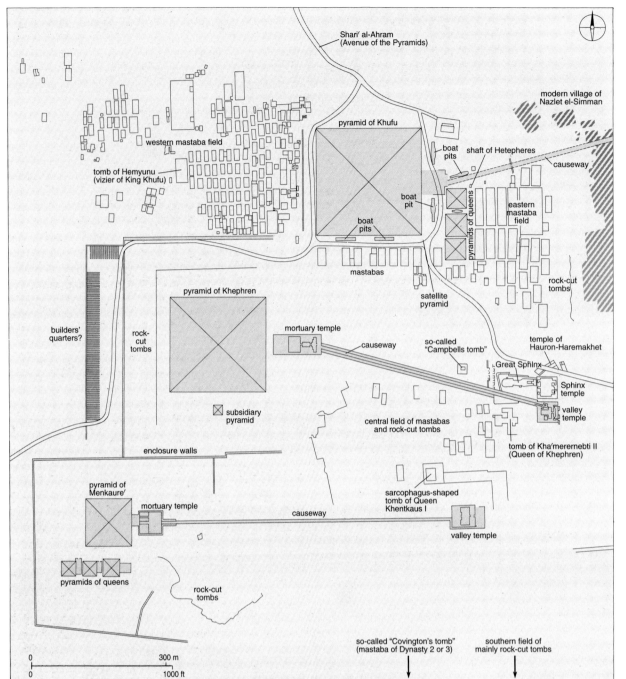

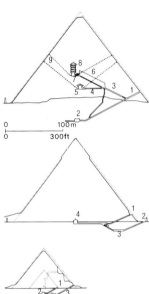

Above Sections of the Giza pyramids looking west: Khufu: 1 descending passage, 2 burial chamber, possibly of the 1st plan, 3 ascending passage, 4 level passage, 5 burial chamber, possibly of the 2nd plan ("Queen's Chamber"), 6 great gallery, 7 burial chamber, possibly of the 3rd plan ("King's Chamber"), 8 weight-relieving rooms, 9 "air shafts" (perhaps of religious significance). Khephren: 1 upper entrance, 2 lower entrance, 3 burial chamber of the 1st plan, 4 burial chamber of the 2nd plan. Menkaure: 1 abandoned descending passage of the 1st plan, 2 burial chamber of the 1st plan, 3 descending passage, 4 burial chamber of the 3rd plan.

Kingdom. Modern explorers found the Great Pyramid empty, with only the massive granite sarcophagus in the burial chamber indicating its original purpose.

During the Middle Ages the outer limestone casing of the pyramid was completely stripped off. Many buildings of old Giza and Cairo probably owe their stone material to the Great Pyramid. Today it is, apart from the small pyramids of Khufu's queens, the only element of the original pyramid complex which remains spectacularly obvious. Basalt blocks from the valley temple have been found under the houses of the village of Nazlet el-Simman. The causeway, discernible on old maps of the site and still visible in the last century, also disappeared when the modern village started growing. Only a patch of a basalt pavement against the east face of the pyramid shows the position of the pyramid temple. The remains of a small satellite pyramid, previously undetected, were found near the south-east corner of Khufu's pyramid in 1991.

The question of whether the interior of the Great Pyramid (see section) underwent alterations in the process of the construction, or whether its final form was planned from the beginning, has not yet been fully answered. The modern visitor enters the pyramid by an opening forced by Caliph Maʿmun's men in the 9th century CE, which is situated below and somewhat west of the original entrance. The descending passage leads to a chamber below ground level. Another chamber (the "Queen's Chamber", although this is a modern term and there is no evidence that it would have been used for the burial of a queen), possibly the burial chamber of the 2nd plan, is in the mass of the pyramid and approached by ascending and level passages. The ascending passage is extended by the great gallery to reach the burial chamber proper (the "King's Chamber"). The great gallery, with its high corbeled ceiling, is easily the most impressive part of the whole interior. One of its purposes was probably to provide space for storing the granite blocks

Right "There is no way to ruin it, but by beginning at the top. It rests upon a basis too firm to be attacked on that part; and whoever would undertake it, would find as much difficulty, as there was to raise it" (F. L. Norden, *Travels in Egypt and Nubia*, i, 1757, p. 72).

which were slid down the ascending passage after the funeral in order to seal it.

Narrow shafts run from the "Queen's Chamber" and the "King's Chamber" in what appears to be the shortest route toward the outside of the pyramid. Their description as "air shafts" is almost certainly incorrect but their purpose has not yet been explained to complete satisfaction. If, as it has been suggested, they are precisely oriented astronomically, they may prove to be important for the dating of the pyramid. In 1993 Rudolf Gantenbrink explored the south shaft in the "Queen's Chamber" by sending a robot equipped with a video camera which established the presence of a limestone slab with copper fittings some 65 meters into the shaft. The suggestion that there is a hidden chamber behind this slab is improbable. It may just mark the point reached when the design of the pyramid was changed during its construction.

Even nowadays building the Great Pyramid would present considerable technological and managerial problems. The project must have been more or less completed by the end of Khufu's 23-year reign, and that meant that every year 100,000 large blocks (i.e. about 285 a day), each weighing on average $2\frac{1}{2}$ tons, must have been quarried, dressed, brought to the building site, and set in place. As the building progressed, the height to which it was necessary to lift the blocks increased, while at the same time the working platform at the top of the pyramid decreased rapidly in size. Once the project was "off the ground," transport of material was almost certainly effected exclusively by human force, because restricted space prevented the use of draft animals. Even such simple devices as the pulley or wheeled carts were yet to be invented, and the problems connected with moving and lifting heavy stone blocks must have been enormous. At least as many people as those actually dealing with the stone blocks must have been engaged in auxiliary works such as construction of inclined ramps along which the blocks were dragged, maintenance of tools, provision of food and water, etc. Because of the uncertainty about the methods the Egyptians actually used, any estimate of the size of the labor force must remain a mere guess.

The sheer size of the task, the accuracy with which the structure was designed and built, the fact that no burial is on record as having ever been found in the Great Pyramid, and the seemingly improbable idea that the object of all this would have been to provide a tomb for one individual, have long worried scholars as well as amateurs. The interest does not seem to be abating.

A remarkable discovery was made in the early 1950s. A rectangular pit close to the south face of the pyramid of Khufu was found to contain parts of a dismantled wooden boat. In the airtight surroundings they remained almost perfectly preserved. The vessel is over 40 meters long and has a displacement of about 40 tons. The location of

Left The great gallery of Khufu's pyramid, as seen by the artists accompanying Napoleon's expedition. "You advance on with crouching. For though it is twenty-two feet in height, and has a raised way on each side, it is, however, so steep and slippery, that if you happen to fail of the holes, made for facilitating the ascent, you slide backwards, and return, in spite of yourself, quite to the resting place" (F. L. Norden, *Travels in Egypt and Nubia*, i, 1757, p. 79). Nowadays the "advance" is much easier.

Right One enters the valley temple of Khephren through one of the two doorways in its eastern facade; short passages lead into a transverse antechamber connected by another short passage with the main T-shaped pillared hall.

Below When C. R. Lepsius and his team visited Giza in 1842–43, Khufu's causeway was still clearly visible. According to Herodotus the causeway was "all of stone polished and carven with figures"; although some decorated blocks have been found, his statement has not yet been fully confirmed.

another pit, also containing a boat, is known, but the pit is still to be opened. The boats were perhaps used to convey the body of the deceased king to the place of purification and embalming and finally to the valley temple.

The pyramid complex of Khephren

Khufu's son and successor Reʿdjedef started constructing his pyramid at Abu Rawash, north of Giza, but the next king, Khephren, another son of Khufu, built his funerary complex beside his father's. Although it was designed on a more modest scale, a slight increase in the incline of the faces of the pyramid produced the effect of a structure comparable in size to the Great Pyramid. The pyramid (usually known as the "Second Pyramid") retains some of its original smooth outer casing near its summit, perhaps due to a change in the method of positioning the blocks.

The valley temple of Khephren's complex, next to the Great Sphinx, is a soberly designed building which, in the absence of almost any decoration, relies on the effect produced by the polished granite casing of the walls of its rooms and its calcite floors. A pit in one of the rooms contained a set of diorite-gneiss and graywacke sculptures of Khephren, deposited there in a later period, among them probably the most famous Egyptian statue, which shows the king seated with a hawk perched on the back slab of the statue.

Left Khephren and Horus, the majesty of the pharaoh and his proximity to gods: an abstract concept expressed in stone. This type of sculpture was probably already introduced by the reign of Khufu, and certainly more than one piece was made for Khephren's temples. Epigones exist, but they all fade into nothingness in comparison. Diorite-gneiss. Height: 1·68 m. Cairo, Egyptian Museum.

Top right Menkaureꜥ with Hathor "Lady of the Sycamore in all her Places (of worship)" and a personification of the 7th Upper Egyptian nome. Graywacke. Height: 96 cm. From the valley temple of Menkaureꜥ. Cairo, Egyptian Museum.

Center right Restored columned portico of the family tomb of Seshemnefer, near the southeast corner of the pyramid of Khufu. Two seated statues and six small obelisks originally flanked the approach. End of the 5th or early 6th Dynasty.

Bottom right The dwarf Seneb with his wife Sentyotes and a small son and daughter. Painted limestone. Height: 33 cm. Mid-6th Dynasty or a little later. From Seneb's tomb west of the pyramid of Khufu. Cairo, Egyptian Museum.

Below "Reserve head" of an unknown lady. Limestone. Height: 25 cm. Reign of Khufu. From the tomb of Kanefer, west of the pyramid of Khufu. Berkeley (CA), Phoebe Apperson Hearst Museum of Anthropology.

The pyramid complex of Menkaureꜥ

The pyramid complex of Menkaureꜥ, another king of the 4th Dynasty, is somewhat dwarfed by its two Giza companions. Although hastily finished in mud brick, its valley temple produced a superb collection of royal statues. Some of these were triads (groups of three figures) and showed the king accompanied by the Memphite goddess Hathor and personifications of nomes (provinces) of Egypt. There was also a standing double statue of the king and one of his wives, the earliest of this type in Egyptian statuary.

The pyramid (known as the "Third Pyramid") was refurbished, probably during the 26th Dynasty when the cult of the kings buried at Giza was revived. The basalt sarcophagus found in the burial chamber was, unfortunately, lost at sea while being shipped to England, but the remains of a wooden coffin, purporting to be that of Menkaureꜥ, were certainly put in the pyramid some 1,900 years later. An inscription discovered in 1968 on the remains of the casing near the entrance of the pyramid probably refers to this remarkable ancient effort of restoration.

Nonroyal tombs

Close to each pyramid complex are fields of tombs of officials and priests. Many of these tombs were presented by the king himself, built by royal craftsmen, and benefited from the redistribution of offerings brought to the nearby pyramid complexes. A large number of people buried in these tombs had held priestly positions connected with the Giza necropolis during their lifetimes.

The most extensive mastaba fields are to the west, south, and east of the pyramid of Khufu. The nuclei of the west and east fields, contemporary with the Great Pyramid, consist of stone-built mastabas of a uniform size and arranged in regular rows. These cemeteries continued to be used through the rest of the Old Kingdom, with smaller tombs often being added in between the larger mastabas. The quarries to the southeast of the pyramids of Khephren and Menkaureꜥ, with their artificially created rock faces, provided ideal conditions for decorated rock-cut tombs, the earliest of this type in Egypt.

A typical mastaba, such as was built at Giza in the reign of Khufu, had a stone-built superstructure with a rectangular plan and slightly sloping faces. A shaft sunk through this superstructure and cut in the rock substratum terminated in a simple burial chamber. This shaft was permanently sealed after the burial had been deposited in the chamber. The original cult chapel consisted of one or two mud brick rooms against the east face of the mastaba. The main element of this chapel was an inscribed slab stela with a representation of the deceased seated at a table and with a list of offerings. Offerings were brought for the *ka* (spirit) of the deceased before this stela on prescribed days.

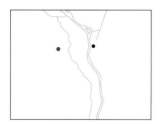

The Great Sphinx before the removal of the sand covering its body: a photograph taken before 1875.

There were no other decorated elements in the tomb.

The mastabas at Giza were among the earliest nonroyal stone-built tombs in Egypt and their original simple design underwent a rapid development. The greatest changes occurred in the chapel. An interior chapel was introduced in some of the tombs in which the offering chamber and subsidiary rooms were contained in the core of the mastaba itself, while other tombs continued to be built with an exterior chapel. The slab stela was replaced by a false door, and the walls of the chapel began to be lined with fine limestone and decorated with reliefs.

The chief royal wives were the only persons apart from the king himself who were granted the privilege of being buried in small pyramids, situated close to the main pyramidal structure. A shaft with a chamber which contained furniture as well as funerary items of Queen Hetepheres, the wife of Snofru and the mother of Khufu, was found to the east of the Great Pyramid in 1925. It lacked a superstructure of any kind and, indeed, the most important object which one would expect in a tomb, the queen's mummy, was not present.

The Great Sphinx
The concept of the sphinx, a creature with a human head and a lion's body, is not known from Egypt before the reign of Redjedef, Khephren's immediate predecessor. The perfection with which these two incongruous elements were blended on a huge scale in the Great Sphinx is admirable, but the idea behind this creation is still rather obscure. The Great Sphinx at Giza is probably associated with the pyramid complex of Khephren (rather than Khufu, as has been suggested), and may represent a guardian deity with the facial features of Khephren. Suggestions that the statue predates the other monuments at Giza by several thousand years carry little conviction. The temple in front of the Great Sphinx bears some resemblance to the later solar temples built by the kings of the 5th Dynasty at Abu Ghurab and Abusir, but it was only some 1,000 years later that the colossal statue started being identified with the god Harmakhis ("Horus on the Horizon"), the local form of the god Horus.

The sand covering the Sphinx has had to be cleared several times. The earliest recorded clearance was undertaken by King Thutmose IV, who left a record of it on the so-called "Dream Stela" erected between its forepaws. In the eyes of many, the Great Sphinx at Giza is a symbol of Egypt and anything connected with it arouses much scholarly as well as public interest. Its restoration is an ongoing project.

Giza after the end of the Old Kingdom
With the end of the Old Kingdom the heyday of Giza's glory was over, and for the next 600 years

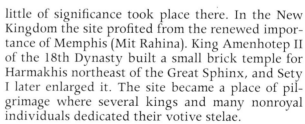

Left Sety I embraced by a goddess, perhaps Isis, on the doorway to the outer hall of the temple of Harmakhis.

Below Lid of the basalt anthropoid sarcophagus of Ptahhotep, a contemporary of Darius I. From "Campbell's Tomb," close to Khephren's causeway. Oxford, Ashmolean Museum.

little of significance took place there. In the New Kingdom the site profited from the renewed importance of Memphis (Mit Rahina). King Amenhotep II of the 18th Dynasty built a small brick temple for Harmakhis northeast of the Great Sphinx, and Sety I later enlarged it. The site became a place of pilgrimage where several kings and many nonroyal individuals dedicated their votive stelae.

During the 21st Dynasty the chapel of the southernmost of the queens' pyramids in the Khufu complex was reconstructed into a temple of Isis "Mistress-of-the-Pyramid." The temple was enlarged during the 26th Dynasty, and the refurbishing of the burial in the Third Pyramid might have been due to the priests of this temple. Several large isolated tombs of this period are scattered along the causeway of Khephren, and doorways leading to the plundered remains of others can be seen in the rock face west of the Great Sphinx.

Abu Rawash

The site of Abu Rawash, which took its name from the village situated to the east, served as the necropolis for an important administrative center at the very beginning of Egyptian history. Excavations have revealed objects inscribed with the names of two kings of the 1st Dynasty, ʿAha and Den.

King Reʿdjedef, who chose the commanding plateau of Abu Rawash for the site of his pyramid complex, did not therefore move on to virgin ground. The pyramid is the northernmost in the Memphite necropolis. Remains of building material visible at the site indicate that it was planned to be at least partly cased with red granite. The causeway, about 1,500 meters long, approaches the pyramid and its temple from the northeast instead of from the customary east, but this was determined by the character of the terrain rather than religious considerations. Because Reʿdjedef reigned for only eight years, his funerary monument hardly got beyond the initial stages of its construction. The Franco-Swiss excavations which began in 1993 have, however, shown that there is no reason to regard the pyramid's design, and so Raʿdjedef's position in the 4th Dynasty, as exceptional.

The pyramid complex produced some excellent examples of royal statuary, though even these are sadly fragmentary. The statues are made of the hard red quartzite of Gebel Ahmar (east of modern Cairo). Apart from providing the probably somewhat idealized features of the king, one of them is an attractive seated statue with a small figure of Reʿdjedef's queen Khentetka shown kneeling holding the leg of her husband. Although eagerly taken up by makers of nonroyal statues, this type was not repeated in royal sculpture.

Abu Rawash never regained its shortlived importance under Reʿdjedef. However, one of the late structures at Wadi Qaren, north of the pyramid, yielded the upper part of a beautiful statuette of Queen Arsinoe II, the sister and wife of Ptolemy II Philadelphus.

Above When discovered during the excavations of the Institut Français d'Archéologie Orientale by F. Bisson de la Roque in 1922–23, this alabaster head of Arsinoe II still possessed an equally attractive torso, now lost. Present height: 12·2 cm. New York, Metropolitan Museum of Art.

Right Quartzite head of King Reʿdjedef wearing the royal *nemes* headcloth with the uraeus: the best-preserved of many fragments of at least 20 statues, originally painted. Found by E. Chassinat in 1900–01. Height: 28 cm. Paris, Musée du Louvre.

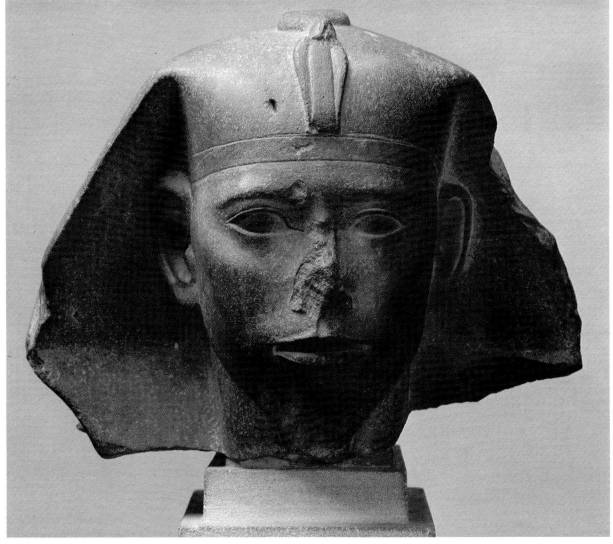

LOWER EGYPT – THE DELTA

Top Silver coffin of Psusennes I, from San el-Hagar. Cairo, Egyptian Museum.

Center Granite naos of Amasis at Tell el-Rub'a.

Bottom Remains of the temples at San el-Hagar.

The delta's prehistory and most ancient history are buried under the silt. Only now is the area beginning to receive the archaeological attention it unquestionably deserves.

The eastern delta was the sensitive shoulder which Egypt rubbed with Asia. In the later Middle Kingdom it was settled by Asiatics and became the center from which they ruled; subsequently it was the Egyptian base for campaigns to Asia.

When the royal residence was moved to Pi-Ri'amsese in the 19th Dynasty, the delta took over the leadership of Egypt. Several of its cities saw their rulers at the helm of Egypt during the 3rd Intermediate and Late Periods. The delta's proximity to the political and economic centers of the ancient world favored its development under the Ptolemies and Romans.

Ausim
Scattered Late Period monuments.
Kom Abu Billo
Early Ptolemaic temple of Hathor. Necropolis with burials from 6th Dynasty to early centuries CE.
Kom el-Hisn
Temple of Sakhmet-Hathor of Middle Kingdom and later.
Old Kingdom town.
Cemeteries of Middle and New Kingdoms.
Naukratis
Greek trading town, with temples of Greek gods, as well as Amun and Thoth.
Alexandria
Ptolemaic and Roman temple of Sarapis (Serapeum).
Catacombs with statuary and relief decoration, including Kom el-Shuqafa.
Many fragmentary remains including palaces.
Abusir (Taposiris Magna)
Unfinished Ptolemaic temple. Animal necropolis.
Sa el-Hagar
Few visible remains of temple of Neith, but many objects in museums.
Tell el-Fara'in
Three mounds, two with town remains, one with temple enclosure.
Behbeit el-Hagar
Temple of Isis of Late and Ptolemaic Periods.
Tell Atrib
Temple of Amasis.
Town, temples, and necropolis of Greco-Roman Period.
Tomb of Queen Takhut.
Tell el-Muqdam
Now almost completely destroyed. Contained remains of temple of Mihos and tomb of Queen Kamama.
Samannud
Remains of temple of Onuris-Shu, of Late and Greco-Roman Periods.
el-Baqliya
Now completely destroyed.
Contained town and temple of Thoth at Tell el-Naqus, necropolis with cemetery of ibises at Tell el-Zereiki, and other remains at Tell el-Rub'a.
Tell el-Rub'a and Tell el-Timai
Late Old Kingdom mastabas, temple of Amasis, tomb of Nepheritis I, and cemetery of rams at Tell el-Rub'a.
Greco-Roman Period structures at Tell el-Timai.

el-Balamun
Late Period enclosure with at least three temples and a fort.
Heliopolis
Temple of Re' and ancillary structures of all periods at Tell Hisn, with obelisk of Senwosret I.
Tombs of High Priests of Heliopolis of 6th Dynasty and others of Late Period.
Ramessid tombs of Mnevis bulls at 'Arab el-Tawil.
Tell el-Yahudiya
Earthwork enclosure of late Middle Kingdom or 2nd Intermediate Period, containing temple and palace of Ramesses II.
Remains of temple and town of Onias.
Cemeteries of Middle Kingdom and later.
Tell Basta
Temple of Bastet by Osorkon II and others.
Smaller temples of 6th, 12th, 18th, and 22nd Dynasties, and Greco-Roman Period.
Cemeteries of animals, especially cats.
Saft el-Hinna
Temple enclosure of Sopd.
el-Khata'na, Tell el-Dab'a, and Qantir
Mounds indicating settlements of Middle Kingdom, 2nd Intermediate, and Ramessid Periods.
Remains of 12th-Dynasty chapel at Tell el-Qirqafa.
Temples, palaces, gardens, and settlement at Tell el-Dab'a (Avaris).
Middle Kingdom town and temple at Ezbet Rushdi el-Saghira.
Palace of 19th and 20th Dynasties at Qantir (Pi-Ri'amsese).
Remains of colossus of Ramesses II at Tell Abu el-Shafi'a.
Tell Nabasha
Enclosure with Ramessid temple of Wadjit and temple by Amasis.
Remains of Greco-Roman town.
Cemetery of Late Period.
San el-Hagar
Enclosure with temple of Amun by Psusennes I and others, with ancillary buildings.
Precinct of Mut, built by Siamun, Apries, and Ptolemy IV Philopator.
Six royal tombs of 21st and 22nd Dynasties.
Tell el-Maskhuta
Temple enclosure.

(Map labels:)
30°
Rosetta Mouth
Abuqir KANOPOS
Alexandria (el-Iskandariya) RAQOTE
Lake Idku
Kafr el-Dauwar
Lake Mariut
Kom el-Kanater
el-Amiriya
Abusir TAPOSIRIS MAGNA
Karm Abu Girg
el-Gharbaniyat
Wadi el-Natru
Qaret

(Legend:)
□ modern settlement
● featured ancient site
● other ancient site
Ⓐ civil airport
Cairo modern name
XOIS classical name
BAST ancient Egyptian name
road
track
railroad
built-up area
fertile area
scale 1:1 000 000
0   30 km
0   20 mi

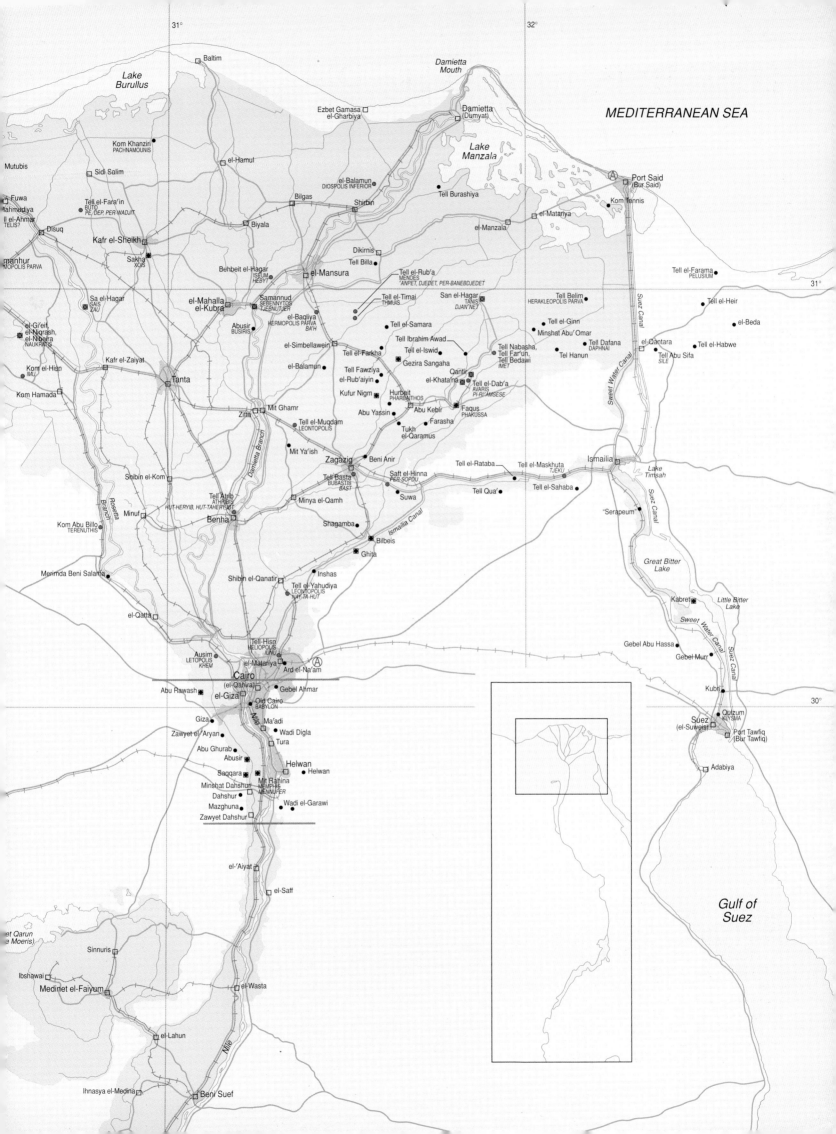

MEDITERRANEAN SEA

Lake Burullus

Baltim

Ezbet Gamasa el-Gharbiya

Damietta Mouth

Damietta (Dumyat)

Lake Manzala

Kom Khanziri PACHNAMOUNIS

Mutubis

Sidi Salim

el-Hamul

Port Said (Bur Said)

Kom Tennis

Fuwa
Mahmudiya
Il el-Ahmar
TELIS?

Tell el-Fara'in
BUTO
PE, DEP, PER-WADJIT

Bilgas

Shirbin

el-Balamun
DIOSPOLIS INFERIOR

Tell Burashiya

el-Matariya

Disuq

Kafr el-Sheikh

Biyala

el-Manzala

Tell el-Farama
PELUSIUM

manhur
MOPOLIS PARVA

Sakha
XOIS

Dikirnis

Tell Billa

Tell el-Heir

el-Beda

Behbeit el-Hagar
ISEUM
HEBYT

el-Mansura

Tell el-Rub'a
MENDES
'ANPET, DJEDET, PER-BANEBDJEDET

Sa el-Hagar
SAIS
ZAU

el-Mahalla
el-Kubra

Samannud
SEBENNYTOS
TJEBNUTJER

Tell el-Timai
THMUIS

San el-Hagar
TANIS
DJAN'NET

Tell Belim
HERAKLEOPOLIS PARVA

el-Qantara

Tell Abu Sifa
SILE

Tell el-Habwe

el-Gi'eif,
el-Niqrash,
el-Nibeira
NAUKRATIS

Abusir
BUSIRIS

el-Baqliya
HERMOPOLIS PARVA
BA'H

Tell el-Samara

Tell el-Ginn

Minshat Abu'Omar

Tell Dafana
DAPHNAI

el-Simbellawein

Tell Ibrahim Awad

Kom el-Hisn
IMU

Kafr el-Zaiyat

Tell el-Farkha

Tell el-Iswid

Tell Nabasha,
Tell Far'un,
Tell Bedawi
IMET

Tel Hanun

el-Balamun

Gezira Sangaha

Qantir

Tanta

Tell Fawziya

el-Khata'na

Tell el-Dab'a
AVARIS
PI-RI'AMSESE

Kom Hamada

el-Rub'aiyin

Kufur Nigm

Hurbeit
PHARBAITHOS

Faqus
PHAKUSSA

Zifta

Mit Ghamr

Abu Yassin

Abu Kebir

Farasha

Shibin el-Kom

Tell el-Muqdam
LEONTOPOLIS

Tukh
el-Qaramus

Mit Ya'ish

Zagazig

Beni Anir

Tell el-Rataba

Tell el-Maskhuta
TJEKU

Ismailia

Lake Timsah

Tell'Basta
BUBASTIS
BAST

Saft el-Hinna
PER-SOPDU

Tell el-Atrib
ATHRIBIS
HUT-HERYIB, HUT-TAHERYIBT

Minya el-Qamh

Suwa

Tell Qua'

Tell el-Sahaba

Minuf

Suez Canal

Benha

Shagamba

"Serapeum"

Kom Abu Billo
TERENUTHIS

Bilbeis

Ghita

Ismailia Canal

Great Bitter Lake

Merimda Beni Salama

Inshas

Little Bitter Lake

Kabret

Shibin el-Qanatir

Tell el-Yahudiya
LEONTOPOLIS
NAY-TA-HUT

el-Qatta

Sweet Water Canal

Gebel Abu Hassa

Gebel Murr

Tell-Hisn
HELIOPOLIS
IUNU

Suez Canal

Kubri

Ausim
LETOPOLIS
KHEM

Cairo
(el-Qahira)

Ard el-Na'am

el-Matariya

Quizum
KLYSMA

Abu Rawash

Gebel Ahmar

Suez
(el-Suweis)

el-Giza

Old Cairo
BABYLON

Port Tawfiq
(Bur Tawfiq)

Giza

Ma'adi

Zawyet el-'Aryan

Wadi Digla

Tura

Adabiya

Abu Ghurab

Abusir

Helwan

Helwan

Saqqara

Mit Rahina
MEMPHIS
MENNUFER

Minshat Dahshur

Dahshur

Wadi el-Garawi

Mazghuna

Zawyet Dahshur

Gulf of Suez

el-'Aiyat

el-Saff

et Qarun
e Moeris)

Sinnuris

Ibshawai

el-Wasta

Medinet el-Faiyum

Nile

el-Lahun

Ihnasya el-Medina

Beni Suef

Ausim

Ancient Egyptian *Khem* (Greek Letopolis), some 13 kilometers northwest of modern Cairo, was the capital of the 2nd Lower Egyptian nome. The nome and its falcon god Khenty-irty (a form of Horus, also referred to as Khenty-Khem, "The Foremost One of Khem") are mentioned in Egyptian texts as early as the 4th Dynasty, but so far only a few late monuments, bearing the names of Necho II, Psammetichus II, Hakoris, and Nectanebo I, have been found at the site.

Kom Abu Billo

At the point where the route leading from Wadi el-Natrun approaches the Rosetta branch of the Nile, there lies the town of Tarrana (from Coptic *Terenouti* and classical Terenuthis). The name derives from that of the serpent goddess Renenutet (Termuthis) who was probably worshiped in the area. The remains of the temple and the necropolis have been found nearby, at the mound of Kom Abu Billo.

The temple of Kom Abu Billo, dedicated to Hathor "Mistress of Mefket" (ancient Tarrana, but *mefket* also means turquoise), was located by F. Ll. Griffith in 1887–88. It was not possible to establish its complete plan, but blocks decorated with exquisite low raised relief showed it to be one of the few surviving works of Ptolemy I Soter, completed by Ptolemy II Philadelphus. Burials of cattle in the vicinity are probably connected with the cult of Hathor.

The large necropolis of Kom Abu Billo contains burials ranging from the 6th Dynasty to the 4th century CE. A number of New Kingdom pottery sarcophagi (called "slipper coffins"), with their lids modeled to imitate often very grotesque faces, have been found. The site is best known for a special type of tomb stela dating to the first four centuries CE (called "Terenuthis stelae"). The deceased, represented in un-Egyptian style, usually stands with upraised arms or reclines on a couch, with a short text in demotic or Greek below.

Kom el-Hisn

A large low mound, measuring some 500 meters across, called Kom el-Hisn, covers the remains of the ancient town of *Imu*. From the New Kingdom onwards this was the capital of the 3rd Lower Egyptian nome, replacing the earlier *Hut-ihyt*, which has not yet been located.

Kom el-Hisn has extensive remains of occupation

dating from the Old and Middle Kingdoms. The most important feature is the rectangular outline of a temple enclosure (about 115 by 64 meters). Statues of Amenemhet III and Ramesses II found there identify the temple as belonging to Sakhmet-Hathor. Hathor was the traditional goddess of the area.

The Middle Kingdom tomb of the "Overseer of Priests" Khesuwer southwest of the temple enclosure is one of the few major nonroyal tombs surviving in the delta. Extensive cemeteries (at least 700 graves) of the Middle and New Kingdoms have been excavated in the vicinity. Many of the Middle Kingdom burials of men contained weapons (battle-axes, spears, and daggers).

Naukratis

A mound near the villages el-Gi'eif, el-Nibeira, and el-Niqrash (the last perhaps preserving the ancient name), in the 5th (Saite) nome of Lower Egypt, is the site of the Greek trading post of Naukratis. The Greeks (initially Milesians) settled in the area some time during the 26th Dynasty, and under Amasis the town was granted a monopoly of Aegean trade.

Naukratis contained several almost entirely lost temples of Greek gods but also an Egyptian temple, dedicated probably to Amun and Thoth, in its southern part (the "Great Mound" within the "Great Temenos"). The Naukratis Stela of Nectanebo I in the Egyptian Museum in Cairo is the most splendid monument surviving from them.

Alexandria

The native Egyptian word for Alexandria was Raqote, a name that occurs in an early text of Ptolemy I Soter and designated an older settlement on the site. Remains of timber works from c. 400 BCE prove the harbor's existence before Alexander. Native Egyptians lived in a quarter, called Rhakotis by the Greeks, that may have contained monuments in an Egyptian style. Another native quarter was a walled settlement on Pharos, near which are Egyptianizing tombs of late Ptolemaic times. Among the lower

Above Early Ptolemaic relief from Kom Abu Billo: Ptolemy I Soter. Oxford, Ashmolean Museum.

Above Basalt royal head, probably of Amenemhet III, found in the tomb of Khesuwer at Kom el-Hisn, though originally from the temple nearby. The identification rests on the discovery of another sculpture of Amenemhet III in the temple. Height: 35 cm. Cairo, Egyptian Museum.

Below Painted tomb from Tigrane Pasha Street, Alexandria, reconstructed at Kom el-Shuqafa; c. 2nd century CE. The ornamentation is Classical, but the main scene is Egyptian-inspired, showing a winged disk above the mummy on a bier, with two mourning figures and two kites; both these pairs derive from Isis and Nephthys.

Right Alexandria. The necropolis areas are quite well preserved, being away from the center and mostly cut in the rock underground. The city center, however, has been constantly rebuilt, and land reclaimed from the sea.

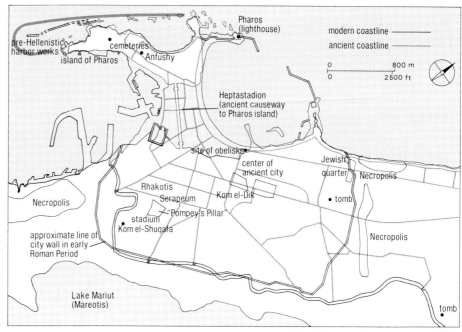

Below Recording a Ptolemaic sphinx found some seven meters underwater at a site near the fort of Qait Bey in Alexandria. Sphinxes of various dates, some as early as the reign of Senwosret III, have been discovered by French archaeologists under the direction of Jean-Yves Empereur.

classes there was widespread intermarriage between Greeks and Egyptians, but otherwise Alexandria was a mixed Greek city whose most important non-Greek element was Jewish. As the Hellenistic world's chief city and port, it was vital in the dissemination of Egyptian lore.

The Serapeum, the principal temple of the Greco-Egyptian god Sarapis, was in Rhakotis. Bilingual plaques date its founding to Ptolemy III Euergetes I. Its foundations survive, along with remains of the Roman replacement of around 200 CE and "Pompey's pillar" of the reign of Diocletian, which still stands. It contained much older Egyptian material, notably sphinxes and other scene-setting statuary. Objects like these, as well as obelisks and smaller pieces, were exported, no doubt through Alexandria, to decorate buildings in the Classical style in Rome, including temples and Hadrian's villa at Tivoli.

Near the Serapeum is the 1st–2nd century CE catacomb of Kom el-Shuqafa, whose burial areas contain Egyptianizing scenes and motifs. Chambers near ground level retain painted decoration; deeper parts have only statuary and relief. Unlike the much older tomb of Petosiris at Tuna el-Gebel, which has Graecizing scenes by Egyptian artists, the catacomb has Egyptian motifs in simplified Classical style, including parallel Greek and Egyptian paintings of the same motifs. For the Isis cult such work, whose style probably originated in Alexandria, was influential in the whole Roman world, at first running parallel with genuine Egyptian objects and later becoming more salient.

Underwater archaeology has uncovered stonework from the Ptolemaic harbor. Work there and near Fort Qait Bey, the site of the Pharos lighthouse, has revealed hundreds of blocks from Classical columns and smaller numbers of Egyptian blocks. The blocks came from such sites as Heliopolis and were reused in Roman and possibly Ptolemaic times. Most were used as building stone rather than for their Egyptian style. The sphinxes include pre-Ptolemaic and Ptolemaic examples. The most important finds are monumental Egyptian-style statues of Ptolemaic kings and their wives that had probably been erected nearby.

Abusir

About 45 kilometers west of Alexandria is Abusir, ancient Taposiris Magna, an important town in the Ptolemaic Period, which has an unfinished temple of Osiris in native Egyptian style. The enclosure, interrupted by an entrance pylon on the east, is in limestone instead of the traditional mud brick, but uses mud-brick building techniques. The temple is uninscribed and cannot be dated precisely. Nearby was a large animal necropolis, which is a further indication of the town's significance as a native center.

The Chief of Physicians Psammetikseneb kneeling with a naos of Neith: basalt statue originally set up in the temple of the goddess at Sa el-Hagar. Heavily restored, probably in the 18th century. Height: 63 cm. 26th Dynasty. Vatican City (Rome), Museo Gregoriano Egizio.

Sa el-Hagar

Sais (ancient Egyptian *Zau*) and its goddess Neith are attested from the very beginning of Egyptian history. The town was the capital of the 5th Lower Egyptian nome, which until the 12th Dynasty also incorporated the area south of it, later the 4th nome. Politically, Sais came to prominence toward the end of the 8th century BCE. Its ambitious leaders Tefnakhte and Bocchoris (later the 24th Dynasty) clashed with the rulers of the 25th (Nubian) Dynasty. Their successors ruled over Egypt; temples, palaces, and royal tombs (all largely undiscovered) bore witness to the success of these kings of the 26th (Saite) Dynasty. Some idea of the topography of Sais can be gleaned from the remarks of Herodotus, who wrote in the middle of the 5th century BCE.

Despite the city's famous past, no monuments except some isolated stone blocks are nowadays visible in the area. Even at the end of the 19th century it was still possible to trace the remains of a huge rectangular enclosure (some 800 by 700 meters, according to the plan published by G. Foucart in 1898) north of the village of Sa el-Hagar, on the right bank of the Rosetta branch of the Nile. Fifty years earlier, in the middle of the 19th century, the artists of Lepsius' expedition recorded a view of the sizable remains of the walls. The relatively recent but very quick disappearance of the enclosure was due to the activities of the sabbakhin who look for old mudbrick structures as a source of cheap fertilizer. Stone blocks had already been removed to be used as building material in the Middle Ages. It has been possible to locate some of them in various towns and villages along the Rosetta branch of the Nile.

Sa el-Hagar has been little explored by archaeologists. The texts of a substantial number of monuments in museums, such as statues, stelae, and sarcophagi show them to come from Sais. The great majority of them date to the 26th Dynasty, and none identified so far is earlier than the 3rd Intermediate Period.

Tell el-Fara῾in

Tell el-Fara῾in ("The Mound of the Pharaohs"), in the 6th Lower Egyptian nome, is the site of Buto (from ancient Egyptian *Per-Wadjit*, "The Domain of Wadjit," Coptic *Pouto*). The town was very important from the very beginning of Egyptian history. It was held to have consisted of two parts, called *Pe* and *Dep*, and was the home of the cobra goddess Wadjit, the tutelary goddess of Lower Egypt. In this function it was paralleled by Upper Egyptian *Nekheb* (el-Kab) and *Nekhen* (Kom el-Ahmar) and the vulture goddess Nekhbet. "The Souls of Pe," falcon-headed figures connected with Buto, may have symbolized the early local rulers ("Lower Egyptian kings") of the area.

The site of Tell el-Fara῾in consists of three mounds, two with town remains and one with a temple enclosure. This corresponds to the expected layout of Buto. Since 1985 the site has been excavated by an expedition of the German Archaeological Institute in Cairo led by T. von der Way and D. Faltings. In extremely difficult working conditions, Predynastic, Early Dynastic, and early Old-Kingdom remains were discovered far below the watertable. These confirm the indications of Buto's early importance which we have from elsewhere, demon-

Above Offering-bearers from the tomb of Harhotep at Tell el-Fara῾in, probably of the 30th Dynasty. Cairo, Egyptian Museum.

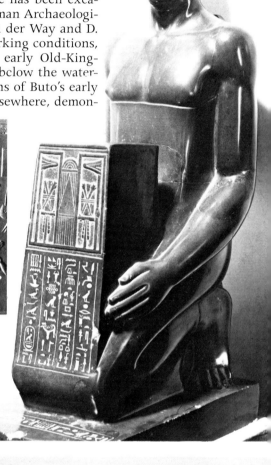

Below The ruins of Sa el-Hagar as seen by the artists of C. R. Lepsius' expedition in 1842.

Below A typical temple statue: Djeho, son of Nebʿankh and Hetepher, kneeling with a naos containing a statuette of Osiris. Hard black stone. Height: 54 cm. Ptolemaic. No recorded provenance, but its inscriptions show that it is from Tell Atrib. Lisbon, Fundação Calouste Gulbenkian.

Early Ptolemaic granite relief from the temple of Isis at Behbeit el-Hagar, showing the king censing before a god with hawk's head and lunar disk, perhaps Khons, with parts of further scenes on either side. Richmond (VA), Museum of Fine Arts.

strating important connections between Buto and the Near East and showing the replacement of the Predynastic delta culture by the Naqada II/III culture of Upper Egypt.

Behbeit el-Hagar

Behbeit el-Hagar is the site of one of the most important temples of Isis in Egypt. It is near Samannud (ancient Sebennytos), the home town of the kings of the 30th Dynasty, who were reputed to have a special devotion to Isis. It is likely that the foundation dates from that period, or that the large temple was built on the site of an unimportant predecessor.

The temple seems to have been built entirely of granite, but other comparable cases have shown that this perception may be due to the pattern of reuse of stone: limestone was more readily recycled as building material than granite. The ruins occupy an area of some 80 by 55 meters and are set in an enclosure measuring 362 by 210 meters whose two sides can still be distinguished. The temple has collapsed completely, either through quarrying activities or after an earthquake, and its plan has not been fully recovered; all that is visible is a disorderly mass of relief blocks and some architectural elements. The reliefs

are very fine work of Nectanebo I–II and of Ptolemy II Philadelphus and III Euergetes I, much more delicate than that of the Greco-Roman temples of Upper Egypt. Reliefs in this style and material played an important part in formulating the Classical image of Egypt. When temples to Isis were built, especially in Rome in the early empire, they were often adorned with these reliefs. Monuments of the Nectanebos and of Isis appear to have been particularly favored, and a block from this temple was found in the chief Isis temple in Rome.

Tell Atrib

Tell Atrib, north of the town of Benha on the right bank of the Damietta branch of the Nile, derives its name from ancient Egyptian *Hut-(ta-)hery(t)-ibt*, Coptic *Athrebi* and Greek Athribis. It was the capital of the 10th Lower Egyptian nome, and the name *Kem-wer* ("The Great Black One," i.e. bull) could equally be applied to the local god, the nome, and its capital. In the Dynastic Period the crocodile (or falcon) god Khentekhtai became the most prominent local deity.

Egyptian texts show that the history of Tell Atrib goes back at least to the early 4th Dynasty, but the remains of the earliest temple found there are dated by foundation deposits to the reign of Amasis. A town, temples, and necropolis of the Greco-Roman Period have also been located. The topography of the little-excavated Tell Atrib still presents difficulties. Isolated monuments of various dates are known from, or have been ascribed to, the site on the basis of their inscriptions; none is earlier than the 12th Dynasty. As with all delta sites, caution is required when dealing with objects that might have been brought from elsewhere and reused. Many monuments have been found by the sabbakhin, whose activities have seriously affected the site: in 1924 they discovered a large cache (some 50 kg) of silver treasure consisting of ingots, amulets, rings, earrings etc., dating to the 25th–30th Dynasties. Other monuments have been uncovered accidentally by peasants or workmen, such as the tombs of Queen Takhut (wife of Psammetichus II), of a woman called Tadubaste, and Pefteuemʿawyamun Tjaiemhorimu of the Late Period, all in the north part of the tell.

Uninscribed statue of the 12th Dynasty from Tell Atrib. Granite. Height: 63·5 cm. London, British Museum.

Tell el-Muqdam

Some of the most extensive man-made mounds in the delta used to be on the right bank of the Damietta branch of the Nile, about 10 kilometers southeast of Mit Ghamr, at Tell el-Muqdam. This is the site of ancient Leontopolis, an important town in the 11th

Lower Egyptian nome and its capital during the Ptolemaic Period. There are indications that Tell el-Muqdam was the seat of a line of kings of the 23rd Dynasty and perhaps their burial place, but so far only the tomb of Queen Kamama, the mother of Osorkon IV, has been found. The tell is now almost completely destroyed.

The temple of the local lion god Mahes/Mihos (Greek Miysis), situated in the east part of the ruins, suffered the fate of many similar buildings in the delta: most of its stone blocks have been removed and reused, leaving even the date of the structure uncertain. Another tell in the neighborhood, Mit Yaʿish, has produced material of the 22nd Dynasty (a stela of Osorkon III) and of the Ptolemaic Period.

Some monuments (particularly statues) of earlier dates were usurped by later rulers and had probably been removed from their original places. At Tell el-Muqdam this certainly applies to a statue of the 13th Dynasty king Nehesy usurped by Merneptah, and possibly to others, particularly some of Senwosret III. The number of monuments found in controlled excavations is small, but the original provenance of others from the reign of Ramesses II or earlier can be established from their inscriptions and other indications. Many objects that were formerly in D. M. Fouquet's private collection (dispersed in 1922), particularly statuettes of lions in bronze and other materials, derived from Tell el-Muqdam.

Manetho, himself a native of Sebennytos, the kings of the 30th Dynasty came from there.

A large mound west of the modern town marks the remains of the temple of the local god Onuris-Shu. The granite blocks bear the names of Nectanebo II, Philip Arrhidaeus, Alexander IV, and Ptolemy II Philadelphus. Some earlier monuments are said to have come from Samannud or its neighborhood, including an Old Kingdom false door of a certain Sesni, an altar of Amenemhet I, a statue dated to Psammetichus I, a fragment of a shrine of Nepherites (probably I), and statuary of the reign of Nectanebo I. No blocks or other architectural elements of buildings earlier than the 30th Dynasty have been reported.

Above Bronze inlay of the lion sacred to the god Mihos, probably part of a piece of temple furniture: early Ptolemaic, from Tell el-Muqdam. Height: 14.7 cm. Formerly in the Fouquet collection, now in the Brooklyn Museum of Art.

Below left Procession of personifications bringing symbolic offerings to the god Onuris-Shu on behalf of Nectanebo II. Granite relief from the temple at Samannud. Baltimore (MD), Walters Art Gallery.

Below Nekhtharhebi, whose "good name" was Nekht-harmenkhib, a contemporary of Psammetichus II, is known from his six statues from various delta sites and his sarcophagus found at Sa el-Hagar. This quartzite kneeling statue, 1·48 m high, probably comes from el-Baqliya. Paris, Museé du Louvre.

Samannud

Ancient *Tjebnutjer* (Coptic *Djebenoute* or *Djemnouti*, Greek Sebennytos), now on the left bank of the Damietta branch of the Nile, was the capital of the 12th Lower Egyptian nome and a town of some importance toward the end of the Dynastic Period: according to

el-Baqliya

South of the modern village of el-Baqliya, three low mounds, rising only a few meters above the cultivated land, marked the site of the ancient *Baʿh* (Hermopolis Parva of the Greco-Roman Period), the capital of the 15th Lower Egyptian nome and a city

Mastaba tombs and houses uncovered by the expedition of the Institute of Fine Arts of New York University at Tell el-Rubʿa in 1977.

The Manager of the Estate Tetu, son of Nekhti; the *hotep-di-nesu* formula running down the front of his long kilt invokes Atum "Lord of Heliopolis" and so indicates the provenance of the statuette. Granite. Height: 27 cm. Berlin, Ägyptisches Museum.

of considerable importance. In the late 20th century this site was leveled completely and nothing is now to be seen there.

Tell el-Naqus probably covered the town and the temple of the local god Thoth. Outlines of an enclosure measuring some 350 by 384 meters were visible, but few remains could be seen inside. There were some granite blocks lying outside the enclosure, including a large bell-shaped capital of a papyrus column which probably gave the tell its name ("The Mound of the Bell").

The necropolis belonging to the town, including a cemetery of ibises, was probably situated at Tell el-Zereiki.

Tell el-Rubʿa covered further, unidentified remains: a quartzite monolithic naos (shrine) dedicated to Thoth by Apries was found there, as well as the torso of a granite statue of Nectanebo I.

Blocks of Psammetichus I and Nectanebo I and a fragment of a basalt sarcophagus of one ʿAhmose of the 26th Dynasty were found near el-Baqliya, as well as another statue of Nectanebo I and a granite block statue of a scribe called Nehesy, a contemporary of Ramesses II. The latter is the earliest monument known to have come from the little-excavated el-Baqliya.

Tell el-Rubʿa and Tell el-Timai

Two mounds several hundred meters apart, northwest of the modern town of el-Simbellawein in the central delta, were in turn the site of the capital of the 16th Lower Egyptian nome: the northern Tell el-Rubʿa (ancient Egyptian *Per-banebdjedet*, "The Domain of the Ram Lord of *Djedet*," Greek Mendes) was in the Greco-Roman Period replaced in this role by the southern Tell el-Timai (Greek Thmuis). The earlier names of Tell el-Rubʿa were ʿAnpet and *Djedet*. Originally, the fish goddess Hatmehyt was the local deity, but in the Dynastic Period the most prominent local cult was that of the Ram (*Ba*) of Mendes (*Djedet*).

A cemetery of sacred rams, with large sarcophagi in which the animals were buried, can be seen in the northwest corner of the enclosure of Tell el-Rubʿa.

The nome is mentioned in texts from as early as the 4th Dynasty, and there are mastaba tombs of the late Old Kingdom at Tell el-Rubʿa. The earliest identified temple of Banebdjedet is Ramessid. Isolated monuments bear the names of Ramesses II, Merneptah, and Ramesses III. A temple attested by its foundation deposits was built by Amasis. A red granite monolithic naos, nearly 8 meters high and dedicated to Shu by the same king, dominates the scene, but apart from the incompletely preserved enclosure walls little is left of the temple itself, and no fragments of temple reliefs have been found in the area. The 29th Dynasty kings were said to have come from Mendes and the city probably functioned as the royal residence. The tomb of Nepheritis I was discovered by an expedition of the Universities of Washington and Toronto in 1992–93.

Tell el-Timai, much spoiled by the sabbakhin, contains remains of brick structures of the Greco-Roman Period.

Heliopolis

Ancient Egyptian *Iunu* (biblical and Coptic *On*), the capital of the 13th Lower Egyptian nome, is at and around Tell Hisn, northwest of the modern el-Matariya (a Cairo suburb, north of Misr el-Gedida). The temples of the sun god Reʿ, Reʿ-Atum or Reʿ-Harakhty at Heliopolis were among the most important and influential religious institutions in the land, economically and still more ideologically. The Heliopolitan doctrine with the creator god Atum and the sun god Reʿ (hence the Greek name of the town, from *helios* "sun") at its center was crucial to the shaping of Egyptian religious and political history. The *benu* bird (phoenix) and the Mnevis bull were worshiped as manifestations of the god, and Hathor "Mistress of Hetpet" and Iusʿas were the goddesses connected with Heliopolis.

No spectacular monuments can be seen in the area nowadays, except a standing obelisk of Senwosret I. Obelisks were particularly characteristic of the temples at Heliopolis and "Cleopatra's Needles" in London and New York, although removed from Alexandria in the second half of the 19th century, originally stood here.

Because Cairo is so near, most of the temples' stone was removed and reused long ago, while the fact that the area is cultivated or built over hinders archaeological work. The main temple and probably also the town at Tell Hisn were surrounded by massive double mud brick walls. The enclosed area has been estimated to measure some 1,000 by 900 meters. The architectural history of the site and its

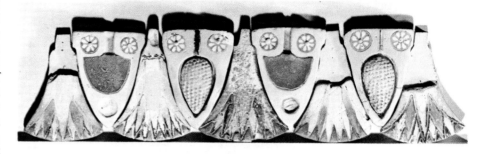

precise topography are not clear. Many isolated
monuments such as statues, reliefs, obelisks, and
offering tables, dating between the 3rd Dynasty
(Djoser) and the Ptolemaic Period, have been
found, and excavations, particularly those carried
out in the late 20th century by the Faculty of
Archaeology of Cairo University, have revealed a
number of religious and other buildings (probably
including a fort) constructed by New Kingdom
kings: Amenhotep III (restored by Ramesses II),
Sety I, several kings Ramesses, and Merneptah. It
remains to be seen whether these belonged to
smaller temples attached to the great temple of Reᶜ
(at least ten of which are known to have existed at
Heliopolis during the New Kingdom), or whether
they are parts of the temple of Reᶜ itself.

Tombs of 6th Dynasty high priests of Heliopolis
have been located some 550 meters southeast of the
obelisk of Senwosret I, near the southeast corner of
the enclosure. At el-Matariya, about 950 meters
from the obelisk, there were tombs of the Late
Period, while objects indicating the presence of
further tombs of the Ramessid and Late Periods
have been found at a distance of some 3 kilometers,
at ᶜArd el-Naᶜam ("The Ostrich Farm").

Tombs of Mnevis bulls, mainly of the Ramessid
Period, have been discovered about 13 kilometers
northeast of the obelisk, at ᶜArab el-Tawil.

Tell el-Yahudiya

Tell el-Yahudiya ("The Mound of the Jews"),
ancient Egyptian Nay-ta-hut, Greek Leontopolis,
lies some 2 kilometers southeast of the village
of Shibin el-Qanatir, within the ancient 13th
(Heliopolitan) nome of Lower Egypt.

The most conspicuous, as well as the most puzzling, feature of the site is the remains of a rectangular earthwork enclosure, the so-called "Hyksos
Camp," measuring some 515 by 490 meters. It probably dates from the late Middle Kingdom or the
2nd Intermediate Period and has been interpreted
as a fortification, but there is a strong possibility
that the structure is religious rather than military,
perhaps imitating the hill on which creation was
believed to have taken place. Inside the enclosure,
in its northeastern part, the discovery of colossal
statues of Ramesses II suggests that this was the
site of a temple of that date. In its western part
there stood a temple of Ramesses III. Faience tiles
decorated with rosettes, rekhyt birds symbolic of
the king's subjects, cartouches, and foreign captives, probably originating in the temple palace, are
now in various museum collections.

Outside the enclosure, near its northeastern
corner, are remains of a temple and town which
the exiled Jewish priest Onias was given per-
mission to build by Ptolemy VI Philometor. The

settlement flourished for more than 200 years until
the temple was closed by the Roman emperor
Vespasian in 71 CE.

Cemeteries of various dates, starting with the
Middle Kingdom, extend to the east of the
enclosure.

Tell Basta

Tell Basta, southeast of Zagazig, is the site of
the ancient Bast (classical Bubastis, from Per-
Bastet, "The Domain of Bastet"), the town of the
lioness goddess Bastet (Bubastis), and the capital of
the 18th Lower Egyptian nome during the Late
Period. The town gained prominence very early, at
least partly because of its strategically important
location controlling the routes from Memphis
to Sinai (Wadi Tumilat) and to Asia. Politically,
its influence peaked during the 22nd Dynasty,
the kings of which came from Bubastis. Bubastis
did not decline significantly until the first
centuries CE.

The main temple, dedicated to Bastet, was excavated by Edouard Naville between 1887 and 1889.
The edifice, some 180 meters long, consisted of a
court of Osorkon II, the sed-festival gate and
hypostyle hall of Osorkon III, and a shrine of
Nectanebo II. A birth house of Mihos (the lion god
regarded as the son of Bastet) dedicated by Osorkon
III, stood to the north of the main temple.

In the middle of the 5th century BCE Herodotus
described the temple as standing on an island, with

Above Obelisk of Senwosret I at
Heliopolis. Granite. Height:
about 20 m.

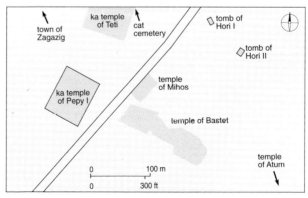

Left Plan of Tell Basta.

Right Bronze statuette of a cat, the sacred animal of Bastet of Bubastis (Tell Basta). Probably Late Period. Oxford, Ashmolean Museum.

Above Silver jug with a goat handle of gold, from a hoard of 19th Dynasty gold and silver vessels and jewelry found at Tell Basta in 1906. Height: 16·8 cm; weight: 602 g. Cairo, Egyptian Museum.

Far right Bronze bust of a king, probably from Qantir. It is usually thought to show Ramesses II, but a much later date seems more likely. Height: 36 cm. Hildesheim, Roemer- und Pelizaeus-Museum.

Below The form and finish brought to perfection, not diminished even by the present fragmentary state of the sculpture: Nectanebo I from Saft el-Hinna. Granite. Height: 67 cm. London, British Museum.

two water channels running on its sides, and being on a much lower level than the city in the middle of which it was located. The excavation confirmed the correctness of both of these statements, though the channels would have been more appropriately described as the two arms of the sacred lake. Blocks of various dates, including some bearing the names of kings of the 4th Dynasty, were found reused in the temple.

Among the other buildings discovered at Tell Basta, there are the *ka* temples of Teti (a structure measuring some 108 by 50 meters, about 250 meters northwest of the temple of Bastet) and Pepy I, the *sed*-festival chapels of Amenemhet III and Amenhotep III, a structure interpreted as a Middle Kingdom palace, and a temple of Atum built by Osorkon II.

The earliest tombs date from the late Old Kingdom. Several burials of important officials have been found, among them the 19th Dynasty vizier Iuti and two viceroys of Kush called Hori, who were father and son, of the end of the 19th and the 20th Dynasties. Extensive cemeteries of sacred animals, particularly cats (associated with Bastet from the 3rd Intermediate Period onwards) have also been located. The site has been excavated by the University of Zagazig since the 1970s.

Saft el-Hinna

The village of Saft el-Hinna, east of Zagazig, stands on the site of ancient *Per-Sopdu* ("The Domain of Sopd"), the earlier capital of the 20th nome of Lower Egypt. In 1885 E. Naville partly uncovered the mud brick enclosure walls of the local temple, measuring 75 (or more) by 40 meters, as well as a number of uninscribed basalt blocks.

Few inscribed monuments have been found at Saft el-Hinna: statue fragments of Ramesses II are among the earliest, but the remains of a granodiorite naos dedicated to Sopd by Nectanebo I, now in the Cairo Museum, are the most impressive.

The district of el-Khataʿna, Tell el-Dabʿa, and Qantir

El-Khataʿna and Qantir are villages some 6 and 9 kilometers respectively north of Faqus, in the northeastern delta. Here many sandy mounds show signs of settlements of the Middle Kingdom and indicate the area's increased importance during the 2nd Intermediate and Ramessid Periods. Avaris, the Hyksos center during the 2nd Intermediate Period, is at Tell el-Dabʿa, and Pi-Riʿamsese, the delta residence of the Ramessids and Raamses of the Book of Exodus, near Qantir.

The remains of a granite gate of a columned chapel of Amenemhet I and Senwosret III were found at Tell el-Qirqafa, north of el-Khataʿna. A Middle Kingdom palace and a temple built by Senwosret II were found at Ezbet Rushdi el-Saghira, further to the north-east.

The occupation at Tell el-Dabʿa probably goes as far back as the Herakleopolitan (1st Intermediate) period. Monuments of Queen Nefrusobk and Kings Harnedjheriotef (Hetepibreʿ) and Nehesy were among the finds of the late 12th and 13th Dynasties. In the Middle Kingdom and 2nd Intermediate Period Tell el-Dabʿa witnessed a large influx of migrants from Asia, leading up to the rise of the

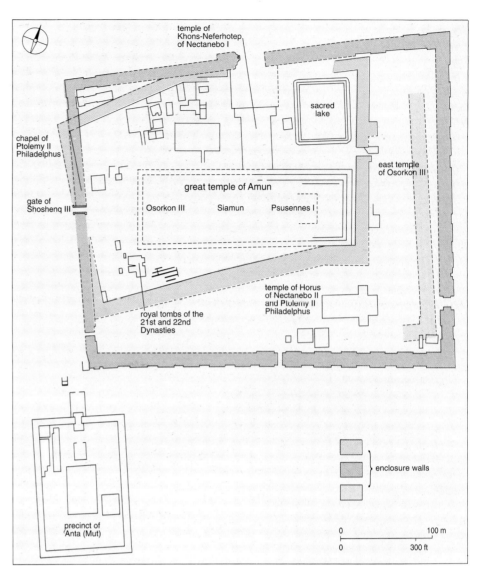

15th (Hyksos) Dynasty. Since the late 1960s, an Austrian expedition led by Manfred Bietak has discovered a town and cemeteries of a local variant of the Palestinian Middle Bronze culture here, including temples, perhaps of Seth-Baʿal and Astarte, similar to those known from Palestine, as well as palaces and other buildings (almost all in brick), and palace gardens. Fragments of palace paintings in an east Mediterranean style known from Syria-Palestine and the Aegean and with subjects associated with the Minoan world, such as acrobats leaping over bulls, have been found; these may date either to the late Hyksos period or the early 18th Dynasty. Building activities were resumed under Haremhab and the Ramessids and included a large temple (180 by 140 meters), probably dedicated to Seth.

In the 1920s a number of decorated glazed tiles bearing floral designs, fish, ducks, plants etc. were reported to have been discovered in the vicinity of Qantir. Excavations conducted since the early 1980s, and still in progress, by a mission of the Roemer- und Pelizaeus-Museum in Hildesheim have uncovered the remains of an extensive city which was at its peak during the Ramessid period, Pi-Riʿamsese, including striking finds such as a royal stable complex. The city flourished from the 18th until the 21st Dynasty.

At Tell Abu el-Shafiʿa, north of Qantir, there is the base of a seated colossus of Ramesses II, perhaps indicating the position of a temple.

Tell Nabasha

A large mound, some 1·5 kilometers across, but now mostly built over, in the northeastern delta, is the site of ancient Egyptian *Imet*. During the New Kingdom this was the capital of a district that was later divided into two Lower Egyptian nomes, the 18th (capital: Bubastis) and 19th (capital: Tanis). The modern names of the locality are Tell Nabasha, Tell Farʿun, or Tell Bedawi.

The earliest finds are late Predynastic and Early Dynastic. The outlines of the mud brick temple enclosure of the goddess Wadjit, measuring some 215 by 205 meters, were still discernible in the 20th century. The enclosure contained at least two temples. The larger one (about 65 by 30 meters), approached from the east, was probably built under the Ramessids (Ramesses II and others are attested). Although Middle Kingdom sphinxes usurped by later kings were found, it is likely that they had been brought from elsewhere. The smaller temple (about 30 by 15 meters), near the northeast corner of the earlier temple and with its longer axis pointing to the north,

may have been a birth house. It is dated to Amasis by its foundation deposits. Reused Middle Kingdom monuments were also discovered here.

Remains of a town of the Greco-Roman Period were located southeast of the temple enclosure, and a cemetery, mostly of the Late Period, lies in the plain further to the east.

San el-Hagar

Situated in the northeastern part of the Nile delta, ancient *Djaʿnet* (Greek Tanis, modern San el-Hagar) was the residence and burial place of the kings of the 21st and 22nd Dynasties. In the Late Period it became the capital of the 19th Lower Egyptian nome. In the present state of archaeological knowledge of the delta it is easily its most impressive ancient site, and one of the largest. The problems encountered in interpreting the monuments of Tanis in order to trace its history epitomize the difficulties connected with all the delta sites. The most prominent excavators at San el-Hagar have been Auguste Mariette in the second half of the 19th century, W. M. Flinders Petrie in 1883–86, and Pierre Montet in 1929–51. The site is currently explored by the *Mission française des fouilles de Tanis* (under Philippe Brissaud).

The salient feature of San el-Hagar is a large rec-

Above San el-Hagar.

Below Seated colossus of Ramesses II, from Tell Nabasha. Granite. Height: 2·02 m. Boston (MA), Museum of Fine Arts.

Brutality personified? Not many Egyptian statues have a more powerful and awe-inspiring effect than this sphinx with its mane closely enveloping the face. Originally a work of the 12th Dynasty (probably of Amenemhet III), it was subsequently "usurped" by kings who added their names on it: Ramesses II, Merneptah, and Psusennes I. The sphinx had been moved several times before it was set up at San el-Hagar by the last-named king. Granite. Length: 2·25 m. Cairo, Egyptian Museum.

tangular mud brick enclosure measuring about 430 by 370 meters. The enclosure walls were, amazingly, some 15 meters thick and probably about 10 meters high. Inside this precinct there are remains of another, inner enclosure, with stamped bricks dating it to Psusennes I. This contains the great temple of Amun.

Nowadays the temple is a mass of inscribed and decorated blocks, columns, obelisks, and statues of various dates, some of them bearing the names of rulers of the Old and Middle Kingdoms (Khufu, Khephren, Teti, Pepy I and II, Senwosret I) and many connected with Ramesses II. The Ramessid and earlier monuments were brought from other places as building material (a near-universal Egyptian practice – in the delta stone monuments often traveled considerable distances) and in order to adorn the newly built temples. Psusennes I is attested by foundation deposits in the sanctuary in the easternmost part of the structure. The most prominent royal builders who contributed to the temple of Amun were Siamun, Osorkon III, and Shoshenq III. Two of the obelisks removed from the temple can be seen in Cairo: one in the Gezira gardens in the heart of the city, the other on the road to the airport.

Apart from the great temple there were other, smaller structures within the inner enclosure. The blocks from several of these buildings, in particular a temple and a sed-festival chapel of Shoshenq V and a temple of Psammetichus I, were later reused by Nectanebo I when he made the sacred lake and built a temple of Khons-Neferhotep nearby. Outside the enclosure, near the approach to the great temple, stood a chapel of Ptolemy II Philadelphus.

Other kings who built in the larger enclosure were Osorkon III ("The East Temple") and Nectanebo II with Ptolemy II Philadelphus (temple of Horus). Outside the enclosure, near its southwest corner, there was a precinct of ʿAnta (Mut), built mainly by Siamun and Apries, and rebuilt by Ptolemy IV Philopator.

In 1939 Pierre Montet found a group of royal tombs of the 21st and 22nd Dynasties near the southwest corner of the great temple. The building of tombs within temple precincts was characteristic of the 3rd Intermediate Period, and may have been dictated by the unstable conditions of the country. In all six tombs were found at San el-Hagar, belonging to Psusennes I, Amenemope, Osorkon III, and Shoshenq III; the owners of the two remaining tombs are unknown.

The underground parts, in most cases consisting of several rooms, were built of limestone (many of the blocks were reused material of an earlier date), granite, or mud brick, and were entered through a shaft. The walls of the tombs of Psusennes I, Osorkon III, and Shoshenq III were decorated with reliefs and inscriptions. Some of the tombs contained several burials, with sarcophagi often made of granite and usurped. Two additional royal burials were found: the sarcophagus used by Takelot II was discovered in a room in the tomb of Osorkon III, while the silver falcon-headed coffin of Shoshenq II was placed in the tomb of Psusennes I. The tomb of Osorkon III may have been used as a cache for several other royal burials. The sarcophagus and coffin of Amenemope were discovered in the tomb of Psusennes I. Silver coffins and gold mummy masks and jewelry, such as pectorals, bracelets, and collars (one of which weighed 19 kilograms), are the most spectacular finds. Apart from the 18th Dynasty tomb of Tutʿankhamun, the royal tombs of San el-Hagar are the only ones that have been discovered essentially intact.

Tell el-Maskhuta

In 1883 Edouard Naville excavated a large mud brick enclosure (some 210 by 210 meters) with a badly damaged temple at Tell el-Maskhuta, in Wadi Tumilat (in the Late Period a canal through this wadi enabled ships to sail from the Nile into the Red Sea). Tell el-Maskhuta is generally identified with ancient Egyptian Tjeku, the capital of the 8th Lower Egyptian nome, and often with Pithom (probably from Per-Atum, "The Domain of Atum") of the biblical Book of Exodus.

NUBIA

Nubia is the area south of the 1st cataract. It formed a buffer zone at Egypt's southern frontier, was a region through which exotic African goods reached the country and an important source of gold (a possible derivation of the name of Nubia is from Egyptian *nub*, "gold"), minerals, and wood (especially hard wood). It provided valued recruits for the Egyptian army and police force.

The crude Early Dynastic and Old Kingdom methods of exploitation consisted of raids aimed at bringing back captives and cattle. In the Middle Kingdom the area under direct military control, exercised through a series of strategically placed fortresses, extended to the southern end of the 2nd cataract. During the New Kingdom the Egyptians went beyond the 4th cataract; in Lower Nubia many rock-cut temples were built, dating chiefly to the reign of Ramesses II. In the Late Period Nubia produced a royal dynasty, the 25th of Egypt, but after an unsuccessful encounter with the Assyrians its Napatan rulers withdrew to the 4th cataract area, ceased to take an active interest in Egyptian affairs, and developed their own, Meroitic, culture. A number of temples were built in the northern part of Lower Nubia during competing phases of dominance in the region by the two cultures in the Ptolemaic and early Roman Periods.

In the 1960s many Nubian temples were removed to new locations in an international cooperation unmatched in the history of archaeology.

Above The Roman Period temple of Sarapis at el-Maharraqa, painted by the French architect Hector Horeau in 1838. The temple was removed to the vicinity of el-Sebuʿa in 1965–66.

Left The temple of Ramesses II at el-Sebuʿa, as it used to be before the creation of the Lake Nasser; (*above*) one of the sphinxes in the outer court.

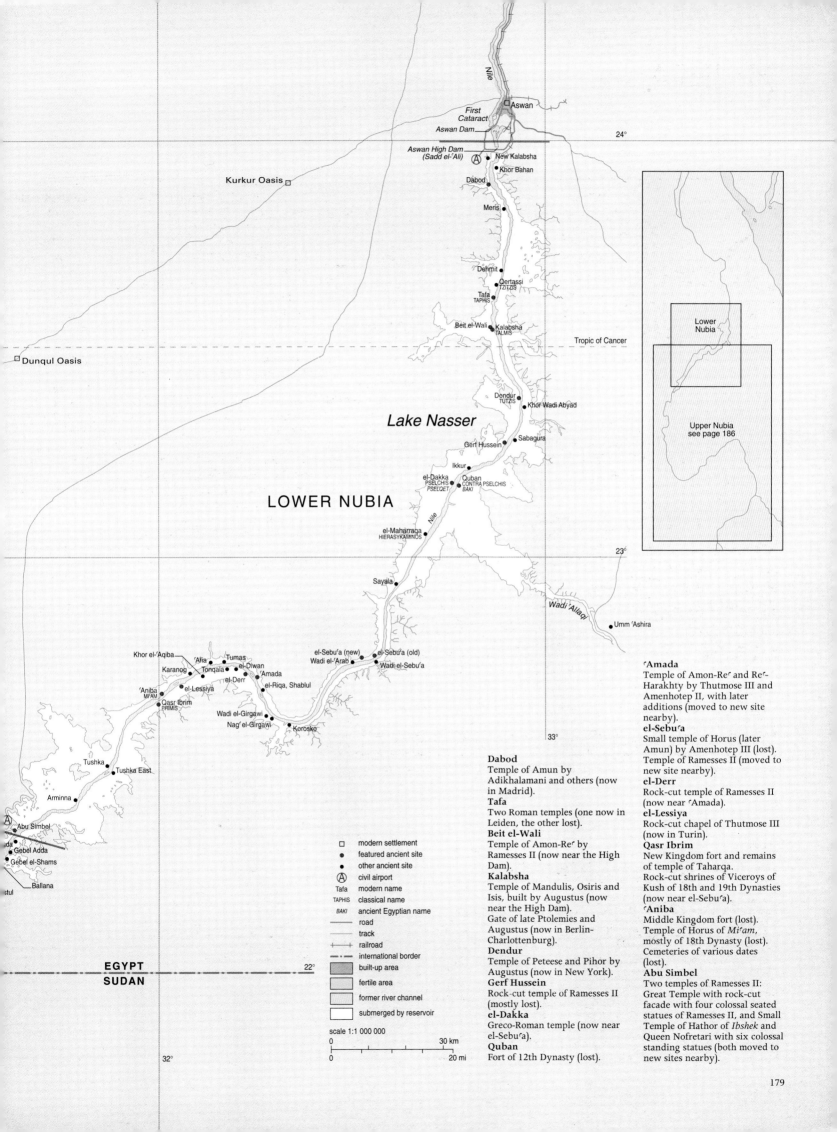

Nile

Aswan

First
Cataract
Aswan Dam

24°

Aswan High Dam
(Sadd el-'Ali)
New Kalabsha
Khor Bahan
Dabod

Meris

Kurkur Oasis

Dehmit
Qertassi
TZITZIS
Tafa
TAPHIS

Beit el-Wali
Kalabsha
TALMIS

Tropic of Cancer

Dunqul Oasis

Dendur
TUTZIS
Khor Wadi Abyad

Lake Nasser

Sabagura
Gerf Hussein

Ikkur
el-Dakka   Quban
PSELCHIS CONTRA PSELCHIS
PSELQET   BAKI

LOWER NUBIA

Nile

el-Maharraqa
HIERASYKAMINOS

23°

Sayala

Wadi 'Allaqi

Umm 'Ashira

Khor el-'Aqiba
'Afia
Tumas
Karanog Tonqala el-Diwan
el-Derr Amada
'Aniba el-Lessiya el-Riqa, Shablul
MI'AM
Qasr Ibrim
PRIMIS
Wadi el-Girgawi
Nag' el-Girgawi Korosko

el-Sebu'a (new)   el-Sebu'a (old)
Wadi el-'Arab   Wadi el-Sebu'a

33°

Tushka
Tushka East

Arminna

Abu Simbel
Gebel Adda
Gebel el-Shams
Ballana
stul

Legend

□ modern settlement
● featured ancient site
● other ancient site
Ⓐ civil airport
Tafa modern name
TAPHIS classical name
BAKI ancient Egyptian name
road
track
railroad
international border
built-up area
fertile area
former river channel
submerged by reservoir

scale 1:1 000 000
0   30 km
0   20 mi

EGYPT   22°
SUDAN

32°

Dabod
Temple of Amun by Adikhalamani and others (now in Madrid).
Tafa
Two Roman temples (one now in Leiden, the other lost).
Beit el-Wali
Temple of Amon-Re' by Ramesses II (now near the High Dam).
Kalabsha
Temple of Mandulis, Osiris and Isis, built by Augustus (now near the High Dam).
Gate of late Ptolemies and Augustus (now in Berlin-Charlottenburg).
Dendur
Temple of Peteese and Pihor by Augustus (now in New York).
Gerf Hussein
Rock-cut temple of Ramesses II (mostly lost).
el-Dakka
Greco-Roman temple (now near el-Sebu'a).
Quban
Fort of 12th Dynasty (lost).

'Amada
Temple of Amon-Re' and Re'-Harakhty by Thutmose III and Amenhotep II, with later additions (moved to new site nearby).
el-Sebu'a
Small temple of Horus (later Amun) by Amenhotep III (lost). Temple of Ramesses II (moved to new site nearby).
el-Derr
Rock-cut temple of Ramesses II (now near 'Amada).
el-Lessiya
Rock-cut chapel of Thutmose III (now in Turin).
Qasr Ibrim
New Kingdom fort and remains of temple of Taharqa.
Rock-cut shrines of Viceroys of Kush of 18th and 19th Dynasties (now near el-Sebu'a).
'Aniba
Middle Kingdom fort (lost). Temple of Horus of Mi'am, mostly of 18th Dynasty (lost). Cemeteries of various dates (lost).
Abu Simbel
Two temples of Ramesses II: Great Temple with rock-cut facade with four colossal seated statues of Ramesses II, and Small Temple of Hathor of Ibshek and Queen Nofretari with six colossal standing statues (both moved to new sites nearby).

Dabod

The early temple of Dabod was built and decorated by the Meroitic ruler Adikhalamani, probably in the first half of the 3rd century BCE, and was dedicated to Amun. In the Greco-Roman Period several Ptolemies (VI Philometor, VIII Euergetes II, and XII Auletes) enlarged it and rededicated it to Isis. The decoration of the vestibule dates to the Emperors Augustus and Tiberius. Old views show a series of three pylons in front of the temple, but only two were to be seen in this century.

In the years 1960–61 the temple was dismantled; since 1970 it has charmed visitors in the lake setting in a park in central Madrid.

Tafa

Two temples of Roman date used to stand at Tafa. The "North Temple," with no relief decoration, was dismantled in 1960 and its reconstruction in the Rijksmuseum van Oudheden in Leiden was completed in 1978. The "South Temple" was lost at the end of the last century.

There were two sanctuaries of Isis of the same date in the area, one of them overlooking the dangerous "minor" cataract of Bab el-Kalabsha.

Beit el-Wali

The small rock-cut temple of Beit el-Wali, on the west bank of the Nile, was built by Ramesses II and dedicated to Amon-Reʿ and other gods. Originally fronted by a mud brick pylon, its simple plan consists of an entrance hall (at one time roofed with a mud brick vault), a columned hall and the sanctuary. The temple was cut into sections and transferred to a new site (New Kalabsha) close to the new Aswan dam in 1962–65.

Kalabsha

The largest freestanding temple of Egyptian Nubia, measuring some 74 meters from the pylon to the rear wall and about 33 meters wide, was built at Kalabsha (ancient Talmis) in the reign of Augustus, and was dedicated to the Nubian god Mandulis, accompanied by Osiris and Isis. In front of the pylon there is a quay and a terrace, and to reach the sanctuary one proceeds through a forecourt, a hypostyle hall,

and two vestibules. Only the three inner rooms are fully decorated with reliefs. The walls of the temple precinct also enclose a birth house (in the southwest corner) and a chapel probably built by Ptolemy IX Soter II (in the northeast corner). The temple contains an inscription of the Nubian ruler Silko, written in Greek, which marks the triumph of Christianity in Nubia in the 6th century CE.

In 1961–63 the temple was dismantled and rebuilt near the new Aswan dam (New Kalabsha). During the dismantling operation reused blocks from a gate built by the late Ptolemies and Augustus were found. The gate, 7·35 m high, is now in the Ägyptisches Museum in Berlin-Charlottenburg.

Dendur

In order to save it from the waters of Lake Nasser, the temple of Dendur was dismantled in 1962 and presented by the Egyptian government to the United States. Its 642 blocks were reassembled at the Metropolitan Museum of Art in New York

The temple of Kalabsha in 1839; watercolor painting by Hector Horeau.

NUBIA

Far right Forecourt of the temple of Ramesses II at Gerf Hussein from the south. View taken before the creation of Lake Nasser.

Below right The temple of Kalabsha at its new site near the Aswan High Dam.

Bottom right The deities of the Kalabsha temple: Mandulis, wearing his characteristic headdress, followed by Isis. Relief on the intercolumnar wall at the back of the forecourt, north of the entrance to the hypostyle hall.

where (since September 1978) the temple forms the Sackler wing of the museum.

Augustus built the small temple (the main building measures about 13·5 by 7 meters) for two local "saints," Peteese and Pihor, sons of Quper. The exact reason for their deification at Dendur is not clear; perhaps they drowned at that spot. The original place of their worship was a speos (rock chamber) behind the temple, which may have dated back to the 26th Dynasty. The temple, fronted by a terrace, has a simple plan: a pylon and the main building some 10 meters behind it. The latter consists of a columned pronaos, a vestibule and the sanctuary. The reliefs in the temple show Augustus before various deities, among them the two deified brothers and the Nubian gods Arensnuphis and Mandulis.

Gerf Hussein

"The Temple of Riʿamsese-meryamun [Ramesses II] in the Domain of Ptah" at Gerf Hussein was built by the viceroy of Kush, Setau, sometime between years 35 and 50 of Ramesses II. The gods to whom it was dedicated were represented by four seated statues in the niche at the back of the sanctuary: Ptah, the deified Ramesses II, Ptah-tanen with a hawk above his head, and Hathor.

The temple, on the west bank of the Nile, was partly free-standing and partly cut in the rock, and its plan was remarkably similar to that of the great temple of Abu Simbel. Unfortunately, most of it disappeared in Lake Nasser; only fragments have been salvaged.

el-Dakka

Several rulers contributed to the building and decoration of the temple of el-Dakka (ancient Egyptian *Pselqet*, classical Pselchis), notably Ptolemy IV Philopator, Ptolemy VIII Euergetes II, the Meroitic King Arqamani of the turn of the 3rd century BCE, and the Roman emperors Augustus and Tiberius.

Between 1962 and 1965 the temple was dismantled and restored at a new site near el-Sebuʿa. During the work a number of reused blocks were found. These come from an earlier temple built by Hatshepsut and Thutmose III for Horus of *Baki* (Quban), probably on the opposite side of the river.

Quban

The fort of Quban (ancient Egyptian *Baki*, classical Contra Pselchis) was built at the beginning of the 12th Dynasty, probably by Senwosret I, but may have had a precursor in the Old Kingdom. During the New Kingdom Quban was the most important settlement in Nubia north of ʿAniba, controlling access to the gold mines of Wadi ʿAllaqi. Several ruined temple structures have been reported from the area.

181

1 el-Derr
2 el-Lessiya

el-Sebuʿa

El-Sebuʿa, on the west bank of the Nile, was the site of two temples of the New Kingdom.

The earlier temple was built by Amenhotep III. In its first stage it consisted of a rock-cut sanctuary (about 3 by 2 meters) fronted by a mud brick pylon, a court, and a hall, partly decorated with wall paintings. Originally the temple seems to have been dedicated to one of the local Nubian forms of Horus, but his representations were altered to Amun at some later point. During the ʿAmarna persecution of images of Amun the decoration suffered, but Ramesses II restored it and also extended the temple by building in front of the pylon of the original plan.

The large temple of el-Sebuʿa, known as "The Temple of Riʿamsese-meryamun (Ramesses II) in the Domain of Amun," was built about 150 meters northeast of the temple of Amenhotep III; monuments and representations of the viceroy of Kush, Setau, indicate that this was done between regnal years 35 and 50 of Ramesses II. The temple is partly freestanding and partly rock-cut.

Proceeding along its central axis, one passes through a series of three pylons and courts to reach the hypostyle hall (later converted into a church), where the rock-cut part of the temple starts. The antechamber opens into two side rooms, two side chapels, and the sanctuary itself. The destroyed statues in the niche of the sanctuary represented Amon-Reʿ, Reʿ-Harakhty, and Ramesses II himself.

In 1964, during the UNESCO campaign to save the monuments of Nubia, the temple was removed to a new site, some 4 kilometers to the west. In its new setting, and with an imposing approaching avenue of sphinxes, it is one of the most impressive sights of Lower Nubia.

ʿAmada

The temple of ʿAmada was originally built by Thutmose III and Amenhotep II for the gods Amon-Reʿ and Reʿ-Harakhty. A hypostyle hall was later added by Thutmose IV. Various kings of the 19th Dynasty, in particular Sety I and Ramesses II, carried out minor restorations and added to the temple's decoration.

There are two important historical inscriptions in the ʿAmada temple. The earlier of them, dated to year 3 of Amenhotep II, describes a victorious military campaign into Asia: "His Majesty returned in joy to his father Amun after he had slain with his own mace the seven chiefs in the district of *Takhesy* (in Syria), who were then hung upside down from the prow of the boat of His Majesty." The other

text concerns the defeat of an invasion of Egypt from Libya in year 4 of Merneptah.

The temple has been re-erected some 65 meters higher and 2·6 kilometers away from its original site. The inner part of the temple, weighing about 900 tons, was transported to its new setting in one piece on temporary railway tracks between January and March 1965.

el-Derr

The only Nubian rock-cut temple built by Ramesses II on the right bank of the Nile used to stand at el-Derr. Its position was probably due to the fact that the river on its approach to the Korosko bend flows in an "unnatural" southeasterly direction. In 1965, in a last-minute rescue, the temple was removed to a new site near ʿAmada.

"The Temple of Riʿamsese-meryamun (Ramesses II) in the Domain of Reʿ" was built in the second half of the king's reign, and in plan and decoration resembles the Great Temple of Abu Simbel (minus the colossal seated statues against the facade). After cleaning, the temple's relief decoration is unusually bright and vivid, contrasting strongly with the more subdued color tones to which we are used from elsewhere. The chief deities worshiped in the temple had seated statues in the sanctuary niche: Reʿ-Harakhty, Ramesses II himself, Amon-Reʿ, and Ptah.

el-Lessiya

At el-Lessiya, on the right bank of the Nile, a small chapel was cut during the reign of Thutmose III. The plan consists of a single room (5·5 by 3 meters) with a niche (2 by 3 meters), and the relief decoration shows the king before various deities, including the Nubian god Dedwen and the deified Senwosret III. The niche originally contained statues of Thutmose III between Horus of *Miʿam* (ʿAniba) and Satis, but these were damaged during the ʿAmarna Period, and Ramesses II had them restored to represent himself between Amon-Reʿ and Horus of *Miʿam*.

The chapel was rescued from the rising waters in 1964–65 and is now in the Museo Egizio in Turin.

Qasr Ibrim

The central of the three sandstone massifs which used to loom south of the village of Ibrim (the name probably derives from the classical Primis), on the

east bank of the Nile, was the most important one. On its top, the fort of Qasr Ibrim ("The Castle of Ibrim" in Arabic) stood on pharaonic foundations (one of the monuments is a stela of year 8 of Amenhotep I) and a temple structure of Taharqa (with a painting showing the king offering to a god). Parts of the fortress were constructed during the short stay of the Roman garrison under the prefect Gaius Petronius in the reign of Augustus, and from then on Qasr Ibrim remained occupied until the beginning of the 19th century. After the completion of the new Aswan dam, the site has become a low island in the midst of Lake Nasser.

Rock-cut shrines (chapels) dedicated to the reigning king and various gods were made by viceroys of Kush of the 18th and 19th Dynasties at the bottom of the cliff. During the salvage operation carried out while the new Aswan dam was being built, their reliefs were cut away and removed to the vicinity of el-Sebuʿa.

The large rock stela of Sety I and his contemporary the Viceroy of Kush, Amenemope, which used to be south of the fort, has been transferred to the neighborhood of the reconstructed Kalabsha temple by the Aswan High Dam.

ʿAniba

ʿAniba, ancient *Miʿam*, was prominent in the New Kingdom, when it served as the administrative center of *Wawat* (Lower Nubia, between the 1st and 2nd cataracts).

The town contained a fort, probably of Middle Kingdom origin, and the temple of Horus of *Miʿam*. The temple may go back to the beginning of the 12th Dynasty (Senwosret I), but most of the evidence dates to the 18th Dynasty (Thutmose III and later kings).

There were cemeteries of various dates in the vicinity, including tombs of the New Kingdom. One of these, the rock-cut tomb of Penniut, the deputy of Wawat under Ramesses VI, has been reconstructed at a new site near ʿAmada.

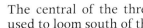

Abu Simbel

Of the seven temples in Nubia built by Ramesses II (Beit el-Wali, Gerf Hussein, el-Sebuʿa, el-Derr, two at Abu Simbel, and Aksha), the rock temples at Abu Simbel (Ibsambul), on the west bank of the Nile, are the most impressive.

The Great Temple was first reported by Johann Ludwig Burckhardt in 1813 and opened by Giovanni Battista Belzoni in 1817. Its ancient name was simply "The Temple of Riʿamsese-meryamun (Ramesses II)." It was probably completed by the king's 24th regnal year.

A gateway leads into a forecourt and on to a terrace. There the visitor is confronted by the temple's rock-cut facade, some 30 meters high and 35 meters wide, with four colossal seated statues of Ramesses II (about 21 meters high), accompanied by smaller statues of relatives standing by his legs. These are as follows:

1st southern colossus: Queen Nofretari by the king's left leg, the king's mother (and the queen of Sety I) Muttuya by his right leg, and Prince Amenhirkhopshef in front.

2nd southern colossus (in the same order as for the previous statue): Princesses Bentʿanta, Nebettawy, and one unnamed, probably Queen Esenofre.

1st northern colossus: Queen Nofretari by the king's right leg, Princess Beketmut by his left leg, and Prince Riʿamsese in front.

2nd northern colossus: Princess Merytamun, Queen Muttuya, and Princess Nofretari.

A niche above the temple entrance contains a symbolic sculptural group representing a cryptographic writing of the praenomen of Ramesses II, Usermaʿatreʿ: the falcon-headed god Reʿ has next to his right leg the hieroglyph showing the head and neck of an animal which is read user, while the goddess by his left leg stands for maʿat. At the top of the temple facade is a row of statues of baboons in adoring attitudes, whose cries were held to welcome the rising sun.

Twice a year, when the rising sun appeared above the horizon on the east bank of the Nile, its rays penetrated the temple entrance, shot through the great hall with eight pillars in the form of colossal statues of the king, the second pillared hall, the vestibule and the sanctuary, and rested on the four statues in the niche at the back, which they illuminated fully. The statues represented the three most important state gods of the Ramessid Period: the Memphite Ptah (first on the left), the Theban Amon Reʿ (second), and the Heliopolitan Reʿ-Harakhty (fourth). The third figure from the left was the king himself.

The Great Temple of Abu Simbel bears witness to the deification of Ramesses II during his lifetime, including scenes showing the king performing rites before the sacred bark of his deified self (on the north wall of the second pillared hall, and on the north wall of the sanctuary). The reliefs in the great hall show scenes of historical or symbolic character: on the long north wall the battle of Qadesh in Syria, and on the south wall the Syrian, Libyan, and Nubian wars.

The Small Temple of Abu Simbel, contemporary with the Great Temple, was dedicated to Hathor of Ibshek and Queen Nofretari. The facade is formed by six colossal standing statues (about 10 meters high) cut in the rock. Four of them represent the king and two the queen, each being flanked by princes and princesses. In its plan the Small Temple is an abbreviated version of the Great Temple: a hall with Hathor pillars, a vestibule with side rooms, and the sanctuary. The niche at the back contains a statue of a Hathor cow protecting the king.

Between 1964 and 1968 both temples were removed to their new location, about 210 meters further away from the river and 65 meters higher. They have become the most popular destination of visitors to the Egyptian part of Nubia and are among the best-known sights of ancient Egypt.

Left The gods of the Great Temple in the niche of the sanctuary.

Right The much more romantic Abu Simbel of the first half of the 19th century (David Roberts, November 1838).

Below right The "Abu Simbel Salvage Operation" was one of the results of the appeal of UNESCO to all its member states to help to rescue the monuments of Nubia threatened by the building of the new dam at Aswan. The protection of the temples at Abu Simbel, cut in the living rock, presented considerable technical and financial difficulties. Several projects were considered; that which was finally chosen consisted of dismantling the temple facades and the walls of their rooms by cutting them into large blocks, removing these, and rebuilding the temples inside concrete dome-shaped structures in a simulated environment. A cofferdam had to he built while the dismantling operation was in progress because of the already rising water of Lake Nasser. The whole huge Lego game was successfully completed, and the resited temples were reopened officially on 22 September 1968.

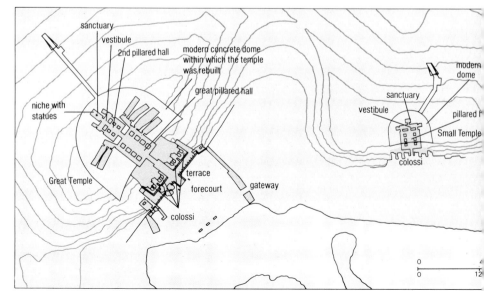

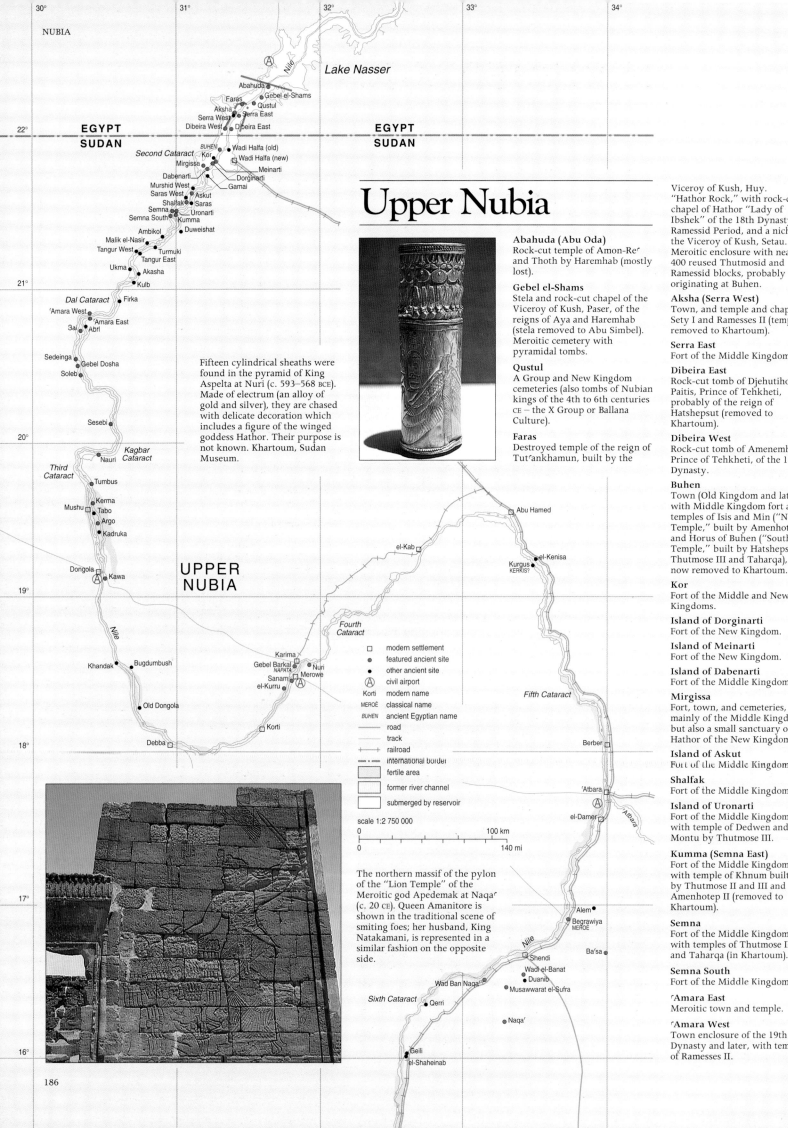

Upper Nubia

NUBIA

EGYPT
SUDAN

Lake Nasser

Second Cataract

UPPER
NUBIA

Dal Cataract

Kagbar Cataract

Third Cataract

Fourth Cataract

Fifth Cataract

Sixth Cataract

Fifteen cylindrical sheaths were found in the pyramid of King Aspelta at Nuri (c. 593–568 BCE). Made of electrum (an alloy of gold and silver), they are chased with delicate decoration which includes a figure of the winged goddess Hathor. Their purpose is not known. Khartoum, Sudan Museum.

Abahuda (Abu Oda)
Rock-cut temple of Amon-Reʿ and Thoth by Haremhab (mostly lost).

Gebel el-Shams
Stela and rock-cut chapel of the Viceroy of Kush, Paser, of the reigns of Aya and Haremhab (stela removed to Abu Simbel). Meroitic cemetery with pyramidal tombs.

Qustul
A Group and New Kingdom cemeteries (also tombs of Nubian kings of the 4th to 6th centuries CE – the X Group or Ballana Culture).

Faras
Destroyed temple of the reign of Tutʿankhamun, built by the Viceroy of Kush, Huy. "Hathor Rock," with rock-cut chapel of Hathor "Lady of Ibshek" of the 18th Dynasty and Ramessid Period, and a niche of the Viceroy of Kush, Setau. Meroitic enclosure with nearly 400 reused Thutmosid and Ramessid blocks, probably originating at Buhen.

Aksha (Serra West)
Town, and temple and chapels of Sety I and Ramesses II (temple removed to Khartoum).

Serra East
Fort of the Middle Kingdom.

Dibeira East
Rock-cut tomb of Djehutihotep Paitis, Prince of Tehkheti, probably of the reign of Hatshepsut (removed to Khartoum).

Dibeira West
Rock-cut tomb of Amenemhet, Prince of Tehkheti, of the 18th Dynasty.

Buhen
Town (Old Kingdom and later), with Middle Kingdom fort and temples of Isis and Min ("North Temple," built by Amenhotep II) and Horus of Buhen ("South Temple," built by Hatshepsut, Thutmose III and Taharqa), both now removed to Khartoum.

Kor
Fort of the Middle and New Kingdoms.

Island of Dorginarti
Fort of the New Kingdom.

Island of Meinarti
Fort of the New Kingdom.

Island of Dabenarti
Fort of the Middle Kingdom.

Mirgissa
Fort, town, and cemeteries, mainly of the Middle Kingdom, but also a small sanctuary of Hathor of the New Kingdom.

Island of Askut
Fort of the Middle Kingdom.

Shalfak
Fort of the Middle Kingdom.

Island of Uronarti
Fort of the Middle Kingdom, with temple of Dedwen and Montu by Thutmose III.

Kumma (Semna East)
Fort of the Middle Kingdom, with temple of Khnum built by Thutmose II and III and Amenhotep II (removed to Khartoum).

Semna
Fort of the Middle Kingdom, with temples of Thutmose III and Taharqa (in Khartoum).

Semna South
Fort of the Middle Kingdom.

ʿAmara East
Meroitic town and temple.

ʿAmara West
Town enclosure of the 19th Dynasty and later, with temple of Ramesses II.

The northern massif of the pylon of the "Lion Temple" of the Meroitic god Apedemak at Naqaʿ (c. 20 CE). Queen Amanitore is shown in the traditional scene of smiting foes; her husband, King Natakamani, is represented in a similar fashion on the opposite side.

Legend:
□ modern settlement
● featured ancient site
• other ancient site
Ⓐ civil airport
Korti modern name
MEROË classical name
BUHEN ancient Egyptian name
road
track
railroad
international border
fertile area
former river channel
submerged by reservoir

scale 1:2 750 000
0 — 100 km
0 — 140 mi

Map labels: Nile, Abahuda, Faras, Gebel el-Shams, Aksha, Qustul, Serra West, Serra East, Dibeira West, Dibeira East, BUHEN, Kor, Wadi Halfa (old), Wadi Halfa (new), Mirgissa, Meinarti, Dabenarti, Dorginarti, Gamai, Murshid West, Saras West, Askut, Shalfak, Saras, Semna, Uronarti, Semna South, Kumma, Ambikol, Duweishat, Malik el-Nasir, Tangur West, Turmuki, Tangur East, Ukma, Akasha, Kulb, Firka, ʿAmara West, ʿAmara East, Ʒai, Abri, Sedeinga, Gebel Dosha, Soleb, Sesebi, Nauri, Tumbus, Kerma, Mushu, Tabo, Argo, Kadruka, Dongola, Kawa, Khandak, Bugdumbush, Karima, Gebel Barkal NAPATA, Nuri, Sanam, Merowe, el-Kurru, Old Dongola, Debba, Korti, Abu Hamed, el-Kab, el-Kenisa, Kurgus KERKIS?, Berber, ʿAtbara, el-Damer, Alem, Begrawiya MEROË, Baʿsa, Shendi, Wadi el-Banat, Duanib, Musawwarat el-Sufra, Wad Ban Naqaʿ, Qerri, Naqaʿ, Geili, el-Shaheinab

PERIPHERAL REGIONS

Island of Sai
Town and fort with temple, 18th Dynasty and Meroitic.

Sedeinga
Temple of Amenhotep III. Meroitic Cemeteries.

Gebel Dosha
Rock-cut chapel of Thutmose III.

Soleb
Temple of Amenhotep III. Cemeteries of the New Kingdom and Napatan Period.

Sesebi
New Kingdom town with temples of the Aten and the Theban triad, built by Akhenaten and Sety I.

Nauri
Rock-cut stela of year 4 of Sety I.

Tumbus
Stelae of Thutmose I and others, including the Viceroy of Kush, Setau, of the reign of Ramesses II.

Kerma
Capital of the Kerma state, reaching greatest extent in the 16th century BCE. Colossal mud brick temple (*deffufa*). Governmental buildings. Remains of large buildings of the Napatan Period. Cemetery with tumuli with reused Egyptian objects.

Island of Argo
Temple at Tabo, of the 25th Dynasty, Taharqa (reusing New Kingdom blocks), and Meroitic. Meroitic cemetery.

Kawa
Temples of Amun, built mainly by Tutʿankhamun, Taharqa, and Napatan and Meroitic kings.

el-Kurru
Pyramid field, including burials of kings of the 25th Dynasty.

Sanam
Palace, storerooms, and cemeteries of the 25th Dynasty, with temple of Amon-Reʿ built by Taharqa.

Gebel Barkal
Meroitic pyramid field. A number of temples and chapels dedicated to Amon-Reʿ, built by kings of the New Kingdom, Piye and Taharqa, and Napatan and Meroitic kings.

Nuri
Pyramid field, including burial of Taharqa and those of various Napatan and Meroitic kings.

Meroe (Begrawiya)
Temples and pyramid fields of the Meroitic Period; site of city with royal palaces.

Baʿsa
Meroitic temple.

Wadi el-Banat
Destroyed Meroitic temple.

Wad Ban Naqaʿ
Destroyed Meroitic temple.

Musawwarat el-Sufra
Meroitic temples.

Naqaʿ
Meroitic temples and unexcavated town site.

The Oases

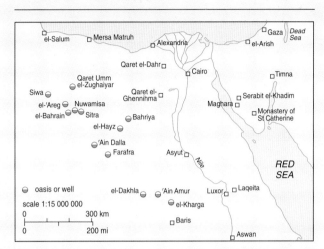

The western oases consist of a series of wind-eroded depressions in the Libyan desert, containing natural springs and wells that are bored up to a thousand meters below ground. The water can support agriculture, but wells are scattered and may fail. The population (more than 100,000 for el-Dakhla in 1999) is spread over wide areas, with barren tracts, often formerly inhabited, between settlements.

The oases have been inhabited since Paleolithic times. The Western Desert has produced traces of early pastoralism and agriculture, and sites comparable to but earlier than Egyptian Predynastic cultures have been found in el-Dakhla. The area was important both as a staging post and for its specialized mineral and agricultural produce, such as wine. Its economy fluctuated with that of the Nile valley, with which the oases traded. Early history is poorly known. For the Old–New Kingdoms all the main oases except for Siwa are mentioned in Egyptian texts and finds have been made notably in el-Dakhla. They were probably all administered by Egypt. From the Late Period remains are more frequent and prosperity increased until the Roman Period, when Greeks and members of new religious communities settled. Siwa was annexed permanently in the 26th Dynasty; its population, now Berber-speaking, was probably always more Libyan than Egyptian.

Late antiquity brought widespread depopulation. The oasis economy did not recover fully, so that the naturally good conditions for preserving sites are enhanced.

Below left Temple of Tutu (Tithoes) at Kellis (Ismant el-Kharab), el-Dakhla Oasis, with a view of the Roman Period desert encampment behind.

el-Kharga
ʿAin Amur Roman Period temple and settlement, halfway between el-Kharga and el-Dakhla oases.
ʿAin Manawir Persian Period temple.
Hibis Temple of Amun, 26th Dynasty, decorated by Darius, Nectanebo II, and Ptolemies.
Qasr el-Ghueida Temple of Amon-Reʿ, Mut, and Khons, 25th Dynasty to Ptolemaic.
Gebel el-Teir Rock inscriptions, 26th Dynasty to Ptolemaic.
Nadura Roman Period temple.
Qasr Zaiyan Ptolemaic and Roman Period temple.
Dush Settlement and temple of Sarapis and Isis, Roman Period.

el-Dakhla
Prehistoric to Old Kingdom and Greco-Roman Period settlements and cemeteries.
Balat Old Kingdom town; 6th Dynasty and 1st Intermediate Period mastabas; temple of Mut, New Kingdom; 3rd Intermediate and Roman Period tombs.
Amheida 1st Intermediate Period cemeteries. Greco-Roman Period temple and settlement.
Mut el-Kharab Occupied from Old Kingdom and capital of the oasis from the New Kingdom on; temple of Seth; cemeteries of Late to Roman Periods.
el-Qasr Temple of Thoth, Greco-Roman; necropolis.
Deir el-Hagar Temple, 1st century CE.
Qaret el-Muzawwaqa Decorated tombs of the Roman Period.
Kellis (Ismant el-Kharab) Ptolemaic–Roman Period town: temples, industrial and government areas, cemeteries, mausolea. Cult center of Tutu and goddesses Tapshay and Neith.

Farafra
Prehistoric remains; evidence for Roman Period occupation.

Bahriya
Monuments near *el-Qasr* and *el-Bawiti* Tomb of Amenhotep Huy (18th–19th Dynasty); chapels and tombs of the reigns of Apries and Amasis; temple of Alexander the Great; major cemetery of the Roman Period; lost Roman "triumphal arch."
el-Hayz Small center of the Roman Period.

Siwa
Aghurmi 26th Dynasty and Ptolemaic temple, assumed to be where Alexander the Great consulted the oracle of Ammon.
Umm el-ʿEbeida Temple of Nectanebo II.
Gebel el-Mawta Necropolis, 26th Dynasty and Greco-Roman, including decorated tombs, cemeteries, and undecorated temples at several further sites.

Small oases with sites: *Qaret Umm el-Zughaiyar, el-ʿAreg, Nuwamisa, el-Bahrain, Sitra.*

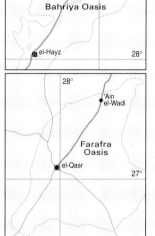

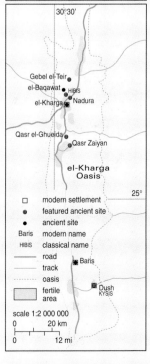

Sinai

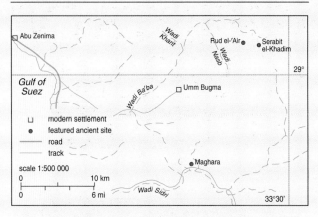

Right Head of a statuette of Teye, the Queen of Amenhotep III, identified by a cartouche bearing her name on the headdress. Green steatite. Height 6·5 cm. Found at Serabit el-Khadim. Cairo, Egyptian Museum.

Below left A relief of King Sekhemkhet, rediscovered at Maghara in 1973. It is almost identical with another, some 35 meters to the south. The two reliefs are among the earliest Egyptian inscriptions in Sinai.

Below A view of the temple of Hathor at Serabit el-Khadim taken in the 1970s, showing some of the stelae that are still standing.

Commercial and military routes connecting Egypt with Western Asia followed the Mediterranean coast or traversed north Sinai. In the late 1980s and early 1990s the west part of north Sinai became the focus of international archaeological effort prompted by a planned large-scale irrigation project. The most spectacular monuments explored during this campaign were forts, mostly of the Late and Greco-Roman Periods: Tell el-Farama (Pelusium), Tell el-Herr, Tell el-Hebua (with material going back as far as the late Middle Kingdom), and Tell Qedwa.

The Egyptians were attracted by the mineral deposits of the valleys of southwest Sinai no later than the 3rd Dynasty. The objective of the expeditions regularly sent out to work the mines during the Old to New Kingdoms was to bring back turquoise and to acquire copper; the copper workings over much of Sinai are mostly not associated with Egyptian finds. Egyptian activities in Sinai ceased at the end of the New Kingdom.

The mines of Maghara were the first to be exploited, with the earliest rock inscriptions and reliefs dating to Djoser, Sekhemkhet, and Zanakht. The last known Old Kingdom expedition was that of Pepy II in the "year of the 2nd census" (around his 3rd year); although Middle and New Kingdom rulers are attested (Amenemhet III and IV, Hatshepsut and Thutmose III, perhaps Ramesses II), the site did not regain its former significance.

The most important site of Egyptian activities in Sinai is Serabit el-Khadim with its temple of Hathor. The temple's earliest part, the rock-cut "Cave of Hathor" preceded by a court and a portico, goes back to the early 12th Dynasty. In the New Kingdom, a shrine for Sopd, the god of the eastern desert, was built, and the temple of Hathor was enlarged (mainly by Hatshepsut and Thutmose III); thousands of votive offerings have been recovered from the site. Thoth was also worshiped locally, together with several deified kings, notably Snofru. Ramesses VI is the last ruler whose name has been encountered. There is a Middle Kingdom rock inscription at Rud el-ʿAir, some 1·5 kilometers to the west.

A rock text of Sahureʿ and a large stela of Senwosret I date the third important center of turquoise mining in the Wadi Kharit. Nearby, in the Wadi Nasb, were found a rock stela of year 20 of Amenemhet III and Middle Kingdom and Ramessid texts.

PART THREE
ASPECTS OF EGYPTIAN SOCIETY

EVERYDAY LIFE

There is no one method of studying the everyday life of the ancient Egyptians, but a mosaic of different approaches. Tomb reliefs and paintings provide a wealth of material. Although only members of the top stratum of society were buried in large decorated tombs, subsidiary scenes afford glimpses of the life of ordinary people, but it would be a mistake to accept this evidence alone. Small wooden figurines ("models") and objects of daily use often form part of funerary equipment; less common but more trustworthy are those found in excavations of settlements. Texts on papyri and ostraca are invaluable because they provide details not available from elsewhere.

Agricultural scenes in Theban tomb TT 1 at Deir el-Medina, belonging to Sennedjem, of the reign of Sety I. The setting is the mythical Fields of Ialu, where Sennedjem, accompanied by his wife Iyneferti, is shown reaping grain, plowing with a pair of dappled cattle, and harvesting flax. Only the heads of grain were cut off with a short-handled wooden sickle, whose serrated blade was formed of sharp flakes of flint; the remaining much-valued straw was pulled up later. Many sickles and whips of the types used by Sennedjem are preserved.

Farms and Vineyards

For sowing, the ground was prepared by plowing, usually done with oxen, or hoeing. The seed was then scattered and cattle, sheep, or goats were used to tread it in.

The monotony of the reapers' work was relieved by a flute player. After cutting, the ears of grain were collected into baskets and either carried or transported on donkeys to threshing floors. The threshing was done by cattle, sheep, or goats which were driven over the ears and trod the grain out. The chaff was separated laboriously by winnowing and sifting. The grain was then deposited in granaries.

Scenes of watering grapevines and picking and crushing grapes are often shown. The crushing was done by men treading grapes in a vat, often to the accompaniment of the rhythmical beating of resonant sticks, and the must was later strained by twisting in a sack. Hieratic labels on wine jars found in excavations give us names of vineyards and vintners as well as the vintage of the wines they originally contained.

Plowing, Middle Kingdom.

Reaping grain, 5th Dynasty.

Granary, Middle Kingdom.

Winnowing and carrying ears of grain to granary, 18th Dynasty.

Threshing with cattle, 18th Dynasty.

Picking grapes, 18th Dynasty.

Herds and Herdsmen

Scenes from the life of herdsmen include cows being mounted by bulls, calving, suckling calves, or being milked; bulls fighting, cattle being fed, and goats browsing on trees or bushes. Inspections of cattle, goats, donkeys, sheep, and fowl by the owner of the estate, during which they were counted and their numbers recorded, were a regular occurrence. Herdsmen may be shown cooking and eating, skinning a goat hung from a tree, or making mats, apparently their favorite pastime. The prestige of stock rearing was reflected in the number of officials bearing titles connected with it.

Inspection of cattle, 18th Dynasty.

Herdsman with goats, 19th Dynasty.

Hunter with dogs, 5th Dynasty.

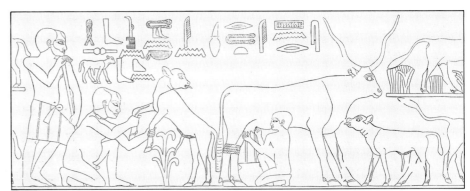

Milking, 5th Dynasty.

Cow calving, 5th Dynasty.

Hunting and Fishing

The contribution of the hunting of desert animals to the Egyptian economy was limited, and the activity soon became the sport of the rich.

Marsh scenes with people fishing, fowling, harvesting papyrus and making papyrus rafts are usually closely associated with cattle-breeding activities. The final stage of seining (or netting) fish by fishermen is often shown, as are several other methods, in particular catching fish in baskets and by means of small hand-held clap-nets. Angling, usually done from a small papyrus raft, must have been regarded as enjoyable relaxation. During the Old Kingdom, hippopotamus hunting was probably a necessary and dangerous task.

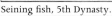
Seining fish, 5th Dynasty.

Fishhook, 18th/19th Dynasties. Angling, 6th Dynasty.

Fishing with clap-net and hippopotamus hunt, 6th Dynasty.

Fishing with clap-net and angling, 6th Dynasty.

Hippopotamus hunt, 5th Dynasty.

Trades and Crafts

Important stages in the manufacture of objects by craftsmen are shown with surprising technical knowledge in tomb reliefs and paintings: a goldworker is weighing gold; joiners are adding final touches to wooden *djed*-signs (symbolizing endurance) for a shrine; boat-builders have nearly completed the hull of a large wooden boat; men with blowpipes are busy smelting metal. Other craftsmen often represented include sculptors (the making of statues was as much a craft as an art), carpenters, leather-workers, potters, makers of stone vessels, rope-makers, and brick-makers. Many models as well as real tools of craftsmen have been found.

Goldsmith, joiners, jewelers, and engravers, 18th Dynasty.

Model tools, 18th Dynasty.

Boat-builders, 5th Dynasty.

Metalworkers, 5th Dynasty.

Because of their role in ensuring that the tomb was provided with meat offerings, scenes and models of butchers were among the commonest.

There were many different qualities and shapes of bread and cakes. The grinding of grain was common to all, but different methods of baking were employed. Sometimes the dough was poured into preheated earthenware pots and gently baked without direct fire.

Egyptian beer was brewed by fermenting part-baked bread; brewers standing in vats treading pieces of bread or leaning over a large vessel straining the mash are a common theme in statuettes, models, and reliefs.

Butchers, 18th Dynasty.

Butchers, bakers and brewers, Middle Kingdom.

Brewer, cook, and woman grinding grain, First Intermediate Period.

Preheating pots for baking bread, 5th Dynasty.

Granaries with grain, 5th Dynasty.

Brewing, Middle Kingdom.

Domestic Life

Musical instruments were known from the earliest times, and many of them have been found in excavations. The flute, double clarinet, double oboe, and trumpet were the most common wind instruments; string instruments included various types of harp, lute, and lyre; the tambourine and drum were the membranophones. On another level, sistra and clappers were used as percussion instruments in rituals.

Occasional finds of model houses usefully complement information gathered from excavations of settlements. Our knowledge of ancient Egyptian domestic architecture is still very incomplete, particularly for the Early Dynastic Period and Old Kingdom, in comparison with what we know about the architecture of temples and tombs.

Details of the day-to-day running of ancient Egyptian households remain little known. The links between individual members of farming communities, the precise form of their relationship to the landowner on whose land they were settled, and details of family life remain imperfectly known. An attempt to reconstruct an ordinary day, month, or year in the life of an ancient Egyptian family would still involve much guessing.

Female musicians and dancers, 18th Dynasty.

Model house, Middle Kingdom.

Reed brush, 18th Dynasty.

Basketwork and matting, Middle Kingdom.

Offering bearers, Middle Kingdom.

Sandals, 18th Dynasty or Greco-Roman Period.

"Place myrrh upon your head, and clothe yourself in fine linen," exhorts the "Song of the Harper." Rich Egyptians appreciated beautiful objects of daily use, in particular toilet articles, such as combs, ointment spoons (often in the form of a musician, a servant carrying a large jar on his shoulders, or a swimming girl), kohl-containers (for eye makeup), vases, and mirrors (made of polished copper or bronze, usually circular, with a decorative handle). They liked to surround themselves with elegant furniture (chairs, stools, beds, chests and boxes) and valued fine clothes, wigs, and jewelry. They also enjoyed good food, drink, music, singing and dancing (they do not seem to have participated actively in dances, but rather watched dancing displays).

Representations of banquets are very common, particularly in Theban tombs of the New Kingdom. One of the features of these merry-making scenes is the cone of a scented greasy substance (the "myrrh" of the "Song of the Harper") placed on the wig of each reveler; as the party progressed, these slowly melted and gave off a pleasant aroma.

Ancient Egyptian children played much the same games and amused themselves in similar ways to Egyptian children of today. A number of simple toys have been found, though wooden horses on wheels are not known before the Greco-Roman Period (the horse was introduced to Egypt in the 1st half of the 2nd millennium BCE).

Detail of banquet scene, 18th Dynasty.

Comb, 19th Dynasty.

Toilet spoon, 18th Dynasty.

Mirror, New Kingdom.

Toy horse, Greco-Roman Period.

Folding stool, 18th Dynasty.

SCRIBES AND WRITING

The spread of writing to record year names around 3000 BCE defines the beginning of Egyptian history more than any other single change. Similarly, literacy set the civilizations of the ancient Near East apart from their contemporaries, opening up new possibilities in social organization and in the transmission, and occasionally criticism, of growing bodies of knowledge. But the script was complex and literacy was confined to a small elite. Only relatively recently has writing spread much more widely in societies.

It seems that there was no separate, nonliterate class of nobility, as a landed aristocracy might be. All high-ranking people had scribal careers in officialdom, army, or priesthood; kings too were literate. Among administrative titles the highest do not allude to writing, but representations show that such people claimed also to be scribes; they had surpassed the level of achievement at which writing was the main occupation, not bypassed it. In all spheres writing formed the basis of official organization.

Learning to read and write was part of training for administration. Sons of important people could begin their careers very young, perhaps about the age of 12. Literary references to schools survive but no materials from basic instruction in writing are known. Secondary education was provided by a scribe's official superior on his first job – normally another scribe. At Deir el-Medina, the only place for which detailed evidence survives, apprentices at work studied under their superiors by copying passages from a cursive hieroglyphic text called *Kemyt* and from classic literature, as well as contemporaneous miscellanies of model letters, satirical compositions, religious and secular poems, and panegyrics, some of which superiors set as daily exercises. Numerous papyri of the miscellanies have been preserved, mainly from Memphis; their preservation suggests that they were ultimately deposited in their owners' tombs.

Two features of training are noteworthy. First, it was mainly in cursive writing, which was from the beginning the commonest form. Further instruction was probably needed for proficiency in the monumental hieroglyphic script, which was comprehensible to rather fewer people, although many may have known the meaning of a few salient signs; in the Late Period the two forms diverged sharply. Second, although the Egyptians analyzed their script into something like a syllabary and had an "alphabetical" order into which lists were sometimes arranged, learning was by copying sentences or words, not by starting from individual signs. Writing was perceived in groups of signs and there was little stimulus to minute subdivision of the script.

Apart from administration and correspondence, cursive writing was used for non-essential purposes, the most interesting of which, from a modern perspective, was works of literature, which are preserved in school copies and from other contexts. They include narrative fiction, instructions and

Top Granite scribe statue of the Chief Lector Priest Petamenope, c. 650 BCE. The figure is in the traditional cross-legged writing pose with a papyrus spread between the knees. The statue form is a conscious revival of an Old Kingdom model by one of the richest men of the Late Period. Quartzite. Height 75 cm. From Karnak. Cairo, Egyptian Museum.

Above Typical scribe's palette with a long slot for reed pens (some original ones are preserved) in addition to depressions with cakes of ink. There are clear signs of use. Middle Kingdom. Wood. From Beni Hasan. Oxford, Ashmolean Museum.

An archaic version of the scribe's basic tools makes up the hieroglyph on the *left*: a palette with depressions for cakes of red and black pigment mixed with gum, a water pot or bag, and a reed pen or papyrus smoother. Ink was made by dabbing a wet pen or brush on the cake of pigment. The scribe painted rather than wrote, with his hand held above the surface. Because of the right-to-left direction of writing, originally in vertical columns, he would have smudged his work if he had let his hand rest. In hieratic he could write about a dozen signs before recharging his pen.

discourses, cult and religious hymns, love poetry, some royal inscriptions and other texts used secondarily as literature, and various genres that are not literary in a narrow sense: medical and mathematical texts, rituals, and some mortuary books. The chief center of production was the "house of life," a scriptorium attached to temples, which made copies of the entire range of traditional writings, not only of religious texts. The tradition continued almost without a break into the 3rd century CE, although few texts were transmitted from hieratic to demotic. Some literary works became generally familiar and were alluded to in later texts, playing on a lettered culture common to writer and reader.

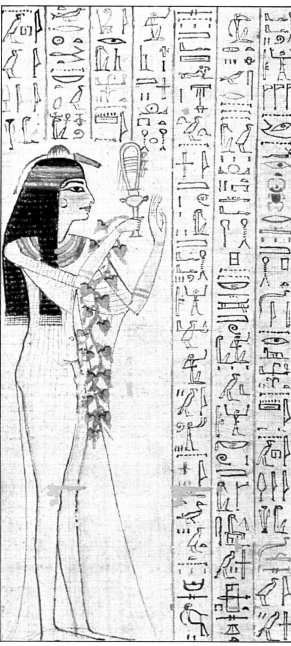

Above Specimen of 12th-Dynasty literary hieratic with transcription into hieroglyphs. Translation: "The vizier Ptahhotep says: 'Sovereign, my lord! Elderliness has occurred, decrepitude has come, old age descended; woe is come and weakness is renewing itself; the heart passes the night in pain, every day; the eyes are shrunk, the ears made deaf; strength perishes because of the heart's weariness. The mouth is silent and cannot speak.'" Paris, Bibliothèque Nationale.

Below Extract from a statement of the misfortunes of Peteese's family, presented as if it was submitted to a high financial official in the reign of Darius I. The text and transcription between the lines read from right to left, but the individual words of the transcription read from left to right. Translation: "The master of harbors dispatched a military officer, saying: 'Arrest anyone Peteese (an ancestor of the author)/tells you to arrest.' The officer came to Teudjoi (el-Hiba), and Peteese had the two priests arrested. He went north with them to the royal palace. /In Pharaoh's presence Peteese recounted everything they had done. Pharaoh passed sentence on the two priests." From el-Hiba. Manchester, John Rylands Library.

p3-dj-jst jw ntj nb rmt n jmhtj m-sm dd mr-ms' w' jw ''-n-mr p' dj

pr-'' pr'p'r jrmw hdjf 2 w'b p' n mhw p'-dj-jst dj t'jw-d'j r jw mr-ms' p' n-jmw mhw mj nk dd r

2 s(?) w'b p' n hp jrw pr-'' dj pr-'' m-b'h jjrw nb md p'-dj-jst dd

There are several forms of the script. Hieroglyphic was used for monumental and ornamental inscriptions, cursive hieroglyphs for religious texts and *Kemyt*, and hieratic, the normal cursive, for everyday purposes. In the 3rd Intermediate Period some monumental inscriptions were written in hieratic, which was also the point of departure for abnormal hieratic, used in the Theban area in the 8th–7th centuries, and for demotic, the cursive of the north after 700 and of all Egypt by 550. Hieratic can always be transcribed into hieroglyphs, in a different arrangement from a text composed in hieroglyphic, but demotic is self-sufficient, referring at most to hieratic. Cursive hieroglyphs died out in the first millennium BCE, whereas hieratic was used to the end for some religious and literary or learned texts; demotic was used for business, literature, some religious texts, and occasional inscriptions on stone.

The spoken language developed continuously, but written forms changed only fitfully, and were linked to the script form used to write them. In no period was written language very close to what was spoken. Between the Old and Middle Kingdoms, the period of Old and Middle Egyptian (the "classical" form of the language), written Egyptian changed relatively little. By the 18th Dynasty spoken and written were far apart. Late Egyptian, a formalization of New Kingdom spoken language, was used for hieratic documents of the 19th–20th Dynasties, while hieroglyphic texts were written in a rather free Middle Egyptian; hieratic forms differed between Middle Egyptian religious texts and Late Egyptian business documents. Demotic, probably derived from the spoken language of the 7th–6th centuries BCE, supplanted Late Egyptian, but Middle Egyptian remained the formal, monumental language until the end. In the 2nd century CE Egyptian magical texts began to be written in Greek letters, and from the 4th century this form developed into Coptic, the language of Christian Egypt, which gradually gave way to Arabic after 640 CE.

Egyptian is one of hundreds of members of the Afroasiatic language family, which range from Semitic in the east to groups in Africa with Berber in the northwest to Chadic around Lake Chad and Kushitic and Omotic in the Horn of Africa. While Egyptian forms a separate branch, it is closest to Semitic. In word formation and phonetics the two have much in common, including triconsonantal roots and the consonants ʿ (ʿayin), q and ḥ, but Egyptian's structure is as far from Semitic's as English is from Latin.

Right Ink hieroglyphs and vignette from the Book of the Dead papyrus of the lady Anhai, 19th Dynasty. The red groups of signs (rubrics) mark the beginnings of sections. The text is corrupt and untranslatable, but derives from a formula for appearing in the form of Ptah and another for eating, drinking, and taking up a throne in the next world. London, British Museum.

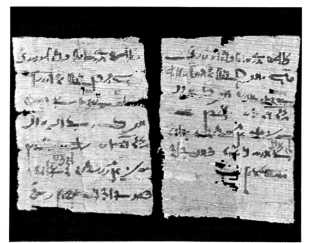

Left Pair of demotic questions to the oracle of Sobek and Isis at Soknopaiou Nesos (Dimai) in the Faiyum; 149 or 138 BCE. The two scraps of papyrus (7·5 × 5·5 cm) were placed before the god, and in some way the relevant one was chosen and removed. The texts are almost identical: the first reads: "Plea of the servant Teshnufe (son of) Mare, who says /before his master Sobek lord of Pay, great god, /and Isis, perfect of throne. If my/ soundest course is to plow /the bank of the lake this year, /year 33, /and I should not sow, let this slip /be brought out to me." The second has the negative provision "if it is not my soundest course . . . ," and omits the reference to sowing, which is not applicable. Oxford, Ashmolean Museum.

All the forms of the script use signs in two overlapping categories: phonograms (phonetic signs) and semograms (conveying meaning). They indicate consonants only, although the vowels associated with particular words or forms may have been understood as being conveyed. Transliterations are into consonantal skeletons. The examples of different types of sign *below* are drawn from the text illustrated *right*. In theory the numbers of possible writings of any word are vast, but in practice words have standard writings, mostly of phonograms with semograms at the end. These are read as groups, not broken down into their components – as is true of fluent reading in an alphabetic script. Standard writings make the script easily legible and are particularly important in hieratic and demotic, with their simplified sign forms.

Inscription on a naos of Tuthmose IV, recording the king's discovery of a stone. The lines of text and transcription give a step-by-step analysis of the Egyptian and its translation into English.
(a) Copy of the hieroglyphs, written from left to right for convenience. Signs enclosed by [ ] are restored.
(b) Sign-by-sign transcription, divided into words, with indication of classifiers and orthograms above the line. (+) marks a phonogram complement, which is not to be read separately. Logograms are written in SMALL CAPITALS; there is no sharp distinction between a single phonogram writing a whole word and a logogram. *nsjt* is a complex historical writing that has to be read as a group.
(c) Conventional Egyptologist's transcription, giving the linguistic structure of the text.
(d) Word-for-word indication of the meaning of the Egyptian.
(e) English translation.

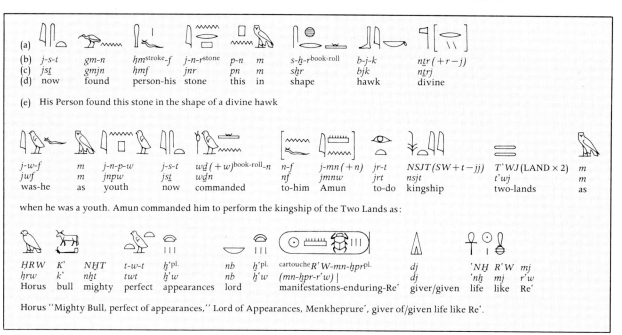

(a)
(b) j-s-t   gm-n   ḥm^stroke-f   j-n-r^stone   p-n   m   s-ḫ-r^book-roll   b-j-k   nṯr(+r−j)
(c) jst   gmjn   ḥmf   jnr   pn   m   sḫr   bjk   nṯrj
(d) now   found   person-his   stone   this in shape   hawk   divine

(e) His Person found this stone in the shape of a divine hawk

j-w-f   m   j-n-p-w   j-s-t   wḏ(+w)^book-roll-n   n-f   j-mn(+n)   jr-t   NSJT(SW+t−jj)   T'WJ(LAND×2)   m
jwf   m   jnpw   jst   wḏn   nf   jmnw   jrt   nsjt   t'wj   m
was-he as youth   now   commanded   to-him Amun   to-do kingship   two-lands   as

when he was a youth. Amun commanded him to perform the kingship of the Two Lands as:

HRW   K'   NḪT   t-w-t   ḫ'^pl.   nb   ḫ'^pl.   cartouche R'W-mn-ḫpr^pl.   dj   'NḪ   R'W   mj
ḥrw   k'   nḫt   twt   ḫ'w   nb   ḫ'w   (mn-ḫpr-r'w)| dj   'nḫ   mj   r'w
Horus bull mighty perfect appearances lord appearances manifestations-enduring-Re'   giver/given life like Re'

Horus "Mighty Bull, perfect of appearances," Lord of Appearances, Menkheprure', giver of/given life like Re'.

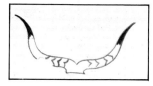

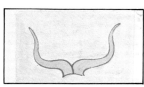

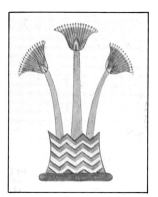

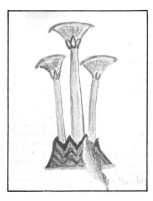

Representational aspects
Most hieroglyphs are pictures and could evolve with the artistic styles of different periods. The group *above* and *left* shows a pair of cattle horns and a clump of papyrus, both in versions of the Old and of the Middle Kingdom, and a reed mat.

Derivation of values
s	from *sw* "length of cloth"
t	from *tj* "loaf of bread"
gm	from *gmt* "black ibis"
r	from *r'* "mouth"
p	from *pj* "mat"
jr	from *jrt* "eye"
ḫ'	from *ḫ'j* "appears (the sun over the horizon)"

A sign's consonantal reading is mostly determined by what it represents, but one sign may have several values, and may function both as a phonogram

and as a semogram. 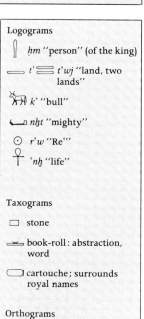, a seated man, may read *rmt* "human being," *zj* "man" or *rḫw* "companion," or may be a taxogram, as in *ḥm-nṯr* "priest."

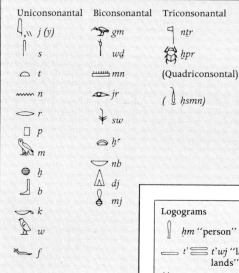

Above Signs can write one to four consonants. Uniconsonantal signs are common, but a set of them is not an alphabet, because it has no special position among phonograms as a whole.

Right There are two types of semogram: logograms, which write complete words, and signs that are placed after the phonograms in a word. The most important of these are taxograms, or determinatives, which indicate the class or area of meaning to which a word belongs. Strokes, which form one category of orthograms – signs functioning purely to aid reading – show that a preceding sign is a logogram; sets of two or three strokes write the dual or the plural.

Uniconsonantal
j (y)
s
t
n
r
p
m
ḫ
b
k
w
f

Biconsonantal
gm
wḏ
mn
jr
sw
ḫ'
nb
dj
mj

Triconsonantal
nṯr
ḫpr

(Quadriconsonantal)
(ḥsmn)

Logograms
ḥm "person" (of the king)
t'wj "land, two lands"
k' "bull"
nḫt "mighty"
r'w "Re'"
'nḫ "life"

Taxograms
□ stone
book-roll: abstraction, word
cartouche; surrounds royal names

Orthograms
| logogram indicator
||| plural indicator

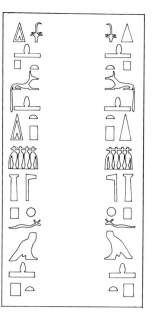

The writing of the signs in a text fixes the direction of reading. Signs facing right – the normal direction – show that the text reads from right to left. Columns or lines may be used. Here an identical text is inscribed once from right to left and once from left to right. Offering formula on a false door in the mastaba of Kahayf. Late 6th Dynasty. Giza.

Ornamental caption to a hunting scene in the tomb of Amenemhet at Thebes (TT 82, reign of Thutmose III). Words containing the name of Amun have been erased, probably during the ʿAmarna Period. The text reads: "Crossing the wadis, treading the hills, taking pleasure, shooting the game of the desert, by the one beloved of his lord, steward of the vizier, scribe accountant of the grain of [Amun, Amenemhet], justified."

Above Outline hieroglyphs in a caption in the tomb of Pereʿ at Thebes (TT 139, reign of Thutmose IV). The text reads: "Going north to the district of Poqer (Abydos); seeing Wennofre (Osiris) at the festival." The sign *m* has been replaced by ⟶, also *m*, in order to make a better grouping. Both versions are now visible.

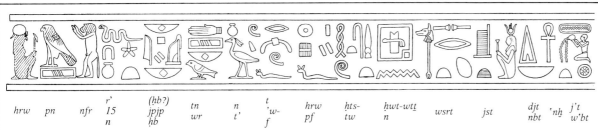

hrw	pn	nfr	rʿ 15 n	(ḥb?) jpjp ḥb	tn wr	n tʾ	ʿwʾ f	hrw pf	ḥts- tw	ḥwt-wtṯ n	wsrt	jst	djt nbt ʿnḥ	jʾt wʾbt

Figurative writing

The use of the script's principles in a playful or oblique way is often called figurative writing or cryptography. This occurs in all periods, chiefly as a challenge to persuade the reader to read a standard formula. During the Late and Greco-Roman Periods, however, the hieroglyphic script was elaborated from a repertory of a few hundred signs to one of several thousand, using every possible method for devising new signs and combinations, and not observing the former economy of means. At this stage hieroglyphs had lost connection with demotic, the everyday script. They could be read only by a tiny elite, mainly of priests, who wished to cultivate complexity and symbolism almost for their own sake.

Above Facsimile of an ornamental inscription of the reign of Tiberius in the birth house at Philae. Translation: "This good day, the 2nd of Epiphi (month name): This festival, the great festival of the entire land; that day when the birth house was completed for the mighty one, Isis, giver of life, mistress of the Abaton (see page 73)." The transliteration follows the grouping of the signs. The writing, especially of the first few words, uses numerous non-traditional sign values. Examples of early and late values are:

p; early *bjk*

n; early *š*

tʾ; early *ʾḥ*

t; early *d*

Some signs do occur in early periods: *nfr*. In other cases

a sign is changed in form: ⟨ ⟩ (human mouth), *r* becomes ℵ. The result of all this is that a single value may be written by many different signs: , all *m* (from a total of more than 25), and one sign can have many values: , *š s ḥ ḫ n m jnr*.

A letter of the 11th Dynasty (c. 1950 BCE) that never reached its destination. The papyrus is folded into a packet (8 × 4 cm), and sealed, with the addressee's name above the seal. The text reads: "The overseer of Lower Egypt, Reʿnofre." From Deir el-Bahri. New York, Metropolitan Museum of Art.

Ostraca were used for writing drafts of texts or as cheap substitutes for papyrus. In this example an illiterate man asks another to write a pledge for him in respect of a debt; the ostracon was probably kept by the creditor until the matter was settled. At this date – between Ramesses III and IX – the tunic was equivalent in value to 1–3 sacks of grain.

Translation: "Year 5, month 3 of *peret* (approx. winter), day 22. What the guardian of the estate Penrenenutet said: 'By Amun and the ruler, if I enter a[nother] week without having given this tunic to Harmin, it (my debt) will be doubled to my debit.' Made (i.e. written) by the foreman of the gang Nekhemmut." From Deir el-Medina. London, Petrie Museum, University College.

THE ARMY

The earliest battle in the history of humankind which can be reconstructed in detail took place near the city of Qadesh on the Syrian river Orontes late in May 1274 BCE. The protagonists were Ramesses II and the Hittite king Muwatallis, and at stake was the control of Syria. In the end, both armies suffered heavily, but neither was annihilated. The encounter was indecisive.

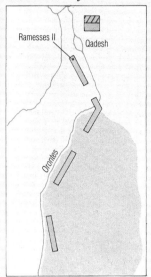

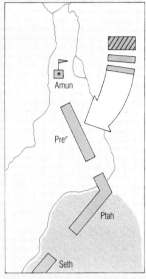

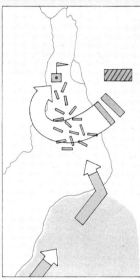

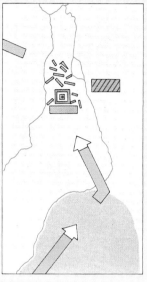

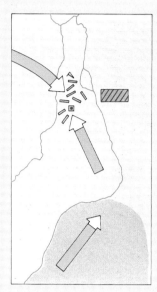

Egyptian infantry and chariotry, total 20,000 men

Egyptian camp

Hittite chariotry 3,500 chariots with 10,500 men

Hittite infantry 8,000 men

1. The Egyptian army consisted of four divisions, with a smaller unit operating independently. Through false information planted on them, the Egyptians were misled into believing that the Hittite host had retreated. The Egyptian divisions advanced northward along the Orontes, unaware that the Hittites lay concealed beyond Qadesh.

2. The Egyptian van, the division of Amun led by the king himself, reached the rendezvous point northwest of the city and set up camp. When the division of Preʿ, suspecting no danger, approached, its right flank was subjected to a devastating charge of Hittite chariotry.

3. The division of Preʿ, caught by surprise, was broken and scattered. Survivors of the Hittite ambush were fleeing northward in the direction of the Egyptian camp, with Hittite chariots in pursuit. The division of Ptah was still emerging from the Robaui forest south of the town of Shabtuna and crossing on to the west bank of the river, and was too far away to render any assistance to the attacked unit.

4. The camp was overrun and the division of Amun suffered heavy losses. The king and his guard desperately tried to fight their way to meet the approaching division of Ptah. Muwatallis committed his chariot reserve in order to bring the battle to a quick conclusion.

5. By his gallant, though forced, action the Egyptian king gained enough time: the special task force appeared at last, and with the division of Ptah now reaching the scene, crushed the Hittite chariotry. Muwatallis' infantry remained inactive beyond the river.

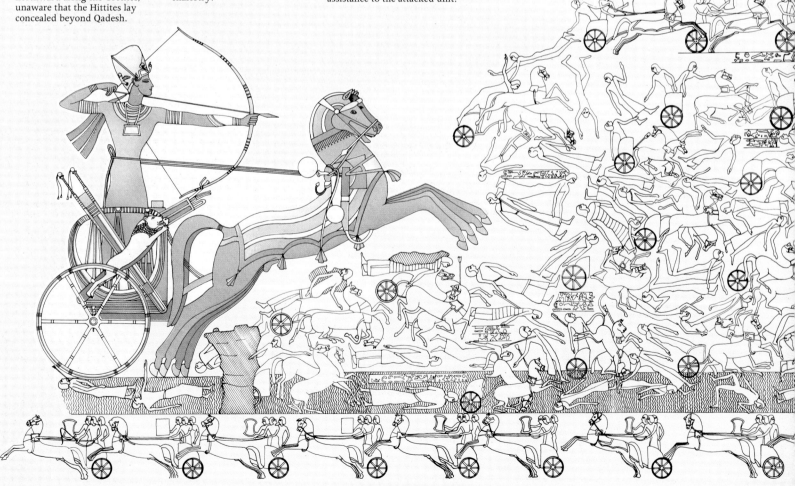

One of the advantages Egypt derived from her unique geographical position was relative safety. Nomadic tribes in the deserts on either side of the Nile valley soon ceased to pose a serious threat to the highly organized and much more powerful Egyptian civilization; only during periods of instability were they a force to be reckoned with. Colonial expansion in the 12th Dynasty led to intensive campaigning and the building of huge fortresses in Nubia, but it was not until the 18th Dynasty that the Egyptians encountered real opposition, when they entered the military arena of the Near East by contending for Syria and Palestine.

The word *mesha*ᶜ, "army," originally described both military forces and peaceful expeditions sent to quarry minerals: "task force" would be the most fitting translation. During the Old Kingdom, when an emergency arose, a body of men was mustered to back the small specialized permanent units. The situation changed in the 1st Intermediate Period: instability brought about the creation of private armies led by nomarchs and the more extensive use of non-Egyptian mercenary troops. The Middle Kingdom knew well-organized standing military units, supplemented when needed by local militia. The force consisted mainly of infantry, with boat personnel integrated into it. The 2nd Intermediate Period and the 18th Dynasty saw an unprecedented advance in the development of weapons, military organization (the appearance of chariotry, organization of infantry into companies of some 250 men led by a standard-bearer), strategy, and tactics. The standing army and professional army officers began to play an important part in internal politics. In the Late Period, foreign mercenaries formed the core.

Ancient Egyptian weapons of various types are known from contemporary representations and models as well as archaeological finds.

The bow, the most important long-range weapon, was used in all periods, either the archaic compound horn-bow, or the wooden, slightly double-convex, "self" bow. During the 2nd Intermediate Period the composite bow was introduced from Asia. It was made of laminated strips of various materials, and had a much improved range and power. When strung, the bow acquired a characteristic triangular shape. *The quiver* was in use from the Old Kingdom onwards.

The spear was employed throughout Egyptian history.

The mace with a stone mace-head of varying form, the most powerful weapon of close combat in the Predynastic Period, was in historic times replaced by *the battle-ax* with a copper ax-head. Some of the early semicircular ax-heads differed little from contemporary tools of craftsmen, but already during the Old Kingdom a specialized shallow type appeared. This, and the scalloped ax-head, were characteristic of the weapons of the Middle Kingdom. In the 2nd Intermediate Period a new type with a narrow ax-blade and therefore much-improved power of penetration appeared, probably an indigenous development. *The scimitar* (sickle sword), an Asiatic weapon used in the same way as the Egyptian battle-ax (as a cutting or piercing rather than thrusting weapon), is also met in the New Kingdom. *Cudgels,*

clubs, and throwing-sticks of various types remained in use as side arms at all times. The *dagger* was used in the same way.

Personal protection was afforded by the *shield*, already attested during the late Predynastic Period. Light *body armor* was known from the New Kingdom but its use remained limited.

The two-wheeled horse-drawn *chariot*, introduced to Egypt from Asia in the 2nd Intermediate Period, was a light vehicle, made of wood with some leather and metal elements. It was manned by two soldiers: the charioteer, and the chariot-warrior armed with a bow and spear and carrying a shield. The chariot's main contribution to the art of warfare was mobility and the element of surprise connected with it: in attack, the chariots approached at full speed and the chariot warriors delivered their arrows while passing the massed enemy ranks. The chariot was not armored in any way and therefore was not suitable for a direct attack. Once the enemy lines were broken, the chariotry was ideally suited for pursuing and harassing the scattered foot soldiers. To judge from the appearance of special titles, the chariotry formed a separate arm of the Egyptian army from the reign of Amenhotep III onward.

WOMEN AND MEN

The position of women in Egyptian ideology is exemplified by their presentation in Old Kingdom tomb decoration and statue groups. At the top of the female hierarchy is the elegantly dressed wife, or sometimes mother, of the tomb owner, who sits at leisure with the owner at a table of offerings, or stands by him. Unlike the elite man, who engages actively in hunting in the marshes, his women are shown uniformly inactive. Men stand with feet apart in a pose of potential movement, while women's legs are statically together. The wife sometimes accompanies her husband when he watches scenes of work, but is more often shown when offerings are presented to them; this distinction may signify that she would normally stay at home. At the other extreme are scenes or statuettes of serving women engaged in domestic tasks, making bread and beer, spinning and weaving. These activities too were probably conducted in a house or estate compound. The female flesh color, yellow, indicates among other things less exposure to the sun than the male red, and therefore a more enclosed existence – as it also does on successful male bureaucrats.

It may have been unsafe for women to venture out. In a posthumous text Ramesses III says "I enabled the woman of Egypt to go on her journey, which was made easy, to where she wanted, without anyone assaulting her on the road" – which implies that this was not always so.

While women are not shown in the most important work and diversions, they are not employed in the heaviest tasks. Men, for example, make wine, which is more strenuous than brewing. Women are present in the fields, for example harvesting flax. Apart from scenes of musicians and of athletic girls' dances, women's roles in early periods are at least superficially decorous. In New Kingdom scenes women are more frequently shown and their clothing is more elaborate. A number of scenes with women have heavily coded erotic content (Old Kingdom scenes may have had such meanings, but they are difficult to identify). The Late Period mostly returned to earlier decorum.

Women did not hold important titles except some

Women in different roles and artistic media
Far left bottom The corpulent Kaʿaper embraces his slender wife. His body depicts wise and prosperous age, hers the blander feminine ideal. Embraces are very rarely depicted. The small musical scenes and the monkey have erotic overtones. In his mastaba at Saqqara. Early 5th Dynasty.

Left Wooden statue of a servant carrying offerings, unusual for its large size (c. 110 cm) and for the coloring of the garments. The type derives from Old Kingdom reliefs of bearers bringing the produce of estates. c. 1950 BCE. From Theban Tomb 280 of Meketreʿ. New York, Metropolitan Museum of Art.

Below left Sketch of a woman performing an acrobatic dance, on a 19th-Dynasty limestone ostracon from Deir el-Medina. Width 16·8 cm. Turin, Museo Egizio.

religious ones, and apart from a few members of the royal family and female kings they had little political power. Their commonest title, "Mistress of the House," is a term of respect that may mean little more than "Mrs." Almost all were illiterate and therefore excluded from the bureaucracy – to which they probably did not aspire – and from the most intellectual high culture. A symptom of this is that age and wisdom were respected in men, who could be represented as corpulent elders, but not in women. Even a man's mother is indistinguishable from his wife in tomb depictions: both are youthfully beautiful. The way women are shown is part of men's definition of them and is a public display of an ideal. In reality their influence may not have been so circumscribed and their roles more varied than might at first appear. Funerary monuments of women, which are known especially from the 1st millennium, are suggestive here; a Middle Kingdom stela from the Faiyum even belonged to a Nubian elite woman.

Family structures as presented are severely simplified. The norms of decoration hardly give room to the widow or widower, the divorcee, homosexuals, or deviations from monogamy, all of which are attested. A tale recounts an affair between a king and a military officer, and the myth of Horus and Seth includes same-sex activity. There was a limited amount of polygyny in the Old and Middle Kingdoms, while kings could have many wives, although only the queen mother and one other bore the title "Great King's Wife."

Marriage, family, and social relations

Egyptians were mostly monogamous. Inheritance passed from father to children, but followed no very rigid pattern. Family property was defined by a marriage settlement, of which examples on papyrus are known from the 3rd Intermediate Period onward, and by deeds of transfer made either between the living or as wills. The woman's role here was important, but not equal to that of her husband. She brought a proportion of property into marriage and had some rights over it in a divorce. At least among property owners, marriage constituted a new household, not an extension of a parental one. A woman could make a will and leave her own property to some extent as she wished. No evidence has been identified either for marriage ceremonies or for judicial processes in divorce. Even so, the legal status of a couple living together was different from that of a married pair. In one case a man is accused for having intercourse with a woman who is living with another man but not married to him, something that might seem unlikely to constitute an offence. Despite relatively free institutions, a woman's adultery was, at least in theory, a serious matter. Community sanctions over unacceptable behavior, as well as accusations of abuse of position to compel married women to have sex, are known from Deir el-Medina.

Apart from complications of these types, general mortality and the seeming frequency of divorce led to involved patterns of property holding and

Above Granodiorite statue group of Thutmose IV and his mother Ti'a. Kings shown with their mothers may not yet have had a chief wife, but this is unlikely here, because Thutmose had three in his ten-year reign. Height 110 cm. From Karnak. Cairo, Egyptian Museum.

Right Mereruka's wife, who wears a counterpoise associated with the goddess Hathor, plays the harp to him on a bed. Beneath are pots and chests containing "the best of the treasures of gold, all sorts of oil, and clothing." These are probably all for the adornment of the couple in their amorous encounters in this world or the next. In his tomb at Saqqara. Reign of Teti.

Left Miy, a lady of the court of Amenhotep III, ebony statuette from a tomb near the royal harem complex at Kom Medinet Ghurab; one of a group of similar works. Height 15·6 cm. Brooklyn Museum of Art.

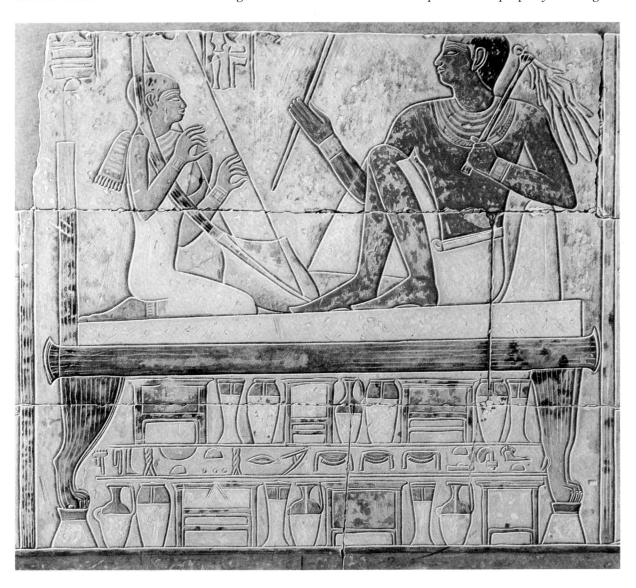

inheritance. Life expectancy was low and it was not unusual to be widowed more than once. A Middle Kingdom deed illustrates the complexity of inheritance. A man retires and hands over his office to his son while disinheriting the son's mother, perhaps because she is deceased, and leaving his remaining property to his children (perhaps not yet born) by another woman; neither woman is stated to be his wife, although both probably were.

The definition of permitted and prohibited marriage partners is not known, but it was possible to marry quite close blood relatives, including on occasion half-siblings. In the royal family there were some brother–sister marriages, but this practice may have deviated deliberately from the norm. From Roman Period Egypt such marriages are well attested among the ethnic Greek population. One difficulty in understanding the social framework lies in Egyptian kinship terms, of which there were very few. A single word could cover brother, mother's brother, brother's son, and more besides. Reconstructed genealogies are therefore difficult to verify.

The age of either partner at marriage is unknown. Genealogies show that some men had children before they were 20, but the clearest cases are royal and may be untypical. Long-term generation spans were 25–30 years. At first marriage women were no doubt younger than their husbands, but this may not have been true of subsequent marriages.

Sexuality, fertility, and succession

Men, who produced the evidence, will have wished to enhance women's sexuality for their own ends, which were religious as well as pleasurable, while limiting its potential as an independent and subversive force. Their attitude toward it was ambivalent. In tales the evil seductress is a common motif, while love poetry of the New Kingdom is often written in the words of the ardent woman, without the same moralistic overtones. Although the tales use religious motifs, both these sources give a secular view. In religious terms, however, sexuality was important because of its relationship with creation, and, by association, with rebirth in the hereafter. It was also significant for the character of such deities as Hathor among goddesses and Min among gods. The covert erotic references in tomb scenes could have three purposes: to ensure rebirth through potency in the next life, to enable the deceased to lead an enjoyable otherworldly existence, and to enhance his standing in this world through the ambiance he could display around him. Scenes with an erotic content include ones of hunting in the marshes, where the deceased is accompanied by his wife, who is implausibly dressed in her most elaborate costume, wears a heavy wig, and holds two symbols of Hathor. Heavy wigs, especially when associated with nudity, could be erotic signals. In a New Kingdom tale an evil wife accuses her husband's young brother of attempting to seduce her by reporting him as saying, "Come, let us spend an hour lying down. Put on your wig."

An example of a comparable motif in an earlier period is a scene in the 6th-Dynasty tomb of Mereruka at Saqqara, where the owner and his wife sit facing each other on a bed and she plays the harp to him. In part the scene created a perpetual erotic ambiance for him. A spell or a female statuette placed in a tomb could have a similar purpose, but was less conjugal in its reference. A Middle Kingdom spell in the

Right Hunting in the marshes. Nebamun and his wife and daughter are on a papyrus boat. All are elaborately dressed. The duck on the front of the boat has erotic associations, as do the wife's wig and the counterpoise and sistrum she holds in her left hand. Nevertheless, the text refers simply to "taking pleasure, seeing good things, trapping birds, as a work of Sekhet (the marsh goddess) ..." Reign of Thutmose IV. London, British Museum.

Below Couple having sex. One of a number of positions of intercourse shown in a humorous and sexually explicit papyrus of the late New Kingdom. As in one other scene, the woman appears to be indifferent to the man. Turin, Museo Egizio.

Coffin Texts has the simple title "Having sex by a man in the necropolis." On a mythological plane the same concerns are seen in the Book of the Dead, where Osiris complains to the creator god Atum that after the end of the world "There will be no sexual gratification there," to which Atum replies, "I have given transfiguration in place of water, air, and gratification" – here the three preconditions of life – "and peace of heart in place of bread and beer" – physical nourishment.

Only one sexually explicit document of any size survives, from the late New Kingdom. This is a set of drawings with brief captions on a papyrus, showing a variety of sexual encounters between a fat, priapic man (or perhaps men) and a woman (or women) dressed in a wig, necklace, armlets, bracelets, and a belt. The papyrus also contains humorous sketches of animals in human roles – a well-known motif – suggesting that the sexual part is also humorous. From about the same time there is a case of apparent prudery, where tomb paintings of nude dancing girls and lightly clothed women in the style of the 18th Dynasty were covered in drapery by a later owner. On Late Period dwelling sites erotic objects, mostly statuettes of men with enormous penises, are common. These are under-represented from earlier periods because of the scarcity of finds from settlements – as well as the qualms of earlier excavators of such

material. They were probably potency charms.

If potency was a man's worry, with a high death rate fertility was important both to women and to men. In all but the wealthiest families the labor of children was vital, particularly in agriculture. On another plane children carried on the family line, whose most obvious feature was the common practice of giving a son the name of his grandfather. The eldest surviving son was expected to perform funerary rituals and maintain a funerary cult, as well as managing his father's inheritance; one inscription is a lament of a childless man that he cannot look forward to a proper afterlife.

In keeping with this concern for fertility, gynecological texts are known, including prescriptions for reproductive disorders, birth prognoses, contraception, and abortion. It is unlikely that any of these, except perhaps those for abortion, were very effective. Shrines of Hathor, dwelling sites, and tombs have produced figurines of women in forms that emphasize the genitals. These, many of which do not conform to the norms of Egyptian representation, probably had a special status outside the canon and were used by a wider range of social groups than most statuary. Some were offered by women who wished the deity to grant them fertility. Until modern times such offerings were probably as effective a way of helping to conceive a child as visiting a doctor.

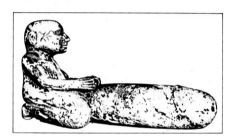

Far left Limestone statuette of a squatting man with an enormous erect penis; probably a fertility or potency charm. Late New Kingdom, from Deir el-Medina. Turin, Museo Egizio.

Left Decorated spoon, perhaps an object for presenting ritual ointments, in the form of a swimming girl holding out a duck. The girl has an elaborate wig, heavy earrings, and a necklace, but is clothed only in a belt with a diagonal strap on the back. The motif of a girl presenting an animal to her lover in order to attract him is known from love poetry. Wood and bone. 18th Dynasty. Length c. 30 cm. Paris, Musée du Louvre.

Left Fertility statuettes of nude women in clay and faience, with a "doll" of reed and linen. The forms of all except the faience figure (3rd from right) emphasize the genitals. The 4th figure from the right (photographed from the back) holds a child, and has an "Isis-knot" amulet, which is associated with life and sexual fertility, hanging around its neck. Middle–New Kingdoms. Height 15–20 cm. London, Petrie Museum, University College.

RELIGION

Wooden figure of a ram-headed demon that probably held a pair of snakes. Like a number of mortuary objects, it was covered in black resin. One of a group from the Valley of the Kings that have parallels in Book of the Dead vignettes and New Kingdom underworld books and mythological papyri; this particular type was not found in the tomb of Tutʿankhamun. Height 45·7 cm. London, British Museum.

Egyptian culture was pervaded by religion and the official presentation of Egyptian history was religious. Much economic activity was channeled through the temples – which does not necessarily mean that it was highly religious, since temples were probably not very different from other landlords. The pattern of secularization, which we tend to take for granted in the development of societies, was absent since temples became more salient in later periods. The central institution of kingship ended by losing much charisma, but in other respects society became if anything more religious. Religion in Egypt can be divided into the official, state aspect, about which much is known, the mortuary sphere, which is also well represented, and the everyday practices of most of the population, which were largely separate from the official cult and are very poorly known.

The king and history

In the official presentation, society consisted of the gods, the king, the dead, and humanity. But humanity is absent from most official pictorial records, which represent history and religion as the interplay of gods and the king. Part of the reason for this lies in rules of decorum governing the compatibility of different types of figure in representation and the contexts in which they may occur; in early periods these did not permit a nonroyal individual and a god to be shown together, and they never allowed normal people to be shown in temples. But in addition the king acted as a mediator, in some respects the only one, between deity and humanity. He represented humanity to the gods and the gods to humanity. He was also the living exemplar of the creator god on earth – an idea that is set forth in a terminology of great richness and complexity – and reenacted the creator god's role of setting order in place of disorder. "History" was a ritual in the cosmos, of which this reenactment is a principal theme.

The king was responsible for the well-being of the people, and took their cares on himself like the "good shepherd" of the Hebrew Bible – a formulation known from Egypt too. Kings sought to enhance their status before people, by identifying with gods, or in some instances by deifying themselves, so that they could be depicted in their normal guise offering to their divine alter egos, as is attested for Amenhotep III and Ramesses II. Finally, kings could be deified after death, more as some private individuals were deified than as if they were true gods. So the king did not have a simple status as god or human being. By virtue of his office he was a being apart; his role differed according to context.

Official and personal religion

Official religion consisted of cult and festivals in the main temples and of the process of "history." The basis of the cult was reciprocity. The king (notionally, in practice the priests) provided for the gods and cared for their cult images. In return, the gods took up residence in the images and showed their favor to the king and hence to humanity. But the gods

had priority since they had created the world in which the king lived and endowed it with benefits; they could withdraw from it at any time. The interdependent nature of their relationship is expressed plainly in offering formulas in the lowest register of temple decoration (see p. 64), which say "The king has come to you (the deity), bringing offerings which he has given to you, so that you may give to him all life (or lands, or a comparable gift)." The same point is made in the main areas of relief, but more discreetly. The compact between deity and humanity does not exclude other facets from their relationship, any more than a marriage contract does. The king expresses his adoration and veneration of the deity, and celebrates the deity's qualities. The deity responds with love for the king and delight in his presence. An enormous vocabulary organizes and expresses these ideas. Human beings or the king cannot "love" a god, but only "respect" or "adore" him. Qualities attributed to kings or deities are often what one might consider reactions to them, so that "fear" means the capacity to arouse fear, and "love" that to inspire love. These distinctions embody the hierarchical character of the relationship between the participants: the subordinate party to a grouping is an active provider of humbler benefits, but a passive recipient of higher ones.

The aim of the cult was the aim of historical action: to maintain and enhance the established order of the world. The chief temples were dedicated to local deities, who were mostly held locally to be the creator and to encompass the vital aspects of the divine world. The cult was carried out by a hierarchy of priests. It did not concern the mass of the population, except for part-time priests, who served one month in four, and people who worked on temple lands. Only priests could enter the temple. The deity left the temple for various festivals and could then be approached by normal people, notably for oracular consultations, but even in processions most cult images were kept hidden in shrines carried on symbolic barks, so that deities were known to be present, but not seen.

Outside these festivals, the official cult was largely irrelevant to the individual. It is impossible to know personal attitudes to it, whether it was viewed as essential but not concerning those not involved, or

Left Entrance to room 31 in the temple of Ramesses III at Medinet Habu. The king holds a mace and scepter, symbols of his divine and ritual role; on both sides the captions beneath his arm say "Everyone who enters the shrine, purify four times."

Above Tubular case of gold made to contain a rolled strip of papyrus with a decree by the god Khons, ratified in an oracle, for the protection of the owner, who would wear it around his neck. The text says "Speech by Khons in Thebes, Neferhotep. He made good protection (of) Shaq, deceased." One of three similar cases. 22nd Dynasty. Height 5·2 cm. Cambridge, Fitzwilliam Museum.

Left Relief of Amenhotep III offering to his deified self, in his temple at Soleb in Upper Nubia. The presentation is that of any normal temple relief. The deified king, "Nebmaʿatreʿ (Amenhotep's praenomen), great god," has a lunar headdress and divine scepter, but wears the royal uraeus, headcloth, and artificial beard.

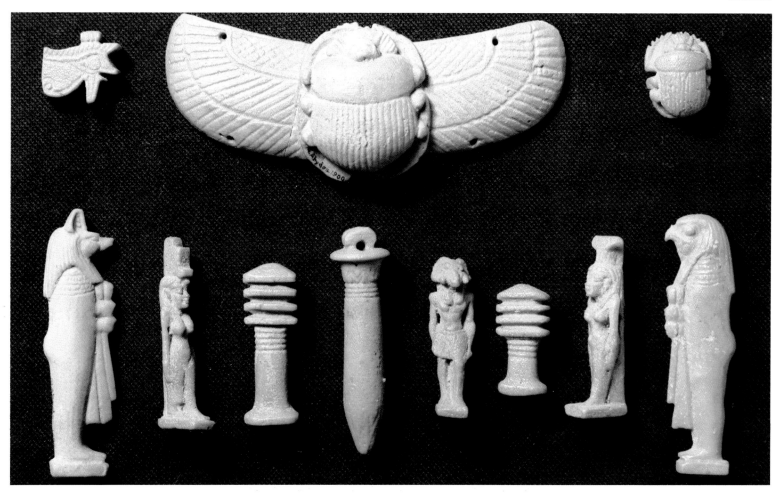

Above Group of faience amulets from a single mummy. Above: *wedjat* eye, winged scarab pectoral, and scarab, all symbols of rebirth. Below, in pairs from outside: mummiform Duamutef and Qehebsenuf, Sons of Horus; Isis and Nephthys, who mourn for Osiris; ram-headed god, probably Amun; two *djeds* and papyrus stem, symbolizing duration and freshness. From Abydos. 30th Dynasty. Width of winged scarab 8·7 cm. Oxford, Ashmolean Museum.

Below Group of animal mummies: elaborately wrapped ibis (with a linen figure of Thoth on the front), cat, and snake; fish in a box. Late or Greco-Roman Period. Oxford, Ashmolean Museum.

as a meaningless extravagance. One or two passages in elite literary texts question the value of offerings, but these must be seen in the context of the general assumption – spelled out explicitly in some religious texts – that they were necessary. Whatever people's attitudes may have been, for their own religious needs they turned elsewhere. Apart from the main temples there were many local shrines to lesser deities, or to minor forms of the main ones, throughout the country, rather as in European cities cathedrals coexist with smaller churches. Normal people went to these shrines, where they made offerings, prayed, or deposited oracular questions. There were also centers of pilgrimage, such as Abydos, whose heyday was in the Middle Kingdom, and Saqqara, where the animal necropolis acted as a focus in the Late and Ptolemaic Periods. If we are to believe letter formulae, people would visit shrines – or possibly pray in their homes – every day in order to intercede for the welfare of the absent correspondent. Such formulae do not necessarily give good evidence, but details in them suggest that they relate to a core of genuine practice.

Activities of this sort existed alongside a host of other practices that range from the more "religious" to the more "magical." Among relevant types of artifacts one may cite, almost at random, amulets, including divine decrees safeguarding their bearers, busts of ancestors in houses, and numerous special objects and modes of dress surrounding childbirth. Texts deal with magical cures for illness, love charms, calendars of lucky and unlucky days, the avoidance of the evil eye, divination through dreams and various rarer practices, letters written to dead relatives who were thought to hold a grudge against the living or could act as intermediaries on their behalf, and much

else besides. Despite the multifarious forms of religious observance and the dozens of deities, some important events in life were notably secular. There is no evidence for rituals performed on the newborn child, only of ones aimed at easing the birth and removing pollution from the mother after it. Similarly, phases of life like the circumcision of boys, apparently just before puberty, or marriage, do not seem to have been strongly sacralized.

One area of popular and official religious life that impressed foreigners in antiquity was animal worship. Animals had always been kept as sacred to particular deities – or possibly worshiped as deities in their own right – and buried ceremonially. In the Late Period these practices proliferated. The species associated with the main deity of an area was often held sacred there, and either a single member of it or all members were mummified and buried. To pay for an animal's burial was a "good deed." In Memphis, whose population was mixed, many species were buried. The best known is the Apis bull, sacred to Ptah, which was buried in one catacomb (the Serapeum) and its mother in a second, while ibises, dogs or jackals, cats, baboons, ichneumons, and rams are all attested in varying numbers. Other species, including several types of fish, snakes, and crocodiles, are known from other parts of the country. A whole town sprang up in the desert at north Saqqara to cater for these needs, and ibises were farmed on an almost industrial scale, before being hastened to their death. All groups in society participated in these practices. Their public character and the decline of grandiose individual tombs in this period may perhaps betoken a weakening of the belief in individual life after death or a more communal vision of religious life and the next world.

The Egyptian Pantheon
Local Gods

La
Ma

It is impossible to arrange Egyptian deities into neat categories; any attempt to do so involves simplification. There are two main reasons for this: the complexity of Egyptian religious ideas, and the long period over which they developed. The religious practices of ordinary people differed considerably from the official religion of the large temples.

In addition to their representations and hieroglyphic forms of their names, the following lists provide three types of information: 1. the main iconographic features by which the deity can be recognized; 2. the character and function of the deity, his or her relationship with other gods etc.; 3. his or her main places of worship.

Many of the gods and goddesses can be described as local deities because from the earliest times they were closely connected with a particular locality. Nonetheless, numerous apparently local deities are found over much of the country from early times. The gods shared the fate of their home towns, and while some of them were ultimately promoted to be Egyptian "state gods" (e.g. the Memphite Ptah, the Theban Amon-Reʿ, and the Heliopolitan Reʿ-Harakhty) whose cult spread over the whole of Egypt, others fell into obscurity and oblivion and were replaced by, or more often assimilated with, the more

vigorous gods of other localities. The latter could be done in two different ways: by adopting another god's attributes (e.g. Osiris took some of his iconographic characteristics from the god ʿAndjety) or by the creation of a composite deity (e.g. Ptah-Sokar-Osiris), a process known to Egyptologists as syncretism. Because of their connection with the resident god or their current importance, various "guest deities" were worshiped in local temples.

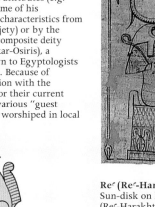
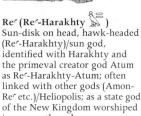

Reʿ (Reʿ-Harakhty **)**
Sun-disk on head, hawk-headed (Reʿ-Harakhty)/sun god, identified with Harakhty and the primeval creator god Atum as Reʿ-Harakhty-Atum; often linked with other gods (Amon-Reʿ etc.)/Heliopolis; as a state god of the New Kingdom worshiped in many other places.

Bastet
Lioness-headed or cat-headed/ war goddess; closely connected with Mut and Sakhmet/Tell Basta.

Neith
Red crown or two crossed arrows and shield on her head (also held in hands)/goddess of war and hunting; closely connected with Sobek; guardian deity/Sa el-Hagar, also Memphis, the Faiyum and Esna.

Thoth
Ibis-headed, often with moon crescent/god of writing, counting, and wisdom in general; patron of scribes; baboon another sacred animal/el-Ashmunein and el-Baqliya, and many Late Period cities.

Harsaphes
Ram-headed or ram/gained importance during the 1st Intermediate Period when Herakleopolis was Egypt's northern capital; closely connected with Reʿ, Osiris, and Amun/Ihnasya el-Medina.

Hathor
Sun-disk, cow's horns. also cow-headed, cow, "Hathor-pillar," or sistrum etc./goddess of women, also sky goddess, tree goddess (Memphis), or necropolis goddess (Thebes)/Heliopolis, Memphis, Atfih, el-Qusiya, Dendara, Thebes, Gebelein, Abu Simbel, Sinai (Serabit el-Khadim).

Montu
Often hawk-headed, sun-disk and two plumes/war god; connected with the Buchis bull of Armant/Armant, but also Karnak, Tod, Nagʿ el-Madamud.

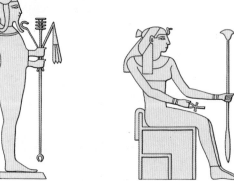
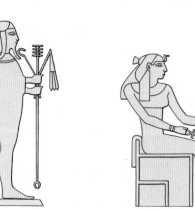

Khons , **Mut** , **and Amun (Amon-Reʿ**)
Khons: child's side-lock of hair, sometimes with moon crescent, often mummiform; Mut: vulture headdress or crowns (white or double), also lioness-headed; Amun (head of the triad): two plumes, sometimes ithyphallic; also ram or goose/Mut a war goddess; Amun's female counterpart Amaunet/Theban triad (Karnak, Luxor), but Amun also important at el-Ashmunein; as a state god of the New Kingdom Amon-Reʿ worshiped in many other places (e.g. Tanis, Memphis, the oases).

212

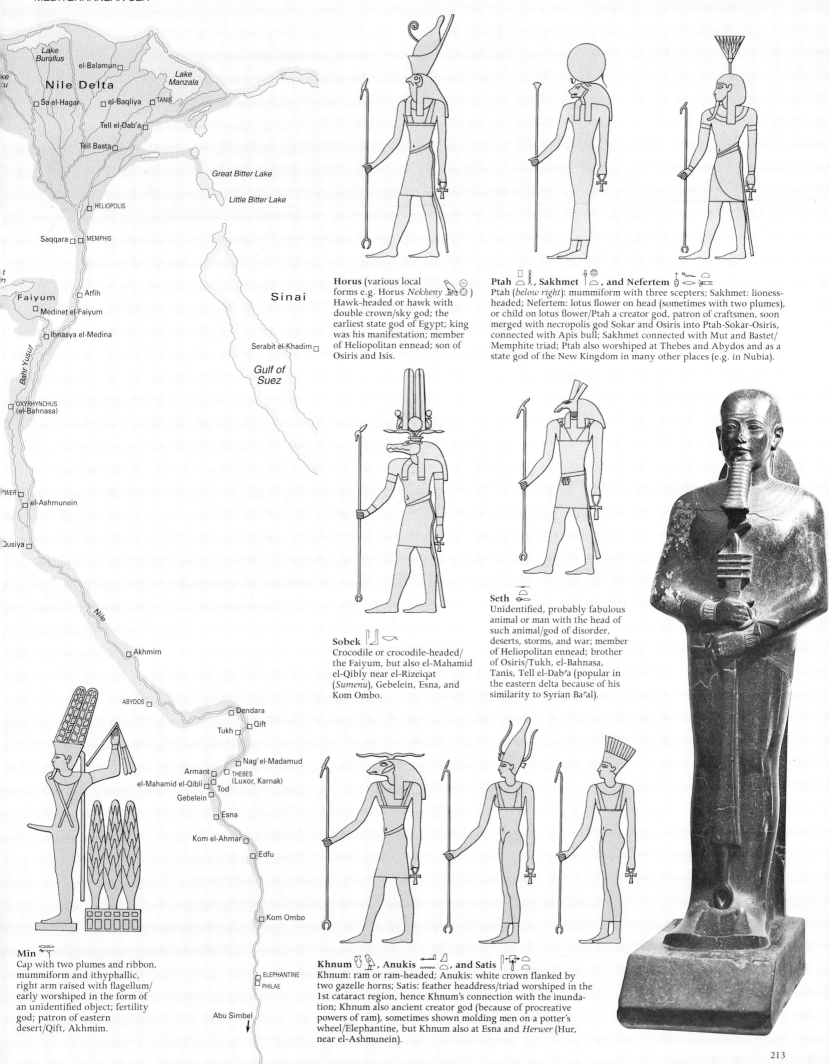

Lake Burullus
el-Balamun
Nile Delta
Lake Manzala
Sa el-Hagar
el-Baqliya
TANIS
Tell el-Dabʿa
Tell Basta
Great Bitter Lake
Little Bitter Lake
HELIOPOLIS
Saqqara
MEMPHIS
Faiyum
Atfih
Medinet el-Faiyum
Sinai
Ihnasya el-Medina
Serabit el-Khadim
Gulf of Suez
Bahr Yusuf
OXYRHYNCHUS (el-Bahnasa)
WER
el-Ashmunein
Qusiya
Nile
Akhmim
ABYDOS
Dendara
Qift
Tukh
Nagʿ el-Madamud
Armant
THEBES (Luxor, Karnak)
el-Mahamid el-Qibli
Tod
Gebelein
Esna
Kom el-Ahmar
Edfu
Kom Ombo
ELEPHANTINE
PHILAE
Abu Simbel

Horus (various local forms e.g. Horus *Nekheny*) Hawk-headed or hawk with double crown/sky god; the earliest state god of Egypt; king was his manifestation; member of Heliopolitan ennead; son of Osiris and Isis.

Ptah, **Sakhmet**, **and Nefertem**
Ptah (*below right*): mummiform with three scepters; Sakhmet: lioness-headed; Nefertem: lotus flower on head (sometimes with two plumes), or child on lotus flower/Ptah a creator god, patron of craftsmen, soon merged with necropolis god Sokar and Osiris into Ptah-Sokar-Osiris, connected with Apis bull; Sakhmet connected with Mut and Bastet/Memphite triad; Ptah also worshiped at Thebes and Abydos and as a state god of the New Kingdom in many other places (e.g. in Nubia).

Sobek
Crocodile or crocodile-headed/the Faiyum, but also el-Mahamid el-Qibly near el-Rizeiqat (*Sumenu*), Gebelein, Esna, and Kom Ombo.

Seth
Unidentified, probably fabulous animal or man with the head of such animal/god of disorder, deserts, storms, and war; member of Heliopolitan ennead; brother of Osiris/Tukh, el-Bahnasa, Tanis, Tell el-Dabʿa (popular in the eastern delta because of his similarity to Syrian Baʿal).

Min
Cap with two plumes and ribbon, mummiform and ithyphallic, right arm raised with flagellum/early worshiped in the form of an unidentified object; fertility god; patron of eastern desert/Qift, Akhmim.

Khnum, **Anukis**, **and Satis**
Khnum: ram or ram-headed; Anukis: white crown flanked by two gazelle horns; Satis: feather headdress/triad worshiped in the 1st cataract region, hence Khnum's connection with the inundation; Khnum also ancient creator god (because of procreative powers of ram), sometimes shown molding men on a potter's wheel/Elephantine, but Khnum also at Esna and *Herwer* (Hur, near el-Ashmunein).

213

Universal Gods etc.

Some Egyptian gods were "universal" in the sense that there was no particular place with which they were connected; this, however, did not prevent them from becoming members of local religious systems (e.g. Isis belonged to the Heliopolitan ennead) and having temples built for them (Isis was the chief deity worshiped at Philae). Conversely, some of the "universal gods" probably started as local deities (e.g. Anubis).

The air god Shu raising his daughter, the sky goddess Nut, above the earth god Geb, adored by various deities and numerous *ba* figures. The owner is shown bottom right, with her *ba* in a doorway in front of her. 21st Dynasty funerary papyrus (P. Greenfield). London, British Museum.

Isis 𓊨𓏏 **and Harpokrates**
Woman, often hieroglyph of her name on her head/member of Heliopolitan ennead: wife of Osiris; guardian and magician.

Harpokrates 𓏏𓏏
Naked child with finger in his mouth, side-lock of hair/member of Heliopolitan ennead; son of Osiris and Isis.

Below **Apis** 𓎛𓊪
Bull with special markings on hide and sun-disk between horns, or bull-headed/connected with Ptah; burial place at Saqqara.

Above **Geb** 𓎼𓃀 , **Shu** 𓈙𓅱 , **and Nut** 𓈖𓏏
Members of Heliopolitan ennead; deities of earth (Geb), air and light (Shu), and sky (Nut).

Osiris 𓊨𓁹
Mummiform, scepter and flagellum, white crown with plumes and horns/dying god of vegetation; ruler of netherworld.

Anubis 𓇋𓈖𓊪𓃢
Recumbent dog ("jackal") or dog-headed, black/necropolis god; connected with mummification.

Bes 𓃀𓋴
Dwarf with mask-like face, often crown of feathers and lion's mane/family god; protector of pregnant women.

Imhotep 𓇋𓐝𓊪
Deified official of Djoser; patron of scribes; healer, sage, and magician; regarded as son of Ptah and a woman Khreduʿankh.

Nephthys 𓉠
Woman with hieroglyphs of her name on her head/member of Heliopolitan ennead; sister of Isis; guardian deity.

Taweret 𓍔𓂋𓏏
Composite of hippopotamus and woman, with lion's paws and crocodile's tail/protectress of pregnant women.

Priesthood and temple institutions

Before the New Kingdom there was no large, full-time priesthood. The expansion of temples in the 18th Dynasty, accompanied by other religious and social changes, saw the rise of the priesthood as a group, a rise that continued with few checks into the Late Period. The basic needs of the cult could be satisfied by an officiant, a ritual specialist or lector priest who might be the same person as the officiant, and the part-time priests who saw to practical and less sacred functions. But the temple of Amon-Reʿ at Karnak, for example, had first to fourth priests of Amun at the head of a huge staff that wielded considerable power. There was a constant tendency, which accorded with a basic Egyptian principle, for son to follow father in priestly office. This was countered by another principle, that the king should freely appoint the best man for the job. By the end of the New Kingdom the former was triumphant, and Egyptian society was developing toward a condition somewhat like that caricatured by Herodotus in the 5th century BCE, with a division into occupational types almost similar to castes. That analogy is reinforced by restrictions priests had to observe in their diet, mode of dress, shaving, and sexual abstinence when they were in service.

Priests received income from temples and often held sinecures at several. Offerings were laid before the god and, "after he was satisfied with them," reverted first to minor shrines and statues of kings and prominent individuals, and then to the priests, who consumed the less spiritual residues. The offerings themselves were, however, only a small proportion of the temples' income, so that much – also notionally offerings – was devoted directly to supporting staff and to barter for products the temple lacked. Temples had workshops, schools, and scriptoria attached to them, which functioned in society as a whole as well as supplying the needs of the institution to which they belonged.

Priests and bureaucrats, including those in the army, were the two basic categories of literate people. The civil administration seems to have lost much of its importance in politics in the course of the Ramessid Period, being replaced by the army and the priesthood (often one and the same). Thus priests became the repository of the cultural heritage. Beneficial magic was the traditional preserve of lector priests. In the Late Period priests assumed a wider cultural importance: most nonroyal monuments are of priests; the elite who performed civil functions presented themselves to deities and to posterity as priests. Greek visitors wrote frequently about them, and they influenced events, chiefly by mobilizing opinion against cuts in their revenues, at vital moments, notably after the death of Cambyses (522) and in the reign of Teos (360). The culture of Greco-Roman Period temples was a priestly culture, of which one feature is the relative devaluation of the king's role: in earlier periods priests came before the deity in the persona of the king, but now the king – who was a purely notional being – approached by virtue of his being a priest. The stereotype of an Egyptian society dominated by priests is not valid for earlier periods, but has some accuracy for later times.

Gods and myths

Egyptian polytheism clothes human response to the world in complex forms. The gods themselves are more prominent than are myths about them; myth was not so striking a feature of the religion as, for example, in ancient Greece. Some gods are circumscribed by myth, others by geographical location and by organization into groups. Most also have a basic association with an aspect of the world, such as Reʿ with the sun, Ptah with crafts, or Hathor with women, but this does not exhaust their characteristics. In specific contexts many gods may exhibit the same features, while any god can take on most aspects of divinity for a particular worshiper.

Scarcely any complete native versions of Egyptian myths survive; some are known only from Classical authors. Most Egyptian religious texts are not narrative in form, and it has been doubted whether there were any longer texts that recounted entire myths. Fragmentary versions of episodes in the conflict between Horus and Seth for the inheritance of Osiris survive from the Old and Middle Kingdoms, the late New Kingdom, and the Greco-Roman Period, but the text is not the same in any two of them and the episodes vary. The texts have in common a rather "secular" tone and an unflattering portrayal of the gods. Several belong as much with fiction as with religious texts, but mythical narratives with a comparable tone also occur in religious and especially magical compositions. Egyptian attitudes toward deities were not necessarily solemn.

Presentations of creation give primacy to the sun god Reʿ, often in the forms Reʿ-Harakhty or (Reʿ)-Atum. The most widespread has the creator appear from the watery chaos on a mound, the first solid matter, and create a pair of deities, Shu and Tefenet, by masturbation or by spitting. Shu and Tefenet in turn produced Geb and Nut, the earth and the sky, whose children were Osiris, Isis, Seth, and Nephthys. This group of nine deities formed the ennead of Heliopolis; other centers had comparable groups. Osiris and Isis are the main actors in the best-known

Right Bronze hawk's head finial, made to be attached to a staff or piece of temple furniture by the inverted T-shaped projection at the back. The flange at the top probably supported a crown in a different material. Late Period. Height 12·1 cm. London, British Museum.

Egyptian myth, which concerns Seth's murder of Osiris, Isis' conception of Horus on Osiris' temporarily revived body, and Horus' eventual defeat of Seth. This was presented in Greek by Plutarch in the 1st century CE; the core of his narrative appears to be authentic.

Perhaps more typically Egyptian than these myths are conceptions of the solar cycle, which vary endlessly a small repertory of basic motifs. It would be wrong to seek complete consistency in the variations; the constant meaning is the cycle itself. The sun god is born anew each morning, crosses the sky in the solar bark (boats being the normal mode of transport), ages, dies – which is never stated explicitly – and during the night travels through the underworld in a cycle of regeneration. Whereas in the creation myth the sky goddess Nut is the granddaughter of the sun god, one image for the cycle is of her as his mother, into whose mouth he enters at night, and from whom he is born in the morning. At the rebirth she may also be Hathor, who is otherwise called the daughter of Reᶜ. Possibly in allusion to these ideas, creator gods, notably Amon-Reᶜ, may be called "bull of his mother." These motifs are mythical situations rather than complete myths, since they are not combined to form narratives. They may, however, generate myths. Two complete ones, the "Destruction of Humanity" and "Isis and Reᶜ," take as their starting point the old age of the sun god, which is one of the basic features of the cosmological cycle, and elaborate it in terms of bodily decay and of its consequences for the god's kingship at the end of the primeval era on earth, when he retreated from the imperfect world to the sky; links between human and divine were thenceforth indirect.

The solar cycle gave rise to a host of linked conceptions, the most striking of which surround the key moment of sunrise. In his travels through the night the god is accompanied in his bark by a group of deities, of whom the most frequently present are personifications of aspects of his being with names like "Magical Power" and "Percipience"; at one point in its journey the bark is towed by a team of jackals. Both the personnel and the furniture of the bark vary in different mixed pictorial–textual compositions about the underworld. When the sun god emerges from the night, the whole of creation rejoices, and he may be greeted by gods and goddesses, the king, personifications of categories of humanity, and baboons called the "eastern souls" that screech acclamation. As in temples, normal humanity is excluded from the scene. All these elements seem almost to be responses to such questions as: "What are the changing aspects of the sun god's being in the night?" or "How is his appearance at dawn heralded?" The answers are more tableaux than myths.

The organization of gods into sets is comparable in its variety and occasional seeming arbitrariness. The commonest grouping is the triad, consisting of two "adult" deities and one youthful one. The triads are, however, only selections, with which other deities may have a connection or may interchange position. Thus, the Theban triad consists of Amon-Reᶜ, Mut, and Khons, the deities of the three main temples at Karnak. It has the form of a family group, but Mut is not the "wife" of Amon-Reᶜ, nor is Khons their son. Rather, three deities with different origins are associated using a family model, whose lack of

Below A version of the sun god's journey through the night. The boat is towed by jackals and uraei with human hands. Seth spears Apopis; behind the seated Reᶜ-Harakhty are mummiform figures of Horus and Thoth. Papyrus of Hirweben. 21st Dynasty. Cairo, Egyptian Museum.

Above The setting sun. Center: the hieroglyph for "west" surmounted by a sun disk and placed in the desert. Top: two winged Horus eyes protect the sun. Below: adoring figures of: "subjects"; groups of deities; baboons (who also evoke sunrise); Isis and Nephthys; the deceased woman's *ba*, shown as a hawk with human head and arms. Papyrus of Anhai. 19th Dynasty. London, British Museum.

Right Bronze statuette of Wadjit with lioness's head and a uraeus above. The uraeus is the normal animal of Wadjit, while the lioness form she commonly bore at Buto embodies her ferocious aspect in myth. The thrones of some of these statuettes contained cat mummies. Height 45 cm. Reign of Apries. Probably from Tell el-Fara'in (Buto). Bologna, Museo Civico.

Below Bronze statuette of Atum. The creator god of Heliopolis is shown in a form modified from the common one for Osiris. The face is that of the aged god of the setting sun. Many bronzes were dedicated in temples by individual worshipers. This one bears a dedication by Peteese son of Harwedja. Height 23·5 cm. Oxford, Ashmolean Museum.

Faience "pilgrim" flask with a scene of Bes with plumed headdress, wings, and pendant breasts, holding a pair of *wedjat* eyes; between his face and arms are two signs of life. There are floral motifs above, below and in the corners, and sun disks or rosettes on either side. Height of figure 5·6 cm. Early 19th Dynasty. From Kom Medinet Ghurab. Oxford, Ashmolean Museum.

realism is clear from the fact that there is only one "child." The symbolic importance of the number three and a principle of economy may together account for this simplification. Amaunet, a female Amun, is another Theban deity, who sometimes occurs in place of Mut, while Montu, probably the original chief god of the Theban nome, had his own temple complex immediately north of the main enclosure at Karnak. At Memphis the four chief deities, Ptah, Sakhmet, Nefertem, and Sokar (the god of the necropolis), were similarly varied in their

association: the first three form a triad, while Sokar was frequently fused with Ptah. Hathor and Neith, whose cults were also important in Memphis, are not part of the main group. At Heliopolis the sun god, whose cult was split into separate ones of Re' and Atum, stood most naturally by himself, but acquired two female companions, Ius'as and Hathor-Nebet-hetepet, who are in essence personifications of the sexual aspect of the solar creation myths.

A further important means of associating deities is termed syncretism by Egyptologists. A deity acquires a multiple name, mostly by taking on the name and some of the attributes of a more important one. Amon-Re' is thus Amun in his aspect as Re', and this can be expanded to form Amon-Re'-Atum, Amun as Re' and Atum, the aged aspect of the sun god. Re' is by far the commonest name in such groupings; this reflects the sun god's universality and central importance. In a slightly different case, at Abydos Osiris was identified, as Osiris-Khentamentiu, with a local god whose cult is known as far back as the 1st Dynasty. Such associations never completely submerged the identities of the deities whose names are linked.

The gods mentioned so far were major deities. Almost all had a cult and an area in which they were sovereign. Some cosmic deities, such as Geb, had no local cult. There were also minor deities found only in restricted contexts. The best known of these are probably Bes and Taweret, "household" figures associated particularly with childbirth. Both have monstrous composite forms of a sort not found among major deities, Bes as a dwarf with an outsize mask-like face, and Taweret as a mixture of hippopotamus and crocodile, with pendant, apparently human, breasts, and a huge belly. In addition, enormous numbers of demons with very diverse names and often grotesque forms are attested in magical and underworld texts. Most seem to be restricted to one or two contexts each, such as a particular text, or one hour of the night. The chief exception was Apopis, a gigantic snake, who was the sun god's enemy as he passed through the crucial phases of his cycle and had to be defeated by Seth, who speared him from the prow of the solar bark.

The world of the dead

The underworld mentioned above is one particular version of the realm of the dead, known mainly from New Kingdom royal tombs; as in most religious domains, there were many alternatives. Conceptions of the afterlife of the king, who was held to join the gods in the realm of the stars, seem initially to have been different from those for the rest of humanity, although they came to be diffused among more and more people. Whatever one's destiny, it was by no means assured. The afterlife was full of dangers, which were mostly to be overcome magically.

The starting point for all these ideas was the tomb. The Egyptians' unparalleled expenditure of elite resources on burial evidently served in part to enhance the tomb owner's prestige while he was alive, but this was a sideline to the ultimate purpose. The deceased might continue to exist in and around the tomb, or could travel through the afterworld. The aim was to identify with gods, in particular Osiris, or to become a transfigured spirit and participate in the solar cycle as a member of the "bark of millions." The bark is never shown with its vast

complement, possibly because human beings were excluded from the type of pictorial material in which it occurs. Both these latter destinies may originally have been restricted to the king: Old Kingdom non-royal texts refer to "walking on the perfect ways of the west (the realm of the dead)."

Between death and incorporation in the divine world came judgment, a theme that is less prominent for kings than for the rest of humanity. From the New Kingdom on, the judgment was depicted often, in tombs, on papyri, coffins, and shrouds. Its central motif is the weighing of the deceased's heart in a balance against Maʿat, the Egyptian conception of right order, which is mostly shown as a hieroglyph, either an ostrich feather or a figure of the personification Maʿat, a goddess with the feather inserted in a band around her wig. Thoth, the scribe god of wisdom and justice, performs the weighing before Osiris, who presides over a judgment hall with 42 judges. If the heart and Maʿat are in equilibrium, the test is successful, and the deceased is presented to Osiris in

triumph. The judgment is of conformity to Maʿat, that is, both order and correct conduct in life. Everyone naturally wished to avoid the judgment and the deceased had ready a declaration of innocence from all manner of misdeeds. Both the declaration and the depiction of a successful outcome were magical ways around the judgment, just as funerary texts and other provisions in the tomb were magical aids to success in the hereafter.

Judgment scenes show a female hybrid monster called "Eater" or "Eater of the Dead." Her role was to consume those who failed the test; a unique Roman Period example shows this happening. For Egyptians, departure from this life was a first stage; the second death, which brought complete annihilation, was what had to be avoided. Here, however, Egyptian categories are unfamiliar to others. Annihilation did not remove victims entirely, but the "dead" – that is, second dead – are shown being punished in the lower registers of the underworld books. They entered a mode of "nonexistence,"

Scene of weighing the deceased's heart in the Book of the Dead papyrus of Hunefer. On the left Anubis leads Hunefer in. A second figure of Anubis checks the balance while Thoth records the result and the "Eater" stands at the ready. Horus then presents Hunefer to Osiris, whose throne is placed on the "Lake of Natron," out of which emerges a lotus with the four "Sons of Horus" on it; behind him are Isis and Nephthys.

In the small register above, Hunefer adores a group of deities consisting of the Heliopolitan ennead without Seth but including Utterance, Perception, and the Southern, Northern, and Western Ways (presumably in the hereafter; east may be omitted because it was sometimes inauspicious). 19th Dynasty. London, British Museum.

which was itself a threat to order and had to be combated.

Scenes on tomb walls were part of the provision for life after death, but the relevance to survival of many of them is not clear and their superficial content is secular. In addition to wall decoration, burials contained material possessions in great variety, including (in very early periods) enormous quantities of food, statues presenting the deceased in a variety of roles that could be inhabited by his person – as a cult statue was by a god – and the mummy itself, elaborately wrapped, protected with amulets, placed in a coffin or nest of coffins, and magically brought to life in a ritual called the "opening of the mouth." Grave goods repeated the motif of rebirth in myriad symbolic forms. Some objects provided for particular needs in the hereafter. As many as 400 shawabty figures, perhaps the commonest of all Egyptian antiquities, accompanied burials. These were substitute figurines of the deceased, one of whose functions was to act as workers, who were to answer a

possible call for corvee duty which involved carrying sand. This conception, which is not well understood, may be an aspect of how the conditions of the next life might continue those of this life.

The accent in mortuary beliefs changed, but few disappeared. Instead, objects corresponding to a number of conceptions could occur side by side. No overall consistency need be sought in them, except insofar as they relate to the hope for rebirth and continued life after death. The most extensive and varied provision preserved is that for Tutʿankhamun, whose funerary equipment was no doubt modest in comparison with that for such kings as Amenhotep III or Ramesses II. Among the nonroyal, the intact 18th Dynasty tomb of Khaʿ from Deir el-Medina exhibits an extraordinary level of provision for a relatively low-ranking member of the elite. By contrast, intact Old Kingdom tombs contained quite modest grave goods. In death as in other contexts, Egyptian practices varied significantly over time and among social groups.

Burial Customs

Mummification

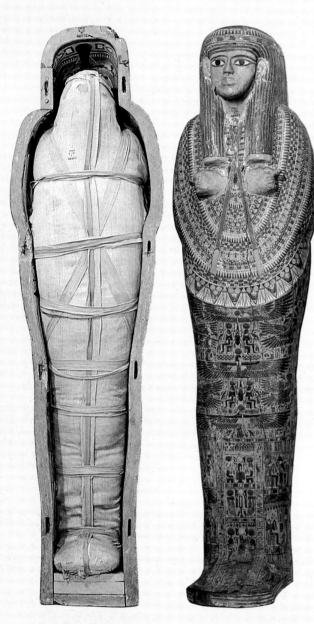

Mummification is a method of preserving artificially the bodies of deceased people and animals. Ancient Egyptian civilization is not the only one in the world to have practiced this custom, but Egyptian mummies are the best known and often, to the chagrin of professional Egyptologists, tend to be regarded as the embodiment of ancient Egypt itself and the main object of interest for those who study it. Mummies can contribute to our knowledge in various ways, in particular by providing information on such subjects as illnesses and conditions of ancient Egyptians, their diet etc. In the case of royal mummies, we can add to our understanding of Egyptian chronology by helping to establish the age of a king at the time of his death; family relationships can also be discovered from examination of mummies and their DNA testing.

Development

Mummification was introduced as a result of human interaction with the environment. It was an attempt to preserve an element by artificial means when new burial customs started threatening natural preservation.

For most of the Predynastic Period burials were very simple. Bodies were placed in shallow graves dug on the edge of the desert and covered with sand. In the dry atmosphere the contact with hot sand produced dehydration (desiccation) very quickly, often before the tissues decomposed, so that bodies were sometimes preserved by entirely natural means. This did not escape attention because such "mummies" were from time to time accidentally uncovered, and a belief developed that the preservation of the body was essential for man's continued existence after death. When at the end of the Predynastic Period some of the graves turned into larger tombs and coffins were introduced, these natural conditions were altered, in particular the contact with sand. It became necessary to look for methods that would achieve by artificial means what nature had previously accomplished unaided, and thus the custom of mummification was introduced. Its history is one of a continuous struggle between two approaches to the problem. The first aimed at a genuine preservation of the body, while the other, more formalistic, concentrated on the mummy's wrappings and packing. The peak of the craft of mummification was reached at the end of the New Kingdom and in the period immediately following; from then on, there was a sharp decline, as if in recognition of the impossibility of the task, and the formalistic approach prevailed.

Procedure

Mummification was carried out in workshops attached to the necropolis; these also supplied most of the funerary equipment. Methods varied according to the period and the wealth of the deceased's family. Although there is no detailed ancient Egyptian description of the procedure, its steps can be reconstructed from the examination of mummies.

The method described here was used at the end of the New Kingdom and during the 3rd Intermediate Period; it took some 70 days, and its most important part was dehydration of the body by burying it in natron, a naturally occurring dehydrating agent (a mixture of carbonate, bicarbonate, chloride, and sulphate of sodium):

1. Extraction of the brain.
2. Removal of the viscera through an incision made in the left flank.
3. Sterilization of the body cavities and the viscera.
4. Treatment of the viscera: removal of their contents, dehydration by natron, drying, anointing, and application of molten resin.
5. Temporary packing of the body with natron and fragrant resins.
6. Covering the body with natron for some 40 days.
7. Removal of the temporary packing materials.
8. Subcutaneous packing of the limbs with sand, clay etc.
9. Packing the body cavities with resin-soaked linen and bags of fragrant materials, such as myrrh and cinnamon, but also sawdust etc.
10. Anointing the body with unguents.
11. Treatment of the body surfaces with molten resin.
12. Bandaging and inclusion of amulets, jewelry etc.

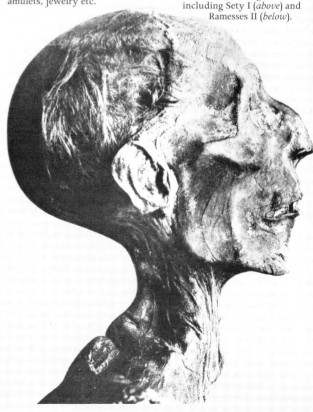

Royal mummies
Egyptologists have the unparalleled advantage of being face to face with the protagonists of their subject. The cache of royal mummies, discovered at Deir el-Bahri in 1881, contained the bodies of some of the most important rulers of the New Kingdom, including Sety I (*above*) and Ramesses II (*below*).

Canopic Jars

The term canopic jars was devised by early Egyptologists from the name of Kanopos, the pilot of Menelaos of the Trojan war. He was said to have been buried at Kanopos (Egyptian *Per-gwati*, present Abu Qir) in the northwestern delta, and was worshiped there in the form of a jar (this was, in fact, a local form of Osiris).

The jars were usually made of calcite ("alabaster"), but also of limestone, pottery, or faience, and contained the viscera removed from the cavities of the body during mummification. They were placed in the burial chamber of the tomb, close to the coffin. Simple lids became human-headed in the Middle Kingdom, and from the Ramessid Period they began to be made in the form of the heads of the four Sons of Horus. Texts on the jars placed each one under the protection of a goddess. Although reliable evidence is scarce, jars probably contained particular organs.

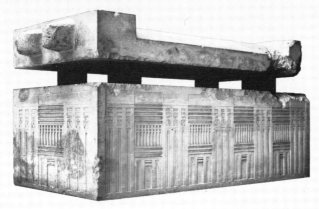

	head	goddess	contents
Imset	man	Isis	liver
Ha'py	baboon	Nephthys	lungs
Duamutef	jackal	Neith	stomach
Qebehsenuf	hawk	Selkis	intestines

Coffins and Sarcophagi

Most of our material for the study of ancient Egypt derives from tombs. Coffins and sarcophagi are thus among the commonest antiquities, though this somewhat somber aspect of Egyptology is brightened by their often very attractive appearance.

The terms *coffin* and *sarcophagus* are used by some as though they were interchangeable; here they denote chests made of wood and stone (limestone, granite, basalt etc.) respectively, regardless of shape. Each consists of the lid and the lower part ("case"). Coffins were often placed inside a sarcophagus, and we find whole sets of them (inner and outer, or 1st, 2nd, and 3rd), though sometimes only a *mummy board* (another "lid") was placed on top of the mummy. A third type of material, particularly common during the 3rd Intermediate and Greco-Roman Periods, was *cartonnage* (the term is also conveniently used in the same way as "coffin" or "sarcophagus"). This was made by successive application of linen (papyrus in the Greco-Roman Period), glue, and gesso around a "model mummy," and painting it with bright watercolors.

Coffins and sarcophagi are of two basic forms: *rectangular*, and *anthropoid* ("mummiform"), but only the latter is known in cartonnage. Anthropoid coffins appeared in the Middle Kingdom as a natural extension of the earlier mummy-masks covering the upper part of the mummy.

Decoration varies according to date. Some of the coffins of the Early Dynastic Period have a "palace facade," as do sarcophagi of the Old Kingdom. In the 1st Intermediate Period and the Middle Kingdom the interior of rectangular coffins was often inscribed with the Coffin Texts, and there were also representations of various items of funerary equipment and an offering-list. Anthropoid *rishi*-coffins (named for the decoration imitating feathered wings of a goddess, probably Isis or Nephthys, protecting the body) are characteristic of the 17th Dynasty, while white coffins with bands suggesting mummy bandages were common in the 18th Dynasty. For the rest of the New Kingdom and later the tendency was to increase the amount of decoration by adding small scenes with various deities and texts. Rectangular coffins and sarcophagi became rare, and enjoyed a limited revival toward the end of the Late Period. The perfection of workmanship and finish of anthropoid sarcophagi of the Late Period are justly famous. They were made of a dark hard stone, usually basalt, but there were also imitations in wood. The decoration and inscriptions on coffins and sarcophagi of the Late and Greco-Roman Periods drew their inspiration from religious texts and their vignettes, including the Book of the Dead, the Pyramid Texts, and underworld books. The outside of the lid was often inscribed with chapter 72 of the Book of the Dead, the "spell for going forth by day and penetrating the netherworld."

Funerary Statuettes

From the end of the Middle Kingdom, one or more funerary statuettes (the Egyptian terms vary between *shabty*, *shawabty*, and *ushebty*) formed an important part of the funerary equipment. In the 18th Dynasty the statuettes started to combine a likeness of the mummified body of the deceased with agricultural or other implements. This was a reflection of the two main ideas connected with these objects: a body substitute, and a worker who acted as the deceased's deputy when he was called upon to perform various corvee tasks in the netherworld. The formula inscribed on the statuettes (Chapter 6 of the Book of the Dead) contained appropriate instructions, but reflected a similar ambiguity concerning the statuette's identity. An increase in the number of funerary statuettes can be detected in the Ramessid Period; in the Late Period there were often several hundred of them in the tomb of one person.

The following are some of the more important clues to the dating of funerary statuettes:
made of dark hard stone probably Middle Kingdom or 25th Dynasty, certainly not later than 26th Dynasty;
made of wood if very crude, end of 17th and early 18th Dynasties; and in no case later than New Kingdom;
tools mid-18th Dynasty or later (statuettes without tools also continued to be made);
baskets held at front, 18th Dynasty; on the back, 19th Dynasty and later;
polychrome (red, blue/green, yellow, black) *decoration on white background* end of 18th Dynasty or Ramessid Period;
flat back and/or head fillet, made of faience 3rd Intermediate Period;
small rectangular base and back pillar mid-26th Dynasty and later.

EGYPT IN WESTERN ART

Although Egyptian culture had influenced various peoples around the Mediterranean since the second millennium BCE, the Romans were the first to show interest in Egyptian objects for their very Egyptianness – an interest colored, as later, by the Greek view of Egypt as the repository of esoteric wisdom, and manifested in a superficial imitation of Egyptian art without comprehension of its basic character.

The appeal of things Egyptian was linked to the worship of the Alexandrian deities Isis and Sarapis, whose cults were established at Rome by the late Republic (1st century BCE). The conquest of Egypt in 30 BCE opened the way for the importation of antiquities to serve as public monuments, to adorn houses and gardens, or to decorate the temples of the Egyptian gods, like this baboon in gray granite, one of a pair from the Iseum Campense, Rome. Roman taste favored the exotic rather than the intrinsically Egyptian. With the creation of

Egyptianizing pieces, like this double-headed herm made for the Nilotic garden, or Canopus, of Hadrian's villa at Tivoli, the bizarre aspect became more pronounced. By the mid–4th century, Rome boasted numerous obelisks, two pyramids, and a variety of statuary.

The monuments exported to Rome and her empire constituted the west's only visual source of Egyptian art until the 18th century. Some remained visible throughout the Dark Ages, like the lions and sphinxes copied in 13th-century Roman sculpture. This one is from the Duomo at Città Castellana. The reemergence of others, and the discovery of Classical texts which included accounts of Egypt, aroused the interest of humanists of the Renaissance.

By classical authors they were told that hieroglyphs embodied abstract concepts in a symbolic, universally intelligible form. Leon Battista Alberti's (1404–72) device symbolizing divine omniscience (*above*) is an early example of the application of this idea.

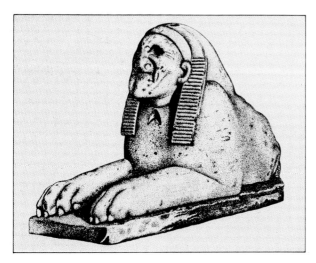

The allegorical use of "hieroglyphs" flourished, perfected in the work of Albrecht Dürer and trivialized in the 16th-century literature devoted to emblems. The major technical feat of the century was the reerection of the Vatican obelisk in front of St Peter's in 1586, illustrated here by Domenico Fontana; the resurrection of others followed, and the obelisk entered the repertory of European architecture, where it soon shed its specifically Egyptian character. More important was the serious interest in Egypt which the event excited; in the following century the hieroglyphs were subjected to fresh examination and the first scholarly publications of Egyptian antiquities appeared, culminating in the great encyclopedic works of the 18th century, where Egyptian objects figured beside Classical. From such sources, and from the first well-illustrated travelers' accounts published around the mid-century, came the inspiration for Egyptianizing works like Johann Melchior Dinglinger's gem-studded Apis Altar (1731), or the exuberant decor created for the Caffè Inglese, Rome (1760), by G. B. Piranesi, whose championship of the majestic Egyptian style was echoed in the work of French and British architects toward the close of the century.

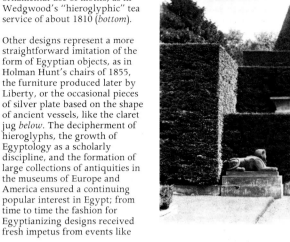

Alongside this new appreciation of Egypt, the mystic tradition continued. The field of *arcana* already prospected by the Rosicrucians was exploited by Freemasonry, and the brotherhood's newly adopted Egyptian rites supplied Schikaneder, librettist of Mozart (himself a Freemason), with some of the ideas expressed in *The Magic Flute*. This frontispiece to the 1791 edition is full of occult gloom.

The French invasion of Egypt seven years later brought with it scholars as well as soldiers, outstanding among them Vivant Denon; his medal cabinet was designed after the picture of a pylon in his own book on Egypt which, together with the expedition's official publication, the *Description de l'Égypte*, provided a wealth of illustrations.

the decorative arts sometimes entailed no more than a playfully ornamental use of motifs, as in Wedgwood's "hieroglyphic" tea service of about 1810 (*bottom*).

Other designs represent a more straightforward imitation of the form of Egyptian objects, as in Holman Hunt's chairs of 1855, the furniture produced later by Liberty, or the occasional pieces of silver plate based on the shape of ancient vessels, like the claret jug *below*. The decipherment of hieroglyphs, the growth of Egyptology as a scholarly discipline, and the formation of large collections of antiquities in the museums of Europe and America ensured a continuing popular interest in Egypt; from time to time the fashion for Egyptianizing designs received fresh impetus from events like

The detailed drawings of the great Egyptian temples, in particular the Greco-Roman with their exaggerated cornices and ornate column capitals, served as models for architecture of a more soberly imitative kind than that advocated by Piranesi. The Egyptian style was considered

appropriate for the massive, the monumental, and the funereal. In Europe and America courthouses, jails, factories, railway stations, bridges, churches and, especially, cemeteries, like this one at Alberobello, south Italy, received Egyptian treatment.

The elegant designs of Napoleon's interior decorators, Percier and Fontaine, were the forerunners in the fashion for *Egyptiennerie* in continental

Europe during the three decades following the French campaign, paralleled by the work of Thomas Hope (1807) and others in England. The Egyptian style in

the opening of the Egyptian Court in the Crystal Palace in London in 1854. This much-admired extravaganza, replete with replicas of the most famous monuments of Egypt, is probably the inspiration behind the later Egyptian garden at Biddulph Grange (*top right*) with its stone sphinxes and topiary pyramid, a trim Victorian descendant of Hadrian's Canopus, Angelo Querini's Egyptian garden at the Villa Altichiero in 18th-century Padua, and Canina's charming Egyptian Portico in the Borghese Gardens, Rome (1827).

The discovery of Tut'ankhamun's tomb in 1922 generated a new wave of Egyptianizing trivia in the decorative arts, but the monumental building style was employed in the 20th century only in the fantasy architecture of the cinema; the pharaonic splendors of Grauman's Egyptian Theater, Hollywood (1922), are reflected in some less grandiose creations in England, like the 1930 Carlton in Islington (*above*).

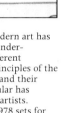

Appreciation of modern art has helped toward an understanding of the different representational principles of the ancient Egyptians, and their sculpture in particular has influenced modern artists. David Hockney's 1978 sets for *The Magic Flute* (*below*) present a starker vision of Egypt than Schinkel's elaborate compositions for the 1815 production, but a sense of majestic spaciousness is common to both.

MUSEUMS WITH EGYPTIAN COLLECTIONS

Although collections of ancient Egyptian antiquities, consisting of curiosities and tourist mementos, had been formed earlier, it was mainly in the first half of the 19th century that museums which displayed Egyptian objects for the delectation and edification of the general public came into existence. Nowadays over 600 of these, scattered over five continents, hold Egyptian objects of importance, and in thousands of others ancient Egypt is represented to some degree. Trained Egyptologists are on the staff of many of these establishments, and museums have also become important centers for the research and study of ancient Egypt. "Excavation" in museum storerooms and basements in order to make available the treasures kept there both to the specialist and to the layman is one of the most urgent tasks of the discipline.

Arab Republic of Egypt
Alexandria
Graeco-Roman Museum
Aswan
Elephantine Museum
Nubia Museum
Cairo
Egyptian Museum
Luxor
Luxor Museum
Museum of Mummification
Mallawi
Mallawi Museum
Minya
Minya Museum
Tanta
Tanta Museum

Australia
Melbourne
National Gallery of Victoria
Sydney
Australian Museum
Nicholson Museum

Austria
Vienna
Kunsthistorisches Museum,
Ägyptisch-Orientalische Sammlung

Belgium
Antwerp
Museum Vleeshuis
Brussels
Musées Royaux d'Art et d'Histoire

Liège
Musée Curtius
Mariemont
Musée Royal de Mariemont

Brazil
Rio de Janeiro
Museu Nacional

Canada
Montreal
McGill University Ethnological
Museum
Musée des Beaux-Arts de Montréal
Toronto
Royal Ontario Museum

Croatia
Zagreb
Archeoloski Muzej

Cuba
Havana
Museo Nacional

Czech Republic
Prague
Náprstkovo muzeum

Denmark
Copenhagen
Nationalmuseet
Ny Carlsberg Glyptotek
Thorwaldsen Museum

Brown quartzite head of a princess, from the so-called sculptor's studio of Thutmose at el-ʿAmarna. Berlin, 21223.

Diorite-gneiss statue of seated Khephren, with Horus-falcon perched on the back panel, from Giza. Cairo, CG 14.

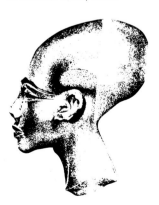

Limestone tomb stela of Wadj, from the king's tomb at Abydos. Paris, Louvre, E.11007.

France
Avignon
Musée Calvet
Grenoble
Musée des Beaux-Arts
Limoges
Musée Municipal
Lyon
Musée des Beaux-Arts
Musée Guimet
Marseilles
Musée d'Archéologie
Nantes
Musée des Arts Decoratifs
Orléans
Musée Historique
Paris
Bibliothèque Nationale
Musée du Louvre
Musée du Petit Palais
Musée Rodin

Strasbourg
Institut d'Egyptologie
Toulouse
Musée Georges Labit

Germany
Berlin
Staatliche Museen Preussischer
Kulturbesitz, Ägyptisches Museum
Dresden
Albertinum
Essen
Museum Folkwang
Frankfurt-am-Main
Liebieghaus, Museum alter Plastik
Hamburg
Museum für Kunst und Gewerbe
Hamburgisches Museum für
Völkerkunde
Hannover
Kestner-Museum
Heidelberg
Ägyptologische Sammlung der
Universität Heidelberg
Hildesheim
Roemer- und Pelizaeus-Museum
Karlsruhe
Badisches Landesmuseum
Leipzig
Ägyptisches Museum
Munich
Staatliche Sammlung Ägyptischer
Kunst
Tübingen
Ägyptologisches Institut der
Universität Tübingen
Würzburg
Martin-von-Wagner Museum

Limestone relief showing a blind harpist, from the Saqqara tomb of the Royal Butler Patenemhab of the end of the 18th Dynasty. Leiden, Inv. AMT.1–35.

Greece
Athens
National Archaeological Museum

Hungary
Budapest
Szépművészeti Múzeum

Ireland
Dublin
National Museum of Ireland

Relief with southern captives, from the Saqqara tomb of Haremhab, probably of the reign of Tutʿankhamun. Bologna, 1887(1869).

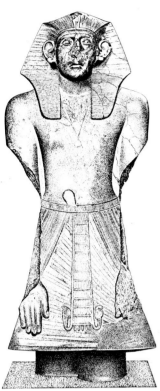

Granodiorite statue of Senwosret III, from Deir el-Bahri. London, British Museum, 684.

Israel
Jerusalem
Bible Lands Museum
Israel Museum

Italy
Bologna
Museo Civico Archeologico
Florence
Museo Archeologico
Mantua
Galleria e Museo del Palazzo Ducale
Milan
Civica Raccolta Egizia, Castello Sforzesco
Naples
Museo Archeologico Nazionale
Palermo
Museo Archeologico Regionale
Parma
Museo Archeologico Nazionale
Rome
Museo Barracco
Museo Capitolino
Museo Nazionale Romano
Rovigo
Museo dell'Accademia dei Concordi

Trieste
Civico Museo di Storia ed Arte di Trieste
Turin
Museo Egizio
Vatican
Museo Gregoriano Egizio
Venice
Museo Archeologico del Palazzo Reale di Venezia

Japan
Kyoto
Museum of the Faculty of Letters

Wall painting of two daughters of Queen Nefertiti, from a palace at el-ʿAmarna. Oxford, Ashmolean, 1893. 1–41(267).

Shigaraki
Miho Museum

Mexico
Mexico City
Museo Nacional de Antropologia

Netherlands
Amsterdam
Allard Pierson Museum
Leiden
Rijksmuseum van Oudheden
Otterlo
Rijksmuseum Kröller-Müller

New Zealand
Dunedin
Otago Museum

Poland
Kraków
Muzeum Narodowe
Warsaw
Muzeum Narodowe

Portugal
Lisbon
Museu Calouste Gulbenkian

Republic of South Africa
Cape Town
South African Cultural History Museum

Russia
Moscow
State Pushkin Museum of Fine Arts
St Petersburg
State Hermitage Museum

Spain
Barcelona
Museu Egipci de Barcelona
Madrid
Museo Arqueológico Nacional

Sudan
Khartoum
Sudan National Museum

Sweden
Linköping
Östergötlands Länsmuseum
Lund
Kulturhistoriska Museet
Stockholm
Medelhavsmuseet
Uppsala
Victoriamuseum för Egyptiska Fornsaker

Switzerland
Basel
Antikenmuseum Basel und Sammlung Ludwig
Cologny
Fondation Martin Bodmer
Geneva
Musée d'Art et d'Histoire
Lausanne
Musée Cantonal d'Archéologie et d'Histoire
Musée Cantonal des Beaux-Arts
Neuchâtel
Musée d'Ethnographie
Riggisberg
Abegg-Stiftung

United Kingdom
Bolton
Bolton Museum and Art Gallery
Bristol
City of Bristol Museum and Art Gallery
Cambridge
Fitzwilliam Museum
Dundee
McManus Galleries
Durham
Oriental Museum
Edinburgh
Royal Museum of Scotland
Glasgow
Art Gallery and Museum
Burrell Collection
Hunterian Museum

Left Blue faience sphinx of Amenhotep III. New York, M.M.A. 1972.125.

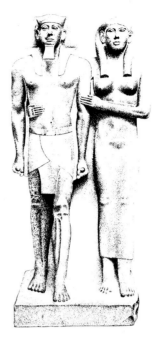

Graywacke pair-statue of Menkaureʿ and Queen Khaʿmerernebty II, from the king's valley temple at Giza. Boston. 11.1738.

Leicester
Leicestershire Museum and Art Gallery
Liverpool
Liverpool Museum
School of Archaeology and Oriental Studies
London
British Museum
Freud Museum
Horniman Museum
Petrie Museum
Victoria and Albert Museum
Manchester
Manchester Museum
Norwich
Castle Museum
Sainsbury Centre for Visual Arts
Oxford
Ashmolean Museum
Pitt Rivers Museum
Swansea
University of Wales, The Egypt Centre

United States of America
Baltimore (MD)
Walters Art Gallery
Berkeley (CA)
Phoebe Apperson Hearst Museum of Anthropology
Boston (MA)
Museum of Fine Arts
Brooklyn (NY)
Brooklyn Museum of Art
Cambridge (MA)
Arthur M. Sackler Museum, Harvard University
Chicago (IL)
Field Museum of Natural History
Oriental Institute Museum
Cincinnati (OH)
Cincinnati Art Museum
Cleveland (OH)
Cleveland Museum of Art
Denver (CO)
Denver Art Museum
Detroit (MI)
Detroit Institute of Arts

Kansas City (MO)
Nelson-Atkins Museum of Art
Los Angeles (CA)
County Museum of Art
Minneapolis (MN)
Minneapolis Institute of Arts
New Haven (CT)
Yale University Art Gallery
New York (NY)
Metropolitan Museum of Art
Palo Alto (CA)
Stanford University Museum
Philadelphia (PA)
University Museum
Pittsburgh (PA)
Carnegie Museum of Natural History
Princeton (NJ)
Art Museum
Providence (RI)
Museum of Art, Rhode Island School of Design
Richmond (VA)
Virginia Museum of Fine Arts
St. Louis (MO)
Art Museum
San Diego (CA)
Museum of Man
San Francisco (CA)
M. H. de Young Memorial Museum
San José (CA)
Rosicrucian Egyptian Museum and Art Gallery
Seattle (WA)
Art Museum
Toledo (OH)
Toledo Museum of Art
Washington (DC)
United States National Museum in the Smithsonian Institution
Worcester (MA)
Worcester Art Museum

Painted limestone head of Queen Nefertiti, from the so-called sculptor's studio of Thutmose at el-ʿAmarna. Berlin, 21300.

GLOSSARY

Wherever possible in this book we avoid using specialized terms. A number that could not be explained within the text are treated in this Glossary. We also offer supplementary information here, especially for administrative and priestly titles. Any terms that are not covered can be found easily in appropriate works listed in the Bibliography. Cross-references within the Glossary are in SMALL CAPITALS.

abacus Cubic block placed between the top of a column capital and the ARCHITRAVE.

ambulatory Roofed pillared or colonnaded walkway, often running around the outside of small New Kingdom temples and bark stations, and of Greco-Roman BIRTH HOUSES.

architrave Horizontal stone beam between columns, or between a column and a wall, that supports a ceiling.

ba One of many terms for aspects of the person, often translated "soul." The *ba* is associated with divinity and with power; gods have many *bas*. It also describes the ability to take on different manifestations, which are themselves *bas*, as the Apis bull is of the god Ptah. The *ba* of the deceased is able to move freely in the underworld and return to earth. See also *KA*.

Badarian From el-Badari, the type site of the earliest certainly identified Predynastic culture of the Nile valley (c. 4500 BCE).

bark shrine Deities were carried in model barks when they went out from temples in procession at festivals; larger divine barks were real boats used on the river. The model barks were kept in shrines in the temples; those at Karnak and Luxor are sizable structures.

birth house Special type of small temple (also called mammisi) in the main temples of the Late and Greco-Roman Periods. These were where the god of the main temple was born, or, if the main temple was dedicated to a goddess, where she bore her son. The birth scenes derive from earlier cycles depicting the birth of kings; kings and young gods shared many aspects.

Book of the Dead A collection of spells mostly written on papyrus and placed with the mummy in a burial, attested from the New Kingdom to the Greco-Roman Period. The texts continue and develop the tradition of the PYRAMID TEXTS and COFFIN TEXTS. The selection of spells, of which about 200 are known, some very long, varies from manuscript to manuscript.

cartouche Circle with a horizontal bar at the bottom, elongated into an ellipse within which kings' names were written from the 3rd or 4th Dynasty on. Detailed examples show that the sign represents a knot of rope, looped so that it is never-ending; it thus symbolizes both protection and cyclical return, probably with solar reference. Kings had two cartouche names, the first a statement about themselves in relation to the god Reʿ (PRAENOMEN) and the second their birth name.

cataract Stretch of rapids interrupting the flow of the Nile, caused by areas of granite interspersed in the Nubian sand-stone belt. There are six numbered and several minor cataracts between Aswan and Khartoum. All are hazards to navigation. The 2nd cataract, the most formidable, was impassable except during the annual inundation. Cataracts 1–4 and the Dal cataract were political frontiers at different times.

cavetto cornice Crowning element of walls, doorways, flat-topped STELAE, and false doors, consisting of a forward flaring curve, with scalloped decoration, often with a winged disk in its middle; probably derived, through mud brick intermediaries, from reed or other plant architectural forms. It was much imitated outside Egypt.

cenotaph Symbolic tombs or mortuary cult places additional to their owner's burial place. The south tomb of the Step Pyramid of Djoser is a cenotaph, as may be the subsidiary pyramids of the 4th–6th Dynasties. At Abydos are many cenotaph chapels for nonroyal individuals of the Middle Kingdom, as well as royal cenotaph temples of the Middle and New Kingdoms. Other sites with cenotaphs are Gebel el-Silsila and Qasr Ibrim.

Chief Steward Middle Kingdom to Late Period title of the administrator of an estate of the temple of a god, of the king or his mortuary temple, of a member of the royal family (e.g. a DIVINE ADORATRICE), or of a nonroyal individual. Because of the function's economic importance, Chief Stewards were very influential. Thus Senenmut combined the offices of Chief Steward of Amun, of Queen Hatshepsut, and of Princess Nefrureʿ, while the powerful Amenhotep Huy, the brother of the vizier Raʿmose, was Chief Steward of Memphis in the reign of Amenhotep III.

Coffin Texts Texts written inside coffins of the Middle Kingdom that are intended to aid the deceased in his or her passage to the hereafter. The texts, which probably originated in the Old Kingdom, are part of the same tradition as the PYRAMID TEXTS, but were used by nonroyal individuals. More than 1,000 spells are known.

colossus Over-lifesize statue, usually of a king, but also of nonroyal individuals and gods; typically set up outside the gates or pylons of temples, and often receiving some sort of cult or acting as intermediaries between human beings and gods.

contrapposto The depiction in statuary of the organic adjustment of the human body to asymmetrical poses; rarely salient in Egyptian art.

Count Translation of a RANKING TITLE of the Old and Middle Kingdoms. As with many titles, the word ceased to refer to a specific function, and modern translations are therefore conventional rather than precise. In the late Middle and New Kingdoms the same title was used for a local administrative function and is better rendered "Mayor."

cuneiform The Mesopotamian script, written with a stylus on clay tablets, with characteristic wedge-shaped (cuneiform) strokes. The script wrote many languages, the most widespread being Akkadian, which was the diplomatic language of the late second millennium BCE. Cuneiform texts have been found in Egypt at el-ʿAmarna, perhaps at Qantir, and on objects of the Persian Period. In the Near East cuneiform tablets written in Egypt have been found at Boğazköy in Anatolia and Kamid el-Loz in Syria.

cursive Rapid, handwritten forms of the script, chiefly HIERATIC and DEMOTIC. Cursive HIEROGLYPHS are special simplified sign forms, similar to hieratic, written in ink and used for religious texts and for the initial training of scribes; the form died out in the first millennium BCE.

demotic From Greek "popular," a further elaboration of HIERATIC, developed in northern Egypt in the 7th century BCE; the normal everyday script of the Late and Greco-Roman Periods. Latest dated text 452 CE.

Divine Adoratrice Chief priestess of Amun in Thebes, an office known from the New Kingdom to the Late Period. Latterly the priestess was celibate. In the 23rd–26th Dynasties princesses held it, notionally "adopting" their successors, and acting as important vehicles of political control by the dynasties of the period.

ennead Group of 9 deities. Enneads are associated with several major cult centers. The number 9 embodies a plurality (3) of pluralities (3, i.e. 3 × 3), and so stands for large numbers in general; hence some enneads have fewer or more than 9 members. The best-known, the Great Ennead of Heliopolis, embodies two myths within its composition, and consists of Reʿ-Atum, Shu, Tefenet, Geb, Nut, Osiris, Isis, Seth, and Nephthys.

Fan-Bearer on the Right of the King Court title alluding to ceremonial attendance, probably with an honorific or ranking function, of high officials of the New Kingdom. The right was the prestigious side.

fecundity figure Type of offering bearer shown at the base of temple walls bringing offerings into the temple; mostly personifications of geographical areas, the inundation, or abstract concepts. The male figures have heavy pendulous breasts and bulging stomachs, their fatness symbolizing the abundance they bring with them.

funerary cones Pottery cones found mostly in Theban tombs of the Middle Kingdom to Late Period, with a flat circular or rectangular base bearing an impression of a stamp with the titles and name of the tomb owner. The cones, some 30 cm long, were originally inserted in the mud brick tomb facade or tomb pyramid to form horizontal rows.

God's Father Common priestly title of the New Kingdom and later, usually further extended by the name of a god (e.g. God's Father of Amun). God's Fathers mostly ranked above ordinary *waʿeb*-priests ("the pure ones") but below "Priests" ("God's Servants").

Herald Middle and New Kingdom title of an official who probably reported to the king and made his commands known, both at court and, for example, on the battlefield.

hieratic From Greek "sacred," the normal form of the script, mostly written on PAPYRUS or OSTRACA, and used throughout Egyptian history. In the Late and Greco-Roman Periods hieratic was restricted to religious texts, hence its name. Hieratic signs largely lost the pictorial character of HIEROGLYPHS, and are often joined together.

hieroglyph Sign in the Egyptian script, from Greek "sacred carving"; used only for the monumental form of the script, in which most signs are identifiable pictures, and signs are not joined together.

High Priest Conventional translation of the title of the head of the priesthood of a particular area. The Egyptian forms of the best known were as follows:
Amun (Thebes): "The First PRIEST of Amun"
Ptah (Memphis): "Greatest of Directors of Craftsmen"
Reʿ (Heliopolis): "Greatest of Seers"
Thoth (el-Ashmunein): "Greatest of the Five."

Horus name The first name in a king's titulary, normally written inside a SEREKH, and consisting of an epithet that identifies the king as manifesting an aspect of Horus.

hypostyle hall Term for columned halls, from the Greek for "bearing pillars." The halls are the outermost, and grandest, parts of the main structures of temples, frequently added after the rest, and exhibit an elaborate symbolism. Many temples have two hypostyle halls. Another term for outer hypostyle hall is "pronaos."

ichneumon A small animal that kills snakes and destroys crocodile eggs, akin to the Indian mongoose. The ichneumon and the shrewmouse formed a pair of animals associated with the sun god. Ichneumons in particular were often buried in the Late and Greco-Roman Periods; many bronze statuettes of them are known.

ithyphallic With erect penis (from the Greek). Various gods were shown in this form, such as Min, Amun (especially at Luxor), and the revitalized Osiris. On Min and Amun the form is associated with a raised arm and probably has a protective symbolism.

ka Concept of an aspect of the person, perhaps associated originally with sexual fertility and with the transmission of identity down the generations. The *ka* was depicted as being born as a "double" of the living person, but came into its own in the afterlife, when it received mortuary offerings and ensured the deceased's survival. See also *BA*.

kiosk Small, open temple structure used as a way station for statues of gods during festivals when they left their main temples, or in the SED-FESTIVAL.

KV with number: tomb in the Valley of the Kings.

Lector Priest Priest (literally "One who bears the ritual book") whose function was to declaim the ritual texts in temple and funerary cult. He wore a distinctive broad white sash diagonally across the chest. Lector Priests were strongly associated with magic and specialized knowledge.

logogram Sign that writes an entire word, often with the addition of a stroke and/or the feminine ending -*t*.

mastaba Arabic word for "bench", used as the term for freestanding tombs of the Early Dynastic Period and Old Kingdom, as well as some later ones. The basic form of a mastaba's superstructure is a rectangle with flat roof and vertical or slightly inclined (or "battered") walls.

Mistress of the House Housewife, title given to married ladies from the Middle Kingdom onwards.

naos Shrine in which statues of deities were kept, especially in temple sanctuaries. A small wooden naos was often placed inside a monolithic one in hard stone; the latter are typical of the Late Period, and sometimes elaborately decorated. Also used as a term for temple sanctuary.

necropolis Greek word for cemetery. "Necropolis" normally describes large and important burial areas that were in use for long periods, "cemetery" smaller and more homogeneous sites; cemeteries may also be subdivisions of a necropolis.

Nilometer Staircase descending into the Nile and marked with levels above low water; used for measuring, and in some cases inscribing, inundation levels. The most famous are on Elephantine Island and on Roda Island in Cairo (of the Islamic Period).

nomarch The chief official of a NOME. In the late Old Kingdom–early Middle Kingdom nomarchs became local, hereditary rulers, who governed their nomes more or less independently of the central authority; the kings of the 11th Dynasty began in this way. During the 12th Dynasty the office ceased to have political importance, but it was revived later, notably in the Greco-Roman period.

nome Administrative province of Egypt, from Greek *nomos*; the ancient Egyptian term was *sepat*. The nome system seems to have developed in the Early Dynastic Period, but did not reach final form until the Ptolemies. During some periods of highly centralized administration (e.g. late Middle Kingdom) the nomes had little real importance.

obelisk Monolithic tapering shaft, mostly of pink granite, with a PYRAMIDION at the top; from a Greek word for a grilling spit. Obelisks are solar symbols, probably similar in meaning to pyramids, and associated with an ancient stone called *benben* in Heliopolis. They were set up in pairs outside the entrances to some Old Kingdom tombs, and outside temples; a single obelisk in east Karnak received a cult.

ogdoad Term describing the group of 8 deities (four male–female pairs) associated with el-Ashmunein (Hermopolis), whose names symbolize the state of the world before creation. The group's composition varies, but its classic form is: Nun and Naunet, the primeval waters; Huh and Hauhet, endless space; Kuk and Kauket, darkness; Amun and Amaunet, that which is hidden.

orthogram Sign in the script whose function is to elucidate the function of another sign or to write a dual or plural.

Osirid pillar Pillar, mostly found in sets in open courts or porticos, with a colossal statue of a king forming its front part; unlike caryatids in Classical architecture, the statues are not structural elements. Many have undifferentiated bodies or are mummiform, but by no means all; their connection with Osiris is doubtful.

ostracon Flake of limestone or potsherd used for writing (from the Greek for potsherd); also fragment from an inscribed jar, such as a wine jar inscribed with the details of a vintage. Ostraca are known from all periods, but 19th- and 20th-Dynasty examples are commonest in hieratic (up to 20,000 have been found). Most texts are in HIERATIC, DEMOTIC (also very common), or Coptic, but there are also CURSIVE HIEROGLYPHIC texts and numerous pictorial compositions, including drafts of hieroglyphic inscriptions.

Overseer of Sealbearers Typical administrative title of the 12th Dynasty borne by a high official of the Treasury. The "Overseer of Sealbearers" was responsible to the head of the Treasury ("The Overseer of the Seal") and his deputies. The term derives from the fact that most containers of produce and goods were sealed when entering or leaving the Treasury magazines. The title also designated expedition leaders.

papyrus The chief Egyptian writing material, and an important export. The oldest surviving papyrus (blank) dates to the 1st Dynasty, the latest to the Islamic Period, when the plant died out in Egypt (it has recently been reintroduced). Sheets were made by cutting the plant's pith into strips laid in rows horizontally and vertically, which were then beaten together, activating natural starches to form an adhesive. Separate sheets were gummed together to form rolls. The better surface of a papyrus (the normal recto) had the fibers running horizontally; letters were normally begun on strips inscribed across the fibers.

peristyle court Colonnaded court with a roof around the sides supported by rows of columns (from Greek *peristylon*) and an open space in the center.

phonogram Sign in the script that records a sound. Only consonants are precisely recorded, and phonograms may write 1–4 consonants.

praenomen A king's first CARTOUCHE name, which he adopted on his accession; also called "throne name." It consists of a statement about the king in relation to the god Reʿ, later with additional epithets, e.g. Menkheprureʿ (Thutmose IV) "The Enduring One of the Manifestations of Reʿ," to which "whom Reʿ begot" can be added.

Priest Priestly title (literally "God's Servant"), ranking above *waʿeb*-priests and GOD'S FATHERS, usually extended by the name of a god (e.g. "Priest of Montu"). The head of the local priesthood, particularly in the provinces, was often called "Overseer of Priests." The high priest of Amun at Thebes was "The First Priest of Amun"; below him were the Second, Third, and Fourth Priests.

pronaos Room in front of the sanctuary (NAOS) of a temple, whose exact location varies with the design of individual temples; also used as a term for outer HYPOSTYLE HALL.

prophet Greek equivalent (literally "one who speaks for" the god) of the Egyptian title rendered here "priest" (see entry above). The Greek probably reflects the role of priests as intermediaries between humanity and deities.

propylon Gateway in a mud brick enclosure wall that stands in front of a PYLON.

pylon Monumental entrance wall of a temple, from the Greek for gate; consists of a pair of massifs with an opening between, mostly elaborated into a doorway. All the wall faces are inclined (or "battered"); the corners are completed with a TORUS MOLDING and the top with torus and CAVETTO CORNICE. Pylons are the largest and least essential parts of a temple, mostly built last. Some temples have series of them, maximally 10 at Karnak, on two axes.

pyramidion Capstone of a pyramid or top of an OBELISK. The pyramidion was decorated and became a symbolic object in its own right, being used also as the most striking feature of the small brick pyramids of nonroyal tombs of the New Kingdom (Thebes, Saqqara) and Late Period (Abydos).

Pyramid Texts Texts on the walls of the internal rooms of pyramids of the end of the 5th and 6th–8th Dynasties, later used by nonroyal individuals for most of Egyptian history. Some texts relate to the king's burial ceremonies and offerings to him, but others are concerned with his celestial destiny, temple ritual, and many further matters.

ranking title Title that indicates status but does not denote any specific function; very important in the Old and to a lesser extent the Middle Kingdom. The typical sequence of titles, in ascending order, is "Royal Acquaintance," "Sole Companion," "COUNT," "Member of the *paʿt* (elite group)."

reserve heads 4th Dynasty tomb sculptures seemingly aiming at a specific representation of the head of the deceased (hence the alternate term "portrait heads"), and perhaps acting as its substitute. Some 30 have been found, mainly at Giza; all seem to have been ritually mutilated.

revetment Cladding of a wall surface or bastion; may be ornamental, e.g. stone covering mud brick, or structural, and intended to give stability to a core of rubble.

sabbakhin Arabic word for diggers of *sabbakh*, nitrogenous earth from ancient sites used as fertilizer; *sabbakh* may be mud brick or remains of organic refuse. *Sabbakhin* are among the chief agents of destruction of ancient sites.

***saff* tomb** Arabic word for "row," describing rock-cut tombs of the early 11th Dynasty that consist of a row of openings – or colonnade – in the hillside.

Sea Peoples Mediterranean invaders of Egypt in the late 19th and early 20th Dynasties, probably associated with a wave of destruction on Near Eastern sites and more remotely with the fall of Mycenaean Greece and the Hittite empire; precise identity, origin, and final dispersal much disputed.

***sed*-festival** Ritual of royal regeneration, almost always celebrated after 30 years of a king's reign, and thereafter at three-yearly intervals, but very occasionally performed earlier; features prominently in the decoration of royal mortuary temples, reflecting the king's wish to rule long in the next world.

semogram Sign in the script that conveys meaning, not sound. Subcategories are LOGOGRAMS, TAXOGRAMS, and ORTHOGRAMS. Also called ideograms.

serekh Image of a brick facade to a palace or enclosure, with a rectangular space above; the facade is in the style of the late Predynastic and Early Dynastic Periods. A falcon (the sign for Horus) perches on top of the rectangle, which encloses a king's HORUS NAME.

sistrum Musical instrument – a kind of rattle – sacred to Hathor. Two types are common: (a) a NAOS shape above a Hathor head, with ornamental loops on the sides (the rattle was inside the naos box); (b) a loop with loose crossbars of metal above a smaller Hathor head; both had long handles. (a) was used from the New Kingdom on as a column capital, making play with the association between the rustle of aquatic plants and the joyful sound of the sistrum (plant and sistrum forms are occasionally combined). At Dendara the sistrum (mostly type a) was a major sacred object.

Standard Bearer of the Lord of the Two Lands Military title of the New Kingdom, borne by an officer of the infantry, chariotry, or one attached to a ship, who was in charge of a company of some 250 men. Companies of the Egyptian army had distinguishing "standards."

stela Slab of stone or wood with textual or pictorial decoration. Commemorative or votive stelae were placed in temples; tomb stelae functioned within the decoration of a tomb. Some stelae formed part of burial rituals.

talatat Arabic word for "three (handbreadths)" describing the length of the typical small stone building blocks of temples of Amenhotep IV/Akhenaten. They are found reused at a number of sites (tens of thousands at Karnak), and are decorated with scenes in the ʿAmarna style. Some complete walls have been reassembled from scattered blocks.

Tasian From Deir Tasa, a Predynastic site in Upper Egypt; Predynastic culture that may not be distinct from BADARIAN.

taxogram Sign in the script that is placed after the PHONOGRAMS in the writing of a word, and indicates the class or area of meaning to which it belongs; also known as determinatives or classifiers.

torus molding Semicircular or cylindrical band forming the edge of a stela or the corner of a stone wall. Detailed examples are decorated with a pattern that suggests lashings around a pole or reed bundle, evoking architecture in flimsy organic materials.

tree goddess A goddess associated with a sacred tree and represented as a tree with arms or a woman emerging from a tree. Hathor, Isis, and Nut are found as tree goddesses, all in the context of mortuary cult.

TT Theban Tomb (nonroyal), followed by its number.

underworld books Mixed pictorial and textual compositions inscribed in New Kingdom royal tombs that present the passage of the sun god through the underworld and the sky; taken over by nonroyal individuals in the Third Intermediate and Late Periods.

uraeus Perhaps the most characteristic symbol of kingship, a rearing cobra worn on the king's forehead or crown that became universal around the end of the Old Kingdom. The cobra was associated with the goddess Wadjit or with the sun, whose "eye" it was held to be. It was an agent of destruction and protection of the king, spitting out fire. New Kingdom and later queens, and Kushite kings, wore two uraei.

Viceroy of Kush Administrator of Nubia during the New Kingdom, at first called "King's Son," from the mid 18th Dynasty "King's Son of Kush." The viceroy was a titular, not a real son of the king. The area he governed extended as far north as Kom el-Ahmar (Hierakonpolis). His two deputies, one for Lower Nubia (Wawat), the other for Upper Nubia (Kush), resided at ʿAniba and ʿAmara respectively.

vizier The highest official in the administration; the post is attested from the Early Dynastic Period on. In the New Kingdom there were two viziers, at Memphis and Thebes. In that period the most important individuals were often not viziers, while the office was less important in the Late Period. A group of New Kingdom texts describes the ideal installation ceremony of a vizier and details his functions.

winged disk A sun disk with an outspread pair of wings attached, attested perhaps from the Old Kingdom on (a 1st Dynasty precursor consists of wings without the disk). It is associated with Horus of Behdet (Edfu), and symbolizes the sun, especially in architecture on ceilings, cornices, and stelae. Often copied outside Egypt.

zodiac The Babylonian and Greek signs of the zodiac were introduced into Egypt in the Greco-Roman Period, "translated" into Egyptian representational forms, and used in the decoration of astronomical ceilings of tombs and temples, and on coffin lids.

LIST OF ILLUSTRATIONS

BIBLIOGRAPHY

Much of the work of Egyptologists is published in specialist journals, of which about twenty are devoted exclusively to the subject. These are listed in the *Lexikon der Ägyptologie* and *Annual Egyptological Bibliography* (see below); the latter has complete listings of publications by year of appearance. The presentation in this book is often based on material in journals or unpublished research, and may differ from that in other books.

*Has been translated into other languages.

General and Reference Works
Annual Egyptological Bibliography, various editors. Leiden 1947– . Since 1992 on the World Wide Web.
K. A. Bard (ed.), *Encyclopaedia of the Archaeology of Ancient Egypt*. London and New York 1999.
F. Daumas, *La Civilisation de l'Égypte pharaonique*. Paris 1965.
S. Donadoni (ed.), *The Egyptians*. Chicago 1997.*
W. C. Hayes, *The Scepter of Egypt*, i–ii. New York 1953, Cambridge (MA) 1959.
W. Helck et al. (eds.), *Lexikon der Ägyptologie*. 7 vols. Wiesbaden 1972–92.
E. Hornung, *Einführung in die Ägyptologie*. 2nd ed. Darmstadt 1992.
B. J. Kemp, *Ancient Egypt: Anatomy of a Civilization*. London and New York 1989.
M. Liverani, *Antico Oriente: storia, società, economia*. Rome 1988.
S. Moscati (ed.), *L'alba della civiltà*, i–iii. Turin 1976.
D. B. Redford (ed.), *The Oxford Encyclopedia of Ancient Egypt*. 3 vols. New York 2000.
J. M. Sasson et al. (eds.), *Civilizations of the Ancient Near East*. 4 vols. New York 1995.
R. Schulz and M. Seidel (eds.), *Egypt: The World of the Pharaohs*. Cologne 1998.*
A. J. Spencer and S. Quirke (eds.), *The British Museum Book of Ancient Egypt*. London 1992.

Part One: The Cultural Setting
The geography of ancient Egypt
W. Y. Adams, *Nubia: Corridor to Africa*. London 1977.
K. W. Butzer, *Early Hydraulic Civilization in Egypt*. Chicago and London 1976.
H. Kees, *Ancient Egypt: A Cultural Topography*. London 1961.*
P. Montet, *Géographie de l'Égypte ancienne*, i–ii. Paris 1957–61.
D. O'Connor, *Ancient Nubia*. Philadelphia 1993.
I. Shaw and P. T. Nicholson (eds.), *Ancient Egyptian Materials and Technology*. Cambridge 2000.

The study of ancient Egypt
M. L. Bierbrier (ed.), *Who was who in Egyptology*. 3rd ed. London 1995.
L. Greener, *The Discovery of Egypt*. London 1966.
Works of travelers to Egypt are available; many are collected in "Voyageurs occidentaux en Égypte," Cairo 1970– .

The historical setting
A. K. Bowman, *Egypt after the Pharaohs*. 2nd ed. London 1996.
Cambridge Ancient History, 1–13. 2nd/3rd ed. Cambridge 1970– .
A. H. Gardiner, *Egypt of the Pharaohs*. Oxford 1961.*
W. Helck, *Geschichte des alten Ägypten*. Leiden and Cologne 1968, 1981.
E. Hornung, *History of Ancient Egypt: An Introduction*. Ithaca (NY) 1999.*
K. A. Kitchen, *The Third Intermediate Period in Egypt (1100–650 B.C.)*. 2nd ed. Warminster 1986.
B. G. Trigger et al., *Ancient Egypt: A Social History*. Cambridge 1983.

Principles of art and architecture
D. Arnold, *Building in Egypt: Pharaonic Stone Masonry*. New York 1991.
——, *Lexikon der ägyptischen Baukunst*. Zurich 1994.
——, *Temples of the Last Pharaohs*. New York and Oxford 1999.
A. Badawy, *A History of Egyptian Architecture*. 3 vols. Giza 1954, Berkeley (CA) 1966–68.
J.–L. de Cenival, *Égypte. Époque pharaonique*. Fribourg 1964.*
K. Lange and M. Hirmer, *Ägypten*. 4th ed. Munich 1967.*
H. Schäfer, *Principles of Egyptian Art*. Oxford 1986.*
J. Malek, *Egyptian Art*. London 1999.
G. Robins, *Proportion and Style in Ancient Egyptian Art*. Austin and London 1994.
——, *The Art of Ancient Egypt*. London 1997.
W. S. Smith, ed. W. K. Simpson, *The Art and Architecture of Ancient Egypt*. 3rd ed., revised. New Haven 1998.
W. S. Smith, *A History of Egyptian Sculpture and Painting in the Old Kingdom*. 2nd ed. London and Boston (MA) 1949.
C. Vandersleyen et al., *Das alte Ägypten*. Berlin 1975.

Stelae
J. Vandier, *Manuel d'archéologie égyptienne*, ii (1). Paris 1954.

Part Two: A Journey down the Nile
For most sites we have faced the almost impossible task of limiting the selection of publications to one or two items. We have chosen those which give the best idea of the current state of knowledge of a site, either by presenting general information or by illustrating a particular feature. Full information is given in B. Porter and R. L. B. Moss, *Topographical Bibliography of Ancient Egyptian Hieroglyphic Texts, Statues, Reliefs, and Paintings*, i–viii, i²– (Oxford 1927–), quoted here as PM. Annual reports on archaeological work in Egypt, Nubia, and Egyptian finds outside Egypt have been published by J. Leclant in *Orientalia* since 1950.

Elephantine and Aswan (PM v.221–44)
E. Bresciani and S. Pernigotti, *Assuan. Il tempio tolemaico di Isi. I blocchi decorati e iscritti*. Pisa 1978.
E. Edel, *Die Felsengräber der Qubbet el-Hawa bei Assuan*, i–ii, 1. Wiesbaden 1967–71.
Elephantine, series published by the German Archaeological Institute in Cairo, especially L. Habachi, *The Sanctuary of Heqaib*, Mainz 1985; G. Dreyer, *Der Tempel der Satet*, Mainz 1986; C. von Pilgrim, *Untersuchungen in der Stadt des Mittleren Reiches und der Zweiten Zwischenzeit*, Mainz 1996.

Philae (PM vi.203–56)
A. Giammarusti and A. Roccati. *File: storia e vita di un santuario egizio*. Novara 1980.
H. Junker and E. Winter, *Philä*, i– . Vienna 1958– .
H. G. Lyons, *A Report on the Island and Temples of Philae*. [London 1897].
S. Sauneron and H. Stierlin, *Die letzten Tempel Ägyptens. Edfu und Philae*. Zürich 1978.*

Kom Ombo (PM vi.179–203)
J. de Morgan et al., *Kom Ombos*, i–ii. Vienna 1909.
A. Gutbub, *Kôm Ombo*, i– . Cairo 1995– .

Gebel el-Silsila (PM v.208–18, 220–21)
R. A. Caminos and T. G. H. James, *Gebel es-Silsilah*, i. London 1963.

Edfu (PM v.200–05; vi.119–77)
M. de Rochemonteix, É. Chassinat et al., *Le temple d'Edfou*, i–xv. Paris 1892–1918. 2nd ed. Cairo 1984– .
S. Cauville, *Edfou*. Cairo 1984.
See also Philae.

Kom el-Ahmar (PM v.191–200)
B. Adams, *Ancient Hierakonpolis*, with *Supplement*. Warminster 1974.
M. A. Hoffman et al., *The Predynastic of Hierakonpolis*. Cairo and Macomb (IL) 1982.
J. E. Quibell (vol. ii with F. W. Green), *Hierakonpolis*, i–ii. London 1900, 1902.

el-Kab (PM v.171–91)
Elkab, i–v. Brussels 1971–95.
Fouilles de el Kab, i–iii. Brussels, 1940–54.

Esna (PM v.165–67 and vi.110–19)
D. Downes, *The Excavations at Esna 1905–1906*. Warminster 1974.
Esna, series published by the Institut Français d'Archéologie Orientale (Cairo), 1959– .

el-Moʿalla (PM v.170)
J. Vandier, *Moʿalla, la tombe d'Ankhtifi et la tombe de Sébekhotep*. Cairo 1950.

Gebelein (PM v.162–64)
A. M. Donadoni Roveri et al., *Gebelein: Il villaggio e la necropoli*. Turin 1994.

Tod (PM v.167–69)
F. Bisson de la Roque, *Tôd (1934 à 1936)*. Cairo 1937.
É. Drioton et al., ed. J.-P. Grenier, *Tôd. Les inscriptions du temple ptolémaïque et romain*, i. Cairo 1980.

Armant (PM v.151–61)
R. Mond and O. H. Myers, *Temples of Armant. A Preliminary Survey*. London 1940.
——, *The Bucheum*, i–iii. London 1934.

Thebes (general, including sites listed below)
N. and H. Strudwick, *Thebes in Egypt*. London 1999.
C. F. Nims, *Thebes of the Pharaohs*. London 1965.

Luxor (PM ii.²301–39)
H. Brunner, *Die südlichen Räume des Tempels von Luxor*. Mainz 1977.
M. Abd el-Raziq, *Die Darstellungen und Texte des Sanktuars Alexander des Großen im Tempel von Luxor*. Mainz 1984.
Reliefs and Inscriptions at Luxor Temple, i– , by the Epigraphic Survey, Chicago 1994– .

Karnak (PM ii.²1–301)
P. Barguet, *Le Temple d'Amon-Rê à Karnak: Essai d'exégèse*. Cairo 1962.
Cahiers de Karnak, i– . Centre Franco-Égyptien d'Étude des Temples de Karnak. Paris, 1980– .
J.-C. Golvin and J -C. Goyon, *Les bâtisseurs de Karnak*. 1987.
Reliefs and Inscriptions at Karnak, i– , by the Epigraphic Survey. Chicago 1936– .

The West Bank (PM i² and ii.²339–537)
J. Assmann et al., *Thebanische Beamtennekropolen: Neue Perspektiven archäologischer Forschung. Internationales Symposion Heidelberg 9.–13.6.1993*. Heidelberg 1995.
H. Carter and A. C. Mace, *The Tomb of Tut·ankh·amen*, i–iii. London etc. 1923–33.*
E. Hornung and F. Teichmann, *Das Grab des Haremhab im Tal der Könige*. Bern 1971.
E. Hornung, *The Tomb of Pharaoh Seti I*. Zurich and Munich 1991.
C. Leblanc, *Ta set neferou. Une nécropole de Thèbes-Ouest et son histoire*, i. Cairo 1989.
Medinet Habu, i–viii, by the Epigraphic Survey. Chicago 1930–70.
E. Naville, *The Temple of Deir el Bahari*, Introductory Memoir and i–vi. London 1894–1908.
J. Osing, *Der Tempel Sethos' I. in Gurna. Die Reliefs und Inschriften*, i– . Mainz 1977– .
N. Reeves and R. H. Wilkinson, *The Complete Valley of the Kings*. London 1996.

G. Thausing and H. Goedicke, *Nofretari. Eine Dokumentation der Wandgemälde ihres Grabes.* Graz 1971.
K. R. Weeks, *The Lost Tomb.* London and New York 1998.

Nagʿ el-Madamud (PM v.137–50)
P. Bisson de la Roque, J. J. Clère et al., *Rapport sur les fouilles de Médamoud (1925–32).* Cairo 1926–36.

Naqada and Tukh (PM v.117–19)
J. de Morgan, *Recherches sur les origines de l'Égypte,* ii, 147–202. Paris 1897.
W. M. F. Petrie and J. E. Quibell, *Naqada and Ballas.* London 1896.

Qus (PM v.135–6)

Qift (PM v.123–34)
W. M. F. Petrie, *Koptos.* London 1896.
C. Traunecker, *Coptos: hommes et dieux sur le parvis de Geb.* Louvain 1992.

el-Qalʿa (PM v.134)
L. Pantalacci and C. Traunecker, *Le temple d'el-Qalʿa,* i– . Cairo 1990– .

Dendara (PM v.109–16 and vi.41–110)
S. Cauville, *Le temple de Dendera: guide archéologique.* Cairo 1990.
E. Chassinat, F. Daumas, and S. Cauville, *Le temple de Dendara,* i– . Cairo 1934– .
F. Daumas, *Dendara et le temple d'Hathor.* Cairo 1969.

el-Qasr and el-Saiyad (PM v.119–22)
T. Säve-Söderbergh, *The Old Kingdom Cemetery at Hamra Dom (El-Qasr wa Es-Saiyad).* Stockholm 1994.

Hiw (PM v.107–09)
W. M. F. Petrie, *Diospolis Parva: The Cemeteries of Abadiyeh and Hu 1898–9.* London 1901.

Abydos (PM v.39–105 and vi.1–41)
A. M. Calverley et al., *The Temple of King Sethos I at Abydos,* i– . London and Chicago 1933– .
G. Dreyer et al., *Umm el-Qaab* I. Mainz 1998.
A. Mariette, *Abydos,* i–ii. Paris 1869–80.
W. M. F. Petrie, *The Royal Tombs of the First Dynasty/Earliest Dynasties.* London 1900–01.
W. K. Simpson and D. B. O'Connor, *Inscribed Material from the Pennsylvania–Yale Excavations at Abydos.* New Haven and Philadelphia 1995.

Beit Khallaf (PM v.37)
J. Garstang, *Mahâsna and Bêt Khallâf.* London 1903.

Akhmim (PM v.17–26)
N. Kanawati et al., *The Rock Tombs of El-Hawawish: The Cemetery of Akhmim,* i–x. Sydney 1980–92.
K. P. Kuhlmann, *Materialien zur Archäologie und Geschichte des Raumes von Achmim.* Mainz 1983.

Wannina (PM v.31–34)
W. M. F. Petrie, *Athribis.* London 1908.

Qaw el-Kebir (PM v.9–16)
H. Steckeweh, *Die Fürstengräber von Qaw.* Leipzig 1936.

Asyut (PM iv.259–70)
E. Edel, *Die Inschriften der Grabfronten der Siut-Gräber in Mittelägypten aus der Herakleopolitenzeit.* Opladen 1984.
F. L. Griffith, *The Inscriptions of Siut and Der Rifeh.* London 1889.

Deir el-Gabrawi (PM iv.242–46)
N. de G. Davies, *The Rock Tombs of Deir el Gebrawi,* i–ii. London 1902.

Meir (PM iv.247–58)
A. M. Blackman, *The Rock Tombs of Meir,* i–vi. London 1914–53.

el-ʿAmarna (PM iv.192–237)
N. de G. Davies, *The Rock Tombs of El Amarna,* i–vi. London 1903–08.
B. J. Kemp et al., *Amarna Reports,* i– . London 1984– .

B. J. Kemp and S. Garfi, *A Survey of the Ancient City of el-ʿAmarna.* London 1993.
G. T. Martin, *The Royal Tomb at el-ʿAmarna,* i–ii. London 1974, 1989.
T. E. Peet, C. L. Woolley, J. D. S. Pendlebury et al., *The City of Akhenaten,* i–iii. London 1923, 1933, 1951.

el-Sheikh Saʿid (PM iv.187–92)
N. de G. Davies, *The Rock Tombs of Sheikh Saïd.* London 1901.

Deir el-Bersha (PM iv.177–87)
E. J. Brovarski et al., *Bersheh Reports.* Boston (MA) 1992.
P. E. Newberry and F. L. Griffith, *El Bersheh,* i–ii. London 1892.

el-Ashmunein (PM iv.165–69)
Excavations at el-Ashmunein, i–iv, series published by the British Museum, especially A. J. Spencer et al., *The Temple Area,* London 1989; D. M. Bailey et al., *Hermopolis Magna: Buildings of the Roman Period,* London 1991; A. J. Spencer, *The Town,* London 1993.
G. Roeder, *Hermopolis 1929–1939.* Hildesheim 1959.

Tuna el-Gebel (PM iv.169–75)
S. Gabra and E. Drioton, *Peintures à fresques et scènes peintes à Hermoupolis ouest (Touna el-Gebel).* Cairo 1954.
D. Kessler, *Tuna el-Gebel II. Die Paviankultkammer G-C-C-2.* Hildesheim 1998.
G. Lefebvre, *Le tombeau de Petosiris,* i–iii. Cairo 1923–24.

el-Sheikh ʿIbada (PM iv.175–77)
Antinoe (1965–1968): Missione archeologica in Egitto dell' Università di Roma. Rome 1974.

Beni Hasan with Speos Artemidos (PM iv.140–65)
P. E. Newberry, F. Ll. Griffith et al., *Beni Hasan,* i–iv. London 1893–1900.
A. G. Shedid, *Die Felsgräber von Beni Hassan in Mittelägypten.* Mainz 1994.*

Zawyet el-Maiyitin (PM iv.134–39)
P. Piacentini, *Zawiet el-Mayetin nel III millennio A.C.* Pisa 1993.
A. Varille, *La Tombe de Ni-Ankh-Pepi à Zâouyet el-Mayetîn.* Cairo 1938.

Tihna el-Gebel (PM iv.127–33)
Akoris: Report of the Excavations at Akoris in Middle Egypt 1981–1992. Kyoto 1995.
R. Holthoer and R. Ahlqvist "The 'Roman Temple' at Tehna el-Gebel," *Studia Orientalia,* 43.7 (1974).

Oxyrhynchus (PM iv.124)
W. M. F. Petrie, *Tombs of the Courtiers and Oxyrhynkhos.* London 1925.
The Oxyrhynchus Papyri, i– . London 1898– .

el-Hiba (PM iv. 124–5)
H. Ranke, *Koptische Friedhöfe bei Karâra und der Amontempel Scheschonks I bei el Hibe.* Berlin and Leipzig 1926.
R. J. Wenke et al., *Archaeological Investigations at el-Hibeh 1980: Preliminary Report.* Malibu 1984.

Dishasha (PM iv.121–23)
N. Kanawati and A. McFarlane, *Deshasha: The Tombs of Inti, Shedu and Others.* Sydney 1993.
W. M. F. Petrie, *Deshasheh 1897.* London 1898.

Ihnasya el-Medina (PM iv.118–21)
E. Naville, *Ahnas el Medineh (Heracleopolis Magna).* London 1894.
M. del Carmen Pérez Die and P. Vernus, *Excavaciones en Ehnasya el Medina (Heracleópolis Magna).* Madrid 1992.
W. M. F. Petrie, *Ehnasya 1904.* London 1905.

Kom Medinet Ghurab (PM iv.112–15)
L. Borchardt, *Der Porträtkopf der Königin Teje.* Leipzig 1911.

el-Lahun (PM iv.107–12)
W. M. F. Petrie, *Kahun, Gurob, and Hawara.* London 1890.
———, *Kahun and Gurôb 1889–90.* London 1891.

The Faiyum (PM iv.96–104)
Di. and Do. Arnold, *Der Tempel Qasr el-Sagha.* Mainz 1979.
E. Bresciani, *Rapporto preliminare delle campagne di scavo 1966 e 1967.* Milan and Varese 1968.
P. Davoli, *L'archeologia urbana nel Fayyum di età ellenistica e romana.* Bologna 1998.
C. W. Griggs et al., *Excavations at Seila, Egypt.* Provo (UT) 1988.
A. Vogliano, *Rapporto degli scavi nella zona di Madînet Mâḍî,* i–ii. Milan 1936–37.

Maidum (PM iv.89–96)
A. el-Khouli et al., *Meidum.* Warminster 1991.
W. M. F. Petrie, *Medum.* London 1892.

el-Lisht (PM iv.77–85)
Di. Arnold et al., *The Pyramid of Senwosret I.* New York 1988.
———, *The Pyramid Complex of Senwosret I.* New York 1992.
H. Goedicke, *Re-used Blocks from the Pyramid of Amenemhet I at Lisht.* New York 1971.

Mit Rahina (PM iii.²830–75)
R. Anthes et al., *Mit Rahineh 1955 and 1956.* Philadelphia (PA) 1959 and 1965.
D. G. Jeffreys, *The Survey of Memphis,* i: *The Archaeological Report.* London 1985.
A. el-Sayed Mahmud, *A New Temple for Hathor at Memphis.* Warminster 1978.
W. M. F. Petrie et al., *Memphis,* i–v. London 1909–13.

Dahshur (PM iii.²876–99)
Di. Arnold, *Der Pyramidenbezirk des Königs Amenemhet III. in Dahschur.* Mainz 1987.
J. de Morgan, *Fouilles à Dahchour,* i–ii. Vienna 1895–1903.
A. Fakhry, *The Monuments of Sneferu at Dahshur,* i–ii. Cairo 1959–61.

Saqqara (PM iii.²393–829)
P. Duell et al., *The Mastaba of Mereruka,* i–ii. Chicago (IL) 1938.
M. Z. Goneim, *Horus Sekhem-khet: The Unfinished Step Pyramid at Saqqara,* i. Cairo 1957.
N. Kanawati and A. Hassan, *The Teti Cemetery at Saqqara,* i–ii. Warminster 1996–97.
J.-P. Lauer, *Saqqara. The Royal Cemetery of Memphis.* London 1976.*
G. T. Martin, *The Tomb of Hetepka.* London 1979.
——— et al., *The Memphite Tomb of Horemheb, Commander-in-Chief of Tutʿankhamûn,* i–ii. London 1989, 1996.
A. M. Moussa and H. Altenmüller, *Das Grab des Nianchchnum und Chnumhotep.* Mainz 1977.
Le Tombeau de Ti, i–iii (i by L. Epron and F. Daumas, ii and iii by H. Wild). Cairo 1939–66.
A. Zivie, *Découverte à Saqqarah: Le vizir oublié.* Paris 1990.

Abusir (PM iii.²324–50)
L. Borchardt et al., *Das Grabdenkmal des Königs Śa3ḥu-rēʿ,* i–ii. Leipzig 1910–13.
H. Ricke et al., *Das Sonnenheiligtum des Königs Userkaf,* i–ii. Cairo 1965, Wiesbaden 1969.
M. Verner, *Forgotten Pharaohs, Lost Pyramids.* Prague 1994.
———, *Abusir I: The Mastaba of Ptahshepses: Reliefs.* Prague 1977.
———, *Abusir III: The Pyramid Complex of Khentkaus.* Prague 1995.

Abu Ghurab (PM iii.²314–24)
E. Edel and S. Wenig, *Die Jahreszeitenreliefs aus dem Sonnenheiligtum des Königs Ne-user-Re.* Berlin 1974.

Zawyet el-ʿAryan (PM iii.²312–14)
D. Dunham, *Zawiyet el-Aryan. The Cemeteries Adjacent to the Layer Pyramid.* Boston (MA) 1978.

Giza (PM iii.²10–312)
D. Dunham and W. K. Simpson, *The Mastaba of Queen Mersyankh III.* Boston (MA) 1974.
H. Junker, *Gîza,* i–xii. Vienna and Leipzig 1929–55.

M. Lehner, *The Pyramid Tomb of Hetep-heres and the Satellite Pyramid of Khufu*. Mainz 1985.
G. A. Reisner, *Mycerinus. The Temples of the Third Pyramid at Giza*. Cambridge (MA) 1931.
——, *A History of the Giza Necropolis*, i–ii. Cambridge (MA) 1942–55.
Giza Mastabas, series published by the Museum of Fine Arts Boston, 1974– .
C. M. Zivie, *Giza au deuxième millénaire*. Cairo 1976.
——, *Giza au premier millénaire*. Boston (MA) 1991.

Abu Rawash (PM iii.²1–10)
F. Bisson de la Roque, *Rapport sur les fouilles d'Abou Roasch (1922–1923)* and *(1924)*. Cairo 1924–25.
M. Valloggia, "Fouilles archéologiques à Abu Rawash (Égypte): Rapport préliminaire de la campagne 1996", *Genava*, 44 (1996), 51–59.

Ausim (PM iv.68)

Kom Abu Billo (PM iv.67–68)

Kom el-Hisn (PM iv.51–52)
D. P. Silverman, *The Tomb Chamber of Ḥsw the Elder: The Inscribed Material at Kom el-Hisn*, i. Winona Lake (IN) 1988.
R. J. Wenke et al., "Kom el-Hisn: Excavation of an Old Kingdom Settlement in the Egyptian Delta", *Journal of the American Research Center in Egypt*, 25 (1988), 5–34.

Naukratis (PM iv.50)
W. D. E. Coulson and A. Leonard, Jr., *Cities of the Delta*, i. *Naukratis: Preliminary Report on the 1977–78 and 1980 Seasons*. Malibu 1981.

Alexandria (PM iv.2–6)
A. Adriani, *Repertorio d'arte dell'Egitto greco-romano*, series C, i–ii. Palermo 1966.
J.-Y. Empereur, *Alexandria Rediscovered*. London 1998.*
P. M. Fraser, *Ptolemaic Alexandria*, i–iii. Oxford 1972.
F. Goddio, *Alexandria: The Submerged Royal Quarters*. London 1998.*

Sa el-Hagar (PM iv.46–49)
R. el-Sayed, *Documents relatifs à Saïs et ses divinités*. Cairo 1975.

Tell el-Fara⁽in (PM iv.45)
E. C. Köhler, *Tell el-Fara⁽în – Buto III*. Mainz 1998.
T. von der Way, *Tell el-Fara⁽în – Buto I*. Mainz 1997.

Behbeit el-Hagar (PM iv.40–42)
C. Favard-Meeks, *Le temple de Behbeit el-Hagara*. Hamburg 1991.

Tell Atrib (PM iv.65–67)
P. Vernus, *Athribis*. Cairo 1978.

Tell el-Muqdam (PM iv.37–39)
E. Naville, *Ahnas el Medineh (Heracleopolis Magna)*. London 1894, 27–31.

Samannud (PM iv.43–44)
G. Steindorff, "Reliefs from the Temples of Sebennytos and Iseion in American Collections," *Journal of the Walters Art Gallery*, 7–8 (1944–45), 38–59.

el-Baqliya (PM iv.39–40)
A.-P. Zivie, *Hermopolis et le nome de l'Ibis*. Cairo 1975.

Tell el-Rub⁽a and Tell el-Timai (PM iv.35–37)
H. De Meulenaere and P. MacKay, *Mendes II*. Warminster 1976.

Heliopolis (PM iv.59–65)
W. M. F. Petrie and E. Mackay, *Heliopolis, Kafr Ammar and Shurafa*. London 1915.
A.-A. Saleh, *Excavations at Heliopolis*, i–ii. Cairo 1981, 1983.
A. el-Sawi and F. Gomaa, *Das Grab des Panehsi, Gottesvaters von Heliopolis in Matariya*. Wiesbaden 1993.

Tell el-Yahudiya (PM iv.56–58)
E. Naville, *The Mound of the Jew and the City of Onias*. London 1890.

G. R. H. Wright, "Tell el-Yehudiyah and the Glacis," *Zeitschrift des Deutschen Palästina-Vereins*, 84 (1968), 1–17.

Tell Basta (PM iv.27–35)
M. I. Bakr et al., *Tell Basta I. Tombs and Burial Customs at Bubastis: The Area of the So-called Western Cemetery*. Cairo 1992.
Labib Habachi, *Tell Basta*. Cairo 1957.
A. el-Sawi, *Excavations at Tell Basta: Report of Seasons 1967–1971 and Catalogue of Finds*. Prague 1979.

Saft el-Hinna (PM iv.10–11)
F. Naville, *The Shrine of Saft el Henneh and the Land of Goshen 1885*. London 1887.

District of el-Khata⁽na, Tell el-Dab⁽a and Qantir (PM iv.9–10).
M. Bietak, *Tell el-Dab⁽a II* and *V*. Vienna 1975, 1991.
——, *Avaris, the Capital of the Hyksos: Recent Excavations at Tell el-Dab⁽a*. London 1996.

Tell Nabasha (PM iv.7–9)
W. M. F. Petrie, *Tanis II, Nebesheh (Am) and Defenneh (Tahpanhes)*. London 1888.

San el-Hagar (PM iv.13–26)
P. Brissaud and C. Zivie-Coche, *Tanis: Travaux récents sur le tell Sân el-Hagar*. Paris 1988.
P. Brissaud (ed.), *Cahiers de Tanis*, i– . (Paris 1987–).
P. Montet, *La Nécropole royale de Tanis*, i–iii. Paris 1947–60.
——, *Les énigmes de Tanis*. Paris 1952.

Tell el-Maskhuta (PM iv.53–55)
J. S. Holladay, Jr., *Tell el-Maskhuta: Preliminary Report on the Wadi Tumilat Project 1978–9*. Malibu 1982.
E. Naville, *The Store City of Pithom and the Route of the Exodus*. London 1903.

el-Dakka (PM vii.40–50)
G. Roeder and W. Ruppel, *Der Tempel von Dakke*, i–iii. Cairo 1913–30.

Quban (PM vii.82–83)

⁽Amada (PM vii.65–73)
H. Gauthier, *Le Temple d'Amada*. Cairo 1913–26.

el-Sebu⁽a (PM vii.53–64)
H. Gauthier, *Le Temple de Ouadi es-Sebouâ*. Cairo 1912.

el–Derr (PM vii.84–89)
A. M. Blackman, *The Temple of Derr*. Cairo 1913.

el-Lessiya (PM vii.90–91)
S. Curto, *Il tempio di Ellesija*. Turin 1970.

Qasr Ibrim (PM vii.92–94)
R. A. Caminos, *The Shrines and Rock-inscriptions of Ibrim*. London 1968.

Dabod (PM vii. 1–5)
M. Almagro, *El templo de Debod*. Madrid 1971.

Tafa (PM vii.8–10)
H. D. Schneider, *Taffeh. Rond de wederopbouw van een Nubische tempel*. The Hague 1979.

Beit el-Wali (PM vii.21–27)
H. Ricke, G. R. Hughes, and E. F. Wente, *The Beit el-Wali Temple of Ramesses II*. Chicago 1967.

Kalabsha (PM vii.10–21)
K. G. Siegler, *Kalabsha: Architektur und Baugeschichte des Tempels*. Berlin 1970.

Dendur (PM vii.27–33)
C. Aldred, "The Temple of Dendur," *Metropolitan Museum of Art Bulletin*, 36.1 (Summer 1978).

Gerf Hussein (PM vii.33–37)

⁽Aniba (PM vii.75–81)
G. Steindorff, *Aniba*, i–ii. Glückstadt etc. 1935–37.

Abu Simbel (PM vii.95–119)
C. Desroches-Noblecourt and C. Kuentz, *Le Petit Temple d'Abou Simbel*, i–ii. Cairo 1968.
W. MacQuitty, *Abu Simbel*. London 1965.

Sinai
A. H. Gardiner et al., *The Inscriptions of Sinai*, i–ii. London 1952–55.
D. Valbelle and C. Bonnet, *Le sanctuaire d'Hathor, maîtresse de la turquoise: Sérabit el-Khadim au Moyen Empire*. Paris 1996.

Boats
D. Jones, *Model Boats from the Tomb of Tut⁽ankhamūn*. Oxford 1990.
B. Landström, *Ships of the Pharaohs: 4000 Years of Egyptian Shipbuilding*. London 1970.
M. Z. Nour et al., *The Cheops Boats*, i. Cairo 1960.

Pyramids
I. E. S. Edwards, *The Pyramids of Egypt*. London. Various editions.*
A. Fakhry, *The Pyramids*. Chicago (IL) and London 1969.
J.-P. Lauer, *Le mystère des pyramides*. Paris 1974.
M. Lehner, *The Complete Pyramids*. London 1997.
R. Stadelmann, *Die ägyptischen Pyramiden*. 3rd ed. Mainz 1997.

Part Three: Aspects of Egyptian Society
Women and Men
L. Meskell, *Archaeologies of Social Life*. Oxford 1999.
G. Robins, *Women in Ancient Egypt*. London 1993.

Scribes and writing
There are numerous grammars of Egyptian by authors including: J. P. Allen; J. B. Callender; J. Černý and S. I. Groll; M. A. Collier and B. Manley; E. Edel; A. H. Gardiner; E. Graefe; H. Junker; G. Lefebvre; F. Lexa; W. Spiegelberg; R. S. Simpson; and dictionaries by: W. Erichsen; A. Erman and H. Grapow; R. O. Faulkner, R. Hannig, L. H. Lesko. The terminology used in the description of the script is that of W. Schenkel.

The army
A. R. Schulman, *Military Rank, Title, and Organization in the Egyptian New Kingdom*. Berlin 1964.
Y. Yadin, *The Art of Warfare in Biblical Lands in the Light of Archaeological Discovery*. London 1963.

Religion
J. Assmann, *Egyptian Solar Religion in the New Kingdom*. London 1995.
H. Frankfort, *Ancient Egyptian Religion*. New York 1948.*
D. Frankfurter, *Religion in Roman Egypt*. Princeton 1999.
E. Hornung, *Conceptions of God in Ancient Egypt*. Ithaca (NY) 1982.*
S. Morenz, *Ägyptische Religion*. Stuttgart 1960.*
D. O'Connor and D. P. Silverman (eds.), *Ancient Egyptian Kingship*. Leiden 1995.
E. Otto, *Osiris und Amun: Kult und heilige Stätten*. Munich 1966.*
S. Quirke, *Ancient Egyptian Religion*. London 1992.

Burial customs
J.-F. and L. Aubert, *Statuettes égyptiennes, chaouabtis, ouchebtis*. Paris 1974.
M.-L. Buhl, *The Late Egyptian Anthropoid Stone Sarcophagi*. Copenhagen 1959.
W. R. Dawson and P. H. K. Gray, *Mummies and Human Remains*. London 1968.
A. M. Donadoni Roveri, *I sarcofagi egizi dalle origini alla fine dell'Antico Regno*. Rome 1969.
H. Schneider, *Shabtis*, i–iii. Leiden 1977.
A. J. Spencer, *Death in Ancient Egypt*. London 1991.
J. H. Taylor, *Egyptian Coffins*. Princes Risborough 1989.

Egypt in Western Art
E. Iversen, *The Myth of Egypt and its Hieroglyphs in European Tradition*. Copenhagen 1961; Princeton 1993.
J.-M. Humbert, M. Pantazzi and C. Ziegler, *Egyptomania: Egypt in Western Art 1730–1930*. National Gallery of Canada 1994.*
J. S. Curl, *Egyptomania. The Egyptian Revival: A Recurring Theme in the History of Taste*, 2nd ed. Manchester 1994.

GAZETTEER

Page numbers refer to maps only. The definite article el- does not affect the alphabetization. Locations are in Egypt unless otherwise stated.

A

Ab'adiya, 26°03'N 32°23'E, 31, 109
Abahuda , 22°19'N 31°38'E, 179, 186
Abdera (*Greece*), 40°56'N 24°59'E, 54
'Abd el-Qadir (*Sudan*), 21°53'N 31°14'E, 31, 179
Abedju *see* el-'Araba el-Madfuna; Kom el-Sultan; Umm el-Qa'ab
Abgig, 29°17'N 30°49'E, 41, 121, 131
Abka (*Sudan*), 21°49'N 22°14'E, 31, 179
Abnub, 27°16'N 31°09'E, 121
Abri (*Sudan*), 20°45'N 30°22'E, 49, 186
Abu Ghurab, 29°54'N 31°12'E, 18, 33, 135, 167
Abu Hamed (*Sudan*), 19°33'N 33°20'E, 21, 186
Abu Kebir, 30°43'N 31°40'E, 167
Abu el-Numrus, 29°57'N 31°13'E, 135
Abuqir (Kanopos), 31°19'N 30°04'E, 53, 166
Abu Qirqas, 27°56'N 30°50'E, 121
Abu Rawash, 30°03'N 31°05'E (village), 30°02'N 31°04'E (pyramid), 18, 31, 33, 49, 53, 135, 141, 167
Abu Seyal, 22°50'N 33°40'E, 41
Abu Simbel, 22°21'N 31°38'E, 43, 49, 179, 213
Abusir (1), 29°53'N 31°13'E (village), 29°54'E 31°12'E (pyramids), 18, 31, 33, 135, 141, 167
Abusir (2), (Taposiris Magna), 30°57'N 29°31'E, 53, 54, 166
Abusir (3), (Busiris), 30°55'N 31°14'E, 15, 18, 33, 47, 49, 167
Abusir (4), (*Sudan*), 21°50'N 31°13'E, 41, 179
Abusir el-Meleq, 29°15'N 31°05'E, 31, 49, 121
Abutig, 27°02'N 31°19'E, 109
Abu Yassin, 30°43'N 31°38'E, 167
Abu Zenima, 29°03'N 33°06'E, 188
Abydos *see* el-'Araba el-Madfuna; Kom el-Sultan; Umm el-Qa'ab
Adabiya, 29°52'N 32°30'E, 167
Adaima, 25°11'N 32°36'E, 31, 71
Aden (*Yemen*), 12°47'N 45°03'E, 13
Addis Ababa (*Ethiopia*), 09°03'N 38°42'E, 13
'Afia, 22°45'N 32°07'E, 31, 179
Afridar (*Israel*), 31°39'N 34°33'E, 31
Aghurmi, 29°12'N 25°32'E, 50, 53, 187
Agilkia (*isl*), 24°01'N 32°53'E, 72
el-'Aguza, 30°03'N 31°12'E, 135
Aidhab (*Sudan*), 22°20'N 36°30'E, 25
Aigina (*Greece*), 37°47'N 23°26'E, 50
'Ain Amur, 25°39'N 30°00'E, 53, 187
'Ain Basor (*Israel*), 31°20'N 34°29'E, 31
'Ain Dalla, 27°19'N 27°20'E, 187
'Ain el-Muftalla, 28°21'N 28°51'E, 49
'Ain el-Wadi, 27°22'N 28°13'E, 187
el-'Aiyat, 29°37'N 31°16'E, 121, 166
Akasha (*Sudan*), 21°05'N 30°42'E, 41, 186
Akhetaten *see* el-'Amarna
Akhmim (Ipu, Khemmis, Khent-min, Panopolis), 26°34'N 31°45'E, 14, 16, 25, 33, 43, 53, 109, 213
'Akko (*Israel*), 32°55'N 35°04'E, 44
Akoris *see* Tihna el-Gebel
Aksha (*Sudan*), 22°10'N 31°24'E, 31, 43, 179, 186
Aksum (*Ethiopia*), 14°10'N 38°45'E, 13
Alalakh (*Syria*), 36°13'N 36°24'E, 44
el-'Alamein, 30°50'N 28°57'E, 43, 44
'Alem (*Sudan*), 16°59'N 33°54'E, 49, 186
Aleppo (*Syria*), 36°12'N 37°10'E, 13, 44, 50
Alexandria (el-Iskandariya, Raqote), 31°12'N 29°53'E, 13, 15, 21, 25, 53, 54, 166, 187
'Amada, 22°43'N 32°15'E, 25, 43, 179
'Amara East (*Sudan*), 20°48'N 30°23'E, 49, 186
'Amara West (*Sudan*), 20°48'N 30°23'E, 41, 43, 186
el-'Amarna (Akhetaten), 27°38'N 30°53'E, 21, 43, 44, 121
Ambikol (*Sudan*), 21°20'N 30°53'E, 31, 186
Amheida, 25°41'N 28°53'E, 33, 187
el-Amiriya, 31°01'N 29°48'E, 166
Amman (*Jordan*), 31°57'N 35°56'E, 13
Amnisos (*Greece*), 35°18'N 25°13'E, 44
Amorgos (*Greece*), 36°49'N 25°54'E, 54
el-'Amra, 26°08'N 31°59'E, 31, 109
Andros (*Greece*), 37°49'N 24°54'E, 54
Anemurion (*Turkey*), 36°06'N 32°48'E, 54
'Aniba (Mi'am), 22°40'N 32°01'E, 41, 43, 44, 49, 179
Ankyronon Polis *see* el-Hiba
'Anpet *see* Tell el-Rub'a
Antaeopolis *see* Qaw el-Kebir
Antinoopolis *see* el-Sheikh 'Ibada
Antioch (*Turkey*), 36°12'N 36°10'E, 50, 54
Aphek (*Israel*), 32°06'N 34°56'E, 44
Aphrodito *see* Kom Ishqaw
Aphroditopolis (1) *see* Atfih
Aphroditopolis (2) *see* Gebelein
Apliki (*Cyprus*), 35°05'N 32°48'E, 21
Apollinopolis Magna *see* Edfu
Apollinopolis Parva *see* Qus
Apollonia (*Libya*), 32°52'N 21°59'E, 54
Apollonos Polis *see* Kom Isfaht
Aqaba (*Jordan*), 29°32'N 35°00'E, 53
el-'Araba el-Madfuna (Abedju, Abydos), 26°11'N 31°55'E, 14, 16, 21, 25, 31, 33, 41, 43, 44, 47, 49, 53, 109, 141, 213
Arados (*Syria*), 34°52'N 35°51'E, 54
Araxa (*Turkey*), 37°03'N 27°56'E, 54
Ard el-Na'am, 30°07'N 31°20'E, 135, 167
el-'Areg, 28°55'N 26°25'E, 53, 54, 187
Argin (*Sudan*), 21°59'N 31°20'E, 31, 49, 179
Argo (*isl*), (*Sudan*), 19°30'N 30°28'E, 44, 49, 186
el-Arish, 31°08'N 33°48'E, 49, 187
Armant (Hermonthis, Iuny), 25°37'N 32°32'E, 14, 16, 25, 31, 33, 41, 43, 49, 71, 109, 213
Arminna, 22°25'N 31°47'E, 41, 43, 49, 54, 179
Arsinoe (1) *see* Koresia
Arsinoe (2) *see* Medinet el-Faiyum
Arsinoe (3) *see* Methana
Arsinoe (4) *see* Patara
Arsinoe (5) *see* Rethymna
Arykanda (*Turkey*), 36°33'N 30°01'E, 54
'Asasif (*hill*), 25°44'N 32°37'E, 85
Asfun, 25°23'N 32°32'E, 16, 71
Ashdod (*Israel*), 31°45'N 34°40'E, 49, 50
Ashkeit (*Sudan*), 22°00'N 31°21'E, 31, 179
el-Ashmunein (Hermopolis Magna, Khmun), 27°47'N 30°48'E, 14, 16, 41, 43, 47, 49, 50, 53, 54, 121, 213
Askalon (*Israel*), 31°39'N 34°35'E, 43, 44, 49, 50
Askut (*Sudan*), 21°38'N 31°06'E, 41, 186
Asmara (*Eritrea*), 15°20'N 38°58'E, 13
Assur (*Iraq*), 35°27'N 43°16'E, 44
Astypalaia (*Greece*), 36°32'N 26°23'E, 54
Aswan (Syene), 24°05'N 32°54'E, 13, 14, 21, 25, 49, 53, 54, 71, 72, 179, 187
Aswan Dam, 24°02'N 32°52'E, 71, 72
Aswan High Dam (Sadd el-'Ali), 23°58'N 32°53'E, 71, 72, 179
Aswan Reservoir Colony, 24°02'N 32°52'E, 72
Asyut (Lykopolis, Zawty), 27°11'N 31°10'E (town), 27°10'N 31°08'E (ancient site), 13, 14, 16, 21, 25, 33, 41, 43, 49, 53, 109, 121, 141, 187
el-Atawla, 27°14'N 31°13'E, 14, 16, 121
'Atbara (*Sudan*), 17°42'N 34°00'E, 186
Atfih (Aphroditopolis (1)), 29°25'N 31°15'E, 14, 16, 47, 53, 121, 213
Athens (*Greece*), 38°00'N 23°44'E, 50, 54
Athribis (1) *see* Tell Atrib
Athribis (2) *see* Wannina
Ausim (Khem, Letopolis), 30°08'N 31°08'E, 15, 18, 33, 47, 49, 135, 167
Avaris *see* Tell el-Dab'a

B

Babylon (1) *see* Old Cairo
Babylon (*Iraq*), 32°33'N 44°24'E, 44, 50
Bacchias *see* Kom el-Asl
el-Badari, 27°00'N 31°25'E, 31, 109
el-Badrashein, 29°51'N 31°16'E, 135
Baghdad (*Iraq*), 33°20'N 44°26'E, 13
Ba'h *see* el-Baqliya
el-Bahnasa (Oxyrhynchus, Per-Medjed), 28°32'N 30°40'E, 14, 16, 47, 53, 121, 213
el-Bahrain, 28°40'N 26°30'E, 53, 187
Bahriya Oasis, 28°20'N 28°50'E, 13, 21, 31, 33, 41, 43, 47, 49, 50, 53, 54, 187
el-Ba'irat, 25°42'N 32°37'E, 85
Baki *see* Quban
Balabish, 26°12'N 32°08'E, 41, 109
el-Balamun (1), (Diospolis Inferior), 31°15'N 31°34'E, 15, 18, 33, 43, 47, 49, 53, 167, 213
el-Balamun (2), 30°49'N 31°26'E, 167
Balansura, 27°55'N 30°42'E, 14, 121
Balat, 25°34'N 29°16'E, 31, 33, 43, 44, 53, 187
Ballana, 22°17'N 31°35'E, 31, 179
Baltim, 31°33'N 31°05'E, 167
Balyana, 26°14'N 32°00'E, 71, 109
el-Baqawat, 25°30'N 30°33'E, 53, 187
el-Baqliya (Ba'h, Hermopolis Parva (2)), 30°57'N 31°25'E, 15, 43, 47, 49, 167, 213
Baris, 24°40'N 30°36'E, 25, 187
Ba'sa (*Sudan*), 16°42'N 33°55'E, 49, 186
el-Basalin, 29°59'N 31°16'E, 135
Basra (*Iraq*), 30°30'N 47°50'E, 13
Bast *see* Tell Basta
Batn Ihrit (Theadelphia), 29°22'N 30°35'E (village), 29°21'N 30°34'E (ancient site), 53, 121, 131
Batu (*mt*), (*Ethiopia*), 06°55'N 39°49'E, 13
el-Bawiti, 28°21'N 28°51'E, 43, 49, 50, 53, 187
el-Beda, 30°55'N 32°35'E, 18, 31, 167
Begrawiya (Meroë), (*Sudan*), 16°54'N 33°44'E, 21, 25, 49, 54, 186
Behbeit el-Hagar (Hebyt, Iseum), 31°02'N 31°17'E, 25, 47, 49, 53, 167
Beirut (Berytos), (*Lebanon*), 33°53'N 35°30'E, 13, 44, 54
Beit Khallaf, 26°19'N 31°47'E, 31, 109
Beit Shan (*Israel*), 32°30'N 35°30'E, 41, 44
Beit el-Wali, 23°33'N 32°52'E, 43, 179
Benghazi (Berenike (2)), (*Libya*), 32°07'N 20°05'E, 12, 54
Benha, 30°28'N 31°11'E, 167
Beni Anir, 30°36'N 31°33'E, 18, 31, 167
Beni Hasan, 27°56'N 30°53'E, 14, 21, 33, 41, 121
Beni Hasan el-Shuruq, 27°49'N 30°51'E, 121
Beni Magdul, 30°02'N 31°07'E, 135
Beni Mazar, 28°30'N 30°48'E, 121
Beni Suef, 29°04'N 31°06'E, 121, 167
Berber (*Sudan*), 18°01'N 34°00'E, 186
Berenike (1), 23°50'N 35°28'E, 21, 53, 54
Berenike (2) *see* Benghazi
Berenike Panchryssos (*Sudan*), 21°49'N 35°32'E, 21, 53
Berytos *see* Beirut
Biba, 28°56'N 30°59'E, 121
Biban el-Harim *see* Valley of the Queens
Biga (*isl*), 24°01'N 32°53'E, 14, 41, 53, 71, 72
Bilbeis, 30°25'N 31°34'E, 49, 167
Bilgas, 31°14'N 31°22'E, 167
Bir 'Abbad, 25°02'N 33°04'E, 43, 71
Bir el-Fawakhir, 26°02'N 33°36'E, 53
Birket Habu, 25°42'N 32°36'E (ancient harbor), 85
Bir Kiseiba, 22°43'N 29°54'E, 31
Bir Menih, 25°35'N 33°35'E, 33, 43
Bir Tarfawi, 22°59'N 28°56'E, 31
Bisutun (*Iran*), 34°59'N 48°42'E, 50
Biyala, 31°11'N 31°13'E, 167
Boğazköy (Hattusas), (*Turkey*) 40°02'N 34°37'E, 44
Bubastis *see* Tell Basta
Bugdumbush (*Sudan*), 18°33'N 30°40'E, 41, 186
Buhen (*Sudan*), 21°55'N 31°17'E, 33, 41, 43, 44, 49, 54, 179, 186
Bulaq, 30°04'N 31°14'E, 135
Bur Sa'id *see* Port Said
Bur Tawfiq *see* Port Tawfiq
Busiris *see* Abusir (3)
Buto *see* Tell el-Fara'in
Byahmu, 29°22'N 30°51'E, 41, 121, 131
Byblos (*Lebanon*), 34°08'N 35°38'E, 41, 44, 50, 54

C

Cairo (el-Qahira), 30°04'N 31°15'E, 13, 21, 25, 135, 141, 167, 187
Carchemish (*Syria*), 36°49'N 38°01'E, 44, 50
Catherine, Mount (*mt*), 28°30'N 33°57'E, 13
Charadros (*Turkey*), 36°06'N 32°34'E, 54
Chios (*Greece*), 38°23'N 26°07'E, 50, 54
Contra Latopolis *see* el-Hella
Contra Pselchis *see* Quban
Cyrene (*Libya*), 32°48'N 21°54'E, 50, 54

D

Dabenarti (*Sudan*), 21°49'N 31°11'E, 41, 179, 186
Dabod, 23°54'N 32°52'E, 25, 31, 53, 179
Daganeg, 25°24'N 33°48'E, 25
Dahshur, 29°48'N 31°14'E , 33, 41, 135, 141, 167
Dairut, 27°34'N 30°49'E, 108, 121
el-Dakhla Oasis, 25°30'N 29°00'E, 13, 21, 31, 33, 41, 43, 47, 49, 53, 54, 187
el-Dakka (Pselchis, Pselqet), 23°11'N 32°45'E, 25, 31, 41, 53, 179
Damanhur (Hermopolis Parva (1)), 31°02'N 30°28'E, 15, 18, 31, 53, 167
Damascus (*Syria*), 33°30'N 36°18'E, 13, 44, 50, 54
el-Damer (*Sudan*), 17°37'N 33°59'E, 186
Damietta (Dumyat), 31°25'N 31°48'E, 25, 167
Daphnai *see* Tell Dafana
Dara, 27°18'N 30°52'E, 33, 121, 141
Darb el-Ba'irat, 25°54'N 32°27'E, 41, 109
Debba (*Sudan*), 18°03'N 30°57'E, 49, 186
Defeia (*Sudan*), 17°44'N 34°00'E, 49
Dehmit, 23°42'N 32°54'E, 31, 179
Deir el-Bahri, 25°44'N 31°36'E, 33, 41, 43, 85
Deir el-Balah (*Israel*), 31°26'N 34°23'E, 43, 44
Deir el-Ballas, 26°03'N 32°45'E, 41, 109
Deir el-Bersha, 27°45'N 30°54'E, 41, 121
Deir Bisra, 27°10'N 31°16'E, 31, 121
Deir Durunka, 27°09'N 31°11'E, 121
Deir el-Gabrawi, 27°20'N 31°06'E, 31, 33, 121
Deir el-Hagar, 25°40'N 28°48'E, 53, 187
Deir el-Malik, 27°46'N 30°52'E, 33, 121
Deir el-Medina, 25°44'N 32°36'E, 43, 85
Deir Rifa, 27°06'N 31°10'E, 31, 41, 121
Deir el-Shelwit, 25°42'N 32°35'E, 85
Deir Tasa, 27°03'N 31°25'E, 31, 109
Dendara (Iunet, Tantere, Tentyris), 26°10'N 32°39'E (village), 26°08'N 32°40'E (temple), 14, 16, 25, 31, 33, 41, 43, 49, 53, 109, 213
Dendur (Tutzis), 23°23'N 32°56'E, 25, 53, 179
Dep *see* Tell el-Fara'in
el-Derr, 22°44'N 32°12'E, 25, 43, 179
Dibeira East (*Sudan*), 22°04'N 31°22'E, 41, 43, 179, 186
Dibeira West (*Sudan*), 22°03'N 31°20'E, 31, 43, 179, 186
Dikirnis, 31°05'N 31°57'E, 167
Dimai (Soknopaiou Nesos), 29°32'N 30°40'E, 31, 53, 121, 131
Dionysias *see* Qasr Qarun
Diospolis Inferior *see* el-Balamun (1)
Diospolis Magna *see* Luxor
Diospolis Parva *see* Hiw
Dishasha, 29°00'N 30°50'E, 33, 121
Disuq, 31°08'N 30°39'E, 167
el-Diwan, 22°43'N 32°13'E, 25, 179
Djamet *see* Medinet Habu
Dja'net *see* San el-Hagar
Djeba *see* Edfu
Djedet *see* Tell el-Rub'a
Djerty *see* Tod
Djew-Qa *see* Qaw el-Kebir
Djibouti (*Djibouti*), 11°33'N 43°10'E, 13
Dongola (*Sudan*), 19°10'N 30°27'E, 186
el-Doqqi, 30°02'N 31°12'E, 135
Dorginarti (*Sudan*), 21°51'N 31°14'E, 41, 43, 179, 186
Dra' Abu el-Naga', 25°44'N 32°27'E, 33, 85
Duanib (*Sudan*), 16°30'N 33°26'E, 49, 186
Dumyat *see* Damietta
Dunqul Oasis, 23°30'N 31°50'E, 13, 21, 31, 33, 41, 43, 49, 53, 179
Dush (Kysis), 24°34'N 30°43'E, 53, 54, 187
Duweishat (*Sudan*), 21°20'N 31°02'E, 41, 43, 186

E

Edfu (Apollinopolis Magna, Djeba, Mesen), 24°59'N 32°52'E (town and tombs), 24°57'N 32°50'E (pyramid), 14, 16, 25, 31, 33, 41, 43, 49, 53, 71, 141, 213
Eileithyiaspolis *see* el-Kab (1)
Ekbatana (*Iran*), 34°48'N 48°30'E, 50
Elephantine (*isl*), 24°05'N 32°53'E, 14, 16, 25, 31, 33, 41, 43, 44, 47, 49, 53, 71, 72, 141, 213
Ephesos (*Turkey*), 37°55'N 27°19'E, 54
Eresos (*Greece*), 39°11'N 25°57'E, 54
Erythrai (*Turkey*), 38°24'N 26°00'E, 54
Esna (Iunyt, Latopolis, Senet, Tasenet), 25°18'N 32°33'E, 14, 16, 25, 41, 43, 49, 53, 71, 109, 213
Euhemeria *see* Qasr el-Banat
Ezbet Bashendi, 25°33'N 29°19'E, 53, 187
Ezbet Gamasa el-Gharbiya, 31°27'N 31°33'E, 167

F

Faqus (Phakussa), 30°44'N 31°48'E, 15, 167
Farafra Oasis, 27°00'N 28°00'E, 13, 21, 33, 41, 47, 49, 53, 54, 187
Faras (*Sudan*), 22°13'N 31°29'E, 31, 41, 43, 49, 54, 179, 186
Farasha, 30°41'N 31°43'E, 18, 41, 167
el-Fasher (Sudan), 13°37'N 25°22'E, 13
el-Fashn, 28°49'N 30°54'E, 121
Firka (*Sudan*), 20°54'N 30°035'E, 49, 186
Fura Wells (*Sudan*), 17°51'N 32°33'E, 49
Fuwa, 31°12'N 30°33'E, 167

G

Gamai (*Sudan*), 21°46'N 31°11'E, 31, 186
el-Gamaliya, 30°03'N 31°16'E, 135
Garden City, 30°02'N 31°14'E, 135
Gaza (*Israel*), 31°30'N 34°28'E, 25, 41, 43, 44, 49, 50, 53, 54, 187
Gebel Abu Hassa, 30°09'N 32°25'E, 167
Gebel Adda, 22°18'N 31°37'E, 54, 179
Gebel Ahmar, 30°03'N 31°18'E, 21, 135, 167
Gebelaw, 26°08'N 32°46'E, 33, 109
Gebel Barkal (Napata), (*Sudan*), 18°32'N 31°49'E, 21, 41, 44, 49, 54, 186
Gebel Dosha (*Sudan*), 20°30'N 30°18'E, 43, 186
Gebel Dukhan (Mons Porphyrites), 27°15'N 33°15'E, 21, 53
Gebelein (Aphroditopolis (2), Pathyris, Per-Hathor), 25°29'N 32°29'E, 21, 25, 31, 33, 41, 53, 71, 109, 213
Gebel el-Hammam, 24°14'N 32°53'E, 33, 71
Gebel Hof (*hills*), 29°55'N 31°21'E, 135
Gebel Manzal el-Seyl, 27°33'N 33°06'E, 21, 31
Gebel el-Mawta, 29°13'N 29°32'E, 50, 187
Gebel Muqattam (*hills*), 30°01'N 31°18'E, 135
Gebel Murr, 30°08'N 32°31'E, 167
Gebel Musa (Mount Sinai), (*mt*), 28°32'N 33°59'E, 13
Gebel Qeili (*Sudan*), 15°21'N 34°40'E, 49
Gebel el-Shams, 22°16'N 31°37'E, 43, 49, 179, 186
Gebel el-Sheikh el-Haridi, 26°46'N 31°34'E, 53, 109
Gebel Sheikh Suleiman (*Sudan*), 21°51'N 31°13'E, 31, 179
Gebel el-Silsila (Kheny), 24°39'N 32°54'E (west bank), 24°39'N 32°56'E (east bank), 14, 21, 25, 43, 49, 71
Gebel el-Teir (1), 28°14'N 30°46'E, 33, 121
Gebel el-Teir (2), 25°32'N 30°33'E, 43, 44, 49, 53, 187
Gebel Tura (*hills*), 29°56'N 31°19'E, 135
Gebel Zeit, 27°56'N 33°26'E, 21, 33, 41, 43
Gebtu *see* Qift
Gedaref (Teawa), (*Sudan*), 14°01'N 35°24'E, 25
Geili (*Sudan*), 16°01'N 32°37'E, 49, 186
Gerf Hussein, 23°17'N 32°54'E, 25, 31, 43, 179
Gesa *see* Qus
Gesy *see* Qus
Gezer (*Israel*), 31°53'N 34°56'E, 43, 44
el-Gezira, 30°03'N 31°13'E, 135
Gezira Dabarosa (*Sudan*), 21°57'N 31°20'E, 31, 49, 179
Gezira Sangaha, 30°50'N 31°39'E, 18, 31, 167
Geziret el-Roda, 29°59'N 31°13'E, 135
el-Gharak el-Sultani (Kerkeosiris?), 29°08'N 30°42'E, 53, 121
el-Gharbaniyat, 30°53'N 29°30'E, 43, 44, 166
Ghita, 30°23'N 31°31'E, 18, 41, 167
el-Ghuriya, 30°02'N 31°16'E, 135
el-Gi'eif (Naukratis), 30°54'N 30°35'E, 18, 49, 50, 53, 167
Girga (Thinis, Tjeny), 26°20'N 31°54'E, 14, 16, 49, 71, 109
Girza, 29°27'N 31°12'E, 31, 121

INDEX

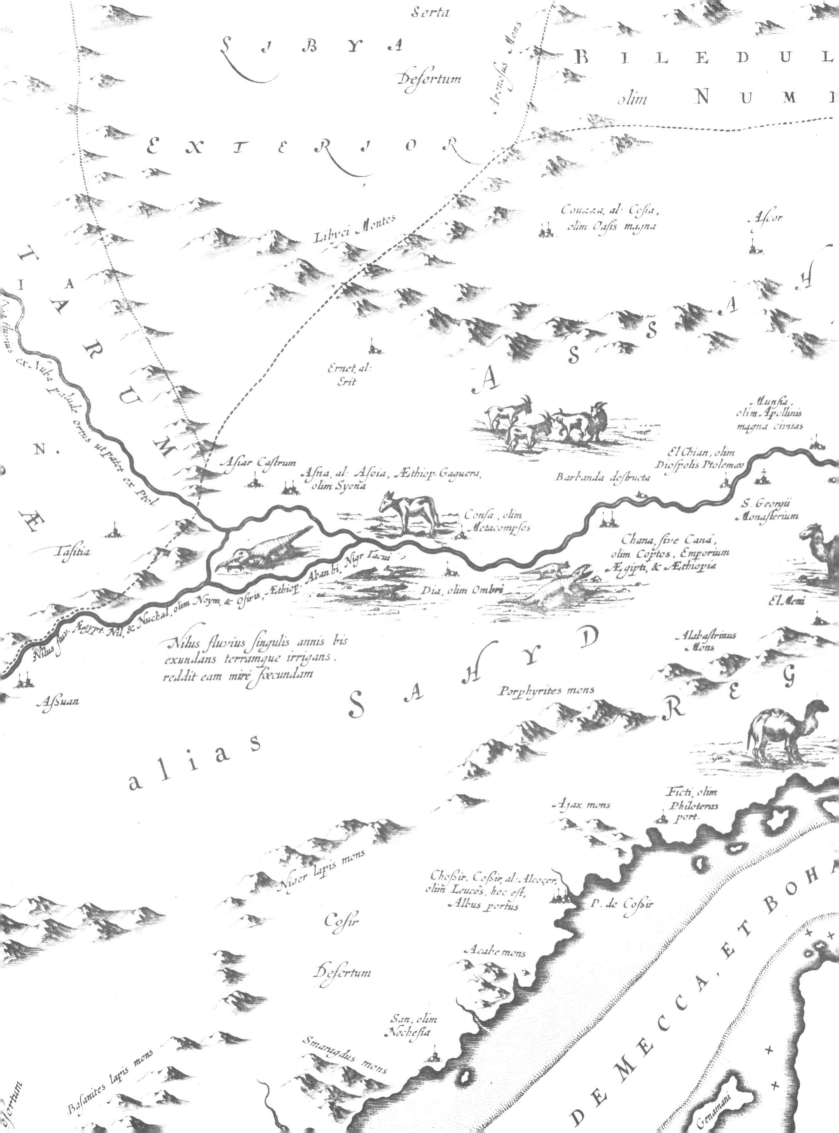

Serta

S I B Y A

Defertum

E X T E R I O R

BILEDUL
olim NUMI

Armiefus Mons

Libyci Montes

Couzza, al. Cofia,
olim Oafis magna

Afcor

A S Ŝ A H

I A R U M

Ernet, al:
Erit

A S

Munfia,
olim Apollinis
magna civitas

Afiar Caftrum

Afna, al. Afoia, Æthiop. Gaguera,
olim Syena

Confa, olim
Metacompfos

El Chian, olim
Diofpolis Ptolemœo

N.

Barbanda deftructa

S. Georgii
Monafterium

Æ

Tafitia

Nilus fluv. Ægypt. Nil, & Nuchal, olim Noym, & Ofiris, Æthiop. Abanhi, Nigr Tacui

Chana, five Cana,
olim Coptos, Emporium
Ægypti, & Æthiopia

Dia, olim Ombri

El Meni

Nilus fluvius fingulis annis bis
exundans terramque irrigans,
reddit eam miré fœcundam

Afuan

S A H Y D

Alabaftrinus
Mons

Porphyrites mons

R E G

alias

Ajax mons

Ficti, olim
Philoteras
port.

Niger lapis mons

Chofsir, Cofsir, al. Alcoçer,
olim Leucos, hoc eft.
Albus portus

P. de Cofsir

DE MECCA ET BOHA

Cofir

Acabe mons

Defertum

San, olim
Nechefia

Bafanites lapis mons

Smaragdus mons

Genamati